CONTENTS

CONTENTS

study holidays

Published by the Central Bureau, Seymour Mews, London
W1H 9PE, England

Sixteenth edition

Distributed in the UK by the Central Bureau, Seymour Mews, London W1H 9PE
Telephone 01-486 5101
Telex 21368 CBEVEX G
BT GOLD 87:WQQ383
Fax 01-935 5741

Distributed in North America by the Institute of International Education, 809 United Nations Plaza, New York, NY10017, United States of America Tel (212) 984 5412

ISBN 0 900087 82 X

Computer typeset by Getset Ltd, Eynsham, Oxford, England

Printed and bound by Hazell Watson & Viney, Aylesbury, England

PRACTICAL INFORMATION

This guide is published by the Central Bureau, the UK national office responsible for the provision of information and advice on all forms of educational visits and exchanges; the development and administration of a wide range of curriculum-related pre-service and in-service exchange programmes; the linking of educational establishments and local education authorities with counterparts abroad; and the organisation of meetings and conferences related to professional international experience. Its information and advisory services extend throughout the educational field. In addition, over 20,000 individual enquiries are answered each year. Publications cater for the needs of people of all ages seeking information on the various opportunities available for educational contacts and travel abroad. The Central Bureau was established in 1948 by the British government and is funded by the Department of Education and Science, the Scottish Education Department and the Department of Education for Northern Ireland.

Seymour Mews House, Seymour Mews, London W1H 9PE *Telephone* 01-486 5101
Telex 21368 CBEVEX G
BT GOLD 87:WQQ383
Fax 01-935 5741

3 Bruntsfield Crescent, Edinburgh EH10 4HD
Telephone 031-447 8024
BT GOLD 87:WCP034

16 Malone Road, Belfast BT9 5BN
Telephone 0232-64418/9

USING THIS GUIDE It should be stressed that whatever type of language course you are applying for, advance preparation is vital. Find out as much as you possibly can about your chosen country by visiting your local library for background reading. Try and get some reading matter actually in the language. Reading newspapers, magazines or novels will not only improve your language skills but will also give you some idea of the customs, social conventions and flavour of the country. The tourist office of your chosen country should be able to provide you with maps and leaflets containing general information on the country or a specific town or area you are going to, and the cultural section of the relevant embassy may also be able to help in providing information.

The entries in this book give a guide to language courses offered by hundreds of private schools, state colleges and universities all over Europe. Once you have decided on a course, and have been in touch with the organisation concerned, you should read their literature and application forms very thoroughly. By doing this you should know in advance exactly what to expect, for example, ability level, hours of study, whether or not recreation opportunities are available, travel arrangements, other expenses, insurance, living conditions and any other requirements. Make sure you know exactly what is covered by the basic fee. If there are any points at all which are unclear, or if you have any other queries, you should contact the school or their agency to receive clarification. It is obviously wise to have a clear idea of the procedure well before you actually apply. Requests for further information and applications should be addressed to the organisations direct, and not to the Central Bureau.

Languages are listed in alphabetical order, with sections on each country where the relevant courses are available. For example there are French courses in Belgium, France and Switzerland, and Russian courses in the USSR and Austria. As far as possible, information on each course includes:

Language levels These range from complete beginners through to advanced, postgraduate level.
Many organisations also offer specific courses, for example, for secretarial, business and technical users, and for teachers.

Ages Most courses are aimed at a specific age group, but many have no particular restrictions.
Generally speaking, anyone aged between 8-80 should be able to find a suitable course within this guide.

Individuals, groups or families Many of the organisations listed, as well as accepting individual applications, will also be able to offer courses for groups. Some schools also offer facilities for families, often with children's courses or activities during the periods of tuition.

Length and dates of courses
Most courses last 2-4 weeks between June and September. Many organisations, however, offer language tuition during the Christmas and Easter holidays as well as all year round, and colleges and universities often run long-term language courses during the academic year.

Intensity and class numbers
Wherever possible the intensity of language tuition is given, and detailed as the number of hours per week, or as a total number of hours over the whole course. The maximum or average numbers of students per class or course is also listed, and where small group or 1:1 or 1:2 tuition is available, this is also noted.

Options Many organisations combine language tuition with study of the culture or history of the country, particular at advanced levels. Language courses can also be combined with sports or activity holidays, particularly for teenagers, or with art, craft or culinary and wine courses. Organisations may also provide a programme of social activities, excursions and sports, either inclusive or as an option. Details of all options are clearly given.

Accommodation Most schools and colleges, if they do not actually offer residential accommodation, will be able to help find the student somewhere to live. Often accommodation is with local families, an ideal environment for language learning and practice.

Costs Wherever possible the full cost of the course is quoted. Prices vary depending on the facilities offered, the intensity of tuition, and whether or not accommodation is included. Where additional costs are involved, for example for excursions, additional courses or textbooks, this is indicated. Most organisations will require a deposit when registering, with the balance to be paid on the first day of the course. The cost is generally given in local currency. Prices may be subject to exchange rate fluctuation, but the following were the rates when this guide was compiled (all rates = £1 Sterling):

Austria 21.72 Sch
Belgium 65.19 BF
Denmark 11.83 Kr
France 10.44 FF
FR Germany 3.09 DM
Greece 242 Drc
Ireland 1.17 £
Italy 2285 Lire
Netherlands 3.51 Fl
Norway 11.35 Kr
Portugal 247 Esc
Spain 203 Pts
Sweden 10.74 Kr
Switzerland 2.56 SF
Yugoslavia 3845 Dnr

Insurance Although many organisations provide insurance cover for their students, this is often solely against third party risks and accidents.
Intending applicants are therefore strongly advised to obtain precise details on this point, and if necessary to take out individual

policies against illness, disablement and loss or damage to personal belongings. Further details are given under the **Health** and **Travel insurance** headings below.

Handicapped participants Certain organisations are able to provide facilities for, or will consider applications from handicapped students, and these are indicated by **PH.** When applying, state the exact nature of the disability and any special care or facilities required. Even if **PH** is not indicated in an entry it is worth making enquiries if you feel that the handicap is not likely to put unreasonable demands on the organisation or their facilities. Some courses unfortunately, are run in buildings unsuitable for disabled access.

BRITISH PASSPORTS A full UK passport costs £15 (£22.50 if particulars of spouse are included) and is valid for 10 years. To obtain a passport you should write in advance to your local regional office (forms are available from post offices). Bear in mind that you should do this well in advance of when you are going to travel as there can be delays. If you have time, it is usually quicker to actually go to your local office and wait for your application to be processed.

Passport Office, Clive House, 70-78 Petty France, London SW1H 9HD Tel 01-279 3434

Passport Office, 5th Floor, India Buildings, Water Street, Liverpool L2 0QZ Tel 051-237 3010

Passport Office, Olympia House, Upper Dock Street, Newport, Gwent NPT 1XA Tel Newport 244500

Passport Office, 55 Westfield Road, Peterborough, Cambridgeshire PE3 6TG Tel Peterborough 895555

Passport Office, 3 Northgate, 96 Milton Street, Cowcaddens, Glasgow G4 0BT Tel 041-332 0271

Passport Office, Hampton House, 47-53 High Street, Belfast BT1 2QS Tel 0232-232371

However, you may not need a full passport to travel to some countries. Within western Europe, excluding the German Democratic Republic and East Berlin, and certain other countries you can travel on a British Visitor's Passport. These cost £7.50 (£11.25 if particulars of spouse are included) and are valid for 12 months. Application forms and BVPs are obtainable from any main post office, Monday-Friday; BVPs are not obtainable from passport offices other than the Passport Office, Belfast, and are only available to British citizens, British Dependent Territories citizens, and British Overseas citizens for holiday purposes of up to three months.

Essential information for holders of UK passports who intend to travel overseas contains notes on illness or injury while abroad, insurance, vaccinations, NHS medical cards, consular assistance overseas, British Customs and other useful advice, and is available from all passport offices.

VISAS For entry to some countries outside the EC a visa or visitor's pass is required, and in many a residence permit will also be required. As regulations are subject to change without warning, you are advised to obtain the current information from the consular sections of the relevant embassies before setting out, particularly if the organisation you are applying through is not responsible for obtaining visas for you.

IDENTITY CARDS The International Student Identity Card scheme is operated by the International Student Travel Conference, a group of major official student travel bodies worldwide. The Card provides internationally accepted proof of the bona fide status of students and consequently ensures that they may enjoy many special facilities, including fare reductions, cheap accommodation, reduced rate or free entry to museums, art galleries and historic sites. Obtainable from officially appointed student travel offices, available to all full-time students at a cost of £4 inclusive of the *International Student Travel Guide* detailing the discounts and facilities worldwide. Valid for up to 15 months (1 October-31 December of the following year). Details in the UK from NUS Services, 2nd floor, Rigby House, 34 The Parade, Watford, Hertfordshire WD1 1LN Tel Watford 55300.

The Federation of International Youth Travel Organisations (FIYTO) aims to promote educational, cultural and social travel among young people and to foster mutual understanding and cooperation between all members. The FIYTO Youth International Educational Exchange Card is a recognised card offering concessions to young travellers including transport, accommodation, restaurants, excursions, cultural events and reduced rates or free entry to many museums, art galleries, theatres and cinemas. Available to all those under 26, cost £3 inclusive of a booklet giving details of the concessions. Details in the UK from STA Travel, 74 Old Brompton Road, London SW7 3LQ Tel 01-581 1022.

HEALTH INSURANCE Students should ensure that they have full insurance cover against risk of accident, illness and possible disability. Most large insurance companies offer comprehensive policies at reasonable cost, and organisations are sometimes able to arrange full cover for students in their programmes. However, the insurance cover provided by organisations is often solely against third party risks and accidents. You are therefore strongly advised to obtain precise details on this point and, if necessary, to take out individual policies against illness, disablement and loss or damage to personal belongings. Even short illnesses abroad can be expensive, so it is well worth taking out medical insurance before you travel, whether or not the country to be visited has a health care arrangement with the UK. In addition to medical expenses, private insurance usually covers incidental expenses such as transportation home, which is never covered by a reciprocal health agreement.

British citizens are only covered by the NHS while in the UK, and will usually have to pay the full costs of treatment abroad themselves. However, there are health care arrangements with all the EC countries (Belgium, Denmark, France, Federal Republic of Germany, Greece, Ireland, Italy, Luxembourg, Netherlands, Portugal and Spain). In most of them free or reduced cost emergency treatment for visitors is provided only on production of form *E111*. Leaflet *SA40, Before You Go – The Traveller's Guide to Health* explains who is covered by the arrangements and how to apply for form *E111*. It lists all the countries where free or reduced cost emergency medical treatment is available, including details of what treatment is free or at reduced cost in EC countries, and gives the procedures which must be followed to get treatment in countries where form *E111* is not needed (usually Denmark, Ireland and Portugal). Form *E111* is issued with an information sheet on how to get emergency medical treatment in other EC countries. Form *E111 or leaflet SA40* must be taken abroad and, if emergency treatment is needed, the correct procedures must be followed. In addition there are reciprocal health care arrangements with other countries, including Austria, Bulgaria, Czechoslovakia, Finland, German Democratic Republic, Hungary, Norway, Poland, Romania, Sweden, USSR and Yugoslavia.

However, private medical insurance may still be needed in these countries; leaflet *SA40* should be read to check the services available. Free or subsidised medical treatment in countries other than those listed above is not available, and it is therefore strongly advisable to take out adequate private medical insurance. Overseas visitors to the UK will be charged the full cost of medical treatment if there are no reciprocal health arrangements between their country and the UK. It is advisable to check what arrangements exist and to take out adequate private medical insurance where necessary. Endsleigh also have policies for overseas students in this position.

UK citizens going away for more than 3 months should hand their NHS medical card to the immigration officer at the point of departure, or send it to the local Family Practitioner Committee (England and Wales), Area Health Board (Scotland) or Central Services Agency (Northern Ireland), with a note of the date of departure. If you have lost or mislaid the card you should write to the same address (see local telephone directory), giving date of departure, last permanent address in this country, name and address of your doctor, and NHS medical numbers. If you are however, going to Bulgaria or Poland you may need the NHS medical card to get free treatment, so should not hand it in. See leaflet *SA40* for details.

The Department of Health and Social Security issue a leaflet *SA40 Before You Go – The Traveller's Guide to Health* with vital information for those travelling overseas. It includes details of compulsory and recommended vaccinations, what else can be done to protect one's health, information on yellow fever, cholera, infectious hepatitis, typhoid, tetanus, polio, malaria rabies and AIDS, precautions to be taken against contracting these diseases, and action to take in an emergency. There is also advice on types of food and on water supplies which may be a source of infection. Available from the DHSS, International Relations Division, Alexander Fleming House, Elephant and Castle, London SE1 6BY Tel 01-407 5522 ext 6711. If you are taking prescribed drugs it is advisable to carry a doctor's letter giving details of the medical condition and the medication, avoiding the possibility of confusion. A certificate of vaccination against certain diseases is an entry requirement for some countries. It is wise to consult embassies on this point, since requirements are continually subject to review; alternatively contact the DHSS. The DHSS also issues leaflet *SA41 While You're Away – The Traveller's Guide to Health* which contains useful information you may need while you are abroad; everything from what to do about insect bites and how to get emergency medical treatment to looking after your health when you return.

TRAVEL INSURANCE The ISIS (International Student Insurance Service) policy, specifically for students, provides a wide range of benefits covering death, disablement, medical and other personal expenses, loss of luggage, personal liability and cancellation, loss of deposits or curtailment. Policies include worldwide travel for up to 6 months including winter sports, and extended stays of over 6 months and up to 2 years. An advantage of this policy is that medical expenses can be settled on the spot in many countries by student organisations cooperating with ISIS; the medical limit for these expenses relates to each claim and therefore the cover is, in effect, limitless. A 24 hour assistance service is provided to handle all medical emergencies. Details in the UK from Endsleigh Insurance Services Ltd, Endsleigh House, Ambrose Street, Cheltenham Spa, Gloucestershire GL50 3NR Tel Cheltenham 36151 or the local Endsleigh Insurance centre, see Yellow Pages.

CURRENCY It is important that you work out just how much money you need to take with you. This will obviously depend on a variety of factors. Is the course residential or non-residential, full board or half board? Is the cost of living in the country that you are going to higher than your own? Are you going to travel after the course has finished? Will you need to pay for any of the places you visit, either as part of the course or on your own? You should also remember to take money to cover any unforeseen circumstances or emergencies. A good guide is to make sure that you take enough to cover one or two nights' hotel accommodation and a long-distance telephone call. If you do run out of money it is possible to arrange for money to be transferred to a bank abroad. In a dire emergency, your embassy or consulate in the country you are visiting will be able to advise on funds, or arrange for direct return by the cheapest possible passage, providing the individual surrenders their passport and gives a written undertaking to pay the travel expenses involved. However, it must be stressed that this should only be turned to as a last resort.

The best way to take large amounts of money is in travellers cheques. When obtaining these from a bank or travel agency you generally need to order them a few days in advance and you will need to show your passport when you collect them. Do not countersign the cheques in advance. Make a note of the numbers and keep it separate from the cheques; in this way, if you lose the cheques they can still be replaced. Some travellers' cheques can be replaced while you are still abroad, others will be honoured by the issuing bank on your return. If you have a current account, you will probably be able to obtain a supply of Eurocheques and a cheque card. These cheques can be cashed abroad at banks displaying the Eurocheque sign, and are also accepted by many shops. A small charge may be levied in some countries, and charges may be higher in bureaux de change. The cheques are drawn against your current account and are guaranteed up to an agreed amount. Don't forget to take some of your own currency with you for use on the outward and return journeys.

In addition to travellers cheques you will of course need some cash. Foreign currency can be obtained before you leave at major travel agents and bureaux de change branches in banks. Banks without a bureaux de change branch may need a few days notice. You can shop around to get the best exchange rate, but remember that commission is always charged.

CUSTOMS Full details of UK Customs regulations are given in *United Kingdom Customs (Customs Notice 1)* which is obtainable from HM Customs and Excise or from Customs at ports and airports in the UK. On arrival in the UK persons with goods in excess of their duty and tax-free allowances or who are in doubt should declare them in the red clearance channel. There are prohibitions and restrictions on the importation of certain goods including controlled drugs, firearms (including gas pistols, electric shock batons and similar weapons); ammunition, explosives (including fireworks); flick knives, horror comics; indecent or obscene books, magazines and video tapes; meat, poultry, plants, vegetables, fruits, certain radio transmitters and cordless telephones not approved for use in the UK; animals and birds and articles derived from endangered species; goods bearing a false or misleading indication of origin (eg Rolex watches marked *Swiss* which are not made in Switzerland). Further details from HM Customs and Excise, CDE5, Room 201, Dorset House, Stamford Street, London SE1 9PS Tel 01-928 0533 ext 2374 or 2528.

Details of Custom formalities in other countries can be obtained from embassies.

BRITISH EMBASSIES There are consular offices at British Embassies in foreign capitals and at Consulates in some provincial cities. Consuls maintain a list of English-speaking doctors and will advise or help in cases of serious difficulty or distress. They cannot provide money (except in certain specific emergencies), telex or telephone facilities, interpretation or legal advice services, or pay bills, whether legal, medical, hotel, travel or any other debts. As a last resort a consul can arrange for a direct return to the UK by the cheapest possible passage, providing the person concerned agrees to have his passport withdrawn and gives written confirmation that he will pay the travel expenses involved. If the consul's urgent help is needed you should telephone or telegraph; the telegraphic address of all British Embassies is *Prodrome* and of all British Consulates *Britain*, followed in each case by the name of the appropriate town. If a passport is lost or stolen while abroad the local police should be notified immediately; if necessary the nearest British Embassy or Consulate will issue a substitute, and it is wise to keep a separate note of the number.

Addresses of other embassies are given under the **Information** headings for each language.

TRAVEL Having organised your admission to a course you will probably have to arrange the travel. Generally there are several options open to you and your choice will depend upon the time you have, the accessibility of the destination, and available funds.

By rail Three UK companies offering low-cost travel in Europe for ages under 26, with a choice of thousands of destinations, plus low add-on fares from any UK stations are:

Eurotrain/London Student Travel, 52 Grosvenor Gardens, London SW1W 0GA Tel 01-730 6525, and local offices

Transalpino, 71-75 Buckingham Palace Road, London SW1W 0QL Tel 01-834 9656

The Miracle Bus Company, 408 The Strand, London WC2 Tel 01-379 6055

All issue BIGE/Eurorail tickets, available to anyone aged under 26, and offering savings of up to 50% on normal rail fares. There are lower fares for those under 14 and on some routes for those under 16. The tickets can only be booked through specialised rail travel operators or through appointed student and youth travel offices. They are valid for two months and stop-overs are possible en route. Destinations include Austria, Belgium, Czechoslovakia, Denmark, France, Federal Republic of Germany, Greece, Ireland, Italy, Netherlands, Poland, Portugal, Spain, Sweden, Switzerland, and Turkey.

For all those under 26 the Inter-Rail Card costs £139 and gives unlimited rail travel for one month through 21 European countries, plus up to 50% discount off travel in Britain and Northern Ireland and reduced price tickets on Hoverspeed hovercraft, most Sealink ships and other ferry services. The Cards are available for those who have been resident in Britain and Northern Ireland for at least 6 months immediately prior to purchase. They are obtainable on production of a passport and completed application form from principal British Rail stations and appointed travel agents. The Card can normally be issued on the spot but it is still wise to apply a week or more in advance. The Inter-Rail and Boat Card costs £169 and offers all the above facilities plus free travel on some Mediterranean, Scandinavian and Irish shipping routes.

The Britrail Pass offers unlimited rail travel in the UK for 8, 15 or 22 days. The Pass can be purchased at half the adult fare for those under 15. If you are between 16 and 25 a Britrail Youth Pass is available. The Passes are only available outside Britain. In mainland Europe they are available from British Rail offices:

Belgium
Rue de la Montagne 52, 1000 Brussels Tel Brussels 511 6685

France
55/57 rue St Roche, 75001 Paris Tel Paris 42 61 85 40

Federal Republic of Germany
Neue-Mainzer-Strasse 22, 6000 Frankfurt/Main 1, Tel Frankfurt 25 20 33

Netherlands
Aurora Gebouw (5e), Stadhouderskade 2, 1054 ES Amsterdam Tel Amsterdam 85 22 02

Italy
Via Pirelli 11, 20124 Milan Tel Milan 655 2297

Switzerland
Centralbahnplatz 9, 4002 Basel Tel Basel 23 14 05 or Limmatquai 78, 8001 Zurich Tel Zurich 47 99 38

For travelling within Britain, anyone under the age of 24 or a full time student in the UK, is entitled to purchase a British Rail Young Person's Railcard, entitling the holder to 30% reduction on a wide variety of tickets. The card costs £15 and is valid for one year. There are some travel restrictions on certain routes at peak times. Further details and application forms are obtainable from principal British Rail stations or most student travel offices. British Rail also offers a variety of discount tickets depending on age, time of day, and travel distance. Make sure to ask for the cheapest available ticket when booking. It is often cheaper to buy a return ticket than a single one, but remember to state how long it will be before you intend undertaking the return journey. Further information can be obtained from British Rail offices or agents in other countries and from any British Rail station.

Rail Rovers are rail passes valid for 7 or 14 days, cost £135 or £215 and permit unlimited travel on the British Rail network. Cheaper Rail Rovers covering limited areas are also available. Apply to any British Rail Travel Centre at least 7 working days before you wish to travel. Ages 5-15, disabled travellers or holders of Young Persons Railcards are entitled to 34% reduction. Children under 5 travel free.

By sea Most ferry companies offer special rates for young people and groups, and there are often lower fares for off-peak travel. Details can be obtained from appointed travel agents, student travel offices or the ferry companies themselves. See also details above on Inter-Rail and Boat Cards.

The main ferry and hovercraft operators and their routes are:

Brittany Ferries
Poole-Cherbourg, Cork-Roscoff, Portsmouth-Roscoff, Portsmouth-St Malo, Plymouth-Santander

The Brittany Centre, Wharf Road, Portsmouth, Hampshire PO2 8RU Tel Portsmouth 827701

Milbay Docks, Plymouth, Devon PL1 3EW Tel Plymouth 227104

Gare Maritime du Naye, 35400 St Malo, France Tel 99 566840

Gare Maritime Roscoff, Port du Bloscom 29211, France Tel 98 690720

Modesto Piniero y Cia, Paseo de Peareda 27, Santander, Spain Tel 942 214500

DFDS Seaways
Harwich-Esbjerg, Newcastle-Esbjerg, Harwich-Hamburg, Harwich-Gothenburg, Newcastle-Gothenburg

Scandinavia House, Parkeston Quay, Harwich CO12 4QG Tel Harwich 554681

Sankt Annae. Plads 30, 1295 Copenhagen K, Denmark Tel 01 156300

Skandiahamnen 402-73, Gothenburg 8, Sweden Tel 031 540300

Jessenstrasse 4, 200 Hamburg 50, Federal Republic of Germany Tel 040 3890371

Fred Olsen Lines
Harwich-Hirtshals, Harwich-Oslo, Harwich-Kristiansand

Victoria Plaza, 111 Buckingham Palace Road, London SW1W 0SP Tel 01-828 7000

Hoverspeed
Dover-Calais, Dover-Boulogne

Maybrook House, Queens Gardens, Dover, Kent CT17 9UQ Tel Dover 240202

Boulogne International Hoverport, Boulogne sur Mer, France Tel 21 302726

Calais International Hoverport, Calais, France Tel 21 966710

North Sea Ferries
Hull-Rotterdam, Hull-Zeebrugge

King George Dock, Hedon Road, Hull HU9 5QA Tel Hull 795141

Beneluxhaven Europort, Box 1123, 3180 AC Rozenburg ZH, Netherlands Tel 01819.62077

Leopold II Dam, Havendam, 8380 Zeebrugge Tel 050 545601

Olau Line *Sheerness-Vlissingen*
Ferry Terminal, Sheerness, Kent M12 1SN Tel Sheerness 663355

Buitenhaven Postbus 231, 4380 AE Vlissingen Tel 01184 65400

Sally Line *Ramsgate-Dunkirk*
Argyle Centre, York Street, Ramsgate, Kent CT11 9DS Tel Ramsgate 595566

Dunkerque Port Ouest, 59279 Loon-Plage, France Tel 1628 684344

Sealink
Folkestone-Boulogne, Dover-Calais, Portsmouth-Cherbourg, Weymouth-Cherbourg, Newhaven-Dieppe, Harwich-Hook of Holland, Stranraer-Larne

163-203 Eversholt Street, London NW1 1BG Tel 01-387 1234

Southern House, Lord Warden Square, Dover, Kent CT16 1JG Tel Dover 203203

Gare Maritime, Dunkerque Ouest, France Tel 668001

Armement Naval SNCF, Gare Maritime, BP85, 6203 Dieppe, France Tel 842260

Armement Naval SNCF, Terminal Gare Maritime, Calais, France Tel 967070

Gare Maritime, BP27, 62201 Boulogne sur Mer, France Tel 302511

By air International air fares and the regulations covering them change frequently. It is therefore advisable to check all possibilities carefully well in advance. Excursion and Advance Purchase Excursion (APEX) fares have a variety of names depending on the airline offering them, and give considerable savings on normal tickets but impose a variety of restrictions, such as the time of purchase before departure, length of stay on arrival, specific routes, restricted stop-overs, time of flight etc. APEX fares are generally cheaper than excursion fares. Two UK companies specialising in low cost air travel are:

STA Travel, 74 Brompton Road, London SW7 3LH Tel 01-581 1022

The Miracle Bus Company, 408 The Strand, London WC2 Tel 01-379 3322

By road If you are not travelling too far afield and you want to save money there is a lot to be said for travelling by coach. Not only is it usually economical but you will also be freed from the burden of carrying your luggage for any great distance since you normally stay with the same vehicle for the entire journey. In the UK contact International Express Services, National Express, Western House, 237-239 Oxford Street, London W1R 1AB Tel 01-439 9368, or associated agencies for details of services throughout Europe. There are 10% discounts for those under 26 on some routes and on others for which any student holding a National Express discount card is eligible. The card is available from student travel offices, National Express and Scottish Citylink agents or by post. In addition to discounts in Europe it will also give 33% off standard fares throughout the British National Express and Scottish Citylink network. The card costs £3.90, is valid for 12 months, and available to any student in full-time education. The Miracle Bus Company, see above, also offer low-cost European coach travel. For details on coach travel within Britain contact National Travel, Victoria Coach Station, London SW1W 9TP Tel 01-730 0202.

USEFUL PUBLICATIONS

Grants and scholarships In the UK local education authorities will often provide enquirers in their area with travel and subsistence grants for approved visits; application should be made through schools or colleges. Information on scholarships available to students wishing to study abroad can usually be obtained from the relevant embassy or high commission. Most of the publications listed here can be found in the reference section of UK public libraries and overseas in the libraries of British Council offices.

The Grants Register 1987-1989 is intended primarily for students at or above graduate level and for people requiring further professional or advanced vocational training. It covers scholarships, fellowships and research grants; exchange opportunities, vacation study awards and travel grants; grants-in-aid, grants for artistic or scientific projects; competitions, prizes, honoraria; professional and vocational awards, and special awards for refugees, minority groups and students in unexpected financial difficulties. Published by Macmillan, Houndmills, Basingstoke, Hants RG21 2XS Tel Basingstoke 29242, price £45.

Study Abroad XXV 1988-1991 lists over 200,000 scholarships, fellowships, assistantships and travel grants at university level throughout the world. Published by UNESCO, 7 Place de Fontenoy, 75700 Paris, France. Obtainable in the UK from HMSO.

Scholarships Abroad is published annually and lists over 300 scholarships tenable for a full academic year to British students by overseas governments and universities as well as a number of bursaries for shorter periods. The majority of awards are for post graduates only. Published by the British Council, Design, Production & Publishing Department, 65 Davies Street, London W1Y 2AA, price £2.95.

Higher Education in the European Community: Student Handbook contains basic information on the availability of grants as well as other information on study, for students of EC member states. Published and available from the Office for Official Publications of the European Communities, 5 rue de Commerce, Boite Postale 1003, L-2985 Luxembourg. Obtainable in the UK from HMSO, price £8.

Employers and Professional Bodies Offering Sponsorship and Supplementary Awards lists many industrial and professional organisations and government departments which administer schemes to assist young people of high academic promise to take higher education courses. Reference copies are available in schools and careers offices. Obtainable from the Manpower Services Commission, Department CW ISCO 5, The Paddock, Frizing Hall, Bradford BD9 4HD Tel Bradford 541391, price £1.60.

Research Grants is a useful free guide listing financial support for research and linguistics/language teaching. It covers details on institutional support, public funds and other sources and gives details on directories of awards, trusts and foundation. Published by the Centre for Information on Language Teaching and Research (CILT), Regent's College, Inner Circle, Regent's Park, London NW1 4NS Tel 01-486 8221.

Travel and accommodation

Touring Guide to Europe £5.95 including UK postage, gives information on 22 countries, what to see, and background details about the people and way of life. *International Youth Hostel Handbook Vol I* £4.95, gives addresses and brief details of all the permanent hostels in Europe, North Africa and the Near East with the principal hostel regulations. Large folding map showing locations. Published annually in March. Both available from YHA Services Ltd, 14 Southampton Street, London WC2E 7HY Tel 01-836 8541 or YHA (England & Wales), National Office, Trevelyan House, St Stephen's Hill, St Albans, Hertfordshire AL1 2DY Tel St Albans 55215.

Europe by Train £6.70 including UK postage, is a paperback guide for young European train travellers, giving advice on where to stay. Published annually in March/April and available from Timetable Publishing Office, PO Box 36, Peterborough PE3 6SB.

Europe – A Manual for Hitch-hikers £3.95, gives country by country information on hitching techniques, route planning, entry procedures and attitudes towards hitch-hikers. Also includes an essential vocabulary in 9 languages, advice on how to cross the channel cheaply and for free, how to read foreign number plates, addresses of hitch-hiking agencies, sources of free maps and how to get help with legal problems. *Travellers Survival Kit Europe* £5.95, is a practical guide covering over 36 European countries, including details on the cost of food and accommodation, rules of the road, how the telephone systems work, car hire, health tips, public transport, shopping hours, customs regulations, the law, where to get help and information and many useful addresses. Both available plus 75p postage from Vacation Work Publications, 9 Park End Street, Oxford OX1 1HJ Tel Oxford 241978.

The Traveller's Handbook £9.95, is an 860 page reference and source book for the independent traveller, with chapters on travel, camping and backpacking, hitch-hiking, health, clothing, luggage and survival kits, where to stay, dealing with people when things go wrong, photography, choosing maps, passports, visas, permits, insurance, currency and customs. Also includes special chapters for students, single women and the handicapped. Published by WEXAS International, 45 Brompton Road, London SW3 1DE Tel 01-589 0500.

YMCA World Directory £3.75 including postage, lists over 2,400 YMCA addresses in 90 countries offering accommodation for men and women. *Pack for Europe* £2, post free, is a handbook containing addresses of hostels and restaurants of the YMCA, YWCA and other recognised youth organisations, offering accommodation within a reasonable price range in Europe and the Middle East. Available from National Council of YMCAs. Supplies Department, 640 Forest Road, London E17 3DZ Tel 01-520 5599.

Further opportunities for work, study and travel

Academic Year Abroad $19.95. Complete guide to 1,250 overseas study programmes offered by accredited US colleges and universities, with a separate section on over 400 foreign university programmes. *Vacation Study Abroad* $19.95, provides information on over 1,000 summer and short-term programmes offered by US and foreign educational institutions. *Study in the United Kingdom* $14.95, guides students and counsellors to over 800 programmes offered throughout the year in the UK and Ireland. All available, postage extra, from the Institute of International Education, IIE Books, 809 United Nations Plaza, New York, NY 10017, United States of America.

Work, Study and Travel Abroad: The Whole World Handbook $8.95. Comprehensive handbook giving information on the basics of going abroad, the cheapest ways to travel, meeting the people, getting work and study opportunities. Published by the Council on International Educational Exchange (CIEE) and available plus $1.50 postage from St Martin's Press, 175 Fifth Avenue, New York, NY 10010, United States of America.

Working Holidays £7.70, is an authoritative annual guide to thousands of short-term paid and voluntary jobs available throughout the year in Britain and over 70 other countries. Full details are given on the type of work involved and the salary, board and accommodation provided, as well as comprehensive practical information on work and residence permits, travel, useful publications and how to advertise for a job abroad.

Volunteer Work £3.55, is a comprehensive guide to voluntary work and service with information on over 100 organisations recruiting volunteers for medium and long-term projects in Britain and 153 countries worldwide. Practical advice is given on selecting an agency, preparation and training, medical requirements, travel, advisory bodies and help for returning volunteers.

Home from Home £3.95, is a guide to international homestays, termstays and exchange visits, with information on over 80 bona fide organisations arranging stays in Britain and 40 other countries in Europe and around the world. Authoritative practical information includes health and insurance requirements, youth travel, dealing with emergencies, and what to expect as a visitor or as a host family.

The *Young Visitors* series of guides provides comprehensive and up-to-date information about living, studying or holidaying in another country. *Young Visitors to Britain* is published in English, French, and Spanish language editions. Also available in English and the host language are *Young Visitors to France, Young Visitors to Spain, Young Visitors to Belgium, Young Visitors to the Netherlands, Young Visitors to the Federal Republic of Germany, Young Visitors to Italy,*

Young Visitors to Luxembourg, Young Visitors to Finland and *Young Visitors to Denmark. Each price £2.*

All prices are inclusive of UK postage and all titles are available from the Central Bureau, Seymour Mews, London W1H 9PE Tel 01-486 5101.

OTHER RESOURCES

The Centre for Information on Language Teaching and Research (CILT), Regent's College, Inner Circle, Regent's Park, London NW1 4NS Tel 01-486 8221 was established in 1966 as a national centre to collect and pass on information on all aspects of languages to anyone who is involved in any way with the learning or teaching of languages. Their Language Teaching Library contains an extensive reference collection on languages, linguistics and language teaching, including coverage of teaching materials in print for French, German, Italian, Russian and Spanish. Materials are also held for English as a second language, and for less commonly taught languages, including those of minority communities in the UK. There is also an enquiry service in operation, on all aspects of language teaching and learning. In addition to language and culture guides, detailed in this guide under the relevant language sections, CILT also regularly publish updated lists of teaching materials, information guides and bibliographies, as well as edited collections of papers and reports on new developments in the theoretical and practical aspects of foreign language teaching. In order to promote language learning and the use of languages in society, specialist conferences and teacher in-service training programmes are also organised.

The Institute of Linguists, 24a Highbury Grove, London N5 2EA Tel 01-359 7445/6386 was founded in 1910, and is a professional association serving the interests of all linguists. Although it does not run courses, it offers a range of public examinations in over 30 languages, and will set a paper for any modern language for which it receives a firm entry. The Institute can also offer resource lists suggesting suitable background reading matter for those taking examinations, in addition to advice on courses and other means of study. The Institute's examinations provide recognised qualifications showing practical competence and applied language skills, from a Preliminary Certificate for beginners through to a Final Diploma for the professional. In the area of community work the Institute provides two examinations, and two levels of examinations for translators. Full details of the examinations and entry procedures are given in the published syllabuses, available, price 75p, from the Institute.

FURTHER OPPORTUNITIES FOR LANGUAGE LEARNING

In addition to the courses offered in this guide there are further opportunities for learning languages, operated by The Central Bureau, which may be open to you.

The Language Assistant scheme enables modern language students from Britain and over 30 other countries to spend a year working in a school or college in a country where their chosen language is spoken. Appointments as Junior Language Assistants are also available in France, the Federal Republic of Germany and Spain for school leavers intending to study French, German, or Spanish at an institution of higher education.

The Teacher Exchange scheme Operated on a post-to-post exchange basis, this scheme for mainland Europe is open to all teachers of modern languages and/or related subjects serving full time in secondary, further or higher education. Denmark is an exception in that there are also opportunities for primary school teachers. Grants are given to assist participants in these programmes and one way placements are available in Bulgaria, Denmark and Hungary.

Short courses are for teachers of modern languages and are held in France, Federal Republic of Germany, Italy and Spain. They are directed by members of HM Inspectorate and are chiefly concerned with maintaining and improving teachers' fluency in the spoken language concerned. In addition, courses for teachers of classical subjects, also directed by a member of HM Inspectorate are held alternate years in Rome and Athens.

International study visits Through the International Study Visit Programme, The Central Bureau provides funds to facilitate the study of aspects of educational provision abroad; to promote the establishment of international links and exchanges in the education field and to develop international educational cooperation. In addition to this programme, the Central Bureau administers in the UK the European Community Scheme of Short Study Visits for Education Specialists. Details of this scheme are available from the Central Bureau but note that participation in the scheme is by nomination of chief officers only.

Project Europe travel bursaries are available for young people aged 16-19 in full or part-time education wishing to carry out a study project in a member state of the European Community. The maximum bursary awarded for any one project will be £150.

School and class linking services put UK schools in touch with partners abroad. A penfriend service for individuals in the 10-18 age group is also available and enquiries about this should be directed to the Northern Ireland office, or if you are a resident of Scotland to the Scottish office.

International services to technical and vocational education Course-related links can be provided on request for FE institutions seeking a partner overseas. A special scheme exists to facilitate project-based links between UK and Dutch colleges and a similar scheme with Denmark is being developed. The International Association for the Exchange of Students for Technical Experience (IAESTE) is administered in the UK by The Central Bureau. It enables students from affiliated institutions of higher education to undertake industrial placements relevant to their courses of study in any of the 50 member countries.

The Bureau provides the secretariats of the British Universities Transatlantic Exchanges Committee (BUTEC) and the Colleges And Polytechnics Transatlantic Exchanges Committee (CAPTEC), both of which encourage staff and student exchange and interchange between the UK and the US and Canada.

Young worker exchange The Central Bureau is both the UK National Coordinating Agency and a promoting body for the EC Young Worker Exchange Programme which is sponsored by the European Commission. The main aim of the programme is to enable young people to gain vocational experience in another EC country through a work placement with a host employer, or through a programme of meetings and visits which focus on a particular industry or aspect of an occupation.

BASQUE

Basque is unique, with no connections between it and any other language. Although it has structural similarities to some Asian languages, it stands completely independent and isolated. Nothing is known of its origins, but it has been fiercly preserved throughout the centuries by Basques, often in the face of official discouragement. As the only western European language not of Indo-European origin it is probably the only survivor of the languages spoken before the arrival of the Indo-Europeans. It is spoken on both sides of the Franco-Spanish border by some 800,000 people. In the Basque region of Spain, which includes the provinces of Guipúzcoa, Vizcaya and Navarra, it is now a flourishing official language, spoken by over 25% of the population. In the French département *of Pyrénées-Atlantiques it has less official recognition but is still taught in schools.*

COURSES IN FRANCE

EUSKALDUNTZE ALFABETATZE KOORDINAKUNDEA (AEK) 17 rue Pontrique, 64100 Bayonne Tel Bayonne 257609

Language courses for all levels in St Jean Pied de Port near Bayonne. Ages 18 + , individuals and groups. 2-6 weeks, July-August. 40 hours per week. Average 8 per class. Audio-visual facilities. Afternoon activities include excursions, visits to local cooperatives, trips to the mountains and meetings with local people. Cost FF1700, FF1100 students/ unemployed, includes course, teaching materials and full board school accommodation.

COURSES IN SPAIN

EUSKALDUNTZE ALFABETATZE KOORDINAKUNDEA (AEK) Diputazio Kalea 3, 48009 Bilbao Tel Bilbao 4231552

Iztueta Kalea 3, 2002 Donostia, San Sebastian Tel San Sebastian 283988

Errege Katonlikuak 15, 01013 Gasteiz, Vittoria Tel Vittoria 288922

Konpainia Kalea 25, 31001 Irune, Pamplona Tel Pamplona 220213

Language courses for all levels in centres throughout the Spanish Basque country. Ages 16+. 1 month, October-June or 2 weeks, July-September. 20-35 hours per week. Average 15 per class. Audio-visual facilities. Excursions, social activities and opportunities to meet local people. Cost Pts25000 winter, Pts22000 summer, includes course, teaching materials, and full board accommodation in pensions, excluding weekend meals in winter.

INFORMATION

Spanish Embassy
24 Belgrave Square, London SW1X 8OA Tel 01-235 1484

British Embassy
Fernando el Santo 16, 28010 Madrid Tel Madrid 4190200

Tourist office

Spanish National Tourist Office, 57/58 St James's Street, London SW1 Tel 01-499 0901

Youth hostels

Red Espanola de Albergues Juveniles, Jose Ortega y Gasset 71, 28006 Madrid

Youth & student information

TIVE, Oficina Nacional de Intercambio y Turismo de Jovenes y Estudiantes, Jose Ortega y Gasset, 28006 Madrid

For information on official organisations in France see under the French *language courses section.*

Travel

STA Travel, 74 Old Brompton Road, London, SW7 3LQ Tel 01-581 8233 operate flexible, low cost flights between London and destinations throughout France and Spain.

Transalpino Ltd, 117 Euston Road, London NW1 2SX Tel 01-388 2267 offer up to 50% off full rail fares to destinations in France and Spain for those under 26.

BULGARIAN

Bulgarian is one of the Slavic language family, other members of which include Russian, Belorussian, Ukrainian, Czech, Polish, Slovak, Bulgarian, Macedonian, Serbo-Croatian and Slovenian. It uses the Cyrillic script, and as the official language of the People's Republic of Bulgaria is spoken by some 9 million people. In the 9th century a Bulgarian dialect was the basis for the first Slavic alphabet. From the 9th-11th centuries the kingdom of Bulgaria enjoyed a Golden Age of letters, with Bulgarian holding the distinction of being the first literary language of the Slavs. The codification of the language as it is known today took place in the 19th century, but due to the long periods of Byzantine and Ottoman domination, Bulgarian possesses features setting it apart from the other Slavonic languages, linking it more with neighbouring languages.

COURSES IN BULGARIA

THE BRITISH COUNCIL Specialist Tours Department, 65 Davies Street, London W1Y 2AA Tel 01-499 8011
Offers places at summer schools under Cultural Exchange Programmes. Ages 18-35. Summer seminars in Bulgarian language and literature for foreign students of Slavonic studies at Kliment Okhridski University of Sofia for advanced levels, with daily language tuition and lectures by senior academics on linguistic problems, literature, folklore, history and

art in Bulgaria. Visits to historical sites and trips to the Black Sea coast. Also similar courses in Veliko Turnovo for younger, less advanced students. 1 month, August. Board and lodging provided, but travel paid by applicant. Bursaries available. Applications should be submitted through an academic or professional referee; candidates applying from a university, college or school must submit their application through a supervisor of studies or head of department. *Closing date mid February.*

INFORMATION

Bulgarian Embassy
186-188 Queen's Gate, London SW7 5HL Tel 01-584 9400

British Embassy
Boulevard Marshal Tolbukhin 65-67, Sofia 1000

Tourist office
Bulgarian National Tourist Office, 18 Princes Street, London W1R 7RE Tel 01-499 6988

Youth hostels
Union Bulgare de Tourisme, Boulevard Marshal Tolbukhin 18, Sofia

Youth & student information
Orbita Youth Travel Bureau, Boulevard Alexander Stamboliski 45a, Sofia

Resources
Centre for Information on Language Teaching and Research (CILT), Regent's College, Inner Circle, Regent's Park, London NW1 4NS Tel 01-486 8221 publish *Bulgarian Language and Culture Guide* £4.25 including postage, with details on the provision and use of language teaching and learning resources, covering an introduction to the language, useful addresses, libraries and special collections to consult, opportunities for learning, and examinations which can be taken.

Travel
Transalpino Ltd, 117 Euston Road, London NW1 2SX Tel 01-388 2267 offer up to 50% off full rail fares for those under 26.

Accommodation
Orbita Youth Travel Bureau, see above, offers accommodation at student hostels in Sofia, Varna, Veliko Turnovo, and in the Rhodope Mountains during July and August.

CATALAN

Catalan is a Romance language, descended from Latin, bearing similarities to both French and Spanish, and a close relation of Provencal. It is the official language of Andorra, and is spoken by over 70% of the population of Catalonia, the northeastern region of Spain. There are regional variations in the Balearic Islands, Valencia, Alicante and the Pyrénées-Orientales province of France. Catalan has a rich cultural history, its own television and radio stations, and is now the official government language in the regions in Spain in which it is spoken. In total there are some 11 million speakers.

COURSES IN SPAIN

CENTRE CARLES SALVADOR C/Moratin 15-6a, Valencia Tel Valencia 3511727

Language courses for all levels in Valencia. Ages 16+, individuals and groups. 1 month, July. 3 hours per week. Average 12-14 per class. Audio-visual facilities. Opportunities to study culture, literature and Valencian history. Also courses in administrative language and for teachers. Examinations of the Department of Catalan Language of the University of Valencia may be taken. Cost Pts4500 includes course and teaching materials. No accommodation provided.

ESTUDIO GENERAL LULIANO DE MALLORCA Instituto de Lenguas Modernas, Estudio General y San Roque 4, 07001 Palma de Mallorca, Balearic Islands Tel Palma 711988

Language courses for all levels on Majorca. Ages 18+, individuals and groups. 3 weeks, July. 20 hours per week. Lectures on history, art and literature, and excursions to places of interest. Cost from Pts54000 includes course and full board hotel accommodation. Half board or breakfast only terms also available. Cost excluding accommodation Pts20000. Textbooks Pts1500. Approved by the universities of Barcelona and the Balearic Islands.

GENERALITAT DE CATALUNYA Departament d'Ensenyament, Escola Oficial d'Idiomes, Avenida Drassanes s/n, 08001 Barcelona Tel Barcelona 29 34 12

Courses for beginners and false beginners. 4 weeks, July. 20 hours per week. Maximum 20 per class. Supplementary programme of lectures and other cultural activities to acquaint students with the culture, literature and lifestyle of Catalonia. Cost Pts14500. For a small fee, students may use University of Barcelona sports facilities. Accommodation list available; cost of living estimated at Pts60000 per month. Also run semi-intensive semester courses during the academic year. 10 hours per week, October-February or February-June.

ÒMNIUM CULTURAL Carrer d'Apodaca 3, 2na Planta, 43004 Tarragona Tel Tarragona 21 66 38

Language courses for all levels in Tarragona, on the coast, south of Barcelona. Ages 18+, groups only. 6 weeks, June-July. 8 hours per week, evenings. 15-40 per class depending on level. Cost Pts3000. No accommodation provided. Approved by Generalitat de Catalunya.

THE SPANISH COUNCIL Department of Castilian Studies, Apartado 2372, 46080 Valencia Tel Valencia 3514011/3514015

Language courses for all levels in the centre of the old part of Valencia. Ages 4+, children's courses and 16+, individuals and groups. 2+ weeks, all year. 10 or 20 hours per week. Maximum 8 per class. Video and audio-visual aids. Also occasional lectures and poetry readings in Catalan. Extra-curricular activities include cultural visits, excursions, fiestas, cinema, theatre, parties, plus opportunities for sports. Participants have free membership of the Valencial Society of Fine Arts with use of its social facilities. Classes available at extra charge in arts and crafts including classical and flamenco guitar and dance. Cost Pts80000, 1 month, includes basic course and half board family accommodation; Pts40000 excluding accommodation. Registration fee Pts8500. Students are met at station or airport on arrival. The teaching staff from the University of Valencia Philology Department. Recognised by the Ministry of the Interior and the Ministry of Education and Sciences. *Scholarships available from the Spanish Council, Programma de Becas, at the above address.* **PH**

UNIVERSITAT BARCELONA Servei de Lengua Catalana, Gran Via de les Corts Catalanes 585, 08007 Barcelona Tel Barcelona 18 42 66
Language courses for all levels in Barcelona, capital of Catalonia. Ages 15+. 1 or 2 months, beginning July or September. 8 hours per week. Maximum 20 per class. Cost Pts5000 per month. Textbooks approx Pts2000. No accommodation provided.

INFORMATION

Spanish Embassy
24 Belgrave Square, London SW1X 8OA Tel 01-235 1484

British Embassy
Fernando el Santo 16, 28010 Madrid Tel Madrid 4190200

Tourist office
Spanish National Tourist Office, 57/58 St James's Street, London SW1 Tel 01-499 0901

Youth hostels
Red Espanola de Albergues Juveniles, Jose Ortega y Gasset 71, 28006 Madrid

Youth & student information
TIVE, Oficina Nacional de Intercambio y Turismo de Jovenes y Estudiantes, Jose Ortega y Gasset, 28006 Madrid

Travel
STA Travel, 74 Old Brompton Road, London, SW7 3LQ Tel 01-581 8233 operate flexible, low cost flights between London and destinations throughout Spain.

Transalpino Ltd, 117 Euston Road, London NW1 2SX Tel 01-388 2267 offer up to 50% off full rail fares to over 50 destinations in Spain for those under 26.

CZECH/SLOVAK

Czech and Slovak are the two official languages of the Czechoslovak Socialist Republic. Czech is spoken by 10 million people in the western and central parts, the former lands of the Czech Crown comprising Bohemia and Moravia. It is closely related to Slovak, spoken by about 5 million people in Slovakia, historically part of Hungary, the eastern third of the country. Although very closely related, enough for Slovak to be considered as a dialect of Czech, the two languages have diverged, partly through the historical division of the territories between Austria and Hungary, and the different alphabets and distinct literatures make them separate languages. The two languages have been exposed to different external linguistic influences on account of the neighbouring languages, Czech showing signs of having been continuous with German, and Slovak displaying a similar strong influence from Hungarian. Czech is a Slavic language written in Roman script, the foundations of the alphabet being laid early in the 15th century by Jan Hus, the religious reformer. The Slovak alphabet is similar, though it lacks three Czech letters, and has three of its own.

COURSES IN AUSTRIA

GESELLSCHAFT FÜR OST UND SUDOSTKUNDE Bismarkstrasse 5, 4020 Linz, Austria Tel 27 33 80
Courses in Czech for all levels at Unterweissenbach, Austria. Ages 14 +. Individuals/groups. 2 weeks, August. Maximum 15 per class. Classes

and lectures on geography and history delivered in Czech, with explanations given in German, English or French if necessary, by university lecturers. Talks, discussions and concerts, opportunities to learn Czech folk songs, plus sports including tennis, riding, swimming, walking and saunas. Cost AS5000 includes tuition and learning materials. Accommodation arranged at guesthouse; cost from AS2100 half board, AS2600 full board. Scholarships available.

COURSES IN CZECHOSLOVAKIA

THE BRITISH COUNCIL Specialist Tours Department, 65 Davies Street, London W1Y 2DA Tel 01-499 8011
Offers places at summer schools under Cultural Exchange Programmes. All levels except beginners. 3/4 weeks, July/August. Ages 18-35. Course for students of Slovak language and literature at Comenius University, Bratislava, and in Czech language at Charles University, Prague, or at JE Purkyne University, Brno. Special intensive courses in Czech or Slovak at elementary level. Lectures on present day Czechoslovakia, and Czech or Slovak linguistics, literary history or the history of Czechoslovakia. Candidates must have had tuition in Czech or Slovak for at least one academic year or possess active knowledge of another Slavic language. Board and lodging provided, but travel paid by applicant. Bursaries available. Applications should be submitted through an academic or professional referee; candidates applying from a university, college or school must submit their application through a supervisor of studies or head of department. *Closing date mid February.*

INFORMATION

Czechoslovak Embassy
25 Kensington Palace Gardens, London W8 4QY Tel 01-229 1255

British Embassy
Thunovska 14, Prague 1

Tourist office
Cedok, 17-18 Old Bond Street, London W1X 3DA Tel 01-629 6058

Youth hostels/youth & student information

Czechoslovak Youth and Students Travel Bureau (CKM), Zitna ulice 12, 12105 Prague 2

Resources

Centre for Information on Language Teaching and Research (CILT), Regent's College, Inner Circle, Regent's Park, London NW1 4NS Tel 01-486 8221 publish *Czech/Slovak Language and Culture Guide* £4.25 including postage, with details on the provision and use of language teaching and learning resources, covering an introduction to the language, useful addresses, libraries and special collections to consult, opportunities for learning, and examinations which can be taken.

The Great Britain/East Europe Centre, 31 Knightsbridge, London SW1X 7NH Tel 01-245 9771 aims to promote closer understanding between the British and the peoples of Bulgaria, Czechoslovakia, Hungary, Romania, Poland and the German Democratic Republic. Organises colloquia, symposia and seminars to permit informal exchanges of views between people who have the same professional interest. Also arranges individual visits for academic and professional people.

Travel

STA Travel, 74 Old Brompton Road, London SW7 3LQ Tel 01-581 8233 operate flexible, low-cost flights to Prague. Cost from £77 return, ex-London.

Transalpino Ltd, 117 Euston Road, London NW1 2SX Tel 01-388 2267 offer up to 50% off full rail fares for those under 26.

DANISH

Danish is the official language of Denmark, one of the two official languages of Greenland, and the main language of communication in the Faroe Islands. It is a member of the Scandinavian group of languages, which share a common root in the Old Norse language spoken throughout Scandinavia from 6th-11th centuries, which make up a branch of the Germanic languages, themselves members of the Indo-European group. Danish, Norwegian and Swedish have remained close to each other, there being strong geographical and historical links. From the late 14th century until 1814, Norway was under Danish rule and Danish was the official language of the court and the bureaucracy. The dialect closer to Danish than Norwegian was spoken in the Norwegian part, and is still in use today, often referred to as Dano-Norwegian. There are also links between the present day English language and Danish, dating back to Danelaw when the Danes ruled over East Anglia and the eastern counties of Britain, and when the Northern Isles and parts of Ireland were in Norwegian hands.

COURSES IN DENMARK

DET DANSKE SELSKAB Kultorvet 2, 1175 Copenhagen K
Tel 01 13 54 48

An independent, self-governing, non-profitmaking institution under the Danish Ministry of Cultural Affairs with the aim of spreading information about Denmark abroad, stimulating cultural relations and

cooperation between Denmark and other countries. Organises courses in Danish language for all levels at Askov Folk High School in the south of Jutland. Ages 18 + , individuals and groups. Maximum 20 per class. Applicants should have some knowledge of Danish. 20 hours tuition per week. 2 weeks, July. Lectures on culture, literature and art. Also courses for translators. Visits to local tourist sights, and opportunities to discuss folk dancing and films with Danes living at the school. Learning materials are sent to participants before the course starts. Cost DKr4400 includes full board single room accommodation, excursions, social events and transfer from station. Can assist with visits after the course, and arrange study tours for groups on specialised themes. **PH**
In the UK applications should be sent to The Danish Cultural Institute, 3 Doune Terrace, Edinburgh EH3 6DY Tel 031-225 7189.

THE FOLK HIGH SCHOOL INFORMATION OFFICE Vartov Opgang 6, Favergade 27, 1463 Copenhagen K Tel 01 13 98 22
Can provide information on Danish language courses available at over 100 Folk High Schools all over Denmark. Folk High Schools traditionally place an emphasis on creating a milieu where dialogue and debate can take place, with freedom in choice of subjects; the form of instruction varying from study circles, discussions, lectures, self study to project groups. All levels. Maximum 18 per class. 6-12 hours tuition per week. 1 + weeks, all year. Ages 17 + . Individuals and families. Participants must be able to understand some Danish. Courses in many different subjects also available. Excursions and social activities at some schools. Cost from Dkr4000 includes course, teaching materials and full board residential accommodation. **PH**

THE INTERNATIONAL PEOPLE'S COLLEGE 1 Montebello Alle, 3000 Helsingor Tel 02 21 33 61
A Danish folk high school in Elsinore acting as an international residential centre for adults, bringing people of different nations and cultures together to foster fellowship and a spirit of global cooperation. Maximum 18 per class. Ages 19 + . Individuals, families and groups. Participants must have a serious intention to take an active part in the life of the school. Danish language classes available for all levels, covering basic elements of structure and developing a basic vocabulary for everyday situations. Language laboratory and audio-visual facilities. Also special summer courses in Danish language, culture and society, organised in conjunction with the Danish Ministry of Education. 2 weeks, June/July, and July/August. Many other courses available during the year. Excursions to historical sites and cultural/social institutions. Library and project materials provided. Scholarships and travel grants available. **PH**

INFORMATION

Royal Danish Embassy
55 Sloane Street, London SW1X 9SR Tel 01-235 1255

British Embassy
Kastelsvej 38/40, 2100 Copenhagen 0

Tourist office
Danish Tourist Board, Sceptre House, 169/173 Regent Street, London W1R 8PY Tel 01-734 2637

Youth hostels
Herbergs-Ringen, Vesterbrogade 39, 1620 Copenhagen V

Youth & student information
Danmarks Internationale Studenterkomite, Skindergade 28, 1159 Copenhagen K

Informationskontoret/Huset, Vester Alle 15, Arhus

Resources
The Danish Cultural Institute, 3 Doune Terrace, Edinburgh EH3 6DY Tel 031-225 7189 was founded in 1940 with the dual purpose of spreading information about Denmark and stimulating cultural relations and cooperation between Denmark and other countries. This is achieved through study tours and seminars, summer schools and conferences, lectures, publications, exhibitions, lectures, concerts, films and reference works. Also organises evening Danish language classes in cooperation with the universities of Edinburgh and Stirling.

Dick Phillips, Whitehall House, Nenthead, Alston, Cumbria CA9 3PS Tel Alston 81440 can provide information and various publications on the Faroe Islands covering historical background, physical environment and Faroese life.

Centre for Information on Language Teaching and Research (CILT), Regent's College, Inner Circle, Regent's Park, London NW1 4NS Tel 01-486 8221 publish *Danish Language and Culture Guide* £4.25 including postage, which provides details on the provision and use of language teaching and learning resources, covering an introduction to the language, useful addresses, libraries and special collections to consult, opportunities for learning, and examinations which can be taken.

The Use-It Youth Information Centre Copenhagen, Radhusstraede 13, 1466 Copenhagen K produce a newspaper *Playtime,* intended as an alternative guide to Copenhagen for low-budget visitors, with advice on travel, food and accommodation, cultural attractions, practical information and a list of alternative organisations.

Travel

The Nordic Tourist Ticket entitles the holder to unlimited travel on trains in Denmark, Finland, Norway and Sweden, and is also valid on some inter-Scandinavian ferries. Valid for 21 days, cost £128. Available from Norwegian State Railways, 21-24 Cockspur Street, London SW1Y 5DA Tel 01-930 6666.

Transalpino Ltd, 117 Euston Road, London NW1 2SX Tel 01-388 2267 offer up to 50% off full rail fares to destinations in Denmark for those under 26.

Map and General Travel Information leaflet provides information on travel, customs and entry formalities, residence and employment, the health service and other practical information. *Greenland* brochure provides brief information on routes to Greenland, domestic transport, accommodation, mountain hiking, boat hire, dog sledges, excursions, entry formalities, health services and other useful facts for visitors. *The Faroe Islands* booklet provides information including details on accommodation, food and drink, transport and activities, plus facts on the Faroes and practical information. All available from the Danish Tourist Board, see above.

Accommodation

The Danish Tourist Board, see above, publish *Camping,* a list of 500 officially approved camping sites, and also a listing of hotels, pensions, inns and youth hostels.

The Use-It Youth Information Centre Copenhagen, see above, publishes *Where to Sleep, Eat and Relax,* a leaflet listing accommodation in Copenhagen, including youth hostels, sleep-ins, cheap hotels, camping sites and pensions. Also *Housing in Copenhagen* giving information on private rooms for rent, flats, bedsits, student halls and communes.

Copenhagen Sleep-In, Per Henrik Lings Alle 6,2100 Copenhagen 0, is a hostel with 432 beds in 4-bedded rooms. Open 22 June-30 August. Cost DKr55 per night, bed and breakfast; take your own sleeping bag.

DUTCH/FLEMISH

Dutch is spoken by 14 million people in the Netherlands and 6 million people in northern Belgium, over half the population, where it is generally known as Flemish. It is one of the Germanic languages, and closest to English of any of the main languages. The earliest written record of Dutch dates back to the 11th century. The proximity of France made it an obvious source of influence on the Dutch language through the Middle Ages until the Napoleonic period and beyond. The Dutch revolt against Spain in the late 16th century had a profound effect both politically and linguistically, and the political independence and unity of the Netherlands meant that an official language became increasingly important; the economic predominance of the western provinces, notably Holland, led to its dialect being adopted as the standard, with a significant contribution from Flemish. As an important maritime nation, many Dutch nautical words have been incorporated into other languages. Flemish is one of the two languages of Belgium, the other being French. Historically Flemish was spoken in the Flanders region, and cultural and religious distinctions over the years have led to the separate terms, Dutch and Flemish, being used for the same language.

COURSES IN BELGIUM

CENTRE LINGUISTIQUE DE THIEUSIES rue du Chateau 26, 7461 Thieusies Tel Mons 72 84 90
Courses in Dutch for all levels at castle in Thieusies, a village near Mons and the French border. Ages 8 + , individuals and groups. 1 + weeks, all

year. 20 or 30 hours per week. Average 8 per class. Language laboratory and video room. Extra-curricular activities include trips, cultural and sporting activities. Cost BF6000, 20 hours, and BF7500, 30 hours, per week includes course, teaching materials and insurance. Accommodation BF1600, half board, student residence or BF2750, full board, family.

CENTRE LINGUISTIQUE DE VELM Halleweg 32, 3806 Velm Tel St Truiden 68 82 60
Courses in Dutch for all levels at castle in Velm, a village near St Truiden, north west of Liege. Ages 8+, individuals and groups. 1+ weeks, all year. 20 or 30 hours per week. Average 8 per class. Language laboratory and video room. Extra-curricular activities include trips, cultural and sporting activities. Cost BF6000, 20 hours and BF7500, 30 hours, per week includes course, teaching materials and insurance. Accommodation BF1600, half board, student residence or BF2750, full board, family.

COURS LAURENT Avenue Brugmann 69, 1060 Brussels Tel 657 11 94
Courses in the Dutch language for all levels in Brussels. No age limits, individuals and groups. All year. 1:1 classes, or for up to 4 people. Also 1:1 crash courses with 2, 3 or 4 hours tuition per day. Cost from BF5650 per week. Also individual courses, cost from BF250 per hour, and courses for business and technical needs. **PH**

INSTITUT PRO LINGUIS Place de l'Eglise 19, 6719 Thiaumont Tel Arlon 22 04 62
Courses in Dutch for all levels in country house at Thiaumont, near Arlon, close to the Luxembourg border. Ages 10+, individuals and groups. 1+ weeks, all year. 4 hours in language laboratory and 4 hours in conversation groups, per day. Maximum 7 per class. Cost from BF8650, 1 week, includes course, textbooks, transfer from station and full board accommodation at school or in village. Also weekend courses, Easter and summer holiday language/sports courses and intensive courses including private tuition for conversation practice. Business and science language programmes available on request.

INSTITUTE OF MODERN LANGUAGES AND COMMUNICATION Avenue de la Toison d'Or 20, Brussels Tel Brussels 512 66 07
Intensive Dutch language training for all levels in Brussels. No age limits, individuals and groups. 2 weeks, July and August. 4 x 45 minute lessons per day. Institute is devoted to developing human resources and refining skills through language and communication training.

Programmes follow a multi-disciplinary approach and are designed primarily for those whose business interests require effective communication in several languages. Cost from BF7950. Also 1:1 courses, and training in progressive oral language, advanced language, general business writing and practical correspondance, report writing, communication and public speaking, and written communication. Students arrange own accommodation.

MINISTERIE VAN DE VLAAMSE GEMEENSCHAP Administratie voor Onderwijszaken, Internationale Samenwerking, Kunstlaan 43, 1040 Brussels Tel Brussels 513 74 64
Summer course in Dutch language and culture at university in Hasselt-Dipenbeek, a town north east of Liege, for speakers of German, English, Finnish, Scandinavian and East European languages. Aimed at students with some knowledge of Dutch, and teachers/lecturers of Dutch. 2 weeks, August. 3 hours language tuition per day, plus classes on Flemish culture and literature. Also discussions on various themes and excursions in the local area. Weekend excursions arranged to Gent and Bruges/Antwerp. Cost BF20000. Family accommodation available. *Some bursaries available.*

COURSES IN THE NETHERLANDS

INTERNATIONALE STUDIEVERBLIJVEN ORGANISATIE KATWIJK (ISOK) De Zeeuw, Jan-Tooropstraat 4, 2225 XT Katwijk aan Zee Tel 01718-13533
Courses in Dutch for all levels at Katwijk aan Zee, a town on the coast, just north of The Hague. No age limits, individuals and groups. 1+ weeks, all year. 10 hours per week. Maximum 12 per class. Private language lessons also available. Excursions to museums and places of cultural interest. Cost Dfl 225 per week, plus Dfl 10 per language session, includes course, teaching materials, transfer from station and full board family accommodation. **PH**

MINISTRY OF EDUCATION AND SCIENCE Bureau Congresses, PO Box 25000, 2700 LZ Zoetermeer Tel 079-53 19 11
Courses in Dutch language, literature and culture for intermediate levels and above at Castle Nijenrode, Breukelen, near Utrecht. Ages 18+,

individuals only. 3 weeks, July/August. 4 x 45 minute lessons per day. Maximum 15 per class. Language laboratory. Additional lectures include politics, economics, art, literature, with background information on culture, land and peoples of the Netherlands, plus Dutch films, music and sports. Excursions to museums at Otterlo, Amsterdam and Enkhuisen, plus sightseeing in Utrecht and Delft. Project material available from teachers; textbooks can be bought at the secretariat. Cost Dfl 850 includes course, excursions and full board residential accommodation. Scholarships available; details from Royal Netherlands Embassy. *Apply by 1 April.* **PH**

INFORMATION

Belgian Embassy
103 Eaton Square, London SW1W 9AB Tel 01-235 5422

Royal Netherlands Embassy
38 Hyde Park Gate, London SW7 5DP Tel 01-584 5040

British Embassy
Britannia House, rue Joseph 11 28, 1040 Brussels

Lange Voorhout 10, 2514 ED The Hague

Tourist office
Belgian National Tourist Office, 38 Dover Street, London W1X 3RB

Netherlands Board of Tourism, 25-28 Buckingham Gate, London SW1E 6LD Tel 01-630 0451

Youth hostels
Centrale Wallonne des Auberges de la Jeunesse, rue Van Oost 52, 1030 Brussels

Vlaamse Jeugdherbergcentrale, Van Stralenstraat 40, 2008 Antwerp

Stichting Nederlandse Jeugherberg Centrale, Professor Tulpplein 4, 1018 GX Amsterdam

Youth & student information
InforJeunes, rue Marche aux Herbes 27, 1000 Brussels

Caravanes de Jeunesse Belge, rue Mercelis 6, 1050 Brussels

Accueil Jeunes, rue Declercq 76, 1150 Brussels

Centre J, rue des Dominicains 11, 4000 Liege

Nationaal Informatiecentrum voor jongeren, Prinsstraat 15, 2000 Antwerp

EXIS, Professor Tulpstraat 2, 1018 HA Amsterdam/PO Box 15344, 1001 MH Amsterdam

Foreign Student Service, Oranje Nassaulaan 5, 1075 AH Amsterdam

Resources

Centre for Information on Language Teaching and Research (CILT), Regent's College, Inner Circle, Regent's Park, London NW1 4NS Tel 01-486 8221 publish *Dutch/Afrikaans* £4.70 including postage, with details on the provision and use of language teaching and learning resources, covering an introduction to the language, useful addresses, libraries and special collections to consult, opportunities for learning, and examinations which can be taken.

Dutch and French Courses in Belgium is a leaflet providing lists of addresses of courses organised by universities and language schools, plus details of who to contact for further information. Published by the Belgian Embassy, see above.

The Royal Netherland Embassy, see above, publish *Private Language Schools in the Netherlands* a listing for intensive Dutch courses.

Dutch Language Courses for Foreign Students is a leaflet giving information on courses for those wishing to study at a university in the Netherlands and thus needing to learn Dutch. Available from the Netherlands Universities Foundation for International Cooperation (NUFFIC), PO Box 90734, 2509 LS The Hague, Netherlands Tel The Hague 510510.

Information centres

ACOTRA Magdalenasteenweg 51, PO Box 3, 1000 Brussels arranges youth and student travel and acts as a transit accommodation centre. Also books tours and excursions, cultural and activity holidays, and issues youth/student reduction and youth hostel cards. The ACOTRA Welcome Desk at Brussels airport provides information and reservations for accommodation and transport.

Bruxelles Accueil, rue de Tabora 6, 1000 Brussels is a Catholic information service for visitors, residents, workers and students, providing advice on education, language classes, social services, legal aid and religion. Free interpreting and translation service. Open Monday-Saturday, 10.00-18.00. Publish *Guide de l'Etranger* BF360.

EXIS, Professor Tulpstraat 2, 1018 HA Amsterdam/PO Box 15344, 1001 MH Amsterdam can provide information and advice on working, activity and special interest holidays, cheap travel and accommodation, courses and exchanges.

Publications

Guide des Vacances Jeunes BF220 including postage, is a comprehensive illustrated booklet describing opportunities in French-speaking Belgium. Includes information on transport, information centres, accommodation, courses, cultural/ sporting activities, jobs and voluntary work. Available from Centre National Infor Jeunes, rue Traversiere 4, 1030 Brussels.

Holland, a young and lively country is a free booklet for young visitors including details of transport, accommodation, eating, sightseeing, events, shopping, entertainment and useful addresses; plus details of organisations providing advice and information on looking for work, legal assistance, medical problems, courses and details of hostels, student hotels, campsites and sleep-ins. *Useful hints for your stay in the Netherlands* is a brochure providing useful information on where to eat and sleep, travel, customs formalities, health care, places of interest, currency, climate, events and museums, plus other general information. Also a booklet listing holiday and recreational opportunities for the disabled, covering travel, accommodation, restaurants and tourist attractions. Both available from the Netherlands Board of Tourism, see above.

Travel

Belgian National Railways, 22-25a Sackville Street, London W1X 1DE Tel 01-734 1491 operate a scheme where a bike can be collected at one of 48 Belgian stations and returned to any one of 101. Advisable to reserve bikes in advance; cost from £1.50 per day.

Abonnement Reseau allows unlimited rail travel throughout the Belgian network. Valid 16 consecutive days, all year, cost £44.50. B-Tourrail Ticket allows unlimited travel for 5/8 days, Easter-September. Cost for ages under 26, £20/£27. Benelux Tourrail allows unlimited travel throughout the Belgium, Luxembourg and Netherlands rail networks; valid for 5 days, March-September. Cost for ages under 26, £33. All available from YHA Travel, 14 Southampton Street, London WC2E 7HY Tel 01-836 8541.

The Miracle Bus Company, 408 The Strand, London WC2 Tel 01-836 3201 are agents for Euro Skyhop, a coach/air service, London-Amsterdam, Rotterdam and the Hague, via Southend and Ostend.

NBBS Travel, Informatiecentrum, Schipholweg 101, PO Box 360, 2316 XC Leiden is the national office for youth and student travel, and administers 33 travel offices including 5 in Amsterdam, and can arrange cheap travel and hotel accommodation.

Rail Rovers entitle the holder to unlimited travel for 3/7 days on the Netherlands Railways network; cost approx £26.50/£36.50. A Public Transport Link Rover, for use in conjunction with Rail Rovers, entitles the holder to unlimited travel on Amsterdam and Rotterdam metro systems and on buses and trams throughout the Netherlands. Costs £3.35/£6.60 for 3/7 days. The Teenage Rover Ticket is available for 4 days within a period of 10 days, June-August, to those aged up to 19; cost approx £13.35. The Benelux Tourrail Card is available for 5 days within a period of 17 days, allowing unlimited travel on the national railway networks of the Netherlands, Luxembourg and Belgium. March-October; cost from £33. Bicycle hire is available at reduced rates for rail ticket holders at many stations. Details from Netherlands Railways, 25/28 Buckingham Gate, London SW1E 6LD Tel 01-630 1735.

Transalpino Ltd, 117 Euston Road, London NW1 2SX Tel 01-388 2267 offer up to 50% off full rail fares to destinations in Belgium and the Netherlands for those under 26.

Accommodation

Camping is a leaflet listing, by province, all camping sites and their facilities is available from the Belgian National Tourist Office, see above.

Le CHAB, Hotel de Jeunes, rue Traversiere 8, 1030 Brussels is an inexpensive international accommodation centre, with 2-8 bedded rooms or dormitories. Cost from BF220 for bed and breakfast plus BF60 linen charge. Cycle hire, walking tours, and information on cultural activities.

Cheap accommodation for young people is available at Maison Internationale, chausée de Wavre 205, 1040 Brussels, based in a former monastery. Cost from BF290 per night includes shower and breakfast.

Also youth camping site situated in a large park, BF200 per night including breakfast.

Rijksuniversiteit Gent, Mrs M Verfaillie, Department of Guest Accommodation, Home A Vermeylen, Stalhof 6, 9000 Gent has cheap accommodation in single rooms in 2 halls of residence, 15 July-15 September. Bed and breakfast BF400 per night. Facilities include restaurant, swimming pool and sports grounds.

EXIS, see above, publishes a list of sleep-ins, offering basic accommodation to young people all over the Netherlands. Cost from Dfl 17.50, bed and breakfast.

Cok Hotels Amsterdam, Koninginneweg 34-36, 1075 CZ Amsterdam offers low-cost accommodation in 3 modern hotels situated in the green heart of Amsterdam. Facilities include self-service restaurant, bars and function rooms. Cost from Dfl 35 per night includes accommodation in 5/6 bedded rooms and breakfast.

Ernst Sillem Hoeve, Soestdykerweg 10b, 3724 MH Den Dolder is an international YMCA conference and holiday centre with 100 beds. Open all year; all ages. Also YMCA camps with 25-60 beds in tents and dormitories, May-September; ages up to 24.

Hans Brinker Hotel, Kerkstraat 136-138, 1017 GR Amsterdam has budget accommodation in a variety of rooms from singles to dormitories of up to 12 beds. Facilities include restaurants, cafe, bar and tourist information. Open all year. Cost from Dfl 23 per night bed and breakfast, summer.

Netherlands Board of Tourism, see above, can provide information on farmhouse, campsite, hotel, summer cottage, holiday chalet, youth hostel and basic accommodation. Booklets include details of facilities available and opportunities for sports and recreational activities. **PH**

ENGLISH

English derives from the Germanic language of the Angle, Jute and Saxon tribes that invaded Britain in the middle 5th century, after the fall of the Roman Empire. They settled, respectively, north of the Thames, in Kent and along the Hampshire coast, and in the rest of southern England. In the following centuries four distinct dialects of English developed, Northumbrian, Mercian, West Saxon and Kentish. Following the Viking invasions in the 9th century, only Wessex remained independent and West Saxon became the official language. The core of English was the Saxon Old English, with Latin, Old Norse and other influences. The language was enriched after 1066 by the French of the Norman conquerors, and until the middle of the 13th century French was the language of the English nobility. Germanic words are more common in ordinary speech with words derived from the French having more subtle or complicated meanings. By the 14th century English was the language of the law and education, with the London dialect becoming the literary standard. Today English is spoken by an estimated 450 million native speakers, and perhaps by as many again as a second language, making it the most spoken language in the world after Mandarin Chinese. It is the official language of countries in all continents except South America, and the main language of international business, finance, air transport and shipping.

COURSES IN BRITAIN & IRELAND

The British Council, 10 Spring Gardens, London SW1A 2BN Tel 01-930 8466 is the official organisation charged with promoting an understanding and appreciation of Britain in other countries through cultural, educational and technical cooperation. As part of this work it inspects language schools and declares them efficient, advises people from foreign countries about language courses through its branches throughout the world, and administers a test in English for those wishing to study at British universities. Recognised schools are indicated here by **BC**

ARELS-FELCO, The Association for Recognised English Language Teaching Establishments in Britain, 125 High Holborn, London WC1V 6QD Tel 01-242 3136 is a non-profitmaking association that ensures high standards are maintained in member schools. All ARELS-FELCO schools are recognised by the British Council. Association schools are indicated here by **AF**

BASCELT, The British Association of State Colleges in English Language Teaching, c/o The BASCELT Secretary, Hampstead Garden Suburb Institute, Central Square, London NW11 7BN is an association of state-run colleges that offer courses in English as a Foreign Language. BASCELT member colleges can be recommended for those learning English for scientific, technical or vocational reasons, as many can offer English language courses together with other specialised courses run for British students. Member colleges are indicated here by **BASCELT**.

There are a wide range of examinations in English as a foreign language, normally taken through the school where the candidate is studying. Schools and colleges offering this facility are indicated together with the range of options:

AEB *The Test in English for Educational Purposes (TEEP), is a writing/reading examination, offered by the Associated Examining Board, an official examining body.*

ARELS *A speaking/listening examination offered by ARELS-FELCO at preliminary, higher and diploma level. March, May and November.*

British Council *The ELTS or English Language Testing Service administered by the British Council is a test for students wishing to follow a course of higher education in Britain. It is often required by universities.*

Cambridge *The most widely recognised qualifications in English as a Foreign Language, administered by Cambridge University. Mainly reading/writing, but including a speaking/listening element. Offered at three levels: Preliminary, First Certificate and Proficiency. June and December.*

ESB *The English Speaking Board, an official examining body, offer this test in spoken English.*

JMB *The Joint Matriculation Board, an official examining body, administers this examination in reading, writing and listening to technical/scientific English. Often required by British universities.*

LCCI *Examinations in speaking, listening, reading and writing in English for business and commercial communication run by the London Chamber of Commerce and Industry. Offered at Elementary, Intermediate and Higher levels.*

Oxford *Writing/reading examinations offered by Oxford University. Preliminary and Higher levels. March and November.*

Pitman *The Pitman Examinations Institute, a private organisation, offer reading/writing examinations at Elementary, Higher Intermediate and Advanced levels.*

RSA *The Royal Society of Arts, who oversee training courses for teachers of English as a foreign language, also run the Examination in the Communicative Use of English. There are separate tests for speaking, listening, reading and writing, offered at Basic, Intermediate and Advanced levels.*

TOEFL *The Test Of English as a Foreign Language is administered by Princeton University for students wishing to study at universities and colleges in the United States.*

Trinity *Spoken English examinations at 12 levels, and a written examination at Intermediate level run by Trinity College, London.*

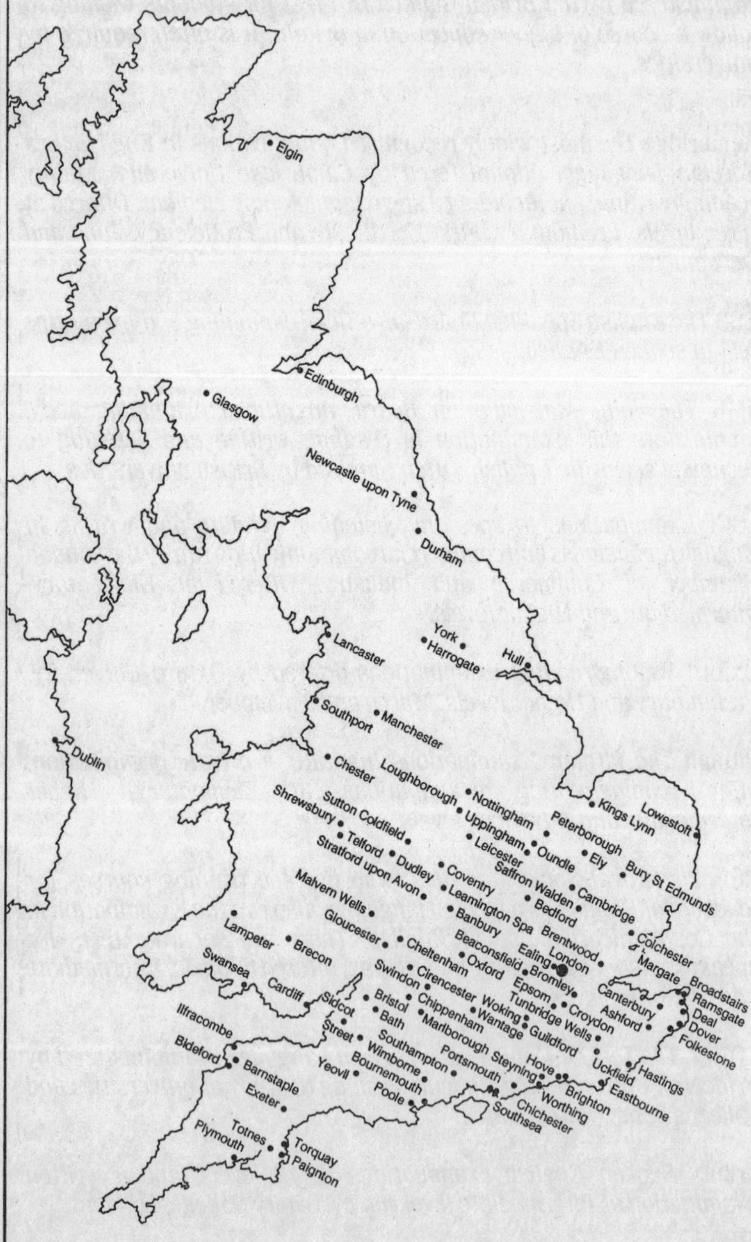
Elgin
Edinburgh
Glasgow
Newcastle upon Tyne
Durham
York
Harrogate
Hull
Lancaster
Southport
Manchester
Dublin
Chester
Loughborough
Nottingham
Kings Lynn
Lowestoft
Shrewsbury
Sutton Coldfield
Uppingham
Peterborough
Telford
Leicester
Oundle
Ely
Stratford upon Avon
Dudley
Coventry
Saffron Walden
Bury St Edmunds
Malvern Wells
Leamington Spa
Bedford
Cambridge
Gloucester
Banbury
Brentwood
Colchester
Lampeter
Brecon
Cheltenham
Beaconsfield
Ealing
London
Margate
Broadstairs
Swansea
Cardiff
Swindon
Oxford
Bromley
Ramsgate
Sidcot
Bristol
Cirencester
Epsom
Canterbury
Deal
Ilfracombe
Bath
Chippenham
Woking
Croydon
Ashford
Dover
Street
Marlborough
Wantage
Tunbridge Wells
Folkestone
Bideford
Southampton
Guildford
Barnstaple
Yeovil
Wimborne
Portsmouth
Steyning
Hove
Uckfield
Hastings
Bournemouth
Exeter
Poole
Brighton
Eastbourne
Worthing
Chichester
Southsea
Totnes
Plymouth
Torquay
Paignton

ABBEY INTERNATIONAL COLLEGE 253 Wells Road, Malvern Wells WR14 4JF Tel Malvern 892300
Language and activity courses for all levels. Ages 11-18, individuals and groups. 3-6 weeks, June-August. 15 hours per week. Average 15 per class. Full programme of sports and activities. Cost £170 includes full board residential accommodation. Also 12 month courses leading to JMB, GCSE and A level examinations. **BC AF**

ACADEMIC TRAVEL LTD The Briar School of English, 8 Gunton Cliff, Lowestoft NR32 4PE Tel Lowestoft 3781
Language and sport courses for all levels. Ages 10-25, individuals and groups. 2-4 weeks, Easter and June-August. 10-15 hours per week. Maximum 15 per class. Sports include watersports, riding and team games. Also mixed activity courses and English and computer studies. Excursions and social activities. Cost from £110 per week includes full board family accommodation. **BC**

ACADEMY INTERNATIONAL 3 Queens Gardens, Bayswater, London W2 3BA Tel 01-262 6982
Courses for all levels. Ages 16+, individuals and groups. 2+ weeks, all year. 15-25 hours per week. Maximum 15 per class. Also 1:1 tuition for business, academic or professional needs. Debates and social activities. Cost £82 per week, 25 hour course. Half board family, residence or bed and breakfast hotel accommodation available. ARELS, Cambridge, Oxford, RSA and TOEFL examinations. **BC AF PH**

ALEXANDERS ENGLISH STUDIES Harlowbury House, Old Road, Old Harlow CM17 OHE Tel Harlow 22122
Courses for all levels. Ages 8-18, individuals and groups. 2-46 weeks, three terms, plus Easter and June-September. 25 hours per week. Average 10 per class. During terms English is taught through school subjects. Easter and summer, intensive English or English with arts and craft activities. Excursions, sports and social programme. Cost £210 per week or £1650 per term includes full board residential or family accommodation. ARELS, Cambridge and Pitman examinations. **BC PH**

ANGLIAN SCHOOL OF ENGLISH 81/83 Norfolk Road, Cliftonville, Margate CT9 2HX Tel Thanet 293700
Courses for all levels. Ages 16+, individuals only. 2+ weeks, all year. 20-25 hours per week. Maximum 12 per class. Courses in business and commercial English. Excursions and social events. Cost £268, 2 weeks, 20 hours per week, includes full board family accommodation. Cambridge, LCCI, Oxford and RSA examinations. **BC**

ANGLO-CONTINENTAL SCHOOL OF ENGLISH 29-35 Wimborne Road, Bournemouth BH2 6NA Tel Bournemouth 27414
Courses for all levels. Ages 16 +, individuals and groups. 2-15 weeks, all year. 20-40 lessons per week. Intensive and examination courses, English for business, banking, computers and tourism, refresher courses for teachers, and senior citizen courses in May and September. 1:1 tuition for special needs. Excursions, social activities and sports. Cost from £359, 2 weeks, includes half board family accommodation. ARELS, Cambridge, LCCI, Oxford, RSA and TOEFL examinations. Also vacation courses with sports coaching for ages 14 +, and junior courses for ages 8-18 with supervised sports and handicrafts. Cost from £126 per week includes family accommodation. **BC AF PH**

ANGLO-WORLD EDUCATION LTD 130-136 Poole Road, Bournemouth BH4 9EF Tel Bournemouth 752288
Courses for all levels in Bournemouth, Cambridge, Oxford and London. Ages 16 +, individuals and groups. 2 + weeks, all year. 15-30 hours per week. Maximum 15 per class. Also courses for ages 8-13 and 13-16 in Dudley, Lampeter and Reading. Special holiday courses, English for business, air traffic control and navigation, and 1:1 tuition. Self-study centres in main schools. Lectures, excursions, social activities and sports. Cost from £276, 2 weeks, includes course, teaching materials and half board family accommodation. ARELS, Cambridge, Oxford, Pitman, RSA and TOEFL examinations. **BC AF PH**

ANGLOSCHOOL 146 Church Road, London SE19 2NT Tel 01-653 7285
Courses for all levels. Ages 16 +, individuals only. 2 + weeks, all year. 30 hours per week. Average 12 per class. Courses for overseas teachers. Excursions, social activities and sports. Cost from £150 per week includes half board family accommodation. Hotels also available. ARELS, Cambridge and TOEFL examinations. **BC AF**

ANNALIVIA SCHOOL OF LANGUAGES Exchequer Chambers 19/23 Exchequer Street, Dublin 2 Tel Dublin 714433
Courses for all levels. Ages 12 +, individuals and groups. 2-6 weeks, all year. 10-30 hours per week. Average 8-12 per class. Also business, professional or technical English for special groups or 1:1. Special course on Anglo-Irish literature. Excursions, social events, and sports. Cost IR£100, 4 weeks, 10 hours per week. Half/full board family, hotel or residential accommodation available. Approved by the Department of Education. Cambridge examinations. **PH**

AVALON STUDENT TRAVEL 46 Withdean Road, Brighton BN1 5BP Tel Brighton 553417
Courses for all levels except complete beginners in Brighton and Hove. Ages 12+, individuals and groups. 2+ weeks, all year. 20 hours per week. Maximum 14 per class. Holiday courses 2-8 weeks, March-April and July-August. 15 hours per week. Cost from £43 per week. Excursions and local visits. Family accommodation from £45 per week. Youth hostel, hotel or university residence accommodation also available. Cambridge examinations.

BEDFORD STUDY CENTRE 15 Goldington Road, Bedford MK40 3JY Tel Bedford 64161
Courses for all levels. Ages 16+, individuals and groups. 2+ weeks, all year. 20 hours per week. Average 8 per class. Tailor-made courses for groups with business, vocational or technical needs. Summer course in English for university entrants. 1:1 tuition. Cost from £115 per week includes half board family accommodation. ARELS, British Council, Cambridge, JMB, LCCI, RSA and TOEFL examinations. **BC**

THE BELL EDUCATIONAL TRUST Hillscross, Red Cross Lane, Cambridge CB2 2QX Tel Cambridge 212333
Courses at private schools in or near Bury St Edmunds, Cambridge, Ely, Eton and Uppingham. All levels; beginners not accepted at some schools. Ages 9-17, depending on school. 3-4 weeks, July-August. 24-28 x 40-45 minute lessons per week. Average 13 per class. Special interest classes in drama, music, art, sport, environmental studies, literature or current affairs. Excursions, sports and social activities. Cost from £840, 3 weeks, includes course, teaching materials, social programme, excursions, transfer from Heathrow airport and full board school accommodation. **BC AF**

THE BELL LANGUAGE INSTITUTE Regents College, Inner Circle, Regents Park, London NW1 4NS Tel 01-487 7411
Courses for all levels. Ages 18+. 4, 8 or 12 weeks, July-September. 21 hours per week. Maximum 14 per class. Also 2 week English and business studies courses, and courses for teachers. Sports, excursions and social activities. Cost from £400. Residential or family accommodation available. **BC**

BELL COLLEGE SAFFRON WALDEN South Road, Saffron Walden CB11 3DP Tel Saffron Walden 22918
Courses for all levels except beginners. Ages 17+. 3-4 weeks, June-September. 21 hours per week. Maximum 14 per class. Language laboratory, self-study centre, video facilities and library. Sports,

excursions and social activities. Cost from £755 includes course, teaching materials, social programme and full board family or residence accommodation. Courses for overseas teachers of English, 1 or 2 weeks, June-August. Cost from £400 includes full board family or residential accommodation. Also courses for all levels except beginners in Felsted. Ages 12-16. 4 weeks, July-August. 28 hours per week. Average 13 per class. Cost £1200 includes course, teaching materials, social programme, excursions, transfer from Heathrow airport and full board school accommodation. **BC AF**

BLUEFEATHER SCHOOL OF LANGUAGES 35 Montpellier Parade, Monkstown, Dublin Tel Dublin 806288
Courses for all levels. Ages 16 +, individuals and groups. 4 weeks, all year. 20-30 hours per week. Maximum 7 per class. Courses have Irish cultural/literary element. Business, literary and other special needs English for special groups or 1:1. Excursions, Irish music and dancing, sports and social activities. Cost from IR£110 per week plus IR£30 registration fee. Full board family accommodation available, IR£8.50 per night. Cambridge examinations.

BOURNEMOUTH INTERNATIONAL SCHOOL 711-713A Christchurch Road, Bournemouth BH7 6AF Tel Bournemouth 33112
Courses for all levels. Ages 15 +, individuals and groups. 4, 8 or 16 weeks, January-November. 20-27 lessons per week. Maximum 15 per class. Cost from £66 per week. 2-3 week courses, Easter and June-August. 16 lessons per week. Cost £55. Business English for groups by arrangement. Lectures, excursions, social activities and sports. Half board family accommodation available, £44 per week. ARELS, Cambridge, LCCI, Oxford, Pitman and RSA examinations. **BC AF**

THE BRIGHTON AND HOVE SCHOOL OF ENGLISH 5-7 Wilbury Villas, Hove BN3 6GB Tel Brighton 738182
Courses for all levels in Brighton. Ages 20 +, individuals and groups. 2-12 weeks, all year. 20-30 hours per week. Maximum 12 per class. Intensive courses, maximum 5 per class. Business and technical English. Lectures and excursions. Cost from £178, 2 weeks, includes half board family accommodation. Hotels on request. Cambridge, Oxford and Pitman examinations. *Some scholarships available.*
Also summer courses for ages 13 +. 4 weeks, June-August. 16 hours per week plus excursions and activities. Cost from £512 includes half board family accommodation. **BC AF**

BRIGHTON POLYTECHNIC Language Centre, Falmer, Brighton BN1 9PH Tel Brighton 606622 extension 337
Courses for intermediate levels and above. Ages 17 +, individuals and groups. 2-24 weeks depending on course, all year. 20-25 hours per week. Average 12 per class. General, business, refresher and pre-university courses. Lectures and discussions on life in Britain, and excursions. Cost from £130, 2 weeks. Half board family accommodation £55 per week. Guest houses and hotels from £10 per night. Cambridge examinations. **BASCELT**

BUCKSWOOD INTERNATIONAL SUMMER SCHOOL Uckfield TN22 3PU Tel Uckfield 61666
Language and activity courses for all levels. Ages 7-16, individuals and small groups. 2-8 weeks, July-August. 15 hours per week. Average 10 per class. Excursions, sports (with coaching), games and social activities. Cost £235 per week includes full board residential accommodation. **BC**

THE CAMBRIDGE CENTRE FOR LANGUAGES Sawston Hall, Cambridge CB2 4JR Tel Cambridge 835099
Courses for all levels. Ages 10 +, individuals and groups. 2-10 weeks, January-November. General English, 18-21 hours per week. Maximum 14 per class. Business English, 30 hours per week. Maximum 6 per class. Also specialised 1:1 tuition and courses for teachers. Self-study centre. Extra special interest courses, excursions, social activities and sports. Cost from £220 per week includes full board family accommodation. ARELS, Cambridge, JMB, LCCI, Oxford, RSA and TOEFL examinations. Also courses for all levels near Grantham. Ages 13-16, individuals and groups. 3-7 weeks, June-August. 20 hours per week. Average 12 per class. Cost from £850, 3 weeks. Course for ages 10-14 at Oakham School, 20 miles away. 3 weeks, July. 18 hours per week. Cost £770. All costs include course, teaching materials, sports, excursions, social programme and full board school accommodation. **BC AF**

THE CANNING SCHOOL 4 Abingdon Road, London W8 6AF Tel 01-937 3233
Business language courses for elementary to advanced levels in Bath and London. 1-4 weeks, all year. 42.5 hours per week. Maximum 6 per class. Also residential summer courses at Oxford University, August and Cambridge, July. Special courses in negotiating and presentation skills. Tailor-made courses for company groups and 1:1 tuition. Social activities and lunches with the teacher. Cost from £1190, 4 weeks, February. Accommodation from £65 per week, bed and breakfast. **BC AF**

CENTRAL SCHOOL OF ENGLISH 1 Tottenham Court Road, London W1P 9DA Tel 01-580 2836
Courses for all levels. Ages 16 +, individuals and groups. 2-24 weeks, all year. 15-30 hours per week. Maximum 16 per class. 1:1 courses for executives. Cost £120 15 hours, £225 30 hours, 2 weeks. Self-study centre. Summer excursions and social programmes. Family accommodation from £53 bed and breakfast, per week. ARELS, Cambridge and Oxford examinations. **BC AF**

CENTRE FOR APPLIED LANGUAGE STUDIES Language Resource Centre, University of Reading, Whiteknights, PO Box 218, Reading RG6 2AA Tel Reading 875123 ext 7673
Course in contemporary English for intermediate to advanced level students of English language and literature at European universities. Ages 18 +, individuals and groups. 3 weeks, July-August. 25 hours per week. Average 12-15 per class. Also courses in language, culture and methodology for overseas teachers of English. Excursions, social events and opportunities to meet local people. Cost from £424 per course includes full board university residence accommodation.

CENTRE FOR APPLIED LANGUAGE STUDIES University College, Singleton Park, Swansea SA2 8PP Tel Swansea 295391
Course for intermediate to advanced levels. The course is aimed, though not exclusively, at European university students. Ages 18 +, individuals and groups. 3 weeks, September. 15 hours per week. Maximum 12 per class. Lectures on the culture and history of Wales and Britain. Excursions and social activities. Cost £330 includes bed and breakfast university accommodation. Also summer and term-time courses in English for academic purposes. Cambridge and RSA examinations. *Some students may qualify for British Council support.*
BC PH

CENTRE OF ENGLISH STUDIES Sybill House, St Paul's College, Raheny, Dublin 5 Tel Dublin 316666
Courses for all levels. Ages 10 +, individuals and groups. 2-6 weeks, all year. 20-30 hours per week. Maximum 12 per class. Summer English and activity courses including crafts and sports for adults and ages 9-17. Also English and computing for teenagers, and English for business and other special purposes for groups or 1:1. Excursions, sports and social activities. Cost from £330 includes full board family accommodation. Hotels on request. Approved by the Department of Education. Cambridge examinations.

CHELTENHAM SCHOOL OF ENGLISH 87 St George's Road, Cheltenham BL50 3DU Tel Cheltenham 570000
Courses for all levels. Ages 16 +, individuals and groups. 12 week terms, starting January, April and September. 3-4 weeks, Easter and June-September. 14-20 hours per week. Maximum 12 per class. Courses for overseas teachers. Excursions, sports and social activities. Cost from £990 per term or £280, 3 weeks, includes full board family accommodation. Cambridge, Oxford and Trinity examinations. **BC AF**

CHICHESTER SCHOOL OF ENGLISH 45 East Street, Chichester PO19 1HX Tel Chichester 789893
Courses for all levels. Ages 16 +, individuals and groups. 2 + weeks, all year. 15-25 hours per week. Average 10, winter and 15, summer, per class. Courses for ages 9 +, June-August. Courses for overseas teachers. 1:1 business/professional tuition. Self-study centre. Cost from £55 per week. Excursions and social activities. Half board family accommodation available, from £45 per week. Cambridge examinations. **BC AF**

CHRIST CHURCH COLLEGE English Language Teaching Unit, Canterbury CT1 1QU Tel Canterbury 458459
Courses for all levels. Ages 17 +, individuals and groups. 10-12 week terms, starting January, April and September. 3-4 weeks July-September. 20-25 hours per week. Average 12 per class. Special afternoon option classes include commerce and British culture. Courses in English for academic purposes. Short and long courses for teachers. Self-study centre. Excursions, sports, social programme and contact with British students. Cost from £95 per week. Half board family accommodation available, £50 per week. Cambridge, LCCI, Oxford and University of Kent examinations. **BASCELT**

CHURCHILL HOUSE SCHOOL OF ENGLISH LANGUAGE 40-42 Spencer Square, Ramsgate CT11 9LD Tel Thanet 586833
Courses for all levels. Ages 12 +, individuals and groups. 2-40 weeks, all year. 16-33 hours per week depending on course. Average 11 per class. Excursions, sports and social activities. Cost from £89 per week includes half board family accommodation, full board at weekends. ARELS, Cambridge, LCCI, Pitman and RSA examinations. **BC**

THE CICERO SCHOOL OF ENGLISH 42 Upper Grosvenor Road, Tunbridge Wells TN1 2ET Tel Tunbridge Wells 47077
Courses for all levels except complete beginners. Ages 16 +, individuals only. 1 + weeks, all year. 15 hours per week. Maximum 10 per class.

Additional afternoon business/cultural classes. English and activities for ages 8-15 at Easter and in summer. Special family courses. 1:1 tuition for executives. Excursions, sports and social events. Cost £65 per week. Option classes £12 per week each. Half board family accommodation available, £65 per week. Cambridge examinations. **BC AF PH**

CITY OF LONDON POLYTECHNIC 84 Moorgate, London EC2M 6SQ Tel 01-283 1030
Courses for intermediate levels and above. Ages 18 +, individuals and groups. 4 weeks, July-August. 20 hours per week. Maximum 20 per class. Courses in general, commercial and business English, and British society. Cost £200. Lectures, excursions and social programme. Separate courses in literature, art, banking, law and shipping. Limited hostel accommodation with breakfast available from £11 per night. **BASCELT PH**

CLARKS INTERNATIONAL SUMMER SCHOOLS 28 Craiglockhart Drive South, Edinburgh EH14 1HZ Tel 031-443 3298
Courses for elementary to advanced levels. Ages 14-24, individuals and groups. 3-4 weeks, June-August. 15 hours per week. Average 12 per class. Courses include a Scottish cultural element. Excursions, sports and social events. Cost from £405, 3 weeks, includes leisure activities and full board family accommodation. **BC AF PH**

COLCHESTER INSTITUTE Sheepen Road, Colchester CO3 3LL Tel Colchester 570271
Courses for elementary to advanced levels. Ages 16 +, individuals and groups. 8-12 weeks, starting September, January and April. 10-20 hours per week. Average 15 per class. Special courses in English for business, or science and technology, courses for specialised groups and 1:1 tuition. Also wide range of technical and vocational courses which may be taken in conjunction with English courses. Cost £5-£16 per week. Excursions and sports facilities. Half board family or residential accommodation from £35 per week. British Council, Cambridge, LCCI and RSA examinations. **BASCELT PH**

CONCORDE INTERNATIONAL Head Office, Hawks Lane, Canterbury CT1 2NU Tel Canterbury 451035/65537
Courses for all levels in centres throughout southern England. Courses for individuals and groups in Ashford, Cambridge and Croydon, and for groups only in Chichester, Cheltenham, Dover and Deal. Ages 10-25 depending on centre. All levels. 2-4 weeks, June-August. 15 hours per week. Maximum 12 per class. Excursions, sports and leisure activities.

Cost from £340, 2 weeks, includes course, teaching materials and half/full board family or residential accommodation. Also courses for all levels at University of Kent, Canterbury. Ages 17 + , individuals and groups. 2-4 weeks, June-September. 25 hours per week. Average 10-12 per class. Commercial and technical English and study of literature, drama and methodology of teaching English. Excursions and social programme. Cost from £410, 2 weeks, includes full board family accommodation. Residential accommodation also available. Also courses for ages 10-20, all levels. 2-4 weeks, Easter and June-August. 15 or 20 hours per week. Maximum 12 per class. Excursions, sports and social events. Cost from £340, 2 weeks, includes full board family accommodation. Residential accommodation also available. **BC AF**

CONCORDE INTERNATIONAL Cheriton Place, Folkestone CT20 2BB Tel Folkestone 56752
Courses for all levels. Ages 16 + , individuals and groups. 4-36 weeks, all year. 15 or 25 hours per week. Average 8-12 per class. English for special purposes, training courses in English and job skills. Excursions, sports and social events. Cost from £57 per week. Half board family accommodation available, £45 per week. ARELS, Cambridge, JMB, LCCI, Oxford, RSA and TOEFL examinations. Also courses for ages 10-20, all levels. 2-4 weeks, Easter and June-September. 15 hours per week. Maximum 12 per class. Excursions, sports and social events. Cost from £318, 2 weeks, includes full board family or residential accommodation. **BC AF**

COUNTRY COUSINS Park School, Bicclescombe, Ilfracombe EX34 8JN Tel Ilfracombe 63304
Language and activity courses in Ilfracombe, Bideford and Barnstaple. Ages 8 + , individuals and groups. 3-4 weeks, Easter and June-August. 12-23 hours per week. Maximum 15 per class. Choice of excursions and sports, or adventure activities for adults and juniors. Cost from £368, 3 weeks, includes full board family accommodation.

COVENTRY INTERNATIONAL ENGLISH STUDIES CENTRE 9 Priory Row, Coventry CV1 8FB Tel Coventry 23379
Courses for all levels. No age limits, individuals and groups. 2 + weeks, all year. 15-25 hours per week. Maximum 12 per class. Courses have a cultural element. Business and other specialised courses for groups or 1:1 on request. Cost from £85 per week. Weekly discos. Summer excursions. Half board family accommodation available, from £41 per week. Cambridge, JMB, Oxford and RSA examinations. **BC AF**

DAVIES SCHOOL OF ENGLISH 56 Eccleston Square, London SW1V 1PQ Tel 01-834 4155
Courses for all levels. Ages 16 +, individuals and groups. 2-21 weeks, all year. 15 hours per week. Maximum 15 per class. Also refresher courses for teachers and 30 hours per week intensive courses, Easter. Excursions and social events. Cost from £230 for 2 weeks includes half board family accommodation. Cost from £130, 2 weeks, course only. Cambridge examinations. **BC AF**

DELTA INTERNATIONAL SCHOOL OF ENGLISH 24 West Hill Road, Bournemouth GH2 5PL Tel Bournemouth 292128
Courses for all levels. Ages 14 +, individuals and groups. 2-15 weeks, all year. 15-25 lessons per week. Maximum 16 per class. Specialised courses for groups. Excursions, social activities and sports. Cost from £94 per week includes half board family accommodation. £25 registration fee. ARELS, Cambridge, LCCI, Oxford, Pitman, RSA and TOEFL examinations. **PH**

DEVON SCHOOL OF ENGLISH 42 Palace Avenue, Paignton TQ3 3HF Tel Paignton 559718
Courses for all levels except complete beginners. Ages 16 +, individuals and groups. 2-16 weeks, all year. 20-30 x 45 minute lessons per week. Maximum 12 per class. Special courses in business, scientific or professional English. Excursions and social activities. Cost from £127 per week includes full board family accommodation. Cambridge, LCCI, Oxford, Pitman and RSA examinations. **BC AF**

DUBLIN SCHOOL OF ENGLISH 10-12 Westmoreland Street, Dublin 2 Tel 773741/773221
Courses for all levels. Ages 10 +, individuals and groups. 2 + weeks, all year. 21-40 lessons per week. Average 15 per class. Also small group courses, courses for au pairs, language courses combined with sports tuition, summer courses for juniors in residential centres, and 1:1 or small group courses for executives or other special purposes. Full programme of excursions, sports and social activities. Cost from IR£345, 2 weeks, 21 hours per week, includes course, extra-curricular programme and full board family accommodation. Textbooks approx IR£8. Approved by Department of Education. ARELS, Cambridge, Oxford and Pitman examinations. **PH** summer only

EAST SUSSEX SCHOOL OF ENGLISH 19 Reynolds Road, Hove BN3 5RJ Brighton 777784
Classes for all levels. Ages 13 +, individuals and groups. 2-9 weeks, June-August. 13-16 hours per week. Maximum 12 per class. Excursions, social activities and sports. Cost £145 per week includes course,

excursions and full board family accommodation. Pitman examinations. **BC AF**

EASTBOURNE SCHOOL OF ENGLISH 8 Trinity Trees, Eastbourne Tel Eastbourne 21759
Courses for all levels. Individuals only. 2-12 weeks, all year. 10-25 hours per week. Average 9 per class. Easter and summer courses, English for retired people, courses for teachers, and specialised courses for groups or individuals. Self-study centre. Excursions, sports and social activities. Cost £136, 2 weeks, 20 hours per week. Half board accommodation available, from £50 per week. ARELS and Cambridge examinations. **BC AF**

EATON HALL INTERNATIONAL Retford DN22 OPR Tel Retford 706441
Courses for all levels. Ages 16 +, individuals and groups. 2-12 weeks, February-December. 20-25 hours per week. Average 10 per class. Vacation courses, executive English in small groups, English for academic purposes, and courses for firemen intending to train in the UK. Specialised courses for groups on request. Excursions, sports and social events, including opportunities to meet local people. Cost from £493 includes half board residential accommodation. Cambridge, Pitman and Trinity examinations. **BC BASCELT PH**

THE ECKERSLEY SCHOOL OF ENGLISH 14 Friar's Entry, Oxford OX1 2BZ Tel Oxford 721268
Courses for all levels. Ages 16 +, individuals and small groups. 4-12 weeks, all year. 20 hours per week. Maximum 14 per class. Summer course for teachers. Self-study centre. Cost from £360, 4 weeks. Half board family or self-catering hostel accommodation available, from £50 per week. ARELS, Cambridge and Oxford examinations. **BC AF**

EDINBURGH LANGUAGE FOUNDATION 11 Great Stuart Street, Edinburgh EH3 7TS Tel 031-225 8785
Courses for all levels. Ages 18 +, individuals and groups. 2 + weeks, all year. 17-20 hours per week. Average 9 per class. English for business, overseas teachers, and other special needs. Cost from £90 per week. Excursions and social activities. Family accommodation available. AEB, ARELS, Cambridge, JMB, LCCI and Oxford examinations. **BC AF**

EDINBURGH SCHOOL OF ENGLISH STUDIES 12 George IV Bridge, Edinburgh EH1 1EE Tel 031-225 3482
Courses for all levels. Ages 16 +, individuals and groups. 2-12 weeks, all year or 3 weeks, summer. 25-28 lessons per week. Average 8 per class. Courses have a Scottish cultural element. Courses for businessmen and

for specialised groups on request. 1:1 tuition. Excursions and social activities. Cost from £318, 2 weeks, includes half board family accommodation. Summer residential accommodation available. ARELS, Cambridge, and Oxford examinations. **BC AF**

EDUCATIONAL GUARDIANS Tymawr, Llangorse, Brecon LD3 7UE Tel Brecon 84383
Language and activity courses for intermediate to advanced levels. 2 + weeks, all year. 15 hours per week in groups of 2-3 students. Activities include riding, canoeing and sailing. Excursions and social activities. Cost £365 per week includes full board family accommodation and transfer from Heathrow airport.

EF LANGUAGE SCHOOLS EF House, 1 Farman Street, Hove BN3 1AL Tel Brighton 723651
Courses for all levels in Brighton, Cambridge and Hastings. General courses, 2-50 weeks, all year. 16 lessons per week. Average 14 per class. Cost from £270, 2 weeks. Main courses, 2-50 weeks, all year. 24 lessons per week. Average 13 per class. Cost from £332, 2 weeks. Also intensive courses, 2-50 weeks, all year. 30 lessons per week. Average 12 per class. Cost from £396, 2 weeks. Also summer courses in Hastings and London, 2-12 weeks, May-August. 20 lessons per week. Average 14 per class. Cost from £286, 2 weeks. Language laboratory and audio-visual facilities. Costs include courses, teaching materials, membership and discount cards, preparatory language cassette, and half board family accommodation. Extra-curricular activities. ARELS, Cambridge, LCCI, Oxford, Pitman and TOEFL examinations.

ELS INTERNATIONAL LANGUAGE CENTRE Meridian House, Royal Hill, Greenwich, London SE10 8RT Tel 01-853 4908
Courses for all levels. Ages 17 +, individuals and groups. 4 weeks, all year. 25 hours per week. Average 12 per class. Cost £585. Executive courses, 2 weeks. 30 hours per week. Average 6 per class. Cost £591. Lectures, excursions and social activities. Costs include half board family accommodation. ARELS, Cambridge and Oxford examinations. **BC AF**

ELT BANBURY 20 Horsefair, Banbury OX16 0AH Tel Banbury 3480
for all levels. Ages 17 +, individuals and groups. 2-10 weeks, throughout the year. 21 hours per week. Maximum 10 per class. Courses for businessmen and overseas teachers. Excursions and social activities. Cost £110 per week. Half board accommodation with families £50. Cambridge and RSA examinations. **BC**

EMBASSY SCHOOL OF ENGLISH Hanover House, Marine Court, St Leonards-on-Sea TN38 ODX Tel Hastings 720282

Courses for all levels in Hastings. Ages 17 +, individuals and groups. 2-12 weeks, all year. 15-30 hours per week. Maximum 15 per class. Also courses for ages 13-16 at Easter, summer and autumn. Business/technical courses can be arranged. 1:1 tuition. Excursions, sports with coaching, and social activities. Cost from £305, 2 weeks, includes half board family accommodation. ARELS, Cambridge, Oxford, Pitman and RSA examinations. **BC AF**

Also courses for all levels in Ashford, Hatfield, Kingston, London, Oxford and Southsea. Ages 12 +, individuals and groups. 2-6 weeks, June-August. 15 or 25 hours per week. Maximum 15 per class. Courses in Oxford for overseas teachers of English. Excursions, sports and social activities. Costs from £500, 3 weeks, including full board college or family accommodation.

ENGLISH IN CHESTER 9/11 Stanley Place, Chester CH1 2LU Tel Chester 318913

Courses for elementary to advanced levels. Ages 16 +, individuals and small groups. 3-12 weeks, all year. 21 hours per week. Maximum 12 per class. Also intensive courses in groups of 6 maximum, and summer courses for ages 12-16. Extra tuition in English for academic purposes. Self-study centre. Cost from £285, 3 weeks. Excursions and social activities. Half board family accommodation available, £50 per week. Cambridge examinations. **BC AF**

ENGLISH AND CULTURAL STUDIES CENTRE 40 Village Road, Enfield, Middlesex EN1 2EN Tel 01-360 4118

Courses for all levels. Ages 10-18, individuals and groups. 3-6 weeks, June-August. 15 hours per week. Maximum 15 per class. Cultural studies, excursions and leisure activities. Also courses for overseas teachers of English. Cost from £479 includes full board family or residential accommodation. Trinity examinations. **BC AF**

THE ENGLISH CENTRE EASTBOURNE Gordon Lodge, 25 St Anne's Road, Eastbourne BN21 2DJ Tel Eastbourne 25887

Courses for all levels. Ages 16 +, individuals and groups. 1-12 weeks, all year. 14-24 hours per week. Maximum 14 per class. Easter and summer courses. Business/technical English on request. Courses include projects outside the classroom for practice of English in real-life situations. Self-study centre. Excursions, sports and social activities. Cost from £75 per week. Full board family accommodation available,

£49 per week. ARELS, Cambridge, Oxford and Pitman examinations. **BC AF**

THE ENGLISH LANGUAGE CENTRE 33 Palmeira Mansions, Hove BN3 2GB Tel Brighton 721771
Courses for all levels. Ages 17 +, individuals and groups. 2 + weeks, all year. 15-45 lessons per week. Average 10 per class. Special courses include English for computers, business, and teachers. Also summer courses. Excursions and social programme. Cost from £65 per week. Half board family accommodation £46 per week. ARELS, Cambridge and Oxford examinations. **BC AF**

ENGLISH LANGUAGE INSTITUTE Admissions Office, Royal Waterloo House, 51/55 Waterloo Road, London SE1 8TX Tel 01-928 1372
Courses for all levels in West Wickham. Ages 14 +, individuals and groups. 3-14 weeks, all academic year. 20 hours per week including academic/business English. Leisure activities. Cost from £80, tuition and £100, full board accommodation, per week. Cambridge examinations. Also courses, 3 weeks, June-July. 15 hours per week. Average 16 per class. Supervised excursions, sports and leisure activities. Cost £635 includes full board residential accommodation. **BC AF**

ENGLISH LANGUAGE SYSTEMS The Old Rectory, Church Lane North, Old Whittington, Chesterfield S41 9QY Tel Chesterfield 450503
Courses for all levels in colleges of the University of Durham. Ages 10-15 and 16 +, individuals and groups. 3 weeks, July-August. 15 (junior) or 21 (senior) hours per week. Average 10 per class. Courses include excursions, topic lessons, sports and social activities. Cost from £525 includes full board residential accommodation. **BC AF**

ESH LANGUAGE COURSES 32 Hyde Gardens, Eastbourne BN21 4PX Tel Eastbourne 647288
Courses for all levels. Ages 8 +, individuals and groups. 2 + weeks, all year. 10-25 hours per week. Maximum 10-15 per class. Holiday courses, courses for juniors, business English, and for teachers from overseas. Self-study centre. Excursions and social activities. Sports coaching. Cost from £40 per week. Half board family accommodation available, £45 per week. Hotels also available. ARELS, Cambridge, English Speaking Board, Oxford and Pitman examinations. *Some scholarships available.* **BC PH**

EURO STUDENTS ORGANISATION 16 McLaren Road, Edinburgh EH9 2BN Tel 031-667 1751
Courses for all levels. 3 weeks, Easter and June-August. 15 hours per week. Average 10 per class. Choice each afternoon of cultural visits or sporting activities. Social programme. Cost from £447 includes full board family accommodation. ARELS examinations. **BC AF**

EUROCENTRE Head Office, Seestrasse 247, 8038 Zurich, Switzerland Tel Zurich 481 61 24
Courses for all levels in Dublin and Torquay and for elementary to advanced levels in Edinburgh and Oxford. Ages 16 +, individuals and groups. 3-9 weeks, July-August. 20-25 hours per week. Maximum 15 per class. Lectures, excursions, sports and social activities. Cost from £411, 3 weeks, includes course, teaching materials and full board family accommodation. Cost £285, 3 weeks, tuition only.

EUROCENTRE 26 Dean Park Road, Bournemouth BH1 1HZ Tel Bournemouth 24426
Courses for all levels. Ages 16 +, individuals and groups. 2-21 weeks, all year. 30 hours per week. Maximum 15 per class. Options in business English, arts and culture. Cambridge examinations. Excursions and social events. Cost from £300, 2 weeks, includes course, teaching materials and half board family accommodation. Cost £206, 2 weeks, tuition only. Also courses for all levels. 4-12 weeks, July-September. 20-25 hours per week. Cost from £544, 4 weeks, includes half board family accommodation. Cost £380, 4 weeks, tuition only. **BC AF**

EUROCENTRE Huntingdon House, 20 North Street, Brighton BN1 1EB Tel Brighton 24545
Courses for all levels. Ages 16 +, individuals and groups. 2-21 weeks, all year. 30 hours per week. Maximum 15 per class. Options in English for business, travel and tourism and English literature. Excursions and social events. Cost from £304, 2 weeks, includes course, teaching materials and half board family accommodation. Cost £206, 2 weeks, tuition only. Cambridge examinations. Also courses for all levels. 3 weeks, July-August. 20-25 hours per week. Cost from £414 includes half board family accommodation. Cost £285, tuition only. **BC AF**

EUROCENTRE 62 Bateman Street, Cambridge CB2 1LX Tel Cambridge 68531
Courses for all levels. Ages 16 +, individuals and groups. 2-21 weeks, all year. 30 hours per week. Maximum 15 per class. Options in English for business, science and technology, plus study of literature, art, history and music. Excursions and social events. Cost from £324, 2 weeks, includes course, teaching materials and half board family

accommodation. Cost £222, 2 weeks, tuition only. Cambridge examinations. Also courses for elementary to advanced levels. 4 weeks, July-August. 20-25 hours per week. Cost from £560 includes half board family accommodation. Cost £380, tuition only. **BC AF**

EUROCENTRE FOREST HILL 36 Honor Oak Road, Forest Hill, London SE23 3SN Tel 01-699 1174
Courses for all levels. Ages 16+, individuals and groups. 3-21 weeks, all year. 30 hours per week. Maximum 15 per class. Options in English for business, life in Britain, plus study of English literature. Excursions and social events. Cost from £462, 3 weeks, includes course, teaching materials and half board family accommodation. Cost £309, 3 weeks, tuition only. Cambridge examinations. Also courses for all levels. 3 or 4 weeks, July-August. 20-25 hours per week. Cost from £420, 3 weeks, includes half board family accommodation. Cost £297, 3 weeks, tuition only. **BC AF**

EUROCENTRE LEE GREEN 21 Meadowcourt Road, Lee Green, London SE3 9EU Tel 01-318 5633
Courses for all levels. Ages 16+, individuals and groups. 2-21 weeks, all year. 30 hours per week. Maximum 15 per class. Options in English for business, science and technology plus study of history, literature, painting and music. Excursions and social events. Cost from £358, 2 weeks, includes course, teaching materials and half board family accommodation. Cost £256, 2 weeks, tuition only. Cambridge examinations. **BC AF**

EUROLANGUAGE LTD Greyhound House, 23/24 George Street, Richmond, Surrey TW9 1HY Tel 01-940 1087
Courses for all levels except beginners in Richmond and Staines. Ages 18+, individuals and groups. 2-6 weeks, July-August. 20 hours per week. Maximum 12 per class. Study of British society. Excursions. Cost £315 includes half board family accommodation. Also courses for ages 10-17 in Brentwood, Welwyn Garden City, Maidenhead, and Sutton Coldfield. 3-4 weeks, July-August. 15 hours per week. Maximum 15 per class. Supervised excursions and sports with coaching. Cost from £445 includes full board family accommodation. **BC AF PH**

EUROPEAN SUMMER SCHOOL OF ARTS AND LANGUAGES AT OXFORD 71 Oxford Street, Woodstock, Oxford OX7 1TJ Tel Woodstock 812547
Language and cultural course for intermediate to advanced levels. Ages 16-30, individuals and small groups. 3-4 weeks, July-August. 13-17 hours per week, average 11 per class. An important part of the course is the additional afternoon activities which include acting plays, film-

making and music classes. Excursions, theatre trips, sports and social events. Cost from £495 includes full board family accommodation. **BC PH**

THE EXETER ACADEMY 64 Sylvan Road, Exeter EX4 6HA Tel Exeter 30303
Courses for all levels. Ages 17 +, individuals and groups. 1 + weeks, all year. 21-30 hours per week. Maximum 12 per class. English for business, technical and scientific purposes. Lectures, excursions and social activities. Cost from £140 per week includes excursions and full board family accommodation. ARELS, Cambridge, LCCI, RSA and TOEFL examinations. **BC**

FITZROY COLEGE OF ENGLISH AND FURTHER STUDIES Northdown House, Margate CT9 3TP Tel Thanet 65547
Courses for elementary to advanced levels. Ages 16 +, individuals and groups. 2 + weeks, all year. 20 hours per week. Average 8 per class. Specialised courses in business and technical language for groups or 1:1. Self-study centre. Excursions, sports and social activities. Cost £145 per week includes full board family accommodation. ARELS, Cambridge, Oxford, Pitman and TOEFL examinations. *Two scholarships available for South American students.* **BC AF**

FOLKESTONE ACTIVITY HOLIDAY CENTRE Marine Crescent, Folkestone CT20 1PS Tel Folkestone 55651
Language and sports courses for all levels. Ages 8 +, individuals and groups. 1-8 weeks, all year. 12 hours per week language tuition. Average 8 per class. Participants choose 4 sports from sailing, canoeing, riding, tennis, cycling and waterskiing. Social activities with British participants. Cost £148 per week includes full board centre or family accommodation.

GLOBE ENGLISH CENTRE The Firs, Queens Terrace, Exeter EX4 4HR Tel Exeter 71036
Courses for all levels. Ages 12-21, individuals and groups. 3-9 weeks, July-August. 14 hours per week. Maximum 12 per class. Excursions, sports and social activities. Cost £160 includes full board family accommodation. Also organise tailor made courses for groups all year. **BC PH**

GLOUCESTERSHIRE COLLEGE OF ARTS & TECHNOLOGY EFL Unit, 73 The Park, Cheltenham GL50 2RR Tel Cheltenham 2128
Courses for all levels except beginners. Ages 18 +, individuals and groups. 4-8 weeks, January-September. 15-25 hours per week.

Maximum 15 per class. Options include business/computer English or study of Britain. Advanced students may also enrol on commercial and technical courses. Self-study centre. Excursions and social activities. Cost from £25 per week. Half board family accommodation available, from £44 per week. ARELS, Cambridge, JMB, LCCI, RSA, TOEFL and Trinity College examinations. **BASCELT**

GORDONSTOUN INTERNATIONAL SUMMER SCHOOL Elgin, Moray IV30 2RF Tel Elgin 830267
Language and activity courses for all levels. Ages 11-16, individuals and groups. 24 days, July. 12 hours per week. Maximum 8 per class. Courses include study of literature, history, computing, crafts, and outward bound sports including sailing, canoeing and climbing in the Scottish mountains. British teenagers also attend the course. Cost £1520 includes all activities and full board school accommodation.

GREENHILL COLLEGE Lowlands Road, Harrow HA1 3AQ Tel 01-422 2388
Courses for elementary to advanced levels. Ages 16 +, individuals only. 4 weeks, July. 6 hours per week. Average 18 per class. Cost £33. Also non-intensive year round courses. Cambridge and Oxford examinations. **BASCELT PH**

THE GREYLANDS SCHOOL OF ENGLISH 315 Portswood Road, Portswood SO2 1LD Tel Southampton 550633
Courses for all levels in Southampton. Ages 14-70, individuals and groups. 2 + weeks, all year. 12-25 hours per week. Maximum 12 per class. Excursions, summer, and social activities. Cost from £48 per week. Half board family accommodation available, £50 per week. ARELS, Cambridge, Oxford, RSA and TOEFL examinations. **BC AF**

THE HARPER SCHOOL OF ENGLISH 7 Warwick Row, Coventry CV1 1EX Tel Coventry 22588
Courses for all levels. Ages 11 +, individuals and small groups. 2 + weeks, January-August and October-December. 15-30 hours per week. Maximum 6 per class. Junior vacation courses. Courses in English for business, engineering or other special purposes. Self-study centre. Social events. Summer excursions and sports. Cost from £253, 2 weeks, includes half board family accommodation. Hotels available. ARELS, Cambridge, LCCI and RSA examinations. **BC AF**

HARVEN SCHOOL OF ENGLISH The Mascot, Coley Avenue, Woking GU22 7BT Tel Woking 23628
Courses for all levels. Ages 15 +, individuals and groups. 3-14 weeks, all year. 18-22.5 hours per week. Maximum 10-15 per class. 1:1 tuition for

special purposes. Excursions and social programme. Cost from £113 per week. Half board family accommodation available, £62 per week. ARELS, British Council, Cambridge, Pitman and Oxford examinations. Courses for ages 10-14, 2 + weeks, July-August. 15 hours per week. Maximum 8 per class. Supervised excursions and activities. Cost £345, 2 weeks, includes full board family acommodation. **BC AF**

HASTINGS ENGLISH LANGUAGE CENTRE St Helens Park Road, Hastings TN34 2JN Tel Hastings 437048
Courses for all levels except complete beginners. Ages 13 +, individuals and groups. 2-12 weeks, March-September. 15-25 hours per week. Average 11 per class. Courses in English for tourism. Lectures, excursions, sports including riding, and social programme. Cost from £111 per week includes leisure activities and full board family accomodation. ARELS and Pitman examinations. **BC AF**

HILDERSTONE COLLEGE St Peter's Road, Broadstairs CT10 2AQ Tel Thanet 69171
Courses for all levels. Ages 17 +, individuals and groups. 2 + weeks, June-August; 3 + weeks, September-June. 21-23 hours per week. Maximum 10 per class. Afternoon business and cultural options. Courses for overseas teachers and pre-university courses. Excursions, social activities and opportunities to meet British people studying at the college. Cost from £142 includes half board family accommodation. Cambridge, LCCI and RSA examinations. **BASCELT**

HOME LANGUAGE LESSONS 12-18 Royal Crescent, Ramsgate CT11 9PE Tel Thanet 590300
1:1 tuition for all levels in teacher's homes in the Cambridge, Colchester, Edinburgh, Kent, London, Oxford and Sussex areas. Also in Dublin and the Irish countryside. 15, 20 or 25 hours per week. 2:1 tuition also possible. Courses for executives, professionals and other special needs. Activities together with teacher. Cost from £320 per week includes full board accommodation in teacher's home. **PH**

HULL COLLEGE OF FURTHER EDUCATION Department of General Education, Humanities and Sciences, Queens Gardens, Hull HU1 3DG Tel Hull 29943 ext 289
Courses for intermediate level. Ages 16 +, individuals and groups. 4 weeks, July. 20 hours per week. Average 16 per class. Excursions and opportunities to meet British people. Cost £100 per week includes half board family accommodation. Also year-round courses for all levels. 3 terms, starting September, January and April. 12 hours per week. English for academic purposes. Cost £685 per term, tuition only. Cambridge and JMB examinations. **BASCELT PH**

INLINGUA COLLEGE COURSES 12 Meadowgate, Urmston, Manchester M13 1LB Tel 061-748 2621
Courses for all levels in Croydon, Lancaster, Newbattle near Edinburgh and Oxford. Ages 17 +, individuals and groups. 2 + weeks, July-August. 25 hours per week. Average 6 per class. Also intensive 1:1 tuition at Lancaster. Tennis, golf and dancing lessons on some courses. Excursions and social activities. Cost from £680, 2 weeks, includes course, teaching materials and full board college accommodation. **BC PH** depending on handicap.

INLINGUA SCHOOLS OF LANGUAGES BRIGHTON AND HOVE 55-61 Portland Road, Hove BN3 5DQ Tel Brighton 735975
Courses for all levels except beginners in Brighton and Hove. 2-16 weeks, all year. 15-25 hours per week. Average 8 per class. Summer courses, courses for overseas teachers, business and office English, and 1:1 courses for special needs. Courses include study of British culture. Self-study centre. Excursions, sports and social activities. Cost from £121 per week includes half board family or residential accommodation. ARELS, Cambridge, LCCI, Oxford and RSA examinations. **BC AF**

INTERLINK SCHOOL OF ENGLISH 126 Richmond Park Road, Bournemouth BH8 8TH Tel Bournemouth 290983
Courses for all levels. Ages 14 +, individuals and groups. 2-15 weeks, all year. 20-25 hours per week. Maximum 16 per class. Courses 2-6 weeks, March-April and June-September. 15-20 hours per week. ARELS, Cambridge, Oxford, RSA and TOEFL examinations. Specialised courses for groups. Excursions, social activities and sports. Cost from £236, 2 weeks, year round, and £198, holiday courses, includes half board family accommodation. **BC AF**

INTERNATIONAL COMMUNITY SCHOOL 10 York Terrace East, Regents Park, London NW1 4PT Tel 01-935 1206
Courses for all levels. Ages 5-17, individuals and groups. 2 + weeks, January-November. 7.5-15 hours per week. Maximum 12 per class. Excursions, sport and cultural activities. Cost from £75 per week. Full board family accommodation available. ARELS, Cambridge and Oxford examinations. **BC AF**

INTERNATIONAL HOUSE 106 Piccadilly, London W1V 9FL Tel 01-491 2598
Courses for all levels. Ages 16 +, individuals and groups. 2 + weeks, all year. 15-20 hours per week. Average 12 per class. Also executive

English in groups of 6 maximum, and courses for overseas teachers. Excursions and social programme. Cost £670, 4 weeks, 15 hours per week, includes half board family accommodation. Bed and breakfast also available. ARELS, Cambridge, LCCI, Oxford and RSA examinations. **BC AF**

INTERNATIONAL HOUSE White Rock, Hastings TN34 1JY Tel Hastings 445777
Courses for all levels except beginners. Ages 16+, individuals and groups. 2+ weeks, all year. 15-20 hours per week. Maximum 15 per class. Also executive English. Excursions and social programme. Cost approx £80 per week. Family accommodation available. ARELS, Cambridge and Oxford examinations. **BC AF**

INTERNATIONAL HOUSE 24 Northumberland Road, Newcastle-upon-Tyne NE1 8JZ Tel 091-232 9551
Courses for all levels. Ages 16+, individuals and small groups. 2+ weeks, throughout the year. 15-25 hours per week. Maximum 15 per class. Summer courses. Business and technical English, 1:1 or for groups. Excursions, sports and social activities. Cost £368, 4 weeks, 15 hours per week. Half board family accommodation available, £45 per week. ARELS, Cambridge, Oxford, RSA and TOEFL examinations. *3 scholarships per year.* **BC AF**

THE INTERNATIONAL SCHOOL 1 Mount Radford Crescent, Exeter EX2 4EW Tel Exeter 54102
Courses for all levels. Ages 15+, individuals and groups. 3-14 weeks, all year. 15-21 hours per week. Average 10 per class. Courses for ages 11-14 and adults, July-August. Courses for ages 60+. Self-study centre. Excursions, sports and social activities. Cost from £74 per week. Half board family accommodation available, £50 per week. Hotels also available. ARELS, Cambridge, ESB, Oxford and RSA examinations. **BC AF**

THE ISCA SCHOOL OF ENGLISH PO Box 15, 4 Mount Radford Crescent, Exeter EX2 4JN Tel Exeter 55342
Courses for all levels. Ages 16+, individuals only. 3-12 weeks, January, March and June-September. 23 hours per week. Maximum 12 per class. Afternoon cultural or commercial options. Self-study centre. Excursions, sports and social activities. Cost £123 per week includes activities and half board family accommodation. Cambridge and Oxford examinations. **BC AF**

ISI LANGUAGE COURSES LTD Belgrave House, 2 Winner Street, Paignton TQ3 3BJ Tel Paignton 524169
Courses for all levels. Ages 14+, individuals and groups. 1+ weeks, all year. 15-30 hours per week. Maximum 12 per class. Easter and summer courses for ages 10-18 including leisure and sports programme. 1:1 English for special purposes. Cost from £69 per week, tuition. Half board family or hotel accommodation available. Cambridge, Pitman and Trinity examinations. **BC AF**

ISI LANGUAGE COURSES LTD 15 Grand Parade, Brighton BN2 2QB Tel Brighton 674121
Courses for all levels. Ages 14+, individuals and groups. 1+ weeks, all year. 15-30 hours per week. Maximum 12 per class. Easter and summer courses for ages 10-18 including leisure and sports programme. 1:1 English for special purposes. Cost from £69 per week. Half board family or hotel accommodation available. Cambridge, Pitman and Trinity examinations. **BC AF**

ITS SCHOOL OF ENGLISH 43-45 Cambridge Gardens, Hastings TN34 1EN Tel Hastings 438025
Courses for all levels. Ages 14+, individuals and groups. 2+ weeks, all year. 15-23 hours per week. Maximum 12 per class. Vacation courses, business English in groups, and 1:1 tuition. Excursions and social activities. Sports in summer. Cost from £55 per week. Half, full board or self catering accommodation available in families, hotels or apartments, from £37 per week. ARELS, Cambridge, LCCI and Oxford examinations. **BC AF**

JORDANHILL COLLEGE Southbrae Drive, Glasgow G13 1PP Tel 041-959 1232
Courses for all levels except complete beginners. Ages 18+, individuals and groups. 4+ weeks, all year. 15-20 hours per week. Maximum 10 per class. Background lectures on Britain, English for special purposes and courses for teachers. Courses for specialised groups. Cost from £70 per week. Excursions and sports facilities. Half board hostel accommodation available, £95 per week. Self-catering rooms also available. Cambridge examinations. **BC BASCELT PH**

KEBLE COLLEGE Mrs Jean Robinson, Administrator, Oxford OX2 7BJ Tel Oxford 272727
Summer school for advanced levels on English language and contemporary Britain. Ages 18+, individuals only. 3 weeks, late July-August. 12 hours per week, consisting of classes on pronunciation and intonation and varieties of English, in groups of 10 students. Additional lectures and seminars on social and cultural aspects of Britain, teaching

English, and grammar. Excursions and social activities. Cost £750 includes full board college accommodation and 1 theatre trip.

KENT LANGUAGE AND ACTIVITY COURSES Aldergate, Aldington Road, Lympne, Hythe CT21 4PD Tel Hythe 67284
Language and activity courses for all levels in Oxford, Harrow, Broadstairs, Canterbury, Goudhurst and Sevenoaks. Ages 8-18, individuals and small groups. 2-6 weeks, Easter and July-August. 15 hours per week language tuition. Average 8 per class. Afternoon activities include sailing, riding and other sports, arts, crafts and music. Excursions and social activities. Cost from £520, 2 weeks, includes full board school accommodation. **BC**

KENT SCHOOL OF ENGLISH 3 Granville Road, Broadstairs CT10 1QD Tel Thanet 68207
Courses for all levels. Ages 12 +, individuals and groups. 1 + weeks, all year. 15-30 hours per week. Maximum 12 per class. Also courses for business/technical staff. Self-study centre. Cost from £160 per week includes course, activities and full board family accommodation. Hotels also available. Cambridge, LCCI, Pitman and RSA examinations. **BC**
Course in English and watersports in Kings Lynn. 3 weeks, July-August. 15 hours per week language plus 15 hours per week watersports tuition. Cost £175 per week includes accommodation. **BC**

KING'S SCHOOLS OF ENGLISH 25 Beckenham Road, Beckenham BR3 4PR Tel 01-650 5891
Courses for all levels except complete beginners. 2-24 weeks, all year. 24-29 lessons per week plus evening lectures. Maximum 16 per class. Cost from £282, 2 weeks, includes half-board family accommodation. Cambridge examinations. Also 2-10 week courses, June-August. 16 hours per week plus 4 evening lectures. Cost from £230, 2 weeks, includes half-board family accommodation. **BC AF**

KING'S SCHOOL OF ENGLISH 58 Braidley Road, Bournemouth BH2 6LD Tel Bournemouth 293535
Courses for all levels except complete beginners in Bournemouth. 4-50 weeks, all year. 24-29 lessons per week. Maximum 16 per class. Also Easter and summer courses, and courses in professional English and business management. Cambridge examinations. Cost from £588 includes half-board family accommodation. Also junior courses in nearby Wimborne. 2-12 weeks, March-August. Includes computer lessons, sports, activities and excursions. Cost from £280, 2 weeks, includes course, teaching materials and full board family accommodation. **BC AF**

KINGSGATE COLLEGE OF ENGLISH/HARROGATE TUTORIAL COLLEGE Kingsgate House, 3/5 North Park Road, Harrogate HG1 5PD Tel Harrogate 501041
Courses for all levels. Ages 15 +, individuals and groups. 3 + weeks, all year. 15-26 hours per week. Maximum 9 per class. Summer courses, English with tuition in riding, golf or tennis, and English for special purposes. Also GCSE and A level courses. Excursions, sports, social programme and opportunities to meet British students. Cost from £55 per week, tuition only. Half board family accommodation available, £45 per week. Cambridge and RSA examinations.

THE LAKE SCHOOL OF ENGLISH 14B Park End Street, Oxford OX1 1HW Tel Oxford 724312
Courses for all levels at teachers' cooperative. Ages 16 +, individuals and groups. 2 + weeks, all year. 21 hours per week. Maximum 14 per class. Also special course for those wishing to undertake academic study in the UK. Self-study centre. Cultural lectures, excursions, sports and social events. Cost £95 per week. Half board family accommodation available, £52 per week. ARELS, Cambridge and Oxford examinations. *One scholarship per term available.* **BC AF**

LANGUAGE AND LEISURE SERVICES 228A High Street, Bromley BR1 1PQ Tel 01-460 4861
Courses for all levels except complete beginners. Ages 14-20, individuals and groups. 2-3 weeks Easter, 2-8 weeks July-August. 14 hours per week. Average 12 per class. Excursions and social visits. Cost £294, 2 weeks, includes excursions and full board family accommodation.

LANGUAGE STUDIES INTERNATIONAL 13 Lyndhurst Terrace, London NW3 5QA Tel 01-435 8552
Courses for all levels in Hampstead and Ealing. Ages 16 +, individuals and groups. 4 + weeks, all year. 20-30 hours per week. Maximum 15 per class. Business/professional English courses and 1:1 tuition. Excursions and social activities. Cost from £200, 4 weeks. Half board family accommodation available, from £60 per week. Also courses, 2-4 weeks, June-August. 20-30 hours per week. Cost from £140, 2 weeks. ARELS, Cambridge, Oxford and TOEFL examinations. **BC AF**

LANGUAGE STUDIES INTERNATIONAL 13 Ventnor Villas, Brighton BN2 2QB Tel Brighton 674121
Courses for all levels. Ages 16 +, individuals and groups. 4 + weeks, all year. 20-30 hours per week. Maximum 15 per class. Business/professional English courses and 1:1 tuition. Excursions and social activities. Cost from £200, 4 weeks. Half board family

accommodation from £50 per week. Also summer courses, 2-4 weeks, June-August. 20-30 hours per week. Cost from £140, 2 weeks. ARELS, Cambridge, Oxford and TOEFL examinations. **BC AF**

LANGUAGE STUDIES INTERNATIONAL Woodstock House, 10-12 James Street, London W1M 5HN Tel 01-499 9621
Summer courses for all levels in Cambridge. Ages 16 +, individuals and groups. 2-4 weeks, July-August. 20-30 hours per week. Maximum 15 per class. Also English for executives. Excursions and social activities. Cost from £150, 2 weeks. Half board family accommodation available, from £60 per week. **BC AF**

LITTLE SCHOOL OF ENGLISH AND COMMERCE Revenue Chambers, 58 Chapel Road, Worthing BN11 1BG Tel Worthing 31541
Courses for all levels. Ages 16 +, individuals and small groups. 4 + weeks, January-November. 20-23 lessons per week. Average 10 per class. 1:1 tuition for special purposes. Excursions, sports and social activities. Cost from £282, 4 weeks. Half board family accommodation available, £42 per week. ARELS, Cambridge, LCCI, Oxford and Pitman examinations. **BC AF**

THE LONDON SCHOOL OF ENGLISH 15 Holland Park Gardens, London W14 8DZ Tel 01-603 1656
Courses for elementary to advanced levels. Ages 18 +, individuals and groups. 4-10 weeks, all year. 22 hours per week. Maximum 12 per class. Cost £515, 4 weeks. Executive and financial courses, 2 weeks all year. 32 hours per week. Average 6 per class. Cost £750. Special courses for company groups. Self-study centre. Lectures and cultural/social events. Family accommodation available, from £60 bed and breakfast per week. ARELS, Cambridge and Oxford examinations. *Some scholarships available.* **BC AF**

LONDON STUDY CENTRE Munster House, 676 Fulham Road, London SW6 Tel 01-731 3549/8298
Courses for all levels. Ages 16 +, individuals and groups. 2 + weeks, July-September and 4 + weeks during academic year. 15 hours per week. Maximum 24 per class. Self-study centre. Courses include study of British society and some visits and excursions. Cost £19 per week. Accommodation available from £40 per week. ARELS and Cambridge examinations. *Occasional scholarships.* **BC AF**

LTC INTERNATIONAL COLLEGE OF ENGLISH Compton Park, Compton Place Road, Eastbourne BN21 1EH Tel Eastbourne 27755
Courses for all levels. Ages 15 +, individuals and groups. 4 + weeks, all year (no beginners July-August). 23-29 hours per week. Maximum 15 per class. Special courses in English for business, hotel management and other special purposes, or with secretarial skills. Self-study centre. Cost from £163 per week. Optional courses in music, sports and practical skills. Cost from £41.40. Excursions and social programme. Half board residential or family accommodation available, cost £46 per week. ARELS, Cambridge, JMB, LCCI, Oxford, Pitman and TOEFL examinations. Also courses for all levels except complete beginners in Lewes. Ages 16-25, individuals and groups. 3-6 weeks, July-August. 17.5 hours per week. Maximum 15 per class. Lectures, sports, excursions and social activities. Cost from £450, 3 weeks, includes full board family accommodation. **BC AF**

MAJOR'S SCHOOL OF ENGLISH 47 Warrior Square, St Leonards-on-Sea TN37 6BG Tel Hastings 440889
Courses for all levels. Ages 17 +, individuals and groups. 2 + weeks, all year. 24 hours per week. Average 6 per class. Courses for groups in business, banking and tourism. Lectures, excursions and social activities. Cost £176 per week includes half board family accommodation. ARELS, Cambridge and Pitman examinations.

MEADS SCHOOL OF ENGLISH 2 Old Orchard Road, Eastbourne BN21 1DB Tel Eastbourne 34335
Courses for all levels. No age limits, individuals and groups. 2 weeks-3 months, all year. 23 hours per week. Maximum 15 per class. Course options include English for business and for secretaries, and English through photography, drama and music. Courses for overseas teachers. 1:1 tuition for executives. Excursions, sports and social programme. Cost from £80 per week. Half board family accommodation available, £50 per week. ARELS, Cambridge and Oxford examinations. **BC AF PH**

MERIDIAN SCHOOL OF ENGLISH 9 Yarborough Road, Southsea, Portsmouth PO5 3DZ Tel Portsmouth 816023
Courses for all levels. Ages 17 +, individuals and small groups. 1 + weeks, all year. 16-24 hours per week. Average 6 per class. Also summer courses for ages 12-14 and small group courses for executives. Excursions and social activities. Cost from £44 per week plus £12.50 enrolment fee. Half board family accommodation available, £45 per week. Self-catering accommodation also available, from £20 per week. ARELS and Cambridge examinations. **BC AF**

MERRION HOUSE CENTRE FOR ENGLISH STUDIES 60 Penn Road, Beaconsfield HP9 2LS Tel Beaconsfield 3769
Courses for intermediate to advanced levels. Ages 19+, individuals only. 11 weeks September-June, 3-4 weeks July-August. 25 hours per week. Maximum 7 per class. Self-study centre. Working excursions, visits designed to deepen understanding of daily life in England, and social activities. Cost £685, 3 weeks, includes excursions and full board family accommodation. ARELS, Cambridge, LCCI and Oxford examinations. **BC AF**

MILESTONE INTERNATIONAL LTD c/o Box 261, 19 South End, Kensington Square, London W8 Tel 01-938 3755
Courses in London, all year and in Cambridge and Oxford, July-August. Ages 16+, individuals and groups. 2+ weeks, 15-30 hours per week. Maximum 15 per class. Lectures, excursions and social activities. Cost from £313, 2 weeks, includes course, teaching materials and half board family accommodation. ARELS, Cambridge, LCCI and Oxford examinations, London only. Also summer courses near Brighton, Cambridge, Chichester, Guildford, London and Sevenoaks. Ages 8-23, individuals and groups. 2-6 weeks, July-August. 23 hours per week plus activities, sports and excursions. Cost from £450, 2 weeks, includes course, teaching materials and full board school or family accommodation.

MILLFIELD VILLAGE OF EDUCATION Millfield School, Street BA11 0YD Tel Street 45823
Courses for all levels. Ages 8+, individuals and groups. 1-4 weeks, July-August. 12.5 hours per week. Average 10 per class. Participants also choose an afternoon course from over 400 sporting, activity and hobby courses. These are mostly attended by British people, and participants mix on excursions and at social events. Cost £221 per week, includes full board school accommodation.

MM OXFORD STUDY SERVICES 44 Blenheim Drive, Oxford OX2 8DQ Tel Oxford 513788
Courses for elementary to advanced levels. Ages 13+, individuals and groups. 2-4 weeks, Easter and July-September. 20 lessons per week. Maximum 15 per class. Lectures on British society. Excursions and social activities. Cost from £395, 2 weeks, includes full board family or college accommodation. **BC AF**

NEWNHAM LANGUAGE CENTRE 8 Grange Road, Cambridge CB3 9DU Tel Cambridge 311344
Courses for elementary to advanced levels. Ages 16+, individuals and groups. 4-12 weeks, all year. 23 hours per week. Maximum 15 per class.

Special courses for groups of businessmen or teachers. Cultural studies and sports in the afternoon. Self-study centre. Excursions and social events. Cost from £360, 4 weeks. Family accommodation from £38, bed and breakfast, per week. ARELS, Cambridge, LCCI, Oxford, RSA and TOEFL examinations. *Some scholarships available to students from Third World countries.*
Also international courses for ages 12-15, in nearby village. 3 weeks, July-August. 16 hours per week language tuition with afternoon activities including arts, crafts, sports, cookery and drama. Opportunities to meet English people. Cost £530 includes course, teaching materials, excursions, leisure activities and full board family accommodation. **BC AF**

NORD-ANGLIA INTERNATIONAL LTD Broome House, 152 Palatine Road, Didsbury, Manchester M20 8QH Tel 061-434 7475
Language and activity courses throughout Britain. Courses for all levels except complete beginners in Cambridge, Cardiff, Chester, Dublin, Edinburgh, London, Manchester, Oxford, Southport and York. Ages 12 +, individuals and groups. 2-4 weeks, Easter and June-September. 15-30 x 50 minute lessons per week. Maximum 15 per class. Excursions, sports and social activities. Cost from £115 per week includes course, teaching materials and half/full board family or residential accommodation. Courses for all levels in Cambridge. Ages 12 +, individuals and groups. 1-12 weeks, all year. 15-25 hours per week. Maximum 15 per class. Also 1:1 tuition and English for special purposes. Cost from £70 per week. Bed and breakfast residential accommodation available, from £36 per week. Cambridge examinations. **BC AF** except Dublin. **PH** depending on centre

NORTH EAST SURREY COLLEGE OF TECHNOLOGY Reigate Road, Ewell, Epsom KT17 3DS Tel 01-394 1731
Courses for all levels. Ages 16 +, individuals only. 10-12 weeks, starting January, April and September. 15 hours per week. Average 15 per class. Also summer school, July, with business and computing modules and courses for overseas teachers of English. Sporting facilities and social activities with British students. Cost £220 per term. Summer school £50 per week. Help given with accommodation; cost approx £40 per week. Cambridge, JMB, RSA and TOEFL examinations. **BASCELT**

OXFORD HOUSE COLLEGE 3-5 Oxford Street, London W1R 1RF Tel 01-734 3880
Courses for all levels. Ages 16 +, individuals and groups. Multiples of 4 weeks, all year. 6-30 hours per week. Average 14 per class. Specialised courses for groups. 1:1 tuition. Cost from £138, 4 weeks, plus £11.50

registration fee. Excursions, sports and social activities. Bed and breakfast family accommodation available from £40 per week. ARELS, Cambridge and RSA examinations. **BC AF**

OXFORD INTENSIVE SCHOOL OF ENGLISH Oise House, Binsey Lane, Oxford OX2 0EY Tel Oxford 249218
Courses in Bedford, Bristol, Cardiff, Chippenham, Cirencester, Gloucester, Hereford, Leamington Spa, Leicester, Loughborough, Marlborough, Newbury, Nottingham, Oundle, Peterborough, Reading, Shrewsbury, Sidcot, St Audries, Swindon, Telford, Teignbridge, Wantage, Winchester and Yeovil. Ages 7-18, individuals and groups. 2-8 weeks, Easter and July-September. 20 x 45 minute lessons per week. Maximum 8 per class. Afternoon activities and sports. Cost from £428, 2 weeks, includes course, teaching materials and full board family or school accommodation. **PH**
Also courses for all levels except complete beginners in Bristol. Ages 17 +, individuals and groups. 2 + weeks, all year. 30 x 45 minute lessons per week, maximum 8 per class. Language laboratory. Excursions and social activities arranged. Cost from £396, 2 weeks, includes course, teaching materials and half board family accommodation, full board at weekends. Also courses for all levels in Oxford. Ages 17 +, individuals and groups. 1 + weeks, all year. 5-40 hours per week, 1:1 tuition. Language laboratory. Special courses for teachers and in English for law, commerce, industry, medicine, business and management. Excursions and social activities arranged. Cost from £190 per week, 5 hours tuition, includes course, teaching materials and half board family accommodation, full board at weekends. ARELS, British Council, Cambridge, LCCI, Oxford, Pitman, RSA and TOEFL examinations. **BC AF**

OXFORD STUDY CENTRE 17 Sunderland Avenue, Oxford OX2 8DT Tel Oxford 515243
Course for all levels except beginners. Ages 16 +, individuals and groups. 3 weeks, July-August. 25 hours per week. Maximum 15 per class. Afternoon seminars on literature and business English. Excursions, sports and social activities. Cost from £148 per week includes full board family accommodation. Also course for beginner to intermediate levels in Abingdon. 3 weeks, July-August. 20 hours per week. Maximum 15 per class. Cost from £145 per week includes full board family accommodation. **BC AF**

PILGRIMS LANGUAGE COURSES LTD 8 Vernon Place, Canterbury CT1 3YG Tel Canterbury 762111
Courses for all levels. Ages 7 +, individuals and groups. 2 + weeks, July-September. 15-22.5 hours per week. Maximum 12 per class. Courses for

ages 17+ at University of Canterbury including seminars on cultural, business and social themes. Language and activity/sport courses for ages 7-16 at residential centres. Excursions and social programme. Cost from £760, 2 weeks, includes full board residential accommodation. Also year-round courses for executives. 2 weeks, 30 hours per week. Courses for groups with special needs and 1:1 courses. Cost from £1000, 2 weeks, includes full board family accommodation.
BC AF PH

POLY-CONTACT INTERNATIONAL LTD 61 Marlborough Road, London N19 4PA Tel 01-263 8663
Courses for all levels in Richmond, Isleworth, Twickenham and north London. Ages 10+, individuals and groups. 2-8 weeks, Easter and June-August. 12-15 hours per week. Average 10 per class. Also courses for under 16s and special courses for groups, all year. Sports and activities for junior courses; excursions for adults. Cost from £430, 3 weeks, includes half board family accommodation. Cost £60 per week, course only. ARELS and Pitman examinations. **BC AF PH**

THE REGENCY SCHOOL OF ENGLISH Royal Crescent, Ramsgate Tel Thanet 591212
Courses for all levels. Ages 16+, individuals and groups. 1+ weeks, all year. 15-30 hours per week. Average 9 per class. Christmas and summer courses. Commercial English in small groups. Self-study facilities in students' bedrooms. Excursions, sports and social activities. Cost from £120 per week includes full board school or family accommodation. Cambridge, LCCI and TOEFL examinations. **BC AF PH**

ST CLARE'S OXFORD 139 Banbury Road, Oxford OX2 7AL Tel Oxford 52031
Courses for all levels. Ages 16+, individuals and groups. 3-4 weeks, June-August. 15 hours per week. Average 12 per class. Additional language laboratory and special options lessons up to 12 hours per week. Also academic year courses. Excursions, sports and social activities. Cost from £275, 3 weeks, includes full board residential accommodation. ARELS, Cambridge, Oxford, Pitman and RSA examinations. *Scholarships offered, one especially for Belgian student.*
BC AF PH

ST GILES COLLEGE Regency House, 3 Marlborough Place, Brighton BN1 1UB Tel Brighton 682747
Courses for all levels. Ages 16+, individuals and groups. Multiples of 4 weeks, all year. 15-30 lessons per week. Average 11 per class. Special courses in English business studies and commercial correspondence. Language laboratory. Excursions and social activities. Cost from £175,

4 weeks, 15 hours per week. Half board family accommodation available, from £41 per week. ARELS, Cambridge, LCCI, RSA and TOEFL examinations. **BC AF**

ST GILES COLLEGE 13 Silverdale Road, Eastbourne BN20 7AJ Tel Eastbourne 29167
Courses for all levels. Ages 16 +, individuals and groups. Multiples of 4 weeks, all year. 20 or 30 lessons per week. Average 11 per class. Language laboratory. Excursions and social activities. Cost from £235, 4 weeks, 20 hours per week. Half board family accommodation available, from £42 per week. ARELS, Cambridge, LCCI, RSA and TOEFL examinations. Also courses for ages 12-16. 3 or 6 weeks, June-August. Cost from £510, 3 weeks, includes course, teaching materials, excursions and full board family accommodation. **BC**

ST GILES COLLEGE 16 Northumberland Avenue, Westminster, London WC2 5AP Tel 01-930 5743/51 Shepherd's Hill, Highgate, London N6 5QP Tel 01-340 0828
Courses for all levels. Ages 16 +, individuals and groups. Multiples of 2/4 weeks, all year. 15-30 lessons per week. Average 11 per class. Special courses in executive English, business and commercial studies. Language laboratory. Excursions and social activities. Cost from £93, 2 weeks, 15 hours per week. Bed and breakfast or half board accommodation available, from £47 per week. ARELS, Cambridge, LCCI, RSA and TOEFL examinations. **BC AF**

ST GODRIC'S COLLEGE 2 Arkwright Road, Hampstead, London NW3 6AD Tel 01-435 9831
Courses for all levels. Ages 16 +, individuals and groups. 3-10 weeks, all year. 21 hours per week. Average 12 per class. Business and other specialised courses. Also year-long courses. Excursions and social events. Sports facilities. Cost from £794, 3 weeks, includes full board residential accommodation. Cost from £541, 3 weeks, course only. ARELS, Cambridge and Oxford examinations. **BC AF PH**

ST HILARY SCHOOL OF ENGLISH 2 & 4 Midvale Road, Paignton TQ4 5BD Tel Paignton 559223
Courses for all levels. Ages 11 +, individuals and groups. 2 + weeks, all year. 16-20 hours per week. Maximum 15 per class. English for business, tourism, computing and overseas teachers for special groups or 1:1. Lectures, excursions and activities on request. Cost £265, 2 weeks, includes full board family accommodation. Cambridge and Pitman examinations. **BC AF PH**

ST JOHN'S WOOD SCHOOL OF ENGLISH 126 Boundary Road, London NW8 ORH Tel 01-624 1925

Courses for all levels. Ages 16-70, individuals and groups. 2-14 weeks, all year. 15-25 hours per week. Maximum 12 per class. Special courses for executives. Self-study centre. Excursions and social programme. Cost from £129, 2 weeks, 15 hours per week. Bed and breakfast/half board family accommodation available, from £45 per week. Cambridge examinations. **BC AF**

SOUTH DEVON COLLEGE OF ARTS AND TECHNOLOGY English Language Centre, Newton Road, Torquay TQ2 5BY Tel Torquay 217553

Courses for all levels except complete beginners. Ages 16 +, individuals and groups. 12 weeks, starting January, April and September. 10 hours per week language tuition plus 6 hours chosen from art and design, hotels and catering, business and computer studies, travel and tourism, or British culture. Average 12-16 per class. Also includes 2 hours per week recreational courses with British students. Courses for overseas teachers. Can also be linked with other technical subjects. Also summer courses. Self-study centre. Excursions and social activities. Cost £130, EC nationals or £950, others, 12 weeks. Half board accommodation available, from £44 per week. Cambridge, LCCI and RSA examinations. **BC BASCELT**

SOUTHBOURNE SCHOOL OF ENGLISH 30 Beaufort Road, Southbourne, Bournemouth BH6 5AL Tel Bournemouth 422300

Courses for all levels. Ages 16 +, individuals and groups. 2 + weeks, all year. 21 hours per week. Maximum 15 per class. Excursions. Sports can be arranged. Cost from £117 per week includes half board family, hotel or flat accommodation. Cambridge and Pitman examinations. **BC AF**

SPECIALIST LANGUAGE SERVICES English in York 38-40 Coney Street, York YO1 1ND Tel York 36771

Courses for all levels. Ages 16 +, individuals and groups. 3 + weeks, all year. 20-35 lessons per week. Maximum 15 per class. Special summer courses. Excursions. Cost from £85 per week. Half board family accommodation available, £55 per week. ARELS, Cambridge and RSA examinations. Also 1:1 and group courses in English for business, scientific or technical purposes. Cost from £320 per week. **BC AF**

STAFFORD HOUSE SCHOOL OF ENGLISH 68 New Road, Canterbury CT1 3EQ Tel Canterbury 453237

Courses for all levels. Ages 14 +, individuals and groups. 4 + weeks, September-June. 25 hours per week. Maximum 10 per class. Also courses, 2 + weeks, Easter and June-September. 15 hours per week. Maximum 12 per class. Special courses, business English, British culture. Excursions, sports and social activities. Cost £150 per week, includes half board family or residential accommodation. ARELS, Cambridge, LCCI and Pitman examinations. **BC AF**

THE STRATFORD UPON AVON SCHOOL OF ENGLISH STUDIES 8/9 Tiddington Road, Stratford upon Avon CV37 7AE Tel Stratford upon Avon 69497
Courses for elementary to advanced levels. Ages 16 +, individuals and groups. 2-8 weeks, all year. 21 hours per week. Average 10 per class. English for academic purposes. Courses for specialised groups on request. Excursions, team games and social activities. Cost from £292, 2 weeks, includes half board family accommodation. Cambridge, JMB, Oxford, Pitman, RSA and TOEFL examinations. *6 scholarships available per year.* **BC AF**

THE STUDIO SCHOOL OF ENGLISH 6 Salisbury Villas, Station Road, Cambridge CB1 2JF Tel Cambridge 69701
Courses for all levels. Ages 17 +, individuals and groups. 2-21 weeks, all year. 28-40 lessons per week. Maximum 15 per class. Courses for overseas teachers, summer courses for adults and ages 15-17, business English and 1:1 tuition. Excursions, sports, and cultural and social activities. Cost from £208, 2 weeks. Family accommodation from £42 per week. Cambridge, LCCI, Oxford and RSA examinations. *Some scholarships granted.*
Also two-centre summer course for advanced students at Cambridge and University of Nottingham, and residential course for ages 10-15 in Letchworth Garden City. **BC AF**

SUMMER SCHOOL IN ENGLAND Mrs K J Johnson, Longlythe, Stairs Hill, Empshott, Liss GU33 6HW Tel Blackmoor 667
Summer school for all levels in Haslemere. Ages 13-19, individuals only. 3-4 weeks, July-August. 15 hours per week. Maximum 10 per class. Lectures on English culture. Excursions, sports including swimming and tennis in the grounds of the house, and social activities with English people. Cost £250 per week includes excursions and full board residential accommodation.

SURREY LANGUAGE CENTRES LTD 39 West Street, Farnham GU9 7DR Tel Farnham 723494
Courses for all levels. Ages 16 +, individuals and groups. 2 + weeks, all year. 15-25 hours per week. Average 8 per class. Summer school for ages 12 + at 4 centres in Surrey. Specialised courses arranged for groups. 1:1

tuition. Excursions, social activities and sports. Cost from £135, 2 weeks, 15 hours per week. Half board family accommodation available, cost £55. Self-catering, residential and hotel accommodation also available. Cambridge, Pitman, RSA and Trinity examinations. **BC AF PH**

SUZANNE SPARROW LANGUAGE SCHOOL LTD Corrofell, Yealm Road, Newton Ferrers, Plymouth PL8 1BL Tel Plymouth 872240
Courses for all levels. Ages 12 +, individuals and groups. 2 + weeks, all year. 15-25 hours per week. Average 6 per class. Also general business English courses, courses for special groups and 1:1 tuition. Summer excursions, sports and social activities. Cost from £148 per week includes full board family accommodation. Cambridge, LCCI and Pitman examinations. **BC AF**

THE SWAN SCHOOL OF ENGLISH 111 Banbury Road, Oxford OX2 6JX Tel Oxford 53201
Courses for all levels. Ages 16 +, individuals only. 2-10 weeks, all year. 23 hours per week. Maximum 14 per class. Courses for overseas teachers, business, technical, literature and translation on request. 1:1 tuition. Excursions and social activities. Cost from £198, 2 weeks. Bed and breakfast or half board family accommodation available, from £37 per week. ARELS, British Council, Cambridge, Oxford and TOEFL examinations. *Some scholarships available.* **BC AF PH**

SWANDEAN SCHOOL OF ENGLISH Oxford Lodge, 7 Oxford Road, Worthing BN11 1XG Tel Worthing 31330
Summer courses in Brighton for elementary to advanced levels. Ages 16 +, individuals and groups. 2-4 weeks, July-August. 20 lessons per week. Average 13 per class. Excursions and social programme included. Cost from £290, 2 weeks includes course, teaching materials and full board family accommodation. **BC AF**

TORQUAY INTERNATIONAL SCHOOL 15 St Marychurch Road, Torquay TQ1 3HY Tel Torquay 25576
Courses for all levels. Ages 16 +, individuals and groups. 1 + weeks, all year. 20 hours per week. Maximum 10 per class. Intensive business course 40 hours per week, with specialised options. Also English for international banking and finance. 1:1 tuition. Excursions, sports and social activities. Cost from £112 per week includes half board family accommodation. Hotels and apartments on request. Cambridge and RSA examinations. **BC AF**

TOTNES SCHOOL OF ENGLISH 51B High Street, Totnes, Devon TQ9 5NP Tel Totnes 865722
Courses for all levels at teachers' cooperative. Ages 18 +, individuals only. 3-10 weeks, all year. 16 hours per week. Average 8 per class. Extra courses in arts, crafts and relaxation techniques, through which students make contact with British people. Excursions and parties. Cost from £55 per week. Half board family accommodation available, £46 per week. Cambridge examinations.

UNIVERSITY COLLEGE CARDIFF English Language Teaching Unit, 2 Museum Place, Cardiff CF1 3DB
Courses for all levels. Ages 17 +, individuals and groups. 10 weeks, starting January, April and July. 21-24 hours per week. Maximum 12 per class. Special courses in English for academic purposes, and language and literature. Lectures on Welsh life and culture. Excursions and social activities. Cost £300 per month. Family or self-catering accommodation available from £28 per week. Cambridge examinations. **BC PH**

UNIVERSITY OF EDINBURGH DEPARTMENT OF EXTRA-MURAL STUDIES 11 Buccleuch Place, Edinburgh EH8 9LW Tel 031-677 1011 ext 6506
Courses for intermediate to advanced levels. Ages 18 +, individuals and groups. 3-4 weeks, July-September. 15-30 hours per week. Maximum 12 per class. Courses include language and literature, language through the arts, and an English course designed to coincide with the Edinburgh Arts Festival in August. Excursions and social activities. Cost from £155, 3 weeks. Advice given on accommodation. *Some scholarships available from the British Council.* **PH**

UNIVERSITY OF EDINBURGH INSTITUTE FOR APPLIED LANGUAGE STUDIES 21 Hill Place, Edinburgh EH8 9DP Tel 031-667 1011 ext 4592
Courses for all levels except complete beginners. Ages 17 +, individuals and groups. 3-33 weeks, all year. 15-20 hours per week. Maximum 12 per class. Courses include general English, and English for university or literary studies, business, law, medicine and teachers. Also tailor-made courses for individuals and groups. Lectures, excursions and social events. Cost from £70 per week. Accommodation with families or in university residences from £35 per week plus £15 booking fee. Cambridge examinations.

UNIVERSITY OF EXETER INTERNATIONAL SUMMER SCHOOL Queens Building, The Queen's Drive, Exeter EX4 4QH
Language and culture course for those with good knowledge of English. Ages 18+, individuals only. 3 weeks, July-August. 5 hours per week language tutorials or literature classes. 9 hours per week lectures and seminars on English life. Art study, excursions, sports and social events. Cost £600 includes full board university accommodation. *Early application advisable.*

UNIVERSITY OF LANCASTER Institute for English Language Education, Bowland College, Lancaster LA1 4YT Tel Lancaster 65201
Courses for intermediate to advanced levels. Ages 18+, individuals and groups. 2-3 weeks, August-September. 20 hours per week. Average 15 per class. Also advanced English for teachers, July, and English for academic purposes, July-August. Courses in teaching methodology. Social activities. Cost from £90 per week. University residence accommodation available. Cambridge and RSA examinations.

UNIVERSITY OF MANCHESTER INSTITUTE OF SCIENCE AND TECHNOLOGY English Language Teaching Centre, PO Box 88, Manchester M60 1QD Tel 061-236 3311 ext 2303
Courses for intermediate to advanced levels. Ages 17+, individuals and groups. 4-12 weeks, September-June; 2-9 weeks July-September. 21-25 hours per week. Average 10-14 per class. Courses include general English, business, technical or scientific English, courses for overseas teachers, English for academic purposes, and academic writing. Excursions and social events. Cost £936 per term, or from £160, 2 weeks. Half board family accommodation available, from £40 per week. Residential summer accommodation available. ARELS, Cambridge, JMB, Oxford. RSA and TOEFL examinations. **BC**

UTS OXFORD CENTRE 2 Gloucester Street, Oxford OX1 2BN Tel Oxford 726745
Courses for all levels. Ages 16+, individuals and groups. 1-11 weeks, all year. 20 hours per week. Maximum 14 per class. 1:1 tuition for special needs. Courses for those about to enter schools or colleges in the UK. Also GCSE and A levels. Social activities. Cost £95 per week. Half board family accommodation available. ARELS, Cambridge and Oxford examinations. **BC AF PH**

VACATIONAL STUDIES Pepys' Oak, Tydehams, Newbury RG14 6JT Tel Newbury 41867
Language and sports courses for all levels except complete beginners. Ages 11-17, individuals only. 4 weeks, July-August. 15 hours per week. Maximum 16 per class. Excursions, supervised sports and activities. Cost £830 includes full board residential accommodation. **BC AF**

VICTORIA SCHOOL OF ENGLISH 28 Graham Terrace, Sloane Square, London SW1 Tel 01-730 1333
Courses for elementary to advanced levels. Ages 16 +, individuals only. 1 + weeks, all year. 20 hours per week. Maximum 12 per class. Cost £50 per week. Excursions. Family accommodation available, from £42 bed and breakfast per week. ARELS, Cambridge, Oxford and TOEFL examinations. **BC AF**

WESSEX ACADEMY SCHOOL OF ENGLISH 84/85 Bournemouth Road, Parkstone, Poole, Dorset BH14 0HA Tel Bournemouth 744700
Courses for all levels in Bournemouth and Poole. Ages 14 +, individuals and groups. 2-24 weeks, all year. 15-30 hours per week. Maximum 15 per class. Supplementary courses in commercial English and British life and culture. Easter and summer courses. Also 1:1 tuition. Excursions, sports and social activities. Cost from £42 per week. Half board family accommodation available from £43 per week. ARELS, Cambridge, LCCI and Oxford examinations. **BC AF PH**

WEST SUSSEX SCHOOL OF ENGLISH 7 High Street, Steyning Tel Steyning 814512
Courses for all levels except complete beginners. Ages 16 +, individuals and families. 2 + weeks, February-December. 20 hours per week. Average 5 per class. 1:1 tuition in English for business. Excursions, parties, films and leisure activities. Cost from £190 per week includes course and full board family or hotel accommodation. ARELS, Cambridge and Pitman examinations. **BC**

WESTERN LANGUAGE CENTRE Forge House, Kemble, near Circencester GL7 6AD Tel Kemble 447
Courses for professional and business people. Ages 23 +. 1-16 weeks, all year. 27 hours per week. Maximum 6 per class. Also 1:1 tuition for special needs. Cost from £242 per week. Half board family accommodation available, £90 per week plus £12 booking fee. Hotels also available. ARELS, Cambridge and LCCI examinations. **BC AF**

WIMBLEDON SCHOOL OF ENGLISH 41 Worple Road, London SW19 4JZ Tel 01-974 1921
Courses for all levels. Ages 16 +, individuals only. 4-12 weeks, all year. 20 hours per week. Average 12 per class. Cost £62 per week. Fortnightly excursions. Half board family accommodation available, £65 per week. Cambridge and Pitman examinations. **BC AF**

WYVERN HOUSE TUTORIAL COLLEGE 77 Landsdowne Road, Bournemouth BH1 1RW Tel Bournemouth 292608
Intensive courses at all levels for students preparing for full-time education in England. Ages 7-18. 3 months-1 year, all year. 30 hours per week. Average 12 per course. Also holiday courses, 16 hours per week. Full time 1 year GCSE courses also available. Excursions, social events and sports. Cost from £1750 per term, £180 per week depending on course, includes full board residential or family accommodation. Cambridge, Pitman and RSA examinations. **BC**

INFORMATION

Irish Embassy
17 Grosvenor Place, London SW1X 7HR Tel 01-235 2171

British Embassy
33 Merrion Road, Dublin 4 Tel Dublin 695211

Tourist offices
British Tourist Authority, Thames Tower, Blacks Road, Hammersmith, London W6 9BL Tel 01-846 9000

Irish Tourist Office, Ireland House, 150 New Bond Street, London W1Y 0AQ Tel 01-493 3201

Scottish Tourist Board, 23 Ravelston Terrace, Edinburgh EH4 3EU Tel 031-332 2433

Wales Tourist Board, Brunel House, 2 Fitzalan Road, Cardiff CF2 1UY Tel Cardiff 499909

Youth hostels
Youth Hostels Association (England & Wales), Trevelyan House, 8 St Stephen's Hill, St Albans, Hertfordshire AL1 2DY

An Oige Irish YHA, 39 Mountjoy Square, Dublin 1 Tel Dublin 745734

Scottish Youth Hostels Association, 7 Glebe Crescent, Stirling FK8 2JA

Youth & student information
International Students House, 229 Great Portland Street, London W1N 5HD Tel 01-631 3223

National Union of Students, 461 Holloway Road, London N7 6LJ Tel 01-272 8900

UKCOSA, 60 Westbourne Grove, London W2 5SH Tel 01-229 9268

Union of Students in Ireland, 16 North Great Georges Street, Dublin 1 Tel Dublin 786020

National Youth Council of Ireland, 3 Montague Street, Dublin 2 Tel Dublin 784122

Information centres
International Travellers' Aid, The Kiosk, Platform 14, Victoria Station, London SW1V 1JT Tel 01-834 3925/3901 is an interdenominational voluntary organisation who help and provide information to travellers, particularly if they have just arrived from overseas, are unfamiliar with English, need advice on accommodation, need to trace friends, relatives or lost possessions, or in distress of any kind. Staffed by volunteers who are willing to help and have time to give travellers their attention.

Publications *Irish Youth Directory* £1.50, is a useful reference and resource aid which provides detailed information on voluntary youth organisations together with a comprehensive list of useful addresses, youth travel and accommodation. *Stepping Out* £3, is a youth handbook providing information on a wide range of topics including training and employment, health and drugs, further education, recreation, the media, politics, the environment and travel. Both published by the National Youth Council of Ireland, 3 Montague Street, Dublin 2 Tel Dublin 784122.

Travel
National Express, Victoria Coach Station, London SW1W 9TP Tel 01-730 0202 operate express coach services between major towns

in Britain. Those under 17 are entitled to up to 50% reduction on adult fares. Full-time students can obtain a card for £3.50 valid 12 months, which entitles them to the same reduction. Those under 24 can purchase a British Rail Young Person's Railcard entitling the holder to 50% reduction on day return tickets and 33% reduction on other tickets. The card costs £12 and is valid for 12 months. Further information on this and other concessions are available at principal British Rail stations or most student travel offices.

Hitch-hikers' Manual Britain £4.70 including postage, is a comprehensive handbook including hints on techniques, route planning, legal matters, and how lifts can be found on boats, planes and hovercrafts. Contains descriptions of how to reach the best hitching points for 200 towns, plus a section on motorway hitching. Published by Vacation Work, 9 Park End Street, Oxford OX1 1HJ Tel Oxford 241978.

CIE Tours International, Ireland House, 150-151 New Bond Street, London W1Y 9FE Tel 01-629 0564 issues the Rambler ticket entitling the holder to unlimited rail and bus travel in Ireland. Cost IR£62/£90 (8/15 days).

Accommodation

The International Friendship League, Peace Haven, 3 Creswick Road, Acton, London W3 9HE Tel 01 992 0221 works to promote a spirit of mutual respect and friendship among the peoples of the world. Offers accommodation at residential centres in London and Gloucester, all year. Cost from £5 per night, bed and breakfast. Advance booking usually necessary. Also offers a hospitality service throughout Great Britain, with households prepared to provide accommodation at a reasonable charge and take visitors to places of interest. Apply at least 8 weeks in advance, enclosing 4 IRCs.

Hackney Camping, Millfields Road, London E5 01 985 7656 is a campsite for those with their own tents. Mid June-end August. Cost £1.60 per night, including the use of hot showers, shop, snack bar and baggage store. From September-May contact Barnaby Martin, Tent City Ltd, 11 Ellesmere Road, Twickenham, Middlesex TW1 2DJ Tel 01-892 3570. **PH**

Tent City, Old Oak Common Lane, London W3 Tel 01-743 5708 offers camping accommodation for young travellers at a football pavilion and park with 400 beds in large or mixed or single sex tents. Bedding available. Also space for those taking their own tents. Early June-late September. Cost £3 per night including use of hot showers, snack bar and baggage store. From September-May contact Barnaby Martin, see above. **PH**

FINNISH

Finnish is one of the official languages of Finland, the mother tongue of approx 93% of the population. It is also spoken in the northwestern USSR and by Finnish emigrés in Sweden and the United States. It is one of the Finno-Ugric languages which include Estonian, Hungarian and Lapp. The Finns came originally from Estonia, migrating to Finland some 2000 years ago. Finland became part of Sweden in the 13th century, was annexed to the Russian Empire in 1809 and finally became independent in 1918. The earliest written Finnish texts appeared in the 16th century, though Swedish remained the sole official language until 1863 when Finnish gained equal status. Finnish is one of the few European languages not a member of the Indo-European family, and though a very regular language it has no articles or gender distinctions and spelling is consistent with pronunciation.

COURSES IN FINLAND

COUNCIL FOR INSTRUCTION OF FINNISH FOR FOREIGNERS Ministry of Education, PO Box 293, Pojhoisranta 4 A 4, 00171 Helsinki Tel Helsinki 134 171

Language and culture courses at the University of Helsinki, the Lappeenranta Institute of Technology, the Rauma College of Navigation, and in Kuopio. Intended primarily for university students of

Finnish language or linguistics. 3 weeks, July. Approx 80 hours instruction in total, comprising text reading, conversation, writing and conversational exercises, grammar and lectures on Finnish culture. Course, teaching materials and accommodation free. Number of participants limited to 30. Application forms also available from Finnish Embassies. *Apply by end February.*

KESÄLUKIOSEURA RY (Summer High School Association), Korkeavuorenkatu 25 A 1, 00130 Helsinki Tel Helsinki 605 239
Summer schools in Finnish language and culture in 33 centres throughout Finland. All levels. Ages 13+, individuals and groups. 10 days-3 weeks, June-mid August. 20-30 hours per week. Average 10-20 per class. Audio-visual facilities and language laboratories. Extra-curricular activities include visits to places of interest, summer theatres, music and dance festivals, barbecues, sports, games and social events. Cost FM900-FM1600 includes course, teaching materials, excursions, social events, insurance and full board accommodation at course centre. Financially supported by Ministry of Education and National Board of General Education. Further information available from Finnish embassies. *Apply by 15 April.* **PH** certain centres.

PÄIJÄT-HÄME SUMMER UNIVERSITY Kirkkokatu 16, 15140 Lahti Tel Lahti 892 400
Courses in Finnish language and culture for beginners and intermediate levels in Lahti, a town north of Helsinki. Ages 18+, individuals and groups. 4 weeks, August. 10 hours per week. Average 10-20 per class. Audio visual facilities and language laboratory. Excursions and study tours can be arranged. Cost FM300. Accommodation not arranged, but school can provide addresses of hotels and hostels, and also gives advice on other services available. Approved by the Ministry of Education. Staff approved by University of Helsinki. *Some grants available; apply to the Executive Board at above address.* **PH**

SUMMER UNIVERSITY OF JYVÄSKYLÄ Seminaarinkatu 15, 40100 Jyväskylä Tel Jyväskylä 216 926
Language and culture courses for elementary and advanced levels at a centre in Korpilahti, south of Jyväskylä. Ages 15-60, individuals and families. Priority given to those needing knowledge of Finnish for career or family reasons. 3 weeks, June-July. 30 hours per week. Maximum 15 per class. Audio-visual facilities and language laboratory. Lectures on Finnish music, culture, society and recent history. Extra-curricular activities include barbecues, hiking, folk singing, slide shows and visits

to local places of interest, museums, open-air theatre and sauna baths. Sports include rowing, tennis and volleyball. Cost FM1600 includes course and teaching materials. Full board school accommodation available, cost FM2250. Students can also arrange own accommodation. Recommended by Ministry of Culture and Education. **PH**

SUMMER UNIVERSITY OF LAPLAND Pohjolankatu 2, 96100 Rovaniemi Tel 60-22621
Course in Inari, in Finnish Lapland, for those with at least one year's study of Finnish. Ages 16 +, individuals and groups. 2 weeks, July. 25 hours per week. Average 10 per class. Opportunity to study Lappish literature and culture. Extra-curricular activities include excursions to surrounding natural wilderness. Cost FM1600 includes course, teaching materials and full board youth hostel accommodation.

TAMPERE SUMMER UNIVERSITY Vuolteenkatu 11 B, 33100 Tampere Tel Tampere 38 433
Courses in Finnish for foreigners for all levels at the University of Tampere. No age limit, individuals and groups. Approx 25 hours per week. Average 10-15 per class. Beginners, 2 weeks, June. Intermediate levels, 10 days, June-July. Advanced levels, 10 days, August. Language laboratory. Opportunity to study Finnish culture. Students arrange own accommodation; list available. Cost FM675, beginners or FM600, intermediate and advanced, includes course and teaching materials. **PH**

INFORMATION

Finnish Embassy
33 Chesham Place, London SW1X 8HW Tel 01-235 9531

British Embassy
Uudenmaankatu 16-20, Helsinki

Tourist office
Finnish Tourist Board, 66/68 Haymarket, London SW1Y 4RF Tel 01-839 4048

Youth hostels
Suomen Retkeilymajajarjesto ry, Yrjonkatu 38B, 00100 Helsinki 10

Youth & student information
Travela-FSTS, Mannerheimintie 5C, 00100 Helsinki 10

Resources

Council for Instruction of Finnish for Foreigners, Ministry of Education, PO Box 293, Pojhoisranta 4 A 4, 00171 Helsinki Tel Helsinki 134 171 gives advice on courses on Finnish and to lecturers in Finnish working abroad. Develops and supervises instruction to foreign students in Finnish language and culture, answers enquiries, grants scholarships and provides information on Finnish summer courses. Publishes an annual guide, *Courses in Finnish Language and Culture,* available from Finnish embassies, giving information on courses organised by the Council and other summer courses.

Suomi-Seura ry (Finland Society), PO Box 213, 00171 Helsinki Tel Helsinki 174 255 is a non-political organisation founded in 1927 and acting as a cultural bridge for Finns all over the world. Organises seminars in Finnish language and culture for descendants of Finnish emigrants.

Centre for Information on Language Teaching and Research (CILT), Regent's College, Inner Circle, Regent's Park, London NW1 4NS Tel 01-486 8221 publish *Finnish Language & Culture Guide* £4.25 including postage, with details on the provision and use of language teaching and learning resources, covering an introduction to the language, useful addresses, libraries and special collections to consult, opportunities for learning, and examinations which can be taken.

Travel

The Finnrailpass entitles the holder to unlimited travel on Finnish State Railways, cost £55/£77/£98 (8/15/22 days). Available from the Finnish Tourist Board, see above, who can also supply timetables for shipping lines, maps and a hiking routes booklet.

The Nordic Tourist Ticket entitles the holder to unlimited travel on trains in Finland, Denmark, Norway and Sweden, and is also valid on some inter-Scandinavian ferries. Valid for 21 days, cost £128. Available from Norwegian State Railways, 21-24 Cockspur Street, London SW1Y 5DA Tel 01-930 6666.

Finland Facts and Map covers travel to and within Finland, accommodation, customs and other useful information. Available from the Finnish Tourist Board, see above.

Accommodation

The Finnish Tourist Board, see above, publish *Camping and Youth Hostels* listing campsites and youth hostels with their facilities and a map, and also *Hotels* which includes a section on hostels.

FRENCH

French is one of the Romance languages, descending from the Latin introduced into Gaul between 58-51 BC, following the conquests of Julius Caesar. Latin replaced the extant Celtic languages as the importance of Gaul as a Roman province became established. In the 12th century Paris became the capital, and Parisian French became dominant over the several dialects that had emerged. From the 17th century onwards French was important as an international language and known as the language of diplomacy. It is now one of the 6 official languages of the United Nations, and of Belgium, Canada, Haiti, Luxembourg and Switzerland, and of over fifteen African countries and French dependent territories. French is spoken as a mother tongue by some 80 million people worldwide, with several more million having it as a second language.

COURSES IN FRANCE

ACTILANGUE Ecole Privée de Langue Francaise, 2 rue Alexis-Mossa, 06000 Nice Tel Nice 96 33 84

Courses for all levels. Ages 16-75, individuals and groups. 2-24 weeks, all year. 20, 25 or 40 x 45 minute lessons per week. Maximum 8 per class. Video facilities and language laboratory. Also small group and 1:1 tuition. Activities include visits to cinema, theatre and concerts, beach parties, bowling, discos and excursions to Monaco, St Tropez, Grasse, Cannes and Antibes. Cost from FF1980, 2 weeks, 20 lessons per week

includes course, teaching materials and activities. Excursions extra. Family accommodation available, cost from FF115 per day bed and breakfast. Hotel accommodation also available. Paris Chamber of Commerce examinations may be taken.
UK applicants can apply to Cultural and Educational Services Abroad, 44 Sydney Street, Brighton, Sussex BN1 4EP Tel Brighton 683304. Cost approx £150-200 per week includes family accommodation. Alternatively, to Language Studies International Ltd, Woodstock House, 10-12 James Street, London W1M 5HN Tel 01-449 9621.

ALLIANCE FRANCAISE Comité de Nice, 1 rue Vernier, 0600 Nice Tel Nice 87 42 11
Courses for all levels. Ages 16+, individuals and groups. 1+ months, all year. 10 hours per week. Maximum 14 per class. Audio-visual facilities. Opportunities to study literature and attend lectures in Nice given by Alliance Francaise. Activities include meeting French people, picnics and visits to places of interest. Cost from FF900 per month, plus FF100 registration fee. Textbooks approx FF100. Advice given on accommodation.

ALLIANCE FRANCAISE Ecole Internationale de Langue et de Civilisation Francaises, 101 boulevard Raspail, 75270 Paris Tel Paris 45 44 38 28
Courses for all levels in the heart of Paris. Ages 16+, individuals and groups. 2+ weeks, all year. 10-20 hours per week. Maximum 22 per class. Multi-media centre. Lectures are held on art, literature, theatre, civilisation and poetry. Also courses for teachers and translators, and courses in business, scientific and technical French. Activities include film club, tour of Paris and excursions to the Loire châteaux, Mont-St-Michel and Reims. Paris Chamber of Commerce and Ministry of Education ratified examinations in French language can be taken. Cost from FF850 per month. Family or residence accommodation available. Approved by Ministry of Education.
UK applicants can apply to Cultural and Educational Services Abroad, 44 Sydney Street, Brighton, Sussex BN1 4EP Tel Brighton 683304. Cost approx £125 per week includes family accommodation.

ALLIANCE FRANCAISE 32 rue de Buffon, 76000 Rouen Tel Rouen 98 55 99
Courses for all levels. Ages 18+, individuals and groups. 3 weeks, all year. 10-20 hours per week. Maximum 12 per class. Lectures and workshops on French wines, cookery, song and literature. Possibility to take Paris Chamber of Commerce examinations. Activities include excursions to Paris, Mont-Saint-Michel, Versailles, the châteaux of the Loire Valley, Deauville and the Normandy coast, plus visits to a

Normandy farm, local firms and local press and radio. Typical cost FF6000, 3 weeks, 15 hours per week, including meals and excursions. **PH**

ALLIANCE FRANCAISE DE TOULOUSE 9 place du Capitole, 31000 Toulouse Tel Toulouse 23 41 24
Courses for all levels. No age limits, individuals and groups. Beginners and elementary: 8 weeks, 7.5 hours per week. Cost FF1300. Intermediate and advanced: 12 weeks, 10 hours per week. Cost FF2700. Very advanced: 16 weeks, 12.5 hours per week. Cost FF5000. Starting dates all year. Average 12 per class. Also conversation classes for advanced levels, cost FF30 per hour. Audio-visual facilities and language laboratory. Study of French culture and civilisation for very advanced level. Activities include visits to places of interest, opportunities to meet local people, videos, films, theatre and concerts. Textbooks approx FF80. Help given with finding accommodation. **PH**
Also canal barge trips with language tuition, on the Canal du Midi, Toulouse to Sète, or the Canal Latéral á la Garonne, Toulouse to Bordeaux. 2 weeks, June-September. 10 hours per week language tuition, with 20 participants divided into 2 work groups. Audio-visual equipment and cassettes. Cost from FF5000 includes full board accommodation.

ARAVI – CAMPUS INTERNATIONAL Université de Toulon/Var, 83130 La Garde Tel Toulon 21 11 86
Courses for elementary levels upwards in the Savoy resort of La Plagne. Ages 18+, individuals and groups. 1-17 weeks, December-April. 24 hours per week in small groups, plus ski course. Cost from FF1400 per week includes tuition and full board chalet accommodation. 6 day ski pass available from FF470.

ASSOCIATION AENEAS 54 Grand' Rue, 89113 Fleury-la-Vallée Tel Fleury-la-Vallée 73 76 85
Courses for all levels in the Burgundy town of Auxerre, on the banks of the river Yonne. Ages 14+, individuals and groups. 2+ weeks, Easter and summer. 15+ hours per week. Maximum 9 per class. Audio-visual facilities. Excursions to places of interest, canal trips, visits to wine cellars and sporting activities arranged. Cost FF1590 per week includes course, teaching materials, insurance and full board family accommodation.

ASSOCIATION LINGUISTIQUE ET CULTURELLE INTERNATIONALE 10 bis rue de l'Egalité, 32000 Auch Tel Auch 05 67 41
Courses for all levels. Ages 15+ individuals, 12+ groups. 2+ weeks, April, July and August. 20 hours per week. Average 10 per class. Aimed

at students intending to take GCSE, International Baccalaureate, A and S level examinations in French. Audio-visual facilities. Also courses in French language, literature and civilisation, French and activity courses, French for business and tourism. Sports include tennis and swimming. Activities include visits to local places of interest, discos and folk evenings. Cost FF3400, Easter, 12 days; FF3600, summer, 14 days or FF5100, 21 days, includes full board family accommodation.

BABEL Cours Privé Audiovisuel de Langues, 22 ter rue de France, 06000 Nice Tel Nice 82 27 44
Courses for all levels. Ages 16-60, individuals and groups. 2-12 weeks, June-August. 15 hours per week. Average 12 per class. Audio-visual facilities, video and language laboratory. Also course in business French, 2 weeks, July. Year round courses for teachers, professionals, business people and companies on request. Excursions, cultural and sports activities on demand. Cost from FF1750, 2 weeks. Bed and breakfast hotel accommodation or self-catering apartments available.

CAVILAM (CENTRE AUDIO-VISUEL DE LANGUES MODERNES) 14 rue Maréchal Foch, BP 164, 03206 Vichy Tel Vichy 32 25 22
Courses for all levels in the spa town of Vichy. Ages 16-75, individuals and groups. 2+ weeks, all year. 25 hours per week. Maximum 18 per class. Audio-visual facilities, computer-assisted learning, video, telematics and language laboratories. Afternoon options include extra language tuition, communication, contemporary French civilisation, literature and history of art, French for business, cookery and sport. Cost FF840 per week. Also courses for teachers of French and in French for special purposes. Opportunity to take Ministry of Education ratified examinations. Social and cultural activities, including excursions, contacts with families, dances, meetings, talks, cinema club, social, professional and artistic events, and sports. All types of accommodation can be arranged, from FF90 per day, bed and breakfast in family. Teaching quality controlled by Universities of Clermont-Ferrand.

CENTRE AUDIO-VISUEL DE ROYAN POUR L'ETUDE DES LANGUES ET DE L'INFORMATIQUE 48 boulevard Franck Lamy, BP 219c, 17205 Royan Tel Royan 05 31 08
Courses for all levels in Royan, north of Bordeaux on the Gironde estuary. Ages 18+, individuals and groups. 4-6 weeks, all year. 25 hours per week. Average 15-16 per class. Audio-visual facilities and language laboratory, plus television studio. Lectures in information technology, and at advanced level, opportunity to study French civilisation. Activities include film club, concerts, social evenings and

excursions. Also special courses in audio-visual methods of French teaching, scientific and technical French, and courses leading to Paris Chamber of Commerce examinations. Cost from FF2335, 4 weeks. Textbooks extra on some courses, from approx FF100. Family, residence or apartment accommodation available. Approved by Ministry of Education, University of Poitiers and town of Royan.

CENTRE D'ETUDES LINGUISTIQUES D'AVIGNON 16 Rue Sainte Catherine, 84000 Avignon Tel Avignon 86 04 33
Courses for all levels in Avignon, an historic town on the banks of the Rhône. Ages 17 +, individuals and groups. 2 + weeks, all year. 20 hours per week. Maximum 12 per class. Audio-visual and audio-oral approach, language laboratory. Cost from approx FF1600 per week includes teaching materials, student discount card and half board family accommodation.

CENTRE D'ETUDES ET DE RECHERCHES AUDIO-VISUELLES D'UNIVERSITAIRES A MONTPELLIER 11 rue de Saint-Louis 34000 Montpellier Tel Montpellier 58 80 68
Courses for all levels. Ages 18 +, individuals and groups. 1 + months, January-September. 25 hours per week. Average 12 per class. Emphasis on audio-visual methods, language laboratory. Lectures on French culture and society. Also courses in French for medical studies and for teachers of French. Activities include visits to places of interest, film shows and social events. Cost FF2700, 4 weeks (FF3000 July-September) includes course, teaching materials and student card allowing access to University facilities and restaurants. All types of accommodation available.

CENTRE INTERNATIONAL D'ENSEIGNEMENT DE LA LANGUE FRANCAISE Etablissement Libre d'Enseignement Supérieur, 100 boulevard Sébastopol, 75003 Paris Tel Paris 42 78 92 98
Courses for all levels. Ages 16 +, individuals and groups. 2 + weeks, June-August. 15 hours per week. Maximum 15 per class. Cost from FF3200, 2 weeks, includes full board family accommodation. Cost FF1400, 2 weeks, tuition only. Lectures on French film and song, Paris architecture and French history. Activities include excursions to Versailles and the Château de Vincennes, plus boat trips on the Seine. Also courses during the academic year, from 4-32 weeks, and courses to suit special needs on request.

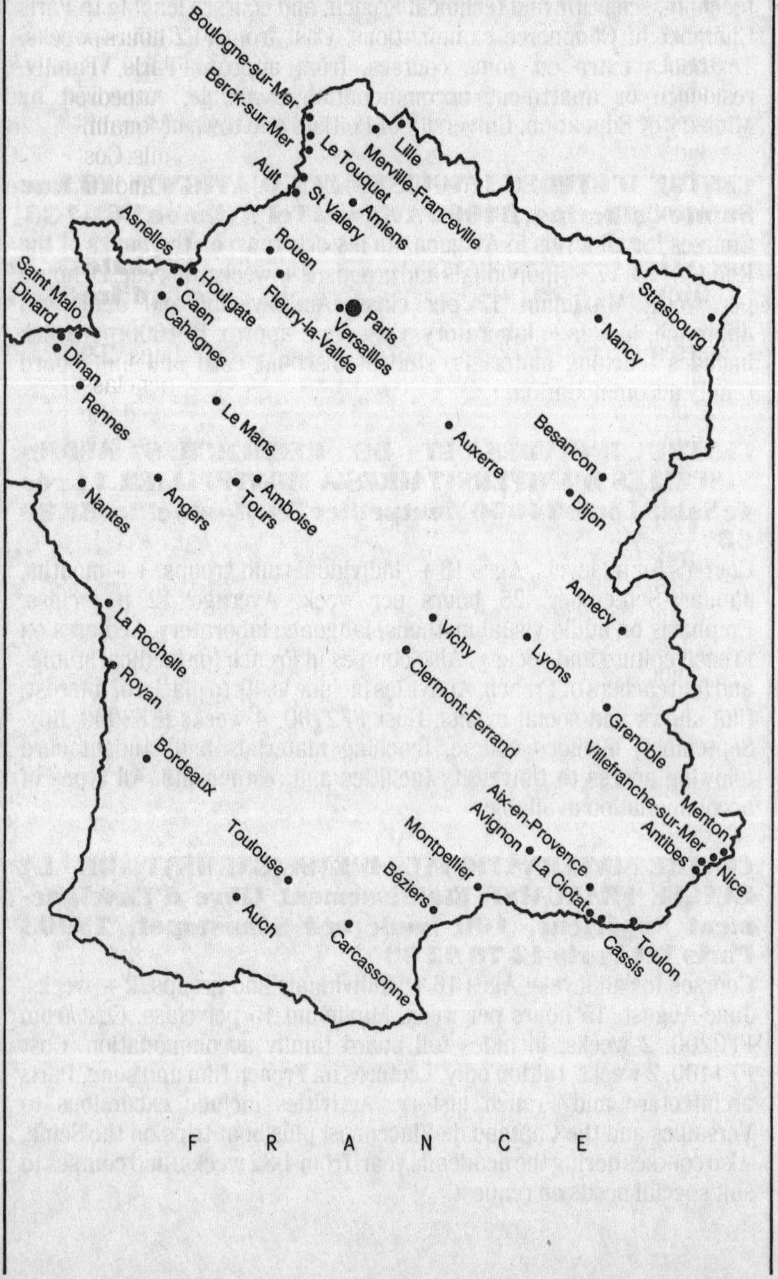
Boulogne-sur-Mer
Berck-sur-Mer
Le Touquet
Ault
St Valery
Lille
Merville-Franceville
Amiens
Asnelles
Rouen
Houlgate
Caen
Cahagnes
Fleury-la-Vallée
Paris
Versailles
Saint Malo
Dinard
Dinan
Rennes
Strasbourg
Nancy
Le Mans
Auxerre
Besancon
Dijon
Nantes
Angers
Tours
Amboise
Annecy
Vichy
Lyons
Clermont-Ferrand
La Rochelle
Royan
Grenoble
Bordeaux
Villefranche-sur-Mer
Menton
Antibes
Nice
Aix-en-Provence
Avignon
La Ciotat
Montpellier
Toulouse
Béziers
Auch
Carcassonne
Cassis
Toulon
FRANCE

CENTRE INTERNATIONAL LINGUISTIQUE ET SPORTIF BP 36, 51700 Dormans Tel Reims 58 82 46
Courses for all levels. Ages 6-17. 3-7 weeks, all year. 15 hours per week. Average 15 per class. Activities include excursions to Paris, Versailles, Chantilly, Reims and Epernay, visits to castles, cathedrals and museums, plus video shows and discos. Sports taught by qualified staff include riding, water skiing, fencing, sailing, golf and tennis. Cost FF320 per day includes course, tuition, activities, excursions and full board residential accommodation.

CENTRE INTERNATIONAL DE VACANCES Château de Bellevue, 49781 Le Bourg d'Ire Tel Le Bourg d'Ire 61 51 42
Courses for all levels. Ages 5-14, individuals and groups. 2-9 weeks, April, July and August. 15 hours per week. Average 15 per class. Tennis and pony riding facilities. Sightseeing activities arranged. Cost from FF4400, 2 weeks, includes course, teaching materials, excursions, insurance and full board accommodation.

CENTRE MEDITERRANEEN D'ETUDES FRANCAISES Chemin des Oliviers, 06320 Cap d'Ail Tel Nice 78 21 59
Courses for all levels in the village of Cap d'Ail, 2km from Monaco. Ages 18+, individuals and groups. 2-13 weeks, all year. 30 hours per week in small groups. Computer-assisted learning and multi-media centre. Afternoon lectures for advanced levels include French history, civilisation, history of art, literature, press and gastronomy. Activities include excursions to places of interest, museum visits, film shows, concerts and social evenings. Cost FF895 per week plus FF35 registration fee. Accommodation available at centre, from FF1050 per week, half board. Also language and sports course for ages 13-17. 2-8 weeks, July-August. Afternoon activities include swimming, windsurfing and tennis. Excursions to Monaco, Grasse, Antibes, Nice and surrounding villages. Cost from FF4200, 2 weeks, includes course, teaching materials, activities and full board accommodation at the centre.

CLUB DES 4 VENTS 1 rue Gozlin, 75006 Paris Tel Paris 43 29 60 20
Language stays for those with at least 2 years' French in Aix-en-Provence, Breuillet, La Ciotat, Dinan, Montpellier and Nantes. Ages 12-20, individuals and groups. 2-4 weeks, Easter (Breuillet only) and July-August. 1 or 2 students of different nationalities live with host families. 10 hours per week morning classes. Maximum 12 per class. Afternoon activities include excursions, local festivals, cycling tours, concerts and sports. Cost from FF3170, 2 weeks, includes course,

excursions, some activities and full board family accommodation. Approved by the Ministry of Youth and Sports and Ministry of Tourism.

CLUB RIVIERA LANGUES INTERNATIONAL Château Laval, 14 Route de la Badine, 06600 Antibes Tel Antibes 74 36 08
Courses for all levels in Antibes on the Côte d'Azur, which dates back to 500 BC. Ages 18+, individuals and groups. 2 or 4 weeks, March, May and July-September. 15 or 30 hours per week. Maximum 12 per class. Audio-visual facilities. Also 1:1 tuition and French for business purposes. Lectures cover the region's art and culture. Sightseeing activities and social evenings arranged. Cost from FF4000, 2 weeks, includes half board school or family accommodation.
UK applicants may apply to Cultural and Educational Services Abroad, 44 Sydney Street, Brighton, Sussex BN1 4EP Tel Brighton 683304. Cost approx £150-£200 per week includes family or residential accommodation.

COMITE D'ACCUEIL/LIGUE D'ENSEIGNEMENT Centres Internationaux, 21 rue Saint-Fargeau, BP 313, 75989 Paris Tel Paris 43 58 95 23
Courses for all levels in Montpellier. Ages 18+. 2-4 weeks, July and August. 15 hours per week. Optional afternoon classes include literature, civilisation, practical and artistic activities. Cost from FF4200, 2 weeks, includes course, teaching materials, excursions, activities and full board university residence accommodation. Also courses for all levels in Aix-en-Provence. Ages 18+. 2-4 weeks, July and August. 15 hours per week. Optional afternoon classes include literature, civilisation, practical and artistic activities. Cost from FF4000, 2 weeks, includes course, teaching materials, excursions and activities, and full board university residence accommodation.

COURS INTENSIFS DE FRANCAIS Professeur Edmond Cros, 87 rue de la Chênaie, 34090 Montpellier Tel Montpellier 61 13 54
Courses for all levels. Ages 17+, individuals and groups. 2+ weeks, July-August. Courses in September for groups only. 25 hours per week. Average 16 per class. Audio-visual facilities and language laboratory. Study of culture, civilisation, cinema, theatre, literature, economy, society, media and politics for higher levels. Opportunity to meet writers, poets and politicians. Activities include barbecues, visits to places of interest, films, transport to the beach 3 times per week, weekly excursions to Nîmes, Avignon, Carcassonne, Arles and the Camargue. Cost from FF3350, 2 weeks, includes course, teaching materials, activities, excursions and half board residential accommodation. Cost

excluding beach trips and excursions FF3100, 2 weeks. Under control of the Université Paul Valéry, Montpellier.

COURS INTERNATIONAUX D'ETE Centre d'Etudes Francaises pour l'Etranger, Université de Caen, Esplanade de la Paix, 14032 Caen Tel Caen 93 26 76
Courses for all levels in Caen, home to William the Conqueror and capital of Lower Normandy. Ages 18+, individuals and groups. 3+ weeks, July-September. 15 hours per week. Maximum 15 beginners, 20 intermediate or 25 advanced, per class. Also courses in business French, literary French and seminars for teachers of French. Cost FF1530, 3 weeks. Also language laboratory and computer assisted learning courses. 15 hours per week, cost FF510. Activities include lectures on French culture, audio-visual presentation of aspects of contemporary French life, social evenings, cinema, music and poetry evenings and talent show. Half day and full day excursions include Bayeux, Honfleur, Deauville, Mont-Saint-Michel, Saint-Malo and Rouen. Cost FF75 half day, FF150 full day. Half board family accommodation available, cost FF75 per day. University residence accommodation also available, cost FF1120, 3 weeks. Also courses for all levels during the academic year. 14 weeks, starting October and February. 15 hours per week. Cost FF1685 per term, plus FF337 optional courses and FF505 registration fee. *Scholarships available through French embassies.*

UK applicants may apply to Cultural and Educational Services Abroad, 44 Sydney Street, Brighton, Sussex BN1 4EP Tel Brighton 683304. Cost approx £125 per week includes tuition and family accommodation. Alternatively, to Euro-Academy, 77A George Street, Croydon, Surrey CR0 1LD Tel 01-686 2363. Cost £478, 3 weeks, including full board residence accommodation and travel from Portsmouth.

COURS UNIVERSITAIRES DE LANGUE, LETTRES ET CIVILISATION FRANCAISES Office Municipal d'Animation et Promotion, Palais d'Europe, avenue Boyer, BP 111, 06503 Menton Tel Nice 57 57 00
Courses for all levels in Menton on the Côte d'Azur, near the Italian border. Ages 15+, individuals and groups. 3 weeks, July and August, or 4 weeks at advanced levels and for teachers. 20 hours per week. Average 15 per class. Language laboratory. Option in literature at advanced levels. Activities include excursions to local places of interest, music festival, sports and social evenings. Cost from FF4500, 3 weeks, includes course, teaching materials, activities and school accommodation, full board with Provencal cuisine. Cost FF1500, course only. Approved by University of Nice.

ECOLE FRANCE LANGUE Etablissement Libre d'Enseignement Supérieur, 2 rue de Sfax, 75116 Paris Tel Paris 45 00 40 15

Courses for all levels in 3 centres in Paris. No age limits, individuals and groups. 2 + weeks, all year. 15 or 30 hours per week. Maximum 18 per class. Lectures in history, literature and history of art, plus visits to tourist sights in Paris. Cost from FF1010, 2 weeks, 15 hours per week. Also long-term courses, 1 term minimum, starting January and April. 4.5 or 9 hours per week. Maximum 25 per class. Cost from FF1300, 1 term, 4.5 hours per week. Also termly course in French for secretaries. Family accommodation available, from FF120 per day, bed and breakfast. Hotel and university residence accommodation also available. Textbooks up to FF100.

ECOLE DE LANGUES JACQUELINE HOBSON 57 Avenue Saint Saëns, 34500 Béziers Tel Béziers 76 70 33

Courses for all levels. Ages 10-60, individuals and groups. 2 + months, starting alternate months. 20 hours per week. Maximum 12 per class. Audio-visual facilities and language laboratory. Also courses in business, cooking, painting, drawing, art history and for teachers of French. Sports include tennis, swimming and skiing. Sightseeing excursions arranged. Cost from FF4000, 2 months, includes textbooks. Hotel or camping accommodation available. **PH** but no facilities for wheelchairs

EF EUROPAISCHE FERIENSCHULE GMBH Annagasse 3, 1010 Vienna, Austria Tel Vienna 512 14 69

Courses in Nice. Ages 16 +, individuals and groups. 2 weeks, Easter or 2-12 weeks, June-August. 20 lessons per week, average 13 per class. Audio-visual facilities and language laboratory. Cost from AS8700, 2 weeks, includes course, teaching materials, map and guided tour, membership and discount cards, preparatory language practice cassette and full board family or residential accommodation. Activities also arranged. Also courses for all levels in Reims, capital of the Champagne-Ardenne region. Ages 16 +, individuals and groups. Main courses: 2-50 weeks, all year. 24 lessons per week. Average 13 per class. Cost AS9880, 2 weeks. Also intensive courses: 2-50 weeks, all year. 30 lessons per week. Average 12 per class. Cost AS11740, 2 weeks. Courses also available for students wishing to take EF and Paris Chamber of Commerce examinations. 8-12 weeks. Examinations take place in January and June. 30 lessons per week. Cost from AS4960, 8 weeks. Language laboratory and audio-visual materials. Costs include course, teaching materials, map and guided tour, membership and discount cards, preparatory language practice cassette and full board family or residence accommodation. Activities also arranged.

ELFCA Institut de Langue Francaise de la Côte d'Azur, 11 boulevard Matignon, 83400 Hyères Tel Toulon 65 03 31
Courses for all levels except complete beginners. Ages 20 +, 18 + July and August, individuals and groups. Multiples of 3 weeks, starting January-July and September-November. 22 hours per week. Maximum 12 per class. Video facilities and language laboratory. Options include French political and social life, geography, literature, economy, French language for banking, study of Provence and Provencal cooking. Activities include parties and excursions. Cost FF1103 per week. Half board family accommodation available, FF749 per week. Approved by Alliance Francaise, who organise 2 examination sessions at the Institute.
UK applicants may apply to Cultural and Educational Services Abroad, 44 Sydney Street, Brighton, Sussex BN1 4EP Tel Brighton 683304. Cost approx £150-£200 includes family accommodation.

L'ETOILE Etablissement Libre d'Enseignement Supérieur, 4 place Saint-Germain-des-Prés, 75006 Paris Tel Paris 45 48 00 05
Courses for all levels in the heart of Paris. No age limits. 4 weeks, July. 20 hours per week including lectures and discussions on history, geography, politics and literature. For advanced levels course includes study of aspects of contemporary France, four works of French literature and cultural diversity in France illustrated by the regions of Alsace, Savoy and Gascony. Courses in geography at all levels include sampling regional dishes. Cost FF1900. Family or residence accommodation available, approx FF3500 per month, half board. Also termly courses, October-June, 8 or 10 hours per week. Cost FF3600 per term.

EUROCENTRE 13 passage Dauphine, 75006 Paris Tel Paris 43 25 81 40
Courses for all levels. Ages 16 +, individuals and groups. 3-12 weeks, all year. 30 hours per week. Maximum 15 per class. Options in French literature and French for business, commerce, science and technology. Lectures on literature, art, social life in France and history. Paris Chamber of Commerce examinations may be taken. Activities include technical and cultural visits and excursions to Versailles, Mont-Saint-Michel, Reims and the châteaux of the Loire Valley. Cost from £507, 3 weeks, includes course, teaching materials and half board family accommodation. Cost £301, 2 weeks, course only. Hotel accommodation also available. Also courses for all levels, 4 weeks, July-August. 20-25 hours per week. Cost £741 includes half board family accommodation. Cost £426, course only. Hotel accommodation also available. Also 3 week summer refresher courses for teachers.

UK applicants can apply to Cultural and Educational Services Abroad, 44 Sydney Street, Brighton, Sussex BN1 4EP Tel Brighton 683304. Cost approx £150-£200 per week includes family accommodation.

EUROCENTRE 10ter rue Amelot, 17000 La Rochelle Tel La Rochelle 505733

Courses for all levels in La Rochelle, a market town on the Atlantic coast, north of Bordeaux. Ages 16 +, individuals and groups. 2-12 weeks, all year. 30 hours per week. Maximum 15 per class. Options in French for business and technology, French songs and current affairs. Students may take Paris Chamber of Commerce examinations. Activities include excursions to the vineyards and fortifications of the southwestern provinces of France. Cost from £366, 2 weeks, includes course, teaching materials and half board family accommodation. Cost £213, 2 weeks, tuition only. Also courses for all levels. 3 or 6 weeks, July-September. 20-25 hours per week. Cost from £549, 3 weeks, includes course, teaching materials and half board family accommodation. Cost £319, 3 weeks, course only.

EUROCENTRE 1 avenue Léonard-de-Vinci, 37400 Amboise Tel Amboise 23 10 60

Courses for all levels. Ages 16 +, individuals and groups. 2-6 weeks, April-December. 30 hours per week. Maximum 15 per class. Options in French art and history, writers and town life. Excursions and social events. Cost from £366, 2 weeks, includes course, teaching materials and half board family accommodation. Cost £213, 2 weeks, tuition only. Also courses for all levels, 3 or 6 weeks, July-September. 20-25 hours per week. Cost from £549, 3 weeks, includes course, teaching materials and half board family accommodation. Cost £319, 3 weeks, tuition only.
UK applicants may apply to Cultural and Educational Services Abroad, 44 Sydney Street, Brighton, Sussex BN1 4EP Tel Brighton 683304.

UK applicants for all Eurocentre courses, above, can apply to Eurocentre, 21 Meadowcourt Road, Lee Green, London SE3 9EU Tel 01-318 5633.

EUROVAC 55 rue Nationale, 37000 Tours Tel Tours 20 20 57

Courses for all levels except beginners in the Loire Valley town of Tours. Ages 14 +, individuals and groups. 2-4 weeks, July. 15 x 50 minute lessons per week. Maximum 15 per class. Also 1:1 tuition. Activities include excursions to châteaux, local visits, discos and meetings with local people. Cost from FF1820 per week includes course, teaching materials, 1 lecture/discussion, 1 half day excursion and half board family accommodation. Full board family or residence accommodation also available. Also courses for all levels except beginners in the seaside resort of Dinard, near Saint-Malo. Ages 14 +, individuals and groups. 2-4 weeks, July. 15 x 50 minute lessons per week. Maximum 15 per class. Also 1:1 tuition. Activities include excursions, local visits, discos and meetings with local people. Cost from FF2090 per week includes course, teaching materials, one full day excursion and full board family accommodation. The Dinard and Tours courses can be combined.

FIAP 30 rue Cabanis, 75014 Paris Tel Paris 45 89 89 15

FIAPAD 19 rue Salvador Allende, BP 631, 92006 Nanterre Tel Paris 47 25 91 34

FIAPEVRY 4 Les Passages (Terrasse de l'Agora), 91000 Evry Tel Paris 60 77 97 20

Courses for all levels in the centre of Paris and the suburbs of La Défense and Evry. No age limits, individuals and groups. 3/4 weeks, July-August, or 4 weeks, November-February. 15 hours per week. Average 15 per class. Activities include guided visits, weekly excursions to the Loire valley, Chartres and Honfleur, discos, cinema and sports including tennis and riding. Cost from FF5100, 3 weeks includes course, teaching materials, cultural programme, guided visits, free public transport card and half board residential accommodation. **PH**

HOME LANGUAGE LESSONS 12-18 Royal Crescent, Ramsgate, Kent CT11 9PE Tel Thanet 590300
1:1 tuition for all levels in the Paris, Côte d'Azur and Provence areas. No age limits. Lessons take place in the teacher's home, where student stays, giving total immersion in the language and no contact with other students. 15, 20 or 25 hours per week. Cost from FF450 per week. 25% reduction for 2 people taking the course together. Weekend crash courses, 5 hours per day, cost FF150. Five star immersion course for business and professional people, 25 hours per week language tuition and superior accommodation, cost FF850 per week. Given notice it is possible to place students with teachers who share their interests, and on immersion courses suitable contacts in the local community can be arranged. Full board accommodation included. **PH**

HOURMONT LTD Brunel House, Newfoundland Road, Bristol BS2 9LU Tel Bristol 426961
Young Reporter courses in Le Touquet, St Valery sur Somme, Berck-sur-Mer, and Houlgate. All levels except beginners. School groups only. 6 + days, all year. Hours vary depending on requirements. Pupils work in teams of 5 to research a chosen theme. Time is spent interviewing, conducting surveys, observing, recording information, sketching and

taking photographs. Material is then reviewed and condensed into a report which reflects aims and linguistic ability of the team. Completed reports can be presented to the rest of the group or back at school. Cost from £133. Also Hi-fi French course for all levels in Berck-sur-Mer, Ault, Asnelle, Merville-Franceville, Cahagnes and Houlgate. School groups only. 5+ days. Pupils are provided with personal hi-fi systems, pre-recorded cassettes and booklets on a selection of topics at varying levels. Cost from £111. Costs are based on 35 pupils and include return coach travel, collective passport, travel insurance, necessary recording and photographic equipment, service of resident courier, teachers' notes and full board guest house accommodation.

INLINGUA SCHOOL OF LANGUAGES 109 rue de l'Université, 75007 Paris Tel Paris 45 51 46 60
Courses for all levels. Ages 18+, individuals and groups. 4+ weeks all year. 25 x 45 minute lessons per week. Average 6 per class. Cost from FF1927 per week. Also courses for all levels, 2+ weeks, Easter and July-August. 20 x 45 minute lessons per week. Average 6 per class. Cost from FF1660 per week. Half board family accommodation available. 1:1 tuition also available.
UK applicants can apply to Cultural and Educational Services Abroad, 44 Sydney Street, Brighton, Sussex BN1 4EP Tel Brighton 683304. Cost approx £150-£200 per week includes family or residence accommodation.

INLINGUA SCHOOL OF LANGUAGES 8 rue de Coëtguen, place de la Mairie, 35000 Rennes Tel Rennes 51 46 60
Courses for all levels. Ages 16+, individuals and groups. 2+ weeks all year. 20 x 45 minute lessons per week. Average 4 per class. Cost from FF1304 per week. Also courses for all levels except complete beginners. 2+ weeks, Easter and June. 24 x 45 minute lessons per week. Average 4 per class. Cost FF1488 per week. Half board family accommodation available. 1:1 tuition also available.

UK applicants for the Inlingua courses, above, can apply to Inlingua School of Languages, 8-10 Rotton Park Road, Edgbaston, Birmingham B16 9JJ Tel 021-454 0204 or 55-61 Portland Road, Brighton, Sussex BN3 5DQ Tel Brighton 721612.

INSTITUT BRITANNIQUE DE PARIS Mrs P J Carpenter, London Office, University of London, Senate House, Room 215, Malet Street, London WC1E 7HU Tel 01-636 8000 ext 3920
Courses in Paris, conducted in French and aimed at university level students with a good knowledge of French. Ages 18+, individuals only.

3 weeks, March includes 19 hours language tuition, two 1 hour lectures and discussions on a play with theatre visit, and two 2 hour lecture tours on Paris architecture and society. Cost FF1450. Also termly courses in translation, business, commercial and economic French, French literature, civilisation and contemporary studies, and courses leading to University of London approved examinations. Cost per term FF2350, EC nationals or FF3450, others. Advice given on finding accommodation.

INSTITUT CATHOLIQUE DE PARIS Cours Universitaires d'Eté, 21 rue d'Assas, 75270 Paris Tel Paris 42 22 41 80 ext 374
Courses for all levels. Ages 18+, individuals and groups. 4 weeks, July. 20 hours per week. Maximum 30 per class. Cost FF1650 plus FF300 registration fee. Optional extra practice in language laboratory, cost FF25 per hour. Also optional courses in conversation and translation, and lectures in civilisation, literature and history of art. Activities include cultural visits and folk evenings, plus excursions to Versailles, Chartres, the châteaux of the Loire Valley and Mont-Saint-Michel. Student residence accommodation available, from FF2100, bed and breakfast. Also courses for all levels during the academic year. 15 weeks, October-February or February-June. 6, 12 or 18 hours per week. Cost FF1945-FF6000 per session, depending on intensity.

INSTITUT D'ETUDES FRANCAISES DE TOURAINE 1 rue de la Grandière, BP 2047, 37020 Tours Tel Tours 05 76 83
Courses for all levels. Ages 16+, individuals and groups. 4, 8 or 12 weeks, July-September. 19 hours per week, beginners or 24 hours per week, other levels. Average 20 per class. Audio-visual facilities and language laboratory. Intermediate and advanced levels also study French literature, civilisation, history of art and French for business. Paris Chamber of Commerce examinations may be taken. Cost from FF2400, 4 weeks. Also courses for secretaries and teachers of French, cost FF2650, 4 weeks. Also course for intermediate and advanced levels. 4 weeks, March-April, 22 hours per week. Cost FF2300. Activities include excursions to Loire châteaux, Mont-Saint-Michel, Chartres and other places of interest, cinema, bicycle trips, walks and visits to wine cellars, and sports. Family or residence accommodation available, from FF700 per month. Also courses for all levels during the academic year. 3 sessions of 12 weeks, October-June. 19-24 hours per week depending on level. Cost from FF5050 per session. Affiliated to the University of Tours.

INSTITUT DE FRANCAIS 23 avenue Général-Leclerc, 06230 Villefranche-sur-Mer Tel Nice 01 88 44
Courses for all levels at the picturesque port of Villefranche-sur-Mer. Ages 21-70. 4 or 8 weeks, all year. 40 hours per week. Maximum 12 per class. Audio-visual facilities and language laboratory. Activities include social evenings, discussions and excursions to local places of interest. Cost from FF11400, 4 weeks, include course, teaching materials and 3 meals per day on class days. Self-catering accommodation available at the Institute, from FF1600, 4 weeks.

INSTITUT FRANCO-SCANDINAVE 3 ter chemin du Belvédère, Val Saint André, 13100 Aix-en-Provence Tel Aix-en-Provence 26 46 08
Courses for elementary to advanced levels. Beginners accepted on certain dates. Ages 17+, individuals and groups. 2-15 weeks, all year. 20-35 x 45 minute lessons per week. Maximum 15 per class. Cost from FF2450, 2 weeks, includes course, teaching materials and excursions. Also specialised courses for professional purposes and 1:1 tuition. Half board family or residence accommodation available, from FF780 per week. Hotel and apartment accommodation also available. **PH**
Also courses for all levels in Montpellier. Ages 17+, individuals, groups and families with children ages 14+. 2-8 weeks, July and August. 20 x 45 minute lessons per week. Maximum 15 per class. Cost from FF1975, 2 weeks, includes course, teaching materials, guided tour and 1 excursion. Half board family accommodation FF830 per week, university residence accommodation FF375 per week.

UK applicants may apply to Cultural and Educational Services Abroad, 44 Sydney Street, Brighton, Sussex BN1 4EP Tel Brighton 683304. Cost from £150 per week includes accommodation.

INSTITUT MEDITERRANEEN D'ETUDES FRANCAISES 11 avenue Professeur-Grasset, BP 6039, 34030 Montpellier Tel Montpellier 52 30 40
Courses for all levels. Ages 17+, individuals and groups. 2+ weeks, June-September. 15 hours per week. Maximum 15 per class. Also 6 hours per week afternoon workshops with options in conversation, grammar, phonetics, slang, aural comprehension, French comics, songs, acting and video. Also field work to encourage communication in French, including opinion polls, interviews and enquiries with French people. Activities include excursions to Nîmes, Arles, the Camargue, the Perrier spring, Sète, the Cévennes, Roquefort and local festivals, plus a night at sea on a fishing boat, visits to local firms, law courts, newspaper and opportunity to produce local radio programme. Also in-house film shows, folk-singing, jazz evenings and yoga. Students have use of the Institute's library. Cost from FF4200, 2 weeks, includes course,

teaching materials, activities and half board university residence accommodation. Registration fee FF600.

UK applicants may apply to Cultural and Educational Services Abroad, 44 Sydney Street, Brighton, Sussex BN1 4EP Tel Brighton 683304. Cost approx £150-£200 per week includes residential accommodation.

INSTITUT NATIONAL DES SCIENCES APPLIQUEES Service d'Enseignement du Francais aux Stagiaires Etrangers, Bâtiment 601, 20 avenue Albert-Einstein, 69621 Villeurbanne Tel Lyons 94 81 12 ext 8483
Courses for all levels in a suburb of Lyons. Ages 18 +, individuals and groups. 4 + weeks, all year. Beginners in January, April, July and October. 25 hours per week. Maximum 12 per class. Audio-visual and audio-oral methods. Cost FF680 per week. Courses in French for special purposes for groups on request. Activities include excursions to places of interest in the Rhône-Alpes region, film shows, membership of student club and visits to local families. Residence accommodation available, FF770 per month. Half board family accommodation also available, from FF2100 per month.

LOGOS ECOLE DE LANGUES 61 boulevard Haussmann, 75008 Paris Tel Paris 42 68 04 02
Courses for all levels in schools in Paris-Opéra and the suburb of La Défense. Ages 16 +, individuals and groups. 1 + weeks, all year. 15 or 20 hours per week. Maximum 5 per class. Video and language laboratory. Cost from FF1250 per week, 15 hours, or FF1500 per week, 20 hours. Also courses at Christmas, Easter and summer, with optional social and cultural activities and weekend excursions. Maximum 8 per class. Cost from FF775 per week, 15 hours, or FF875 per week, 20 hours. Also 1:1 tuition, cost from FF2400 per week, 20 hours. Paris Chamber of Commerce examinations may be taken. All types of accommodation available, from FF80 per day, residential. **PH** on request

REGENCY LANGUES 1 rue Ferdinand Duval, 75004 Paris Tel Paris 48 04 99 97
Courses for all levels. Ages 11 +, individuals and groups. 1 + weeks, all year. 15 or 30 hours per week. Maximum 8 per class. Cost FF1050 per week, 15 hours, or FF2100 per week, 30 hours. Also maximum 5 per class, cost FF1350 per week, 15 hours, or FF2700 per week, 30 hours. Also 2:1 and 1:1 tuition, refresher courses for teachers and French for special needs. Audio-visual facilities and video. Study of culture and civilisation from intermediate level; literature courses offered at advanced levels. Paris Chamber of Commerce examinations may be taken. In summer, excursions to places of interest in Paris; other outings

available on request. Hotel or family accommodation available, from FF980 bed and breakfast. **PH**

UK applicants can apply to Mrs J Beech, Regency School of English, Royal Crescent, Ramsgate, Kent Tel Ramsgate 591212.

LA SABRANENQUE CENTRE INTERNATIONAL Saint Victor La Coste, 30290 Laudin Tel Laudin 50 05 05
Courses for all levels in the village of Saint Victor la Coste, 25km from Avignon. Ages 18+, individuals only. 12 weeks, February-May and September-December. 13 hours per week. Average 6 per class. Also courses in French history, politics, government, society and regional life, and Mediterranean culture. Students also take part in all aspects of French village life, including tree planting, restoration work, fruit picking, chestnut gathering, mushroom picking, jam and wine making, plus the opportunity to meet local craftsmen, cheese and honey producers and the mayor. Cost approx FF18000 includes course, teaching materials, visits, all extra-curricular activities and full board accommodation.

SCHOOL JOURNEY ASSOCIATION 48 Cavendish Road, London SW12 0DG Tel 01-673 4849
Courses in Paris for students taking GSCE French. Ages 15-20, individuals and groups. 9 days, March-April. 21 hours per week. Maximum 16 per class. Excursions arranged in Paris area. Cost approx £230 includes escorted travel, tuition, insurance, excursions and full board school accommodation. Also courses in Dieppe for students taking A level French. Ages 15-20, individuals and groups. 10 days, April. 14 hours language tuition plus 12 hours literature study, per week. Maximum 17 per class. Activities include films, meeting local people and excursions to Paris, Rouen and Le Havre. Cost approx £230 includes escorted travel, tuition, insurance, excursions and full board hotel accommodation. **PH**

TASIS FRANCE Château de Beauchamps, Villaines-la-Gosnais, 72400 La-Ferté-Bernard Tel Le Mans 93 22 68
Language programme for all levels, northwest of Le Mans. Ages 12-18, individuals only. 4 weeks, June-August. 3 hours language tuition per day, plus 2 hours per day of music, art, drama or French civilisation. Centre is equipped with small library, art studio and playing fields. Activities include meeting people from the local community, art and drama, crêpe-making sessions, picnics, film shows and cycle trips. Excursions to Le Mans, Chartres, the Loire Valley, Normandy, Mont-Saint-Michel and Paris. Sports facilities. Cost FF13000 includes course, teaching materials, excursions, full board school accommodation, accident insurance and laundry.

TRAINING TOUR CULTURAL 4 rue Gaston-de-Saporta, 13100 Aix-en-Provence Tel Aix-en-Provence 21 21 23
Courses for all levels in Aix-en-Provence, Avignon, Cassis, Montpellier and Toulon. 3 weeks, July-August. 15 hours per week. Extra-curricular activities include full day excursions to places of interest, and weekly parties. Cost FF4200 includes full board family accommodation.

TREASURE TOURS INTERNATIONAL Département Eurolangues, 15 rue de l'Arcade, 75008 Paris Tel Paris 42 65 05 69
Courses for all levels in Paris suburbs, on the Mediterranean coast, and in the Loire Valley. Ages 12-25, individuals and groups. 2-3 weeks, Easter and July-August. 15 hours per week. Maximum 15 per class. Afternoon activities include visits to places of interest, sports and excursions. Cost from FF5250, 2 weeks, includes course, activities and full board family accommodation. Also French plus skiing courses for groups only in the French Alps. 2-3 weeks, January-February. 10 hours language tuition plus 12 hours ski tuition per week. Maximum 15 per class, language, 10 per class, ski. Cost from FF7770, 2 weeks, includes course, ski lifts and equipment and full board hotel or chalet accommodation. *Apply 2 months in advance.*

UK applicants can apply to Eurolanguage Ltd, Greyhound House, 23-24 George Street, Richmond, Surrey TW9 1HY Tel 01-940 1087.

UNIVERSITE D'AIX-MARSEILLE III Institut d'Etudes Francises pour Etudiants Etrangers, 23 rue Gaston-de-Saporta, 13625 Aix-en-Provence Tel Aix-en-Provence 23 28 43
Courses for all levels. Ages 18 + , individuals and groups. 4 weeks, June-September. 30 hours per week. Average 15-20 per class. Audio-visual facilities and language laboratory. Also business French, French for teachers and courses on literature and civilisation. Social activities with local people and excursions to places of interest. Access to University sports facilities. Cost from FF3200, 4 weeks, includes course, teaching materials and excursions. University residence accommodation available, approx FF750 per month. Also academic year course which includes classes in literature, poetry, theatre, regional studies, the press, history, judicial and political institutions and French civilisation. Cost FF6044, 2 terms. Family or studio apartment accommodation available, from FF1600 per month.

UNIVERSITE DE BORDEAUX III Département d'Etudes Francaises pour l'Etranger Domaine Universitaire, 33405 Talence Cedex Tel Bordeaux 84 50 44
Courses for all levels. Ages 18+, individuals and groups. 3-4 weeks, July-September. 20 hours per week. Maximum 20 per class. Audio-visual facilities and language laboratory. Daily lectures on French culture. Also courses in French for teachers and business French. Sightseeing excursions and films. Students may use sports facilities. Cost from FF1500, 3 weeks. University residence accommodation available, cost approx FF1000 per month. Also courses during academic year, cost FF1500 per semester or FF3200, whole year.

UNIVERSITE DE BOURGOGNE Centre International d'Etudes Francaises, 36 rue Chabot-Charny, 21000 Dijon Tel Dijon 66 20 49
Language courses for all levels in Dijon, in the heart of the Burgundy wine region. Ages 17+, individuals and groups. Families also catered for, with special classes for children ages 7-13, whose parents have enrolled. 4-8 weeks, July-August. 23 hours per week. Average 15-23 per class depending on level. Audio-visual facilities and language laboratory. Lectures on French literature, philosophy, history, history of art and contemporary France for advanced level students. Other courses open to all students include choral song, folk dancing, theatre, cookery and the history of art in Burgundy. Activities include visits to families, film shows, theatre, parties and excursions in the Burgundy region. Also 2-3 day optional visits to Paris, Champagne, Provence and the châteaux of the Loire Valley. Cost FF1600, 4 weeks. Also course for teachers of French. 4 weeks, July. 20 hours per week. Cost FF1900. University residence accommodation available, from FF770, 4 weeks. Half board family accommodation also available, approx FF150 per day. Registration fee FF250. Also courses during the academic year for all levels. 28 weeks, October-June. 18 hours per week. Cost FF3850 plus FF350 registration fee. Also 4 week preparation course, September, cost FF1850. **PH** depending on handicap
UK applicants may also apply through Cultural and Educational Services Abroad, 44 Sydney Street, Brighton, Sussex BN1 4EP Tel Brighton 683304. Cost approx £125 per week includes residential accommodation.

UNIVERSITE CATHOLIQUE DE L'OUEST Centre International d'Etudes Francaises, 3 Place André-Leroy BP 808, 49005 Angers Tel Angers 88 30 15
Intensive courses for all levels. Ages 16+. 4 weeks, July. 21 hours per week. Average 24 per class. Language laboratory. Cost FF1940, textbooks extra. Optional classes in literature, civilisation and French

affairs, cost approx FF210, 2 hours. Specialised course for teachers of French, cost FF2310. Also pre-university course, to help those intending to study in France. 4 weeks, September, cost FF2600. One year language course also offered. Activities include visits to local places of interest, museums and monuments, concerts, folk evenings and local festivals. Sports include tennis, yachting, and swimming. Full board university residence accommodation available, cost FF3220, 4 weeks.

UNIVERSITE D'ETE DE TOULON ET DU VAR avenue de l'Université, 83130 La Garde Tel Toulon 21 11 86
Courses for all levels except complete beginners. Ages 16+, individuals, groups and families, with supervision of children aged 3-7 every weekday morning, cost FF60 per day including midday meal. 2-4 weeks, July-September. 20 hours per week language tuition, plus 10 hours per week afternoon workshops. Maximum 20 per class. Audio-visual facilities and language laboratory. Workshops include history of art, French press, written French, theatre, photography, painting on silk, French cuisine and wine-making. Also 2 lectures per week on French literature and economic and social life. Intermediate and advanced levels also choose options from various aspects of French language and literature. Activities include guided visits of the region, weekend excursions to Nice, Monaco, St Tropez or local villages, plus theatre, concert, cinema or party evenings, and sports. Cost from FF4600, 2 weeks, includes course, teaching materials, activities, excursions, bicycle hire and full board university residence accommodation. Hotel accommodation also available. Cost from FF1600, 2 weeks, course only. Also courses for teachers of French and preparation courses for Paris Chamber of Commerce examinations.

UNIVERSITE DE FRANCHE-COMTE Faculté de Lettres et de Sciences Humaines, Centre de Linguistique Appliqué, 47 rue Mégevand, 25030 Besancon Tel Besancon 82 25 01 ext 371
Language and civilisation courses for all levels. Ages 18+. 4 weeks, all year. 25 hours per week. Cost FF615 per week. Also courses in oral expression, sport and languages, French for special purposes and for teachers of French. Cost from FF2215, 4 weeks. Activities include film club, sporting and cultural trips and social activities. Students may use University accommodation service.

UNIVERSITE DE GRENOBLE III Centre Universitaire d'Etudes Francaises, BP 25 X, 38040 Grenoble Tel Grenoble 42 48 37
Courses for all levels. Ages 17+. 4 weeks, July-September. 20 hours per week, using audio-visual method. Cost FF2200. Also courses in French

language, literature and civilisation for those with some knowledge of French. 23 or 28 hours per week. Cost from FF1650, 4 weeks. Also courses in French for specific purposes and for teachers of French. Cost from FF2450, 4 weeks. Activities include social events, excursions, trips to the mountains and sports. University residence or family accommodation available. Also 11 week and 2 termly courses during academic year. Cost from FF525 per week, FF3580 per term.

UNIVERSITE INTERNATIONALE D'ETE Palais des Congrès, 10 rue de la Chancellerie, 78000 Versailles Tel Versailles 51 46 30
Language and civilisation courses for intermediate and advanced levels. Ages 18+. 4 weeks, July and August. 12 hours per week language tuition in small groups, plus lectures on French civilisation, the Ile-de-France region, and workshops on French theatre, song, and written and spoken French. Cost FF2600. Also course on 18th century French civilisation, for French and foreign participants. 4 weeks, July, covering 65 hours lectures in total. Participants may also attend lectures offered by the other course. Suitable for teachers of French. Cost FF1900. Costs cover course, teaching materials, guided visits of Paris and Versailles, theatre, concert, cinema and dance evenings, parties, excursions and sports. Family or residence accommodation available. Operates in liaison with the University of Paris X-Nanterre. *Applications sent before 1 May qualify for FF100 reduction.*

UNIVERSITE DE LILLE III Département des Etudiants Etrangers/Université d'Eté, BP 149, 59653 Villeneuve d'Ascq Tel Lille 91 92 02
Courses for all levels in Lille, near the Belgian border. No age limits, individuals and groups. 15 weeks beginners and elementary levels, or 29 weeks, other levels, starting October. 15 hours per week. Average 25 per class. Audio-visual facilities, computer-assisted learning and language laboratory. Study of French literature, history of ideas, political institutions, geography, economy and history for advanced levels. Activities include excursions to Paris and Brussels, visits to local places of interest, theatre and concert evenings. Cost £200 15 weeks or £400, 29 weeks. Accommodation service available. **PH**
Also course for all levels in Boulogne-sur-Mer. Ages 16+, individuals and groups. 3+ weeks, July and August. 18 hours per week. Maximum 15 per class. Audio-visual facilities, computer assisted learning and language laboratory. Courses for teachers of French, commercial and administrative French and a full time economics course. Lectures on French literature and civilisation for advanced levels, and study of French songs and poetry for all levels. Extra-curricular activities include excursions to places of interest, sports, bicycle trips, films,

conferences and visits to local festivals. Cost from FF3000 includes course, teaching materials, insurance, and full board residential accommodation. Family accommodation also available. Cost FF350, course only.
Between July and September apply to Université d'Eté, Cité Technique, 2 rue de la Porte-Gayole, 62200 Boulogne-sur-Mer

UNIVERSITE LUMIERE LYON 2 Centre International d'Etudes Francaises, 16 quai Claude Bernard, 69007 Lyons Tel Lyons 69 24 45 ext 435
Courses for all levels except beginners. Ages 18 +, individuals only. 4 weeks, July. 20 hours per week using audio-visual methods. Average 5 per class. Cost FF1450. Also course in French language, literature and civilisation for advanced students. 8 hours language tuition plus 10 hours options from grammar, literature, contemporary history, press, sociology, economy, communication, translation, drama, video, journalism, teaching French, business French and information technology, per week. Cost FF1450. Activities include swimming, tennis and excursions to Paris and the Avignon festival. University residence accommodation available, approx FF750 per month. Family accommodation also available. Also courses for all levels during the academic year. 28 weeks, starting October. 12 hours per week. Cost FF1950. *Enclose IRC when requesting information.*

UNIVERSITE DE NANCY II Cours d'Eté pour Etudiants Etrangers, 23 boulevard Albert-1er, 54000 Nancy Tel Nancy 96 53 56 ext 1400
Courses for all levels. Ages 15 +, individuals and groups. 2-4 weeks, July-August. Approx 25 hours per week. Maximum 15 per class. Audio-visual facilities. Afternoon lectures for advanced levels on French civilisation, politics, Government, education, institutions, culture, press, art, gastronomy and wine. Also courses for teachers of French. Activities include visits to museums, local firms, press and a brewery, theatre, dance and musical evenings, and excursions to Metz, the Vosges mountains, Alsace, Champagne and Burgundy. Cost from FF3100, 2 weeks, includes course, teaching materials, activities, excursions and full board university residence accommodation. Cost FF650 per week course only. *When requesting information enclose 3 IRCs.*

UNIVERSITE DE NICE Centre International d'Etudes Francaises, Faculté des Lettres, 98 boulevard Edouard-Herriot, 06200 Nice Tel Nice 86 66 43
Courses for all levels. Ages 17 +, individuals and groups. 2 sessions of 24 days, July and August. 20-30 hours per week. Maximum 10-25 per class depending on level. Audio-visual facilities and video rôle-play.

Lectures for advanced levels in contemporary French literature, sociology, politics and culture. Cost from FF2420 per session. Also special audio-visual courses, business and commercial French and courses for teachers of French. Cost from FF2640 per session. Activities include concerts, visits to the theatre and local museums, and workshops in music, painting and sculpture. Also guided tours and excursions along the coast and to other places of interest. Full board residential accommodation available, FF3850 per session. Also courses for elementary levels and above during the academic year. 2 terms, beginning October. 16 hours per week, with options from a wide variety of themes from French language, literature and society. Cost FF2700 per term. Also 3 week introductory course in October for students embarking on study of literature. 25 hours per week. Cost FF1350.

UNIVERSITE DE PARIS-SORBONNE (PARIS IV) Cours de Civilisation Francaise de la Sorbonne/Cours Universitaires d'Ete, Centre Expérimental d'Etude de la Civilisation Francaise, 47 rue des Ecoles, 75005 Paris Tel Paris 43 29 12 13 ext 3430
Courses for all levels. Ages 18+. 4, 6 or 8 weeks, July-August. Beginners: intensive preparatory courses, 25 hours per week including audio-visual work. Cost from FF2800, 4 weeks. Other levels: 10 hours per week plus 9 hours of lectures on aspects of French civilisation. Cost from FF2000, 4 weeks. Also special sessions preparing for Paris Chamber of Commerce examinations or university study. Also language and civilisation course for intermediate levels and above. Recommended for those wishing to continue their higher education in France. Ages 18+. 6 weeks, July-August. 90 hours in total, with options from various aspects of French language, literature, art, history and civilisation. Cost FF4900. Also refresher course for teachers of French. 4 weeks, July, 30 hours in total. Cost FF1950. For both courses, weekend excursions include Mont-Saint-Michel, châteaux of the Loire Valley, Reims and Normandy, cost from FF200. Help given with finding accommodation.

UNIVERSITE DE PICARDIE Centre de Liaison et d'Echanges Internationaux BP 0339, 80003 Amiens Tel Amiens 91 47 54
Courses for intermediate and advanced levels. Ages 18+, individuals and groups. 3 weeks, July. 12 hours per week. Average 15 per class. Extra-curricular activities include excursions to places of interest, social evenings and meetings with local families. Cost approx FF1750 includes course, textbooks and accident insurance cover. University residence accommodation available, cost FF2100. Hotel and family accommodation may also be arranged. **PH** on request

UNIVERSITE DE POITIERS Institut d'Etudes Francaises de La Rochelle, avenue du Général de Gaulle, 17340 Châtelaillon Tel La Rochelle 56 45 11
Courses for all levels in La Rochelle. Ages 18 +, individuals and groups. Intensive courses: 2 weeks, January-May. 30 hours per week. Average 15 per class. Cost FF1950. Summer courses: 4 weeks, June-August. 20 hours language tuition, plus 8 hours options in literature, civilisation, history of art and conversation. Cost FF3350. Also courses for teachers, and in economic and business French in preparation for Paris Chamber of Commerce examinations. Cost FF3600, 4 weeks, plus up to FF300 examination fee. Family accommodation available, from FF75 per day, bed and breakfast. Also Easter intensive courses for all levels except complete beginners: 1-5 weeks, March-April. 30 hours per week, maximum 12 per class. Cost FF2,975 per week includes course and half board family accommodation. Cost FF1,950 per week course only. Audio-visual facilities and language laboratory. Activities for all courses include excursions to places of interest, cinema and video club, contact with local radio stations, conversation club and sports.

UNIVERSITE DE REIMS Service Universitaire des Etudiants Etrangers, Bureau 2002, UFR de Droit et Science Politique, 57bis rue Pierre Taittinger, 51096 Reims Tel Reims 04 10 82
Course for intermediate to advanced levels. Aimed mainly at university level students wishing to improve their standard of French. 4 weeks, September. 25 hours per week, with choice of translation courses in English and German. Cost FF2200. Also 14 week courses for all levels, beginning October and February. Ages 18 +. 15 or 16 hours per week, depending on level. Language laboratory and audio-visual facilities. Intermediate and advanced level courses include study of French literature, civilisation, history and translation. Cost FF3000. Textbooks FF50. Activities include guided visits in Reims, excursions in the Champagne region, cinema, theatre and sports. Cost FF65. University residence accommodation available, cost FF1200 per month.

UNIVERSITE RENNES 2 HAUTE BRETAGNE Cours Universitaire d'Eté de Saint-Malo, 6 Avenue Gaston-Berger, 35043 Rennes Tel Rennes 54 99 55
Courses for all levels at Saint-Malo on the Brittany coast. Ages 16 +. 2 or 4 weeks, July-August. Beginners: 4 weeks, 25 hours per week, cost FF2350. Elementary and intermediate levels: 15 hours per week, cost FF850, 2 weeks or FF1500, 4 weeks. Advanced levels: 15 hours per week including options in French literature, civilisation or society. Cost FF850, 2 weeks or FF1500, 4 weeks. Advanced levels may also take extra course in history, geography and culture of Brittany. 2 afternoons

per week, cost FF250, 2 weeks. Activities include films, sports and excursions to places of interest. Family accommodation available, from FF65 per day, bed and breakfast. Hotel and camping accommodation also available.

UNIVERSITE DE SAINT-ETIENNE Service Universitaire des Etudiants Etrangers, 2 rue Basse des Rives, 42100 Saint-Etienne Tel Saint-Etienne 25 22 02 ext 419
Courses for all levels. Ages 18 +, individuals and groups. Beginners: 12 weeks, starting January. 18 hours per week. Average 12 per class. Cost FF2640. False beginners: 12 weeks, starting October and January. 18 hours per week. Average 12 per class. Cost FF2640. Intermediate and advanced levels: 10 weeks, starting January, April, May. 18 hours per week including study of French civilisation. Average 12 per class. Cost FF2200. Audio-visual facilities and language laboratory. Students may attend lectures organised by other faculties of the University and use sports facilities. Activities include film shows, visits to the theatre and monthly excursions to places of interest including Lyons, Vienne, Le Puy and a trip in a steam train around the Ardèche region. Accommodation service available, cost approx FF650 per month, university residence.

UNIVERSITE DE SAVOIE Institut Savoisien d'Etudes Francaises, Service des Cours d'Eté à Annecy, 27 rue Marcoz, BP 1104, 73011 Chambéry Tel Chambéry 69 00 56
Courses for all levels in Annecy, a lakeside town in the mountains of eastern France. No age limits. 4 weeks, July and August. 18 hours per week. Audio-visual and audio-oral teaching. Study of literature and civilisation at intermediate and advanced levels. Also courses for teachers of French. Activities include excursions to places of interest, walks in the mountains, summer skiing, tennis, swimming, skating, riding and watersports. Cost FF1400. Self catering university residence accommodation available, cost approx FF1000.

UNIVERSITE DES SCIENCES HUMAINES DE STRASBOURG Institut International d'Etudes Francaises et Cours d'Eté, Palais Universitaire, 9 place de l'Université, 67000 Strasbourg Tel Strasbourg 35 53 22
Courses for all levels. 4 weeks July. Ages 18 +. Beginners: 25 hours per week. Maximum 18 per class. Audio-visual method used. Other levels: 15 hours per week language tuition, plus 15 hours per week lectures on phonetics, literature and civilisation for advanced levels. Also seminars for teachers of French. 20-30 hours per week including linguistics, phonetics, French literature, civilisation and institutions. Activities include parties, guided tours of Strasbourg and visits to places of

interest in Alsace. Cost from FF1300-FF1750, depending on level. University residence accommodation available, approx FF1000, 4 weeks. Also language courses for all levels during the academic year. 25 weeks, October-May. 15 hours per week. Cost from FF4000. *Apply by mid May.*

UNIVERSITE DE TOULOUSE-LE MIRAIL Mission à la Formation Continue, Département Extension Universitaire du Centre d'Etudes Francaises pour Etrangers, 5 allée Antonio Machado, 31058 Toulouse Tel Toulouse 40 12 22 ext 345
Courses for all levels. Ages 17 + . 4 weeks, July-September. 15 hours per week. Cost FF1080. Also courses for teachers of French and for groups of 15. Cost FF300 per hour, per group. Also options in French for special purposes, French civilisation and literature. Residence accommodation available. Also courses during the academic year for all levels. 2 sessions, October-February and March-June. Cost FF2650 per session, 180 hours tuition in total.

UNIVERSITE DE TOULOUSE-LE MIRAIL Centre d'Eté de Carcassone, 5 allée Antonio Machado, 31058 Toulouse Tel Toulouse 41 11 05
Courses for all levels in Carcassone, a medieval town on the river Aude. Ages 18 + , individuals and groups. 3 weeks, July-August. 30 hours per week. Average 15 per class. Audio-visual facilities, computer assisted learning and language laboratory. Activities include visits to Cathar châteaux, excursions to places of interest, local festival and opportunities to meet wine-producers. Cost FF5100, 3 weeks, includes course, teaching materials, activities and full board residential accommodation.

VACANCES INTERNATIONALES EN FRANCE 20 rue André Moinier, 63000 Clermont-Ferrand Tel Clermont-Ferrand 36 22 97
Courses for all levels in Clermont-Ferrand, Lyons, Nice and Paris. Ages 12 + , individuals and groups. 2 + weeks, March-April and June-August. 12 hours per week. Average 15 per class. Audio-visual facilities. Activities include weekly excursions to places of interest, visits to museums, historic sites and factories, and sports. Cost from FF3435, 2 weeks, includes course, activities, insurance and full board family accommodation. Also small groups tuition, Clermont-Ferrand, and 1:1 tuition, all year.

VACANCES-JEUNES 88 rue de Miromesnil, 75008 Paris Tel Paris 42 89 39 39
Courses for all levels 20km from Paris, near Orly airport and the Senart forest. Ages 10-16, individuals and groups. 3 weeks, June-August. 15 hours per week. Maximum 15 per class. Activities include tennis, swimming, cultural evenings, films and games, plus 1 full-day excursion per week. Cost FF6600 includes course, teaching materials, activities, excursions and full board school accommodation. Transfer to and from airport arranged at extra cost. Also courses for all levels at a school near Verneuil, in the Eure region of Normandy. Ages 12-18, individuals and groups. 3 or 4 weeks, July-August. 18 hours per week in small groups. Activities include tennis, swimming, gymnastics, cultural evenings and films, plus 1 day excursion per week to Paris or in Normandy. Cost from FF6800, 3 weeks, includes course, teaching materials, activities, excursions and full board school accommodation. Transfer to and from Paris airport arranged at extra cost. **PH**

UK applicants may apply through Jenny Braden Holidays Ltd, 800 Fulham Road, London SW6 5SL Tel 01-736 3202.

COURSES IN BELGIUM

ALLIANCE FRANCAISE DE BRUXELLES 6 place Quételet, 1030 Brussels Tel Brussels 218 25 66
Courses for all levels. Ages 16+. 1+ months, all year. 6-15 hours per week. Maximum 20 per class. Audio-visual facilities and language laboratory. Additional lectures on French literature, plus films and visits. Also courses for teachers of French and evening classes. Cost from BF2900 per month, 6 hours per week, plus BF500 registration fee. Textbooks from BF540. Students arrange own accommodation.

CENTRE LINGUISTIQUE DE THIEUSIES rue du Château 26, 7461 Thieusies Tel Mons 72 84 90
Courses for all levels in Thieusies, a village near the French border. Ages 8+, individuals and groups. 1+ weeks, all year. 20 or 30 hours per week. Average 8 per class. Language laboratory and video room. Activities include trips, cultural and sporting activities. Cost BF6000, 20 hours and BF7500, 30 hours, per week includes course, teaching materials and insurance. Accommodation from BF1600, half board, student residence.

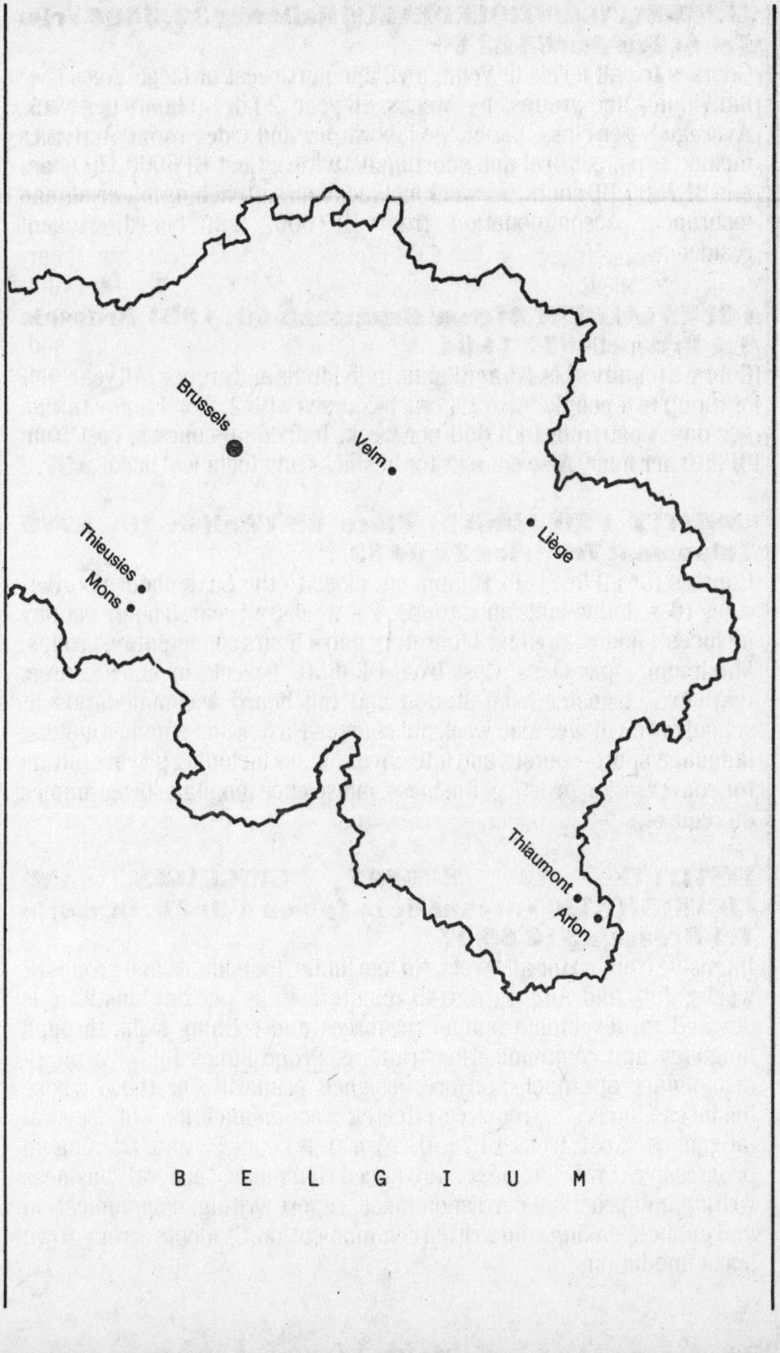
Brussels
Velm
Liège
Thieusies
Mons
Thiaumont
Arlon
B E L G I U M

CENTRE LINGUISTIQUE DE VELM Halleweg 32, 3806 Velm Tel St Truiden 68 82 60

Courses for all levels in Velm, a village northwest of Liege. Ages 8 +, individuals and groups. 1 + weeks, all year. 20 or 30 hours per week. Average 8 per class. Language laboratory and video room. Activities include trips, cultural and sporting activities. Cost BF6000, 20 hours and BF7500, 30 hours, per week includes course, teaching materials and insurance. Accommodation from BF1600, half board, student residence.

COURS LAURENT Avenue Brugmann 69, 1061 Brussels Tel Brussels 657 11 94

Courses for all levels. No age limits, individuals and groups. All year. 1:1, or for up to 4 people. Also 1:1 crash courses with 2, 3 or 4 hours tuition per day. Cost from BF5 650 per week. Individual courses, cost from BF250 per hour. Also courses for business and technical needs. **PH**

INSTITUT PRO LINGUIS Place de l'Eglise 19, 6719 Thiaumont Tel Arlon 22 04 62

Courses for all levels in Thiaumont, close to the Luxembourg border. Ages 10 +, individuals and groups. 1 + weeks, all year. 8 hours per day includes 4 hours language laboratory and 4 hours conversation groups. Maximum 7 per class. Cost from BF8650, 1 week, includes course, textbooks, transfer from station and full board accommodation at school or in village. Also weekend courses Easter and summer holiday language/sports courses and intensive courses including private tuition for conversation practice. Business and science language programmes on request.

INSTITUTE OF MODERN LANGUAGES AND COMMUNICATION avenue de la Toison d'Or 20, Brussels Tel Brussels 512 66 07

Intensive courses for all levels. No age limits, individuals and groups. 2 weeks, July and August. 4 x 45 minute lessons per day. Institute is devoted to developing human resources and refining skills through language and communication training. Programmes follow a multidisciplinary approach and are designed primarily for those whose business interests require effective communication in several languages. Cost from BF7950. Also 1:1 courses, and training in progressive oral language, advanced language, general business writing and practical correspondance, report writing, communication and public speaking, and written communication. Students arrange own accommodation.

UNIVERSITE LIBRE DE BRUXELLES Cours de Vacances de Langue et Littérature Francaises, Avenue F Roosevelt 50, CP 165, 1050 Brussels Tel Brussels 642 40 80
Course for intermediate levels and above. Ages 18-60, individuals and groups. 4 weeks, August. 20 + hours per week. Audio-visual facilities and language laboratory. Lectures on economy and civilisation, French literature in Belgium, art, music and contemporary problems. Students may use University library. Activities include excursions to places of interest, visits to museums and industrial sites, walks, bicycle trips and film shows, and sports. Cost approx BF4750. Self-catering residence accommodation available, from BF4250.

COURSES IN SWITZERLAND

THE AMERICAN SCHOOL IN SWITZERLAND Admissions Office, 6926 Montagnola-Lugano Tel Lugano 546471
Language programme for all levels on campus in village near Lugano. Ages 12-18, individuals only. 4 weeks, June-August. 3 hours language tuition per day, supplemented by computer-assisted language-learning programmes, plus 2 hours per day of activity periods, including language laboratory work, drama classes, video film-making, art and singing. Maximum 12 per class. Excursions and activities include mountain hikes, visits to open-air markets and trips to Milan and Locarno. On-campus social activities include weekly videos and feature films, discos, cook-outs, picnics, games, boat-trips and firework displays. Optional weekend trips to main cities. Daily sports programme. Facilities include library, theatre, students' recreation centre and snack bar, arts centre and photographic studio, gym, swimming pools, hard courts and playing fields. Cost SF3600 includes full board campus accommodation, excursions, books, accident insurance and laundry.

COLLEGE LA CORDEE, 1912 Ovronnaz, Valais Tel Sion 862963
Language, music and sports courses for all levels in the alpine resort of Ovronnaz, above Sion. Ages 10-18, individuals and groups. 4 weeks, July and August. 24 hours per week language tuition. Maximum 10 per class. Overnight stays in mountain huts with optional mountain ascents, bird watching, and photo safari also organised. Excursions include visits to local tourist sights, local industries, and an excursion to

Burgundy. Other activities include barbecues, fondue evenings, discos, videos, competitions, chess, Scrabble, billiards and weekly trips to the cinema. Cost SF2200 includes course, teaching materials, social events and full board school accommodation. Excursions extra. Also optional 3 hours per week music lessons in piano, guitar, flute or recorder, cost SF250 per course. Also sports lessons and extra tutorial lessons, from SF30 per hour.

DIAVOX 19 avenue de Beaulieu, Case 138, 1000 Lausanne 9 Tel Lausanne 37 68 15
Courses for all levels. Ages 16+, individuals and groups. 4-11 weeks, starting January, April, July and October. 30 x 45 minute lessons per week. Maximum 12 per class. Audio-visual facilities, computer-assisted learning and language laboratory. Literature offered at advanced levels. Cost from SF1260, 4 weeks. Textbooks from SF80. Also small group and 1:1 courses. Alliance Francaise and Federation of Swiss Private Schools examinations may be taken. Help given with finding accommodation.

ECOLE LEMANIA 3 chemin de Préville, 1001 Lausanne Tel Lausanne 20 15 01
Courses for all levels. Ages 15+, individuals and groups. 3+ weeks, June-October. 24-28 hours per week. Maximum 10 per class. Audio-visual facilities and language laboratory. Cost from SF331 per week, 24 hours. Also termly courses of 10 weeks minimum, starting January, April, August and October. Cost from SF3310 per term, 24 hours per week. Textbooks from SF20. Alliance Francaise and Federation of Swiss Private Schools examinations may be taken. Activities include excursions to local towns, the Jura and the Alps, visits to factories and museums, theatre, cinema and concert evenings. Accommodation available at the school, from SF4380 per term. **PH**

ECOLE DE SECRETARIAT ET DE LANGUES 15 avenue de Naye, Case Postale Territet 77, 1820 Montreux Tel Lausanne 963 08 80
Courses for all levels in Montreux. Ages 15+, individuals, families and groups of 6-12. 3-6 weeks, July-August. 20 lessons per week. Average 4-8 per class. Excursions to places of interest and sports. Cost from SF2000, 2 weeks, includes course, sports and full board school accommodation. Also courses throughout the year for all levels, ages 16+. 1-31+ weeks, all year. 20 lessons per week. Average 4-8 per class. Cost from SF550 per week includes language tuition, loan of teaching materials and full board school accommodation. Students can prepare for exams of the Alliance Francaise and the Université Populaire de Lausanne. Approved by local government.

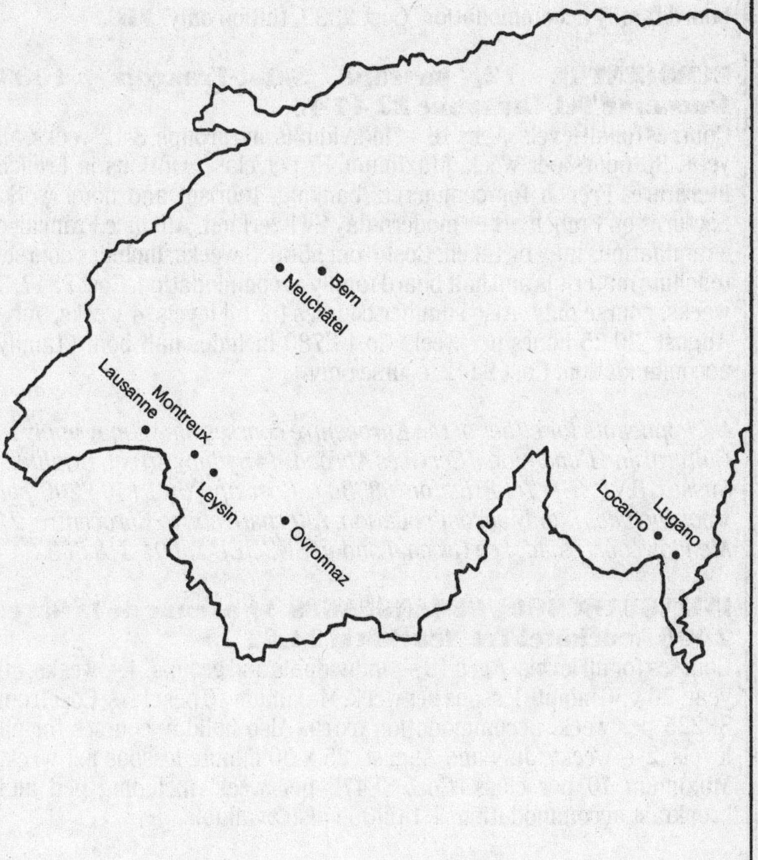

SWITZERLAND

EUROCENTRES Head Office, Seestrasse 247, 8038 Zurich Tel Zurich 4816124
Courses for all levels in Neuchâtel at the foot of the Jura mountains. Age 16 +, individuals and groups. 3 weeks, July-August. 20-25 hours week. Maximum 15 per class. Audio-visual facilities and language laboratory. Special options include business language, Swiss life and institutions, literature and cinema. Activities include barbecues, films, visits to wine cellars, factories, museums and other places of interest, plus sports. Cost from £577 includes course, teaching materials, activities and half board family accommodation. Cost £332, tuition only. **PH**

EUROCENTRE 12 passage Saint-Francois, 1003 Lausanne Tel Lausanne 22 47 45
Courses for all levels. Ages 16 +, individuals and groups. 3-12 weeks, all year. 30 hours per week. Maximum 15 per class. Options in French literature, French for commerce, banking, tourism and hotel work. Lectures on French art or modern-day Switzerland. Alliance Francaise examinations may be taken. Cost from £569, 3 weeks, includes course, teaching materials and half board family accommodation. Cost £317, 3 weeks, course only. Also summer courses for all levels. 4 weeks, July-August. 20-25 hours per week. Cost £780 includes half board family accommodation. Cost £442, course only.

UK applicants for either of the Eurocentre courses above may apply to Cultural and Educational Services Abroad, 44 Sydney Street, Brighton, Sussex BN1 4EP Tel Brighton 683304. Cost approx £150-£200 per week includes family accommodation. Alternatively, to Eurocentre, 21 Meadowcourt Road, Lee Green, London SE3 9EU Tel 01-318 5633.

INLINGUA SCHOOL OF LANGUAGES 41 avenue de la Gare, 2000 Neuchâtel Tel Neuchâtel 24 62 29
Courses for all levels. Ages 18 +, individuals and groups. 4 + weeks, all year. 20 x 50 minute lessons per week. Maximum 10 per class. Cost from SF225 per week, accommodation extra. Also holiday courses for all levels. 2 + weeks, July and August. 25 x 50 minute lessons per week. Maximum 10 per class. Cost SF475 per week, including bed and breakfast accommodation.. 1:1 tuition also available.

UK applicants can apply to Inlingua School of Languages, 8-10 Rotton Park Road, Edgbaston, Birmingham B16 9JJ Tel 021-454 0204 or 55-61 Portland Road, Brighton, Sussex BN3 5DQ Tel Brighton 721612

INSTITUT RICHELIEU Ecole de Langue et Culture Francaise, 7 rue du Clos-de-Bulle, 1004 Lausanne Tel Lausanne 23 27 18

Courses for all levels. Ages 15 +, individuals and groups. 3, 6 or 9 weeks, July-September. 20 hours per week. Maximum 12 per class. Audio-visual facilities, video and language laboratory. Study of contemporary problems, media and literature at advanced levels. Cost from SF620, 3 weeks. Also termly courses of 11 weeks, 4 or 20 hours per week. Ages 16 +. Cost per term SF450, 4 hours per week, or SF2200, 20 hours per week. Textbooks from SF20. Alliance Francaise examinations may be taken. Activities include optional excursions to other towns, visits to archaeological or artistic sites and skiing days in the Alps. Help given with finding accommodation. **PH**

UK applicants can apply to Gabbitas, Truman and Thring, Broughton House, 6-8 Sackville Street, Piccadilly, London W1X 2BR Tel 01-734 0161.

INSTITUT VALCREUSE 26 chemin Isabelle de Montolieu, 1010 Lausanne Tel Lausanne 32 10 36 Courses for all levels. Ages 10-20, individuals and groups. 4 or 8 weeks, July-August. 20 hours per week. Maximum 15 per class. Audio-visual facilities, computer-assisted learning and language laboratory. Afternoons are taken up with sports. Weekly excursions to places of interest and local attractions. Entertainment programme includes barbecues and a music club. Cost SF3260 per month includes course, teaching materials, sports, excursions, insurance, transfer from Lausanne railway station or Geneva airport and full board school accommodation.

UNIVERSITE DE LAUSANNE Secrétariat des Cours de Vacances, BFSH 2 Dorigny, 1015 Lausanne Tel Lausanne 46 45 19

Language and culture courses for intermediate levels and above. Ages 16 +, individuals only. Multiples of 3 weeks, July-September. 13 hours per week language tuition, plus study of French civilisation, aspects of daily life and history. Maximum 20 per class. On the same dates, course in French language, literature and civilisation for advanced students. Ages 18 +, individuals only. 6 hours language tuition and 7 hours study of French and Swiss literature per week, plus aspects of French civilisation, art, literature and language. Cost from SF350, 3 weeks. Students of either course may also opt for pronunciation course including language laboratory work. 5 hours per week, cost SF170, 3 weeks. Activities include excursions to places of interest, cost from approx SF30, wine and fondue-tasting, and meetings with local councillors. Students may enrol in sports club, cost SF10. List of available accommodation provided, cost from approx SF14 per day. **PH** depending on handicap.

UNIVERSITE DE NEUCHATEL Faculté des Lettres, Cours de Vacances, 26 avenue du Premier-Mars, 2000 Neuchâtel Tel Neuchâtel 25 38 51
Courses for all levels and for teachers of French. Ages 17 +, individuals and groups. 4 weeks, July. 70 x 45 minute lessons total. Average 20 per class. Audio-visual facilities and language laboratory. Lectures for advanced levels on French and Swiss literature and civilisation, plus Swiss history, geography and institutions. Cost SF400. 7 excursions arranged to places of interest in Neuchâtel and surrounding cantons, cost SF200. Activities also include dance evenings, films, concerts and walks. Full board student residence accommodation available, SF720, 4 weeks. Also course in modern French during the academic year for university level students with at least O level/GCSE French or equivalent. Ages 18 +. Cost SF1110 per year. **PH**

VILLAGE CAMPS Route du Jura, 1296 Coppet Tel Geneva 76 20 59
Language and activity camps for all levels in the mountain resort of Leysin, above Montreux. Organised in association with the Berlitz School of Languages. Ages 13 +, individuals, families and groups. 2 weeks, July-August. 20 hours per week language tuition. Average 7 per class. Outside classes, participants may choose instruction in tennis, riding, mountaineering or multi-activity programme. 2 hours per day, 8 days. Weekend excursions arranged to Château Chillon, Montreux, France by boat across Lake Geneva, Gruyères and its cheese factory and the peaks of Les Diablarets. Evening programmes include barbecues, discos, games and campfire activities. Cost from SF1925 includes full board accommodation in local college for ages 13-19, or in local hotel for adults.

INFORMATION

French Embassy
58 Knightsbridge, London SW1X 7JT Tel 01-235 8080

Belgian Embassy
103 Eaton Square, London SW1W 9AB Tel 01-235 5422

Swiss Embassy
16-18 Montagu Place, London W1H 2BQ Tel 01-723 0701

British Embassy
35 rue de Faubourg St Honoré, 75008 Paris

Britannia House, rue Joseph II 28, 1040 Brussels

Thunstrasse 50, 3005 Bern

Tourist office
French Government Tourist Office, 178 Piccadilly, London W1V 0AL Tel 01-491 7622

Belgian National Tourist Office, 38 Dover Street, London W1X 3RB Tel 01-499 5379

Swiss National Tourist Office, Swiss Centre, 1 New Coventry Street, London W1V 8EE Tel 01-734 1921

Youth hostels
Fédération Unie des Auberges de Jeunesse, 6 rue Mesnil, 75016 Paris

Ligue Française pour les Auberges de la Jeunesse, 38 boulevard Raspail, 75007 Paris

Centrale Wallonne des Auberges de la Jeunesse, rue van Oost 52, 1030 Brussels

Vlaamse Jeugdherbergcentrale, Van Stalenstraat 40, 2008 Antwerp

Schweizerischer Bund fur Jugenherbergen, Postfach 2232, Wildhainweg 19, 3001 Bern

Youth & student information
Accueil des Jeunes en France, 12 rue des Barres, 75004 Paris (for correspondence) or 16 rue du Pont Louis-Philippe/119 rue Saint-Martin, 75004 Paris (for personal callers)

Centre d'Information et de Documentation Jeunesse (CIDJ), 101 quai Branly, 75740 Paris Cedex 15

Organisation pour le Tourisme Universitaire, 137 boulevard St Michel, 75005 Paris

InforJeunes, rue Marché aux Herbes 27, 1000 Brussels

Caravanes de Jeunesse Belge, rue Mercelis 6, 1050 Brussels

Accueil Jeunes, rue Declercq 76, 1150 Brussels

Swiss Student Travel Office, SSR-Reisen, Backerstrasse 40, PO Box, 8026 Zurich

Resources

Alliance Francaise de Londres, 6 Cromwell Place, London SW7 2JN Tel 01-723 6439 was founded in 1883 with the aim of spreading French language and culture around the world. It now has over 1000 branches in 101 different countries, and is one of the world's largest French language teaching associations. The London branch runs language courses at all levels and for all ages. Alliance Francaise and Paris Chamber of Commerce examinations may be taken. Also organises events and activities designed to broaden students' experience of France and French culture, including lectures, exhibitions, films and trips to France.

Institut Francais, 14 Cromwell Place, London SW7 2JR Tel 01-581 2701, is the official centre for French language and culture in London, depending directly on the French Ministry for Foreign Affairs. It offers courses in French for all levels and an extensive programme of cultural activities attended by a large number of French speakers. Students registered at the Institut Francais have free access to its library of 74,000 volumes and 250 periodicals, as well as its video library, film club, cafeteria and exhibitions.

Cours de Francais pour Etudiants Etrangers, published by the French Ministry of Foreign Affairs, is a booklet giving information on all types of courses in French as a foreign language. 2 editions, one dealing with summer courses, the other with courses available all year, both updated annually. Available from the French Embassy Cultural Service, 23 Cromwell Place, London SW7 Tel 01-235 8080.

The Swiss Universities is a guide to university education in Switzerland, giving information on enrolment, duration of studies, degrees, study fees, living costs, scholarships, holiday courses and detailed information on each university. *Private Schools in Switzerland* is published in conjunction with the Federation of Swiss Private Schools and provides information on examinations as well as detailing location, courses and fees of each school. *Holidays and Language Courses* is an annual table of holiday opportunities available in Swiss private schools state schools, holiday camps and universities. All available from the Swiss National Tourist Office, see above.

Information centres

Accueil des Jeunes en France, 12 rue des Barres, 75004 Paris is a general information and advisory service for young travellers. Can provide vouchers for low-cost restaurants and arrange cheap accommodation, see below, and also supply cheap rail and coach tickets.

Centre d'Information et de Documentation Jeunesse (CIDJ), 101 quai Branly, 75740 Paris Cedex 15 provides a comprehensive information service for young people, with branches throughout France. Information is available on accommodation, social, cultural, artistic, scientific and sports facilities, activities and holidays plus practical information on staying, travelling and studying in France and facilities for the disabled. Services include free legal aid, consumer protection and a hitch hikers rendezvous.

ACOTRA rue de la Madeleine 51, PO Box 3, 1000 Brussels arranges youth and student travel and acts as a transit accommodation centre. Also books tours and excursions, cultural and activity holidays, and issues youth/student reduction and youth hostel cards.

Bruxelles Accueil, rue de Tabora 6, 1000 Brussels is a Catholic information service for visitors, residents, workers and students, providing advice on education, language classes, social services, legal aid and religion. Free interpreting and translation service.

Travel

Rent-a-bike scheme available at 287 stations, bookable in advance; FF250 deposit, cost FF35 per day, increasing as the number of rental days increases. Two youth cards available to ages 12-25: Carte Jeune offers 4 single or 2 return journeys at up to 50%; valid for 1 year; Carte Jeune offers up to 50% reduction, June- September. Cost £15 each. Holiday Return Ticket concession of 25% if the journey covers more than 1000km, and if the holder stays for more than 5 days. Valid 2 months; cost £50. France Vacances Pass gives unlimited travel on 4 days during a period of 1 month, all year, plus, among other concessions, 50% reduction on Hoverspeed Channel crossings. Cost £105/£130. Jeune Voyageur Service looks after unaccompanied children on 37 routes across France, covering 150 stations. Cost from £16-£20 depending on length and time of journey. Available from two Channel ports only, St Malo and Roscoff. Details of all from SNCF French Railways Ltd, French Railways House, 179 Piccadilly, London W1V 0BA Tel 01-409 1224.

Transalpino Ltd, 117 Euston Road, London NW1 2SX Tel 01-388 2267 offer up to 50% off full rail fares to nearly 150 destinations in France, Belgium and Switzerland for those under 26.

Belgian National Railways, 22-25a Sackville Street, London W1X 1DE Tel 01-734 1491 operates a scheme where a bike can be collected at one of 48 Belgian stations and returned to any one of 101. Cost from £1.50 per day; advisable to reserve in advance.

Abonnement Réseau allows unlimited rail travel throughout the Belgian network. Valid 16 consecutive days, all year, cost £44.50. B-Tourrail Ticket allows unlimited travel for 5/8 days, Easter-September. Cost for ages under 26, £20/£27. Benelux Tourrail allows unlimited travel throughout the Belgium, Luxembourg and Netherlands rail networks; valid for 5 days, March-September. Cost for ages under 26, 333. All available from YHA Travel, 14 Southampton Street, London WC2E 7HY Tel 01-836 8541.

Swiss National Tourist Office, see above, issues the Swiss Holiday Card which gives unlimited travel on rail, lake boat and postal coach networks, plus reductions on mountain railways and cable cars. Cost SF145-SF285, 4-31 days.

Swiss Student Travel Office, SSR-Reisen, Backerstrasse 52, 8026 Zurich offers reduced fares by rail and air for youth and students. Daily departures, London to Zurich, Geneva or Basle from £79 return.

Accommodation

Accueil des Jeunes en France, 12 rue des Barres, 75004 Paris is a central booking office for youth accommodation with access to 11000 beds in the summer. Has 4 offices which guarantee to find any young traveller decent, cheap accommodation in Paris, with immediate reservation. Cost approx FF75 per night. Contact AJF Beaubourg, 119 rue St-Martin, 75004 Paris; AJF Hôtel de Ville, 16 rue du Pont Louis-Philippe, 775004 Paris; AJF Quartier Latin, 139 boulevard Saint-Michel, 75005 Paris; and AJF Gare du Nord, Arrival Hall, 75010 Paris.

Bureau des Voyages de la Jeunesse, 20 rue JJ Rousseau, 75001 Paris has 4 youth accommodation centres in Paris at Les Halles, Opéra, Latin Quarter and Louvre. Cost FF75 bed and breakfast, FF120 half board, FF165 full board, per night, 1-8 bedded rooms.

Centre d'Information et et de Documentation Jeunesse (CIDJ), 101 quai Branly, 75740 Paris Cedex 15 publish information sheets providing addresses of reasonable accommodation in youth centres, university halls and pensions, mainly in the Paris region: *Centres d'Hébergement Temporaires Paris et Région Parisienne; Hôtels Bon Marché et Pensions de Famille à Paris; Logement des Jeunes Travailleurs;* and *Le Logement de L'Etudiant.*

Centre International de Séjour de Paris, 6 avenue Maurice-Ravel, 75012 Paris offers accommodation available at 2 residential centres. Facilities include sports hall, workshops, swimming pools, library and restaurants. Cost from FF46 per night includes dormitory accommodation. Reservation should be made at least 3 months in advance.

Union des Centres de Rencontres Internationales de France (UCRIF), 21 rue Beranger, 75003 Paris publishes a list of 77 youth accommodation centres and hostels, each providing a comprehensive tourist service in a friendly atmosphere. Facilities include swimming, riding, sports grounds, cycling, skating, skiing, sailing and language courses. Cost from FF60 per night for bed and breakfast in 1-6 bedded rooms. **PH**

Le CHAB, Hôtel de Jeunes, rue Traversiére 8, 1030 Brussels is an inexpensive international accommodation centre, with 1-8 bedded rooms or dormitories. Cost from FB220 bed and breakfast plus FB60 linen charge. Cycle hire, walking tours and information on cultural activities.

Rijksuniversiteit Gent, Mrs M Verfaillie, Department of Guest Accommodation, Home A Vermeylen, Stalhof 6, 9000 Gent has cheap accommodation in single rooms in 2 halls of residence, 15 July-15 September. Bed and breakfast FB400 per night. Facilities include restaurant, swimming pool and sports grounds.

Student Lodgings at University Cities in Switzerland is a booklet giving the addresses of student accommodation in Basle, Bern, Fribourg, Geneva, Lausanne, Neuchâtel, St Gall and Zurich. Available from the Swiss National Tourist Office, see above.

Swiss Student Travel Office, see above, offers cheap but comfortable accommodation in international student hotels at Klosters, St Moritz, Scuol, Lucerne, Wengen and Davos. 2-6 bedded rooms with self-catering facilities. Cost approx SF36 per day, half board.

GAELIC

A member of the Indo-European group, Gaelic is one of the Celtic languages that were spoken from Scotland to the Mediterranean before the spread of the Roman Empire. The Germanic invasions which followed the Empire's fall pushed these languages to the western fringes of Europe, and subsequent Anglicisation led to a further decline in the number of Gaelic speakers. During the 5th century Gaelic was carried from Ireland to Scotland, where it evolved into a separate dialect, and the traditional alphabet evolved from the Latin. Irish Gaelic or Irish is recognised as the first official language of the Republic of Ireland and is spoken by approx 28% of the population, although most of these have English as their mother tongue. Scottish Gaelic is spoken by fewer people, some 82,000 or under 2% of the Scottish population. Recently there has been a revival of interest, with television and radio broadcasts in Gaelic and the increased teaching of the language in schools.

COURSES IN IRELAND

FORAS NA GAEILGE 26 Cearnóg Mhuirfean, Dublin 2
Tel Dublin 767283

Irish Gaelic courses in Dublin for beginner to intermediate levels. No age limits, individuals and groups. 5 weeks, all year. 24 hours per week, beginners, 10 hours per week, other levels., Average 12-15 per class.

Audio-visual facilities. Cost from IR£135, beginners or from IR£60, other levels, includes course and teaching materials. Also summer courses for all levels, 2 or 3 weeks, June-August. Cost from IR£45, 2 weeks, includes course and teaching materials. Accommodation can be found with families or in hotels. Also residential summer courses for teenagers in Baile Mhúirne, County Cork and Machaire Rabhartaigh, County Donegal, both in *Gaeltacht* (Gaelic-speaking) areas. 2 or 3 weeks, June-August. Extra-curricular activities include singing, dancing and games. Cost from IR£120, 2 weeks, includes course, teaching materials and full board family or school accommodation. *Some scholarships available for children from Northern Ireland.* **PH**

COURSES IN SCOTLAND

SABHAL MOR OSTAIG An Teanga, Sleite, Isle of Skye IV44 8RQ Tel Ardvasar 373
Courses in Scottish Gaelic for all levels on the island of Skye, in the Inner Hebrides. Ages 16 +, individuals and groups. 10 days, June-September. 30 hours per week. Average 12-15 per class. Courses involve visiting lecturers, trips to local communities, visits to places of interest and *ceilidhs,* folk dancing evenings. Cost £110. Local accommodation list provided. Also short cultural courses in piping, fiddle, clarsach, Hebridean dance, Hebridean genealogy and Gaelic song and story. Cost £55-£65, 5 days. Also 2 year full time HND courses in business and Gaidhealtachd studies, and business and information technology studies, both taught in Gaelic. Approved by Scottish Education Department.

UNIVERSITY OF EDINBURGH Department of Extra-Mural Studies, 11 Buccleuch Place, Edinburgh EH8 9LW Tel 031-667 1011 ext 6686
Language and culture course for all levels in Edinburgh. Ages 18 +, individuals and groups. 2-3 weeks, August-September. 35 hours per week. Maximum 12 per class. Courses include study of place names at elementary level, and literature and folk music at intermediate/advanced levels. Audio-visual facilities. Extra-curricular activities include excursions, parties and *ceilidhs,* and participants can attend events of the Edinburgh Festival. Cost £110-£160. Textbooks approx £10. Advice given on accommodation. **PH**

INFORMATION

Irish Embassy
17 Grosvenor Place, London SW1X 7HR Tel 01-235 2171

British Embassy
33 Merrion Road, Dublin 4 Tel Dublin 695211

Tourist office
Irish Tourist Office, Ireland House, 150 New Bond Street, London W1Y 0AQ Tel 01-493 3201

Scottish Tourist Board, 23 Ravelston Terrace, Edinburgh EH4 3EU Tel 031-332 2433

Youth hostels
An Oige Irish YHA, 39 Mountjoy Square, Dublin 1 Tel Dublin 745734

Scottish Youth Hostels Association (SYHA), 7 Glebe Crescent, Stirling FK8 2JA

Youth & student information
Union of Students in Ireland, 16 North Great Georges Street, Dublin 1 Tel Dublin 786020

Union of Students in Ireland Travel Service (USIT), 7/9 Anglesea Street, Dublin 2 Tel Dublin 778117

National Youth Council of Ireland, 3 Montague Street, Dublin 2 Tel Dublin 784122

Resources
Centre for Information on Language Teaching and Research (CILT), Regent's College, Inner Circle, Regent's Park, London NW1 4NS Tel 01-486 8221 publish *Gaelic (Scottish) Language & Culture Guide* £4.25 and *Irish Language & Culture Guide* £4.75, both including postage, with details on the provision and use of language teaching and learning resources, covering an introduction to the language, useful addresses, libraries and special collections to consult, opportunities for learning, and examinations which can be taken.

Travel
CIE Tours International, Ireland House, 150-151 New Bond Street, London W1Y 9FE Tel 01-629 0564 issues the Rambler ticket entitling

the holder to unlimited rail and bus travel in Ireland. Cost IR£62/£90, 8/15 days.

Transalpino Ltd, 117 Euston Road, London NW1 2SX Tel 01-388 2267 offer up to 50% off full rail fares to 14 destinations in Ireland for those under 26.

Publications

Irish Youth Directory £1.50, is a useful reference and resource aid which provides detailed information on voluntary youth organisations together with a comprehensive list of useful addresses, youth travel and accommodation. *Stepping Out* £3, is a youth handbook providing information on a wide range of topics including training and employment, health and drugs, further education, recreation, the media, politics, the environment and travel. Both published by the National Youth Council of Ireland, 3 Montague Street, Dublin 2 Tel Dublin 784122.

GERMAN

German is descended from the language of the tribes that bordered the northwestern frontier of the Roman Empire, and today is spoken by about 115 million people in Austria, the Democratic and Federal Republics of Germany, Liechtenstein and Switzerland, as well as in eastern France, formerly Alsace-Lorraine, and in Luxembourg and border areas of Italy and Belgium. Traditionally written in Fraktur, a Gothic style dating from the 14th century, this was replaced by Roman characters after the Second World War. Although written German is fairly uniform, spoken dialects vary to some extreme. High German, the standard written language, is spoken in the southern highlands. Low German, sounding more like Dutch and English, is spoken in the north lowlands. German is one of the most logical and regular of all the European languages, and still retains many grammatical structures that have been lost in other languages. In its ability to make long compound words, German is an ideal language for science and philosophy where precise expression of concepts is essential.

COURSES IN AUSTRIA

ANGLO-AUSTRIAN SOCIETY 46 Queen Anne's Gate, London SW1H 9AU Tel 01-222 0366
Language course for GCSE and A level students of German in Lunz am Zee, near Vienna. Ages 15-18. 10 days, Easter. 3 hours per day. The course is designed to give young people from Britain and Austria the

chance to meet and learn each other's language, and extra-curricular shared activities include walks, discussions, activities and excursions, including a day trip to Vienna. Cost £369 includes course, textbooks, full board hostel accommodation, all social activities and excursions, insurance, and air/coach travel, London to Lunz via Vienna. *Limited number of travel bursaries of up to £100 available.*

DEUTSCH IN GRAZ Internationale Kurse und Seminare für Deutsch als Fremdsprache, Kalchberggasse 1, 8010 Graz Tel Graz 79 038
Intensive language courses for all levels in the ancient university town of Graz. Ages 18+, individuals and groups. 3, 4, 6 and 10 weeks, June-October. 28 hours per week. Maximum 12 per class. Cost from AS5600, 3 weeks includes language tuition, teaching materials, and extra-curricular activities such as folk dancing, Vienna Waltz evening, video evening and use of sports facilities. Optional extras include grammar lessons, use of language laboratory, and lessons in Austrian literature and contemporary history. Bed and breakfast accommodation provided in student homes or with families, from AS2530, 3 weeks. Also special interest courses for advanced students, combining commercial and economic German with lectures in contemporary Austrian society and culture, and 20th century Austrian literature. 2 weeks, July-September. Cost AS7120 covers language tuition and extra-curricular activities. Bed and breakfast accommodation provided in student homes or with families, from AS1700, 2 weeks. Approved by local government. **PH**

DEUTSCH INSTITUT TIROL (DIT) Am Sandhügel 2, 6370 Kitzbühel Tel Kitzbühel 57932
Language courses for all levels in the Austrian Tyrol. Ages 16+, individuals and groups. 1 week upwards, starting every Monday (for beginners, only the first Monday in each month), all year. 20 hours per week, maximum 7 per class. The course also includes 4 afternoon activities a week such as sports, cultural activities, excursions (at extra cost) and walking in the mountains, all conducted in German and accompanied by a teacher. Skiing, including accompanied touring and ski lessons, also available on slopes around the town (winter) or on glaciers (summer). In the evening special interest courses are organised 3 times a week in areas such as geography, history, music, literature, grammar, spelling, idiomatic expressions, easily confused words and conversation, plus Tyrolean evenings. Tapes available for private language practice. Special courses also offered for businessmen and teachers of German, and for children aged 12-16. Cost from AS5100 per week includes half board school/guest house accommodation and course, plus teaching materials. Member of the Federation Europeene des Ecoles.

Applications in the UK can be made to the Anglo-Austrian Society, 46 Queen Anne's Gate, London SW1H 9AU Tel 01-222 0366, cost from £357 per week including travel and insurance, or to Cultural and Educational Services Abroad, 44 Sydney Street, Brighton, Sussex BN1 4EP Tel Brighton 683304.

DEUTSCH IN ÖSTERREICH Universität für Bildungswissenschaften, Universitätsstrasse 65, 9020 Klagenfurt Tel Klagenfurt 24180

Language courses for all levels in Klagenfurt and Pörtschach. Ages 17 +, individuals and groups. 3-4 weeks, May-September. 24 hours per week, maximum 12 per class. Cost AS3900, 3 weeks or AS5300, 4 weeks. Teaching methods involve the use of language laboratories and audio-visual material. All teaching materials and a day excursion included. Also special programme comprising business correspondence and Austrian culture, history and literature; 4 hours per week. Cost AS400, 3 weeks or AS500, 4 weeks. Extra-curricular activities include theatre, film shows, concerts, sports, parties and further excursions. Self-catering/bed & breakfast accommodation arranged in local student halls, youth centre or guest house; cost AS2100-AS3700, 3-4 weeks. Meals available in canteen and self-service restaurant. Students arrange own insurance. Five day seminars in July/August also available for teachers and advanced students of German, covering Austria in the 19th and 20th centuries, methodology in German language teaching, commercial and business German, and German in tourism. Cost AS3900 includes bed & breakfast student accommodation. Ski-school and informal language course in Bad Kleinkirchheim. 13 days, March-April. 30 hours language classes. Maximum 12 per class. Cost AS5840 covers language tuition, 10 day ski pass, 5 day ski school. Half board guest house accommodation arranged. Facilities include TV, gym and own shower; cost AS4200. Students arrange own insurance.

Applications in the UK can be made to Cultural and Educational Services Abroad, 44 Sydney Street, Brighton, Sussex BN1 4EP Tel Brighton 683304.

GARS KREATIV INTERNATIONAL Obkirchergasse 38/3/3, 1190 Vienna Tel Vienna 326808

Summer language course for all levels at Gars am Kamp, 50 miles north of Vienna. Ages 17 +, individuals and groups. 3-4 weeks, July/August. 15-25 hours per week. Average 6 per class. Optional seminars on politics, art, literature and history and lectures on health and fitness, plus lunchtime debates during the week. Extra-curricular activities include excursions twice a week, guided tours, parties, visits to *Gasthausen* and *Moststub'n*, a local festival and folk dancing. Sports

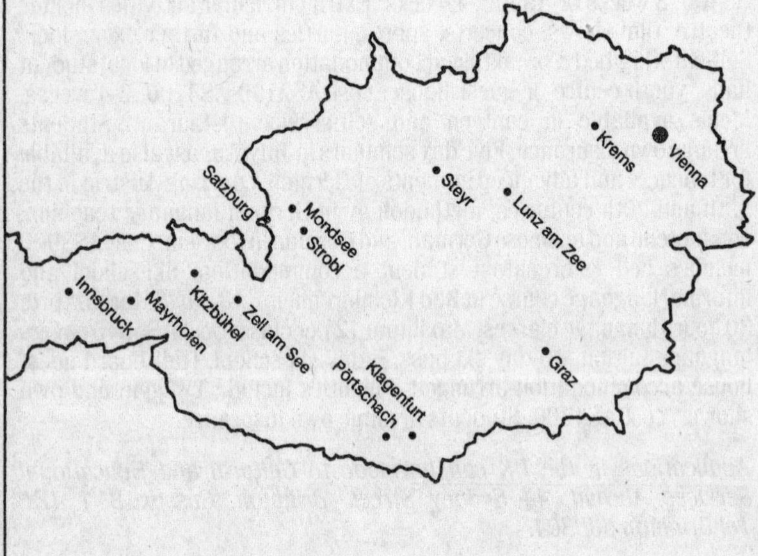
Krems
Vienna
Steyr
Lunz am Zee
Salzburg
Mondsee
Strobl
Innsbruck
Mayrhofen
Kitzbühel
Zell am See
Klagenfurt
Pörtschach
Graz

A U S T R I A

available include tennis, riding and swimming. Self-study room available during leisure time. Cost AS12400, 3 weeks or AS16200, 4 weeks includes course, textbooks and materials, extra seminars and debates, 2 excursions a week, parties, full board family/guest house accommodation and transfer to and from Vienna airport. Can provide help with cheap flights or arranging accommodation in Vienna for extended stays; also on opportunities to study in Vienna or other towns. *Scholarships available from the Austrian Institute, see below.* **PH**

IFK – INTERNATIONALE FERIENKURSE FÜR DEUTSCHE SPRACHE UND GERMANISTIK Franz-Josef-Strasse 19, 5020 Salzburg Tel Salzburg 76595
Language courses in Salzburg for all levels. Ages 16 +, individuals and groups. 10 weeks, starting January, March, October. 20 lessons per week. Maximum 16 per class. Audio-visual facilities and language laboratory. Cost AF10800 including textbooks and materials. Lectures on Austrian history, literature, music, arts and folklore. Extra-curricular activities include guided tours and visits, social evenings, and folklore performances. Reduced priced tickets for theatre and concerts. Bed and breakfast accommodation available in private homes, from AS115 per day. Self catering accommodation can also be found, and advice on cheap restaurants in Salzburg is given. Insurance available at AS6 per day. Also special summer language courses for all levels, with lectures on Austria. Ages 16 +, individuals and groups. 3-4 weeks, July-August. Intensive German with seminars on language training, business and commerce, theatre, arts and music (intermediate and advanced levels only). Also technical courses on philology and literature, for teachers of German and for repeat students (advanced levels only). Special courses arranged for groups on request. Costs AS8420-AS11895 including bed and breakfast student/family accommodation. Also German on Skis course at Zell am See, in the Alps south of Salzburg, for all levels. Ages 16 +, individuals and groups. 3 weeks, January. 15 hours language teaching plus 15 hours ski instruction, per week. Cost AS17100-AS20900 includes course, books, ski instruction, ski pass, half board hotel/guest house accommodation and access to indoor swimming pool, sauna and ice-rink. A summer course, German by the Lake, also available at Zell am See in July with language classes plus hiking, tennis, golf, sailing and windsurfing. Cost AS14500-AS13700 includes language and sports tuition, course materials and bed and breakfast guest house accommodation. Social/cultural activities for both courses cover folklore, lantern lectures, skating, bowling and social evenings. Enrolment fee for all courses AS750. *Scholarships available for the Salzburg summer course; apply by 31 March.* Approved by the University of Salzburg.

Applications in the UK may be made to the Anglo-Austrian Society, 46 Queen Anne's Gate, London SW1H 9AU Tel 01-222 0366. Cost for 3 week summer course £559 including accommodation, medical insurance and air travel from London; £459 excluding travel.

INNSBRUCKER HOCHSCHULKURSE DEUTSCH (IHD) Universität Innsbruck, Innrain 52, 6020 Innsbruck Tel Innsbruck 724/3437

Language courses for all levels in Innsbruck. Ages 17 + , individuals and groups. 3/6 weeks, July-August. 17.5 hours per week, mornings only. Maximum class size 15. Teaching methods include use of language laboratory. Cost AS4500, 3 weeks or AS7500, 6 weeks includes language tuition, cultural and social activities, use of library and sports/recreational facilities. For 3 afternoons a week students can take extra language classes, cost AS750, 3 weeks, or a course in modern German literature, cost AS950, 3 weeks. Accommodation arranged in self-catering student home or hostel, from AS2000, 3 weeks.

INTERNATIONALE FERIENKURSE MAYRHOFEN, 6290 Mayrhofen, Zillertal, Tirol Tel Mayrhofen 2305

Language courses for all levels in Mayrhofen in the Austrian Tyrol. Ages 15 + , or 12 + if accompanied by a parent, individuals and groups. 3 weeks, July-September. 15 hours per week. Maximum 20 per class. Students may take an examination leading to the language certificate of the University of Innsbruck. 10 hours of lectures per week on economic, political and cultural topics, covering history, poetry, fine arts, music, theatre and folklore. Extra-curricular activities include community singing, folk dancing, films, excursions to Vienna, Salzburg and Innsbruck, walks in the mountains, skiing on glaciers and other sports. Cost AS5970 includes language course, education materials, activities, excursions, and bed and breakfast guest house accommodation. Cost AS3390, language course only.

INTERNATIONALES KULTUR-INSTITUT Opernring 7, 1010 Vienna Tel Vienna 567321

Language courses for all levels in Vienna. Ages 16 + , individuals and groups. 10 weeks, starting January, April, July and October. Students may also attend a half course of 5 weeks. 15 hours per week. Maximum 16 per class. Audio-visual facilities. In the summer, the course includes lectures on Austrian literature, history and art. Extra-curricular activities include barbeques, parties, rowing on the Danube, football, walking in the Vienna woods, and visits to museums, theatres and concerts. Cost AS5400, 10 weeks, including textbooks. Accommodation can be found in rooms in private flats from AS1500, or in student dormitories from AS2500, 5 weeks.

ÖSTERREICHISCH-AMERIKANISCHE GESELLSCHAFT Stallburggasse 2, 1010 Vienna Tel Vienna 523982/ 524784

Summer course in Salzburg for all levels. Ages 18-50. 6 weeks, July-August. 24 hours per week. Maximum 20 per class. Includes afternoon seminars on German style, 20th century Austrian literature, and German for business, conducted in German, and Austrian music, Austrian history, and art in Salzburg, conducted in English. Extra-curricular activities include sports, parties and other social activities, films and the Salzburg Festival. Cost AS20800 includes tuition, all books and materials, full board campus accommodation, a tour of Salzburg and a ticket to a Festival performance. Accommodation with families also available, cost AS4500. Sponsored by the University of Salzburg. *Limited number of scholarships available through the Austrian Institute.*

Also language courses in Vienna for all levels. Ages 16 + . 4 weeks, June-September. 24 hours per week. Maximum 20 per class. It is recommended to enrol for at least 8 weeks. Cost AS3100, 4 weeks or AS6100, 8 weeks, including textbooks. Also year round courses for 8 weeks, starting February, April, October and November. 24 hours per week. Maximum 20 per class. Cost AS6100 including textbooks. Courses include one self-study lesson, a day in the language laboratory and home study. Accommodation can be arranged in student houses from AS3300 per month. Examinations of the Goethe-Institut may be taken at the end of some courses.

Applications in the United States to US Student Programs, Institute of International Education, 809 United Nations Plaza, New York, NY 10017.

ÖSTERREICHISCHE VEREINIGUNG FÜR AUSTAUSCH UND STUDIENREISEN (ÖVAST) Dr Gschmeidlerstrasse 10/4, 3500 Krems Tel Krems 5743

Language courses at all levels in Krems and Steyr. Ages 10 +, groups only. 3-6 weeks, all year. 15-30 hours per week. Maximum 15 per group. Cost from AS2000 per week includes language course and full board family accommodation. Cost from AS2600 per week for groups of 7 or less. Also Anglo-Austrian educational holidays for all levels in Altenmarkt, near Salzburg. Ages 6-18, individuals and groups. 2 weeks, July-August. 15 hours per week. Maximum 15 per class. The British participants learn German while the Austrians learn English. Cost AS5380 includes tuition, excursions, walking tours and full board shared accommodation. Skiing holidays in Altenmarkt, with language course. Ages 10-25, groups only. 1 week, in season. 10 hours per week, maximum 15 per class. Cost AS3040 includes language tuition, skiing instruction and full board shared accommodation. Ski and boot hire each AS800 extra. Can arrange escorted travel.

ÖSTERREICHISCHES KOMITEE FÜR INTERNATIONALEN STUDIENAUSTAUSCH (ÖKISTA) Türkenstrasse 4, 1090 Vienna Tel 347526/318681
Language course for all levels at Strebersdorf, near Vienna. Ages 9-13 and 14-18. Individuals, groups on request. 3 weeks, July. 15 hours per week. Average 15 per class. In the afternoon facilities are available for table tennis, football, volleyball and swimming and there is also a programme of excursions, cycling, walking or boating trips and social activities. Cost AS8960 includes language tuition, textbooks, full board hostel accommodation and leisure activities, but not insurance or excursions. *Apply by 31 May.*
Also language and sport course at Mondsee, a lakeside village near Salzburg. Ages 14-19, individuals, groups on request. 3 weeks, August. 15 hours per week. Average 15 per class. In the afternoons participants can practise tennis, windsurfing and sailing. Sports tuition available from AS495; international certificates in windsurfing or sailing may be obtained. Programme of walks, games, campfire events and barbecues. Cost AS9900 includes language tuition, textbooks, full board accommodation in country inn, use of sporting equipment and leisure activities. *Apply by 30 June.*

PEGASUS REISEN Seilergasse 16, 1010 Vienna Tel Vienna 515450
Summer language course for all levels in Vienna, using the Berlitz method. Ages 14+, individuals and groups. 3 weeks, July-August. 19 hours per week. Maximum 12 per class. Half day tours of Vienna and the Vienna Woods and an evening cruise on the Danube. Reductions offered on other excursions and at restaurants. Cost from AS9890 includes language classes, excursions and hotel accommodation. Textbooks extra. Also 1:1 courses, tailored to individual needs, in Vienna and Graz.

SALZBURG INTERNATIONAL LANGUAGE CENTRE Moosstrasse 106, 5020 Salzburg Tel Salzburg 846511/844485
Language courses for all levels in Salzburg. Ages 12+ summer, 17+ winter, individuals and groups. 2-6 weeks, July-September and 12 weeks, September-December and January-March. 20 hours per week. Average 15 per class. Special courses for ages 12-17, and for teachers of German. For advanced levels literature classes are included in the course. Audio-visual, language laboratory and computer facilities. Extra-curricular activities include excursions, cultural events in Salzburg, tennis, sailing, windsurfing, all year skiing and mountain

climbing. Students have the opportunity to meet with local people attending the school. Cost AS9000, 2 weeks or AS49900, 12 weeks, includes language classes, full board campus accommodation, textbooks and materials, and social events. Excursions extra. Medical insurance can be arranged, cost AS400 per month. Ski programme AS800 and sailing/wind surfing programme AS400, per day. Advice given on all aspects of the student's stay, and assistance provided in enrolling at Salzburg University. Approved by the Department of Education.

SPRACHSCHULE LERCH Kapuzinergasse 10, 6020 Innsbruck Tel Innsbruck 28957

Language courses for all levels in Innsbruck. Ages 14 +, individuals and groups. 4 weeks, July-September and also during the academic year. 20 hours per week. Maximum 14 per class. At Christmas and Easter, courses can be combined with skiing. Also courses in phonetics, German for journalism and tourism, literature, and Austro-German civilisation, plus courses for teachers of German. Social events include excursions, concerts, Tyrolean evenings, theatre performances, lectures, music circles, dancing, and sports. Cost AS4600 per week includes lessons and half board family accommodation. Full board AS500 per week extra. Hotel/student hostel accommodation also available. Registration fee AS500, textbooks AS250. Can arrange cheap travel and medical insurance. Recognised by the local government. **PH**

SPRACHSCHULE WESTENDORF Oberwindau 4, 6363 Westendorf Tel Westendorf 677113

Language courses for all levels at a small school in a village in the Austrian Tyrol. Ages 16 +, individuals and groups. 2, 3, or 4 weeks, January-December. 17.5 hours per week. Average 5-10 per class. Video facilities. Lectures on Austrian history and geography. In winter there are opportunities to ski, with reductions on ski hire. Summer programme of excursions, plus optional afternoon study of folk songs, grammar, literature or Austrian wine. Social events include sing-songs, Tyrolean evenings, films and barbecues. Facilities for swimming, riding and tennis. Cost AS8900, 2 weeks, AS13300, 3 weeks or AS17800, 4 weeks, includes language classes, textbooks and materials, supplementary lectures and social activities, and full board accommodation in the school or with families. Cost AS1700 per week, course only.

SUMMER SCHOOL OF THE UNIVERSITY OF VIENNA, Summer School Office, Wahringerstrasse 17, 1090 Vienna Tel Vienna 436141 extn 60

Summer language courses for all levels at Strobl, at a campus of parkland and lakes. Ages 19 +, individuals only. Applicants must have completed 1 year's study at a European university. 6 weeks, July-August. Intensive courses 15 hours per week, or non-intensive, 5 hours per week. Average class size 15. Also weekly seminar for teachers of German. Language laboratory available. Academic programme covers international relations and law, world finance, socio-political topics especially related to Eastern Europe, and Austrian culture and history. Extra-curricular activities include sports, watersports and fitness classes. Also mountain walking, special lectures on political-economic affairs, cultural programme, excursions and opportunities to visit the Salzburg Festival. Cost AS20800 includes all tuition, full board campus accommodation, plus social and sports activities. *Scholarships offered by the Austrian government via Austrian cultural institutes and embassies. For students applying before March a limited number of scholarships also available from the school. Apply by 31 May.*

WIENER INTERNATIONALE HOCHSCHULKURSE Universitat, 1010 Vienna Tel Vienna 421254/424737
Summer language school for all levels at the University of Vienna. Ages 16+, individuals and groups. 4 weeks, July-August, and 3 weeks, September. 15 hours per week. Maximum 25 per class. Also courses for teachers of German. Language laboratory available for out-of-class study. During July and August special courses are run on the literature, music, linguistics and socio-politics of Austria, and during all courses extra afternoon sessions can be taken in translation or pronunciation, business correspondence, or the Viennese Waltz. Social events include excursions, tours of Vienna, wine parties and boat trips on the Danube. Cost AS7560 includes course and student hostel accommodation. Textbooks up to AS400 per course, special courses AS200-AS440. Excursions extra. 25% reduction for refugees.

Applications in the UK can be made to the Anglo-Austrian Society, 46 Queen Anne's Gate, London SW1H 9AU Tel 01-222 0366. Cost £517, 4 weeks, includes course, accommodation, medical insurance and flight from London; £351 excluding travel. Also to Cultural and Educational Services Abroad, 44 Sydney Street, Brighton, Sussex, BN1 4EP Tel Brighton 683304. Cost £553, 4 weeks, includes course, accommodation, insurance and flight from London.

COURSES IN THE GERMAN DEMOCRATIC REPUBLIC

Application forms for all courses are obtainable from the Embassy of the German Democratic Republic, see below. Those interested should contact the Embassy before the end of November each year. Completed application forms are sent direct to the institution where the course is held; closing dates are given at the end of each entry. As indicated on some courses, a limited number of Britsih Council scholarships are available for British applicants; contact the British Council, 10 Spring Gardens, London SW1A 2BN Tel 01-930 8466.

FRIEDRICH-SCHILLER UNIVERSITÄT JENA Universitätshochhaus, 4 Obergeschoss, 6900 Jena Tel Jena 822 4121
Courses in Weimar for Germanists, teachers, lecturers and translators of German. Sektion Literatur- und Kunstwissenschaft organises course in language and literature, concentrating on contemporary literature. 3 weeks, July. Sektion Sprachwissenschaft organises course in language and linguistics, with some study of literature. 3 weeks, August. Extra-curricular activities for both courses include discussions with people from political, cultural and economic life, visits to the theatre, cinema, concerts, museums and art galleries, and excursions to Thüringen and local places of interest. Cost $325 includes course, teaching materials, activities, excursions and full board hotel/private accommodation. British Council scholarships available. *Apply by 31 May.*

HOCHSCHULE FÜR ÖKONOMIE BRUNO LEUSCHNER, BERLIN Institut für Fremdsprachen, Hermann-Duncker-Strasse 8, 1157 Berlin Tel Berlin 5 04 25 31
Language course in Berlin, for all levels. Applicants with an interest or education in economics preferred. Ages 18-70, individuals and groups. 2 or 4 weeks, July-August. 30 hours per week language tuition, with options in German for business or economics. Extra-curricular activities include visits to theatres, museums and other places of interest, discussion groups with public figures and weekend excursions to Potsdam and Dresden. Cost $300, 2 weeks or $550, 4 weeks covers course, teaching materials, activities, excursions and full board accommodation at the college. Students may also take an examination at the end of the course, cost $20.

HUMBOLDT-UNIVERSITÄT ZU BERLIN Sektion Fremdsprachen, Internationaler Hochschulferienkurs, Reinhardstrasse 7, 1040 Berlin Tel Berlin 2093 2846
Language and methodology course in Berlin for teachers and lecturers of German. 3 weeks, July. As well as language and phonetics, course includes lectures on GDR literature and problems of foreign language teaching, plus workshops on various aspects of language teaching, including the use of audiovisual material and computers. Extra-curricular activities include visits to the theatre, cinema, museums and concerts, plus excursions to Potsdam, Dresden, Luther's birthplace in Wittenberg and a trip on the Berlin lakes. Also arrange evenings of authors reading their own works, and group discussions with public figures. Cost $325 includes course, teaching materials, activities, excursions and full board student residence accommodation. British Council scholarships available. *Apply by 31 May.*

HUMBOLDT-UNIVERSITÄT ZU BERLIN Sektion Germanistik, Internationaler Hochschulferienkurs/ Studenten, Clara-Zetkin-Strasse 1, 1086 Berlin Tel Berlin 20 93 28 46
Language, literature and culture course in Berlin for students of German with at least a basic knowledge. 3 weeks, July. 15 hours language tuition per week plus work on phonetics and in language laboratory. Lectures and seminars held on modern literature, history, culture and society of the GDR. Extra-curricular activities include visits to concerts, museums, art galleries and the theatre, film shows and excursions to Dresden, Güstrow, Potsdam and the surroundings of Berlin. Opportunities to meet writers, scientists and artists. Cost $325 includes course, teaching materials, activities, excursions and full board student residence accommodation. *Apply by 31 May.*

INTERNATIONALER HOCHSCHULFERIENKURS FÜR GERMANISTIK IN DER DDR Ernst-Moritz-Arndt-Universität Greifswald, Bahnhofstrasse 46/47, 2200 Greifswald Tel Greifswald 25 46
Language, literature and culture course for students of German in Greifswald, on the Baltic coast. The university dates back to the 15th century, and the course has been running for longer than any other. 3 weeks, July. Includes language tuition plus aspects of GDR literature, fine arts, music and cultural policy, and GDR past and present. Extra-curricular activities include group discussions with people from political, economic and cultural life, social evenings and excursions, including visits to the Baltic islands of Rügen and Hiddensee. Cost $280 includes course, teaching materials, activities, excursions and full board student residence accommodation. British Council scholarships available. *Apply by 31 May.*

KARL-MARX-UNIVERSITÄT LEIPZIG Herder-Institut, Internationaler Hochschulferienkurs für Germanistik, Lumumbastrasse 4, 7022 Leipzig Tel Leipzig 5 63 20
Courses in Leipzig for Germanists, teachers, lecturers and translators. 3 weeks, July. As well as language tuition, lectures cover problems of methodology, linguistics and geography encountered in teaching German, plus aspects of GDR development, literature and culture. Also workshops on various themes of linguistics, methodology, geography and literature. Extra-curricular activities include discussions with industrial and agricultural workers, and with public figures, authors reading from their own work, cultural events and film shows, plus excursions to Dresden and Weimar. Excursions to Quedlinburg and Meissen also available at extra cost. Cost $325 includes course, teaching materials, activities, excursions and full board private accommodation. British Council scholarships available. *Apply by 31 May.*

Also intensive course in general German and German for legal and education purposes, for elementary to advanced levels. 4 weeks, July-August. 30 hours language tuition per week. Extra-curricular activities include excursions, talks on political, economic, scientific and cultural topics, and social evenings. Cost $550 includes course, teaching materials, activities, excursions and full board college accommodation. Students may also take an examination at the end of the course, cost $20.

MARTIN-LUTHER-UNIVERSITÄT HALLE-WITTENBERG Sektion Germanistik und Kunstwissenschaften, Internationaler Hochschulferienkurs, Universitätsring 4, 4010 Halle (Saale) Tel Halle 83 23 48
Language, linguistics and literature course for Germanists, teachers, lecturers and translators, in Halle, near Luther's birthplace in Wittenberg. 3 weeks, July. As well as language tuition, course includes study of theory and methodology of literature and linguistics, foreign language teaching, and new developments in language and literature in the GDR. Extra-curricular activities include group discussions with public figures, authors reading from their own works, visits to the theatre, puppet theatre and cinema, and an excursion to Weimar. Excursions to Berlin, Dresden, Leipzig, Erfurt, Wittenberg, Eisleben and Naumburg also available at extra cost. Cost $325 includes course, teaching materials, activities, excursions and full board student residence accommodation. British Council scholarships available. *Apply by 31 May.*

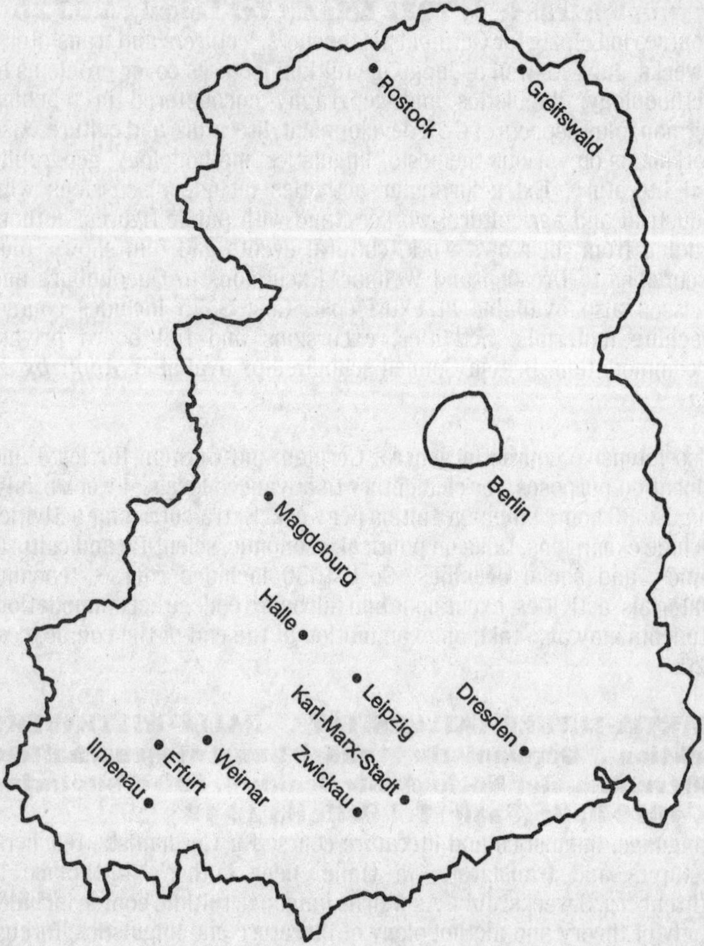

DEMOCRATIC REPUBLIC OF GERMANY

PÄDAGOGISCHE HOCHSCHULE ERNST SCHNELLER ZWICKAU Internationale Beziehungen, Scheffelstrasse 39, 9560 Zwickau
Language and literature course for students, teachers and lecturers of German, in Zwickau, birthplace of the composer Schumann. 3 weeks, July. As well as language tuition students choose a special programme from: Bertold Brecht – work and impact, development of GDR literature with emphasis on children's and juvenile books, German language and literature of the early Bourgeois period or trends and problems in the development of modern German. Extra-curricular activities include visits to the theatre, cinema, museums and concerts, musical and literary evenings, slide shows, group discussions with people from cultural and political life, and an excursion to the Erzgebirge mountains. Cost DM650 includes course, teaching materials, activities, excursion and full board student residence accommodation. British Council scholarships available. *Apply by 30 March.*

PÄDAGOGISCHE HOCHSCHULE DR THEODOR NEUBAUER ERFURT/MÜHLHAUSEN Abteilung Ausländerstudium, Nordhäuser Strasse 63, PSF 848, 5101 Erfurt Tel Erfurt 536 237
Courses in language, literature and culture for advanced level students, teachers and lecturers of German in Erfurt, a town over 1000 years old. 3 weeks, July and August. Basic courses cover language tuition and study, and GDR development, art, literature and culture. Students also choose a special programme from modern German language, GDR literature, practical phonetics or GDR society. Evening group discussions, cultural and social events organised. Excursions arranged to Weimar, Eisenach and Buchenwald. Cost DM580 includes course, activities, excursions and full board student residence accommodation. British Council scholarships available. *Apply by 30 March.*

TECHNISCHE HOCHSCHULE ILMENAU Internationaler Hochschulferienkurs für Germanistik, PSF 327, 6300 Ilmenau Tel Ilmenau 74 741
Language course for intermediate levels upwards in Ilmenau, a town to the north of the Thüringer Wald. Ages 18-30, individuals only. 3 weeks, July. 12 hours per week language tuition, plus lectures on themes from literature, culture, history, economics, politics and science in the GDR. Extra-curricular activities include visits to a hospital and kindergarten, conversation with writers and artists, film, theatre, concert and singing evenings, informal discussions on the development of socialism in the GDR, and excursions to Erfurt and Weimar. Excursions to Eisenach, Naumburg, Leipzig, Jena and Dresden also available at extra cost. Cost $280 includes course, teaching materials, activities, excursions and full

board student residence accommodation. British Council scholarships available. *Apply by end of May.*

TECHNISCHE UNIVERSITÄT DRESDEN Sektion Angewandte Sprachwissenschaft, Internationale Hochschulkurs für Deutsche Sprache und Germanistik, Mommsenstrasse 13, 8027 Dresden Tel Dresden 463 6015

Language and culture course for advanced levels in the historic city of Dresden. Ages 18 +, individuals only. 3 weeks, July. 25 hours per week. Maximum 12 per class. The emphasis is on scientific and technical German. Teaching methods involve the use of language laboratory and audiovisual facilities. Also lectures on artistic and literary development, internal and foreign policy and education in the GDR. Extra-curricular activities include theatre, film, concert and literary evenings, discussions with people from political, cultural and scientific spheres, visits to a kindergarten, art gallery and castle, plus excursions to Meissen, Freiburg and surrounding mountains. Cost $325 includes course, teaching materials, activities, excursions and half board student residence accommodation. No meals provided at weekends. *Apply by 31 May.*

TECHNISCHE UNIVERSITÄT KARL-MARX-STADT Sektion Fremdsprachen, Internationaler Hochschulferienkurs für Germanistik, Strasse der Nationen 62, PSF 964, 9010 Karl-Marx-Stadt Tel Karl-Marx-Stadt 5 61 42 47

Language, methodology and culture course in Karl-Marx-Stadt for teachers, lecturers and methodologists of German. 3 weeks, July. Course covers modern German language and usage, didactics and methodology of teaching German as a foreign language, plus literature, art and culture of the GDR. Extra-curricular activities include group discussions on themes from politics, economics and culture, visits to the theatre, cinema and concerts, social and literary evenings, and excursions to Dresden and Weimar. Cost $325. British Council scholarships available. *Apply by end of May.*

Also intensive course in general German and German for special purposes, for elementary to advanced levels. 4 weeks, September-October. 30 hours language tuition per week. Course intended for scientists, engineers, economists and those engaged in higher education, research, management, industry and commerce. Extra-curricular activities include excursions, talks on political, economic, scientific and cultural topics, and social evenings. Cost $550. Students may also take an examination at the end of the course, cost $20. All costs include course, teaching materials, activities, excursions and full board college accommodation.

TECHNISCHE UNIVERSITÄT OTTO VON GUERICKE MAGDEBURG Institut für Fremdsprachen, Internationaler Hochschulferienkurs für Germanistik, Boleslaw-Beirut-Platz 5, PSF 124, 3010 Magdeburg Tel Magdeburg 59 29 83
Language and culture course for advanced level students of German in Magdeburg, a modern industrial town on the Elbe. Ages 18 + . 3 weeks, July. 2-3 hours language tuition per day, average 10 per class. Teaching methods involve the use of language laboratory. Also lectures on the politics, art, literature and customs of today's GDR. Extra-curricular activities include group discussions with public figures, folklore evenings, conversations with writers and artists, visits to the theatre, concerts and art galleries, and excursions to Weimar, Berlin, Potsdam and the Harz region. Cost $280 includes course, teaching materials, activities, excursions and full board student residence accommodation. British Council scholarships available. *Apply by end of May.*

WILHELM-PIECK-UNIVERSITÄT ROSTOCK Internationaler Hochschulferienkurs für Germanistik, Kröpeliner Strasse 26, 2500 Rostock Tel Rostock 36 92 78
Language and literature course in Rostock, on the Baltic Coast, for students of German. 3 weeks, July. As well as language tuition, course includes study of linguistics and modern GDR literature, and lectures and discussions on GDR education, economy, ecology, philosophy, history and art. Extra-curricular activities include group discussions with authors, music, theatre, film and cabaret evenings, visits to a factory and kindergarten, and excursions to Schwerin, Güstrow, Bad Doberan and the Baltic island of Hiddensee. Cost $280 includes course, teaching materials, activities, excursions and full board student residence accommodation. *Apply by 31 May.*

WILHELM-PIECK-UNIVERSITÄT ROSTOCK Institut für Fremdsprachen, Richard-Wagner-Strasse 4, 2500 Rostock Tel Rostock 36 95 95
Intensive course in general German and German for medicine, for elementary to advanced levels. 4 weeks, July-August. 30 hours language tuition per week. Extra-curricular activities include excursions, talks on political, economic, scientific and cultural topics, and social evenings. Cost $550 includes course, teaching materials, activities, excursions and full board college accommodation. Students may also take an examination at the end of the course, cost $20.

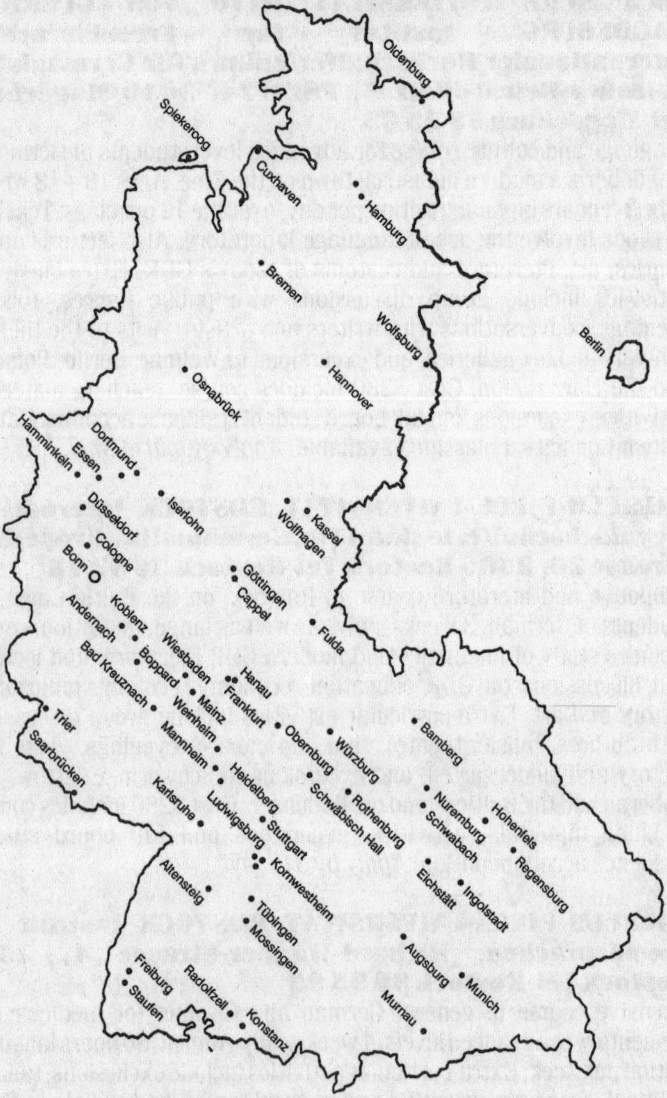

FEDERAL REPUBLIC OF GERMANY

COURSES IN THE FEDERAL REPUBLIC OF GERMANY

AKADEMIE KLAUSENHOF Klausenhofstrasse 100, 4236 Hamminkeln 2 Tel Hamminkeln 89328/89329

Language course for all levels in Hamminkeln, a village to the north east of Essen, near the Dutch border. Ages 16-50, individuals and groups. 4 or 8 weeks, February, April, June, August, October and December. 36 hours per week. Average 17 per class. Also special courses for teachers of German and for business German. Entrance examinations to German universities and the Deutsch als Fremdsprache certificate of the International Certificate Conference may be studied for. Video, language laboratory, computer facilities and large library for student use. Extra-curricular activities include trips to theatres, museums and exhibitions; excursions to Cologne, Bonn and other places of interest; supervised activities including pottery, handicrafts and films; and supervised sports such as tennis, table-tennis, football, volleyball, gymnastics and billiards. Cost DM980, 4 weeks includes course, all activities and full board residential accommodation. Textbooks DM50 per course. Recognised by the Ministry of Culture of North Rhine-Westphalia and supported by the Catholic Church.

BENEDICT SCHOOL BERLIN Kurfürstendamm 229, 1000 Berlin 15 Tel Berlin 8826245

Language courses for all levels. Ages 12+, individuals and small groups. 1+ weeks, starting monthly. 15 or 30 hours per week. Maximum 10 per class. Cost from DM195, 15 hours or DM390, 30 hours. Also 1:1 courses of up to 50 hours per week including lunch with a teacher. Also classes for special business or technical needs. Textbooks from DM20; free to 1:1 students. No extra-curricular programme, but tourist packages for minimum of 7 can be arranged, including 2 sightseeing tours, a history lecture, and opera/theatre trip or meeting with Berliners. Accommodation arranged in families from DM245, or pensions/hotels from DM420, per week. Travel can be arranged.
Benedict Schools of Languages is an international organisation with 69 language schools in 7 countries. Addresses of other schools in the Federal Republic include:

Ehrenfeldstrasse 30-34, 4630 Bochum Tel Bochum 33 02 00

Gürzenichstrasse 17, 5000 Cologne 1 Tel Cologne 21 22 03

Graf-Adolfstrasse 73, 4000 Düsseldorf 1 Tel Düsseldorf 37 11 35

Kettwiger Strasse 5, 4300 Essen Tel Essen 22 13 93

Georgstrasse 22, 3000 Hanover Tel Hanover 32 71 29

Cusanusstrasse 9, 5400 Koblenz Tel Koblenz 40 86 90

Bayerstrasse 21, 8000 Munich Tel Munich 55 56 45

Goethering 16, 4500 Osnabrück Tel Osnabrück 2 21 11

Kaiserstrasse 15, 6600 Saarbrücken 3 Tel Saarbrücken 3 72 24

Marienstrasse 9, 7000 Stuttgart 1 Tel Stuttgart 60 83 73

Wilhelmstrasse 12, 6200 Wiesbaden Tel Wiesbaden 30 67 22

BERLITZ Marienplatz 18/19, Munich 2 Tel Munich 268036
Language courses for all levels in Munich, capital of Bavaria, by the Berlitz method. Berlitz club courses take place in a social atmosphere, with 20 or 40 hours classes per week. 6-8 per class. Special crash courses are more intensive, with 20 or 40 hours per week. 4 per class. Also 1:1 tuition, and courses in business German, monthly, all year. Approx cost of 160 lessons in a group of 8, £570. Assistance given in finding accommodation.

The Berlitz Schools of Languages is an international organisation with over 200 language centres in 24 countries. Addresses of other schools in the Federal Republic include:

Grottenau 6, 8900 Augsburg Tel Augsburg 3 61 51/2

Kurfürstendamm 74, 1000 Berlin Wilmersdorf Tel Berlin 3 23 90 47/48

Bongardstrasse 21, 4630 Bochum Tel Bochum 6 01 08/9

Gerhard-v-Are-Strasse 4-6, 5300 Bonn Tel Bonn 5 50 05

Obernstrasse 38-42, 2800 Bremen Tel Bremen 32 15 07/8

Schildergasse 72-7, 5000 Cologne Tel Cologne 23 06 19

Hüttenstrasse 4, 4000 Düsseldorf Tel Düsseldorf 37 60 66/7

Kennedyplatz 6, 4300 Essen Tel Essen 22 21 57/8

Kaiserstrasse 66, 6000 Frankfurt/Main 2 Tel Frankfurt 27 10 00 44

Friedrichring 37, 7800 Freiburg/Breisgau Tel Freiburg 27 30 74/5

Kurze Mühren 2, 2000 Hamburg Tel Hamburg 32 70 24/5

Ständehausstrasse 2-3, 3000 Hanover Tel Hanover 32 76 06/7

07, 13 An den Planken, 6800 Mannheim Tel Mannheim 2 19 95/6

Am Plärrer 29, Nuremburg Tel Nuremburg 26 50 88/9

Kaiserstrasse 25, 6600 Saarbrücken Tel Saarbrücken 3 05 18/9

Kreigsbergstrasse 28, 7000 Stuttgart Tel Stuttgart 22 10 94

Adolfstrasse 4, 6200 Wiesbaden Tel Wiesbaden 37 10 61/2

CARL DUISBERG CENTRES Referat 13, Hansaring 49-51, 5000 Cologne 1 Tel Cologne 1626240

Language courses for all levels in Cologne, Dortmund, Munich, Radolfzell and Saarbrücken. Ages 18+, individuals and groups. 4 weeks, starting beginning of each month. 28 hours per week. Average 15 per class. Also courses for foreign managers of German companies, teachers of German, and courses for specialist technical fields. Video facilities and language laboratory. Extra-curricular activities include excursions, social events, discussion groups, films, games and dances. Cost DM1050 per month includes course, teaching materials and activities. Full board or bed and breakfast accommodation can be arranged in families, hotels or boarding schools; cost from DM590 per month. Some centres have self-service restaurants. Examinations recognised by German universities.

COLLEGIUM PALATINUM Hölderlinweg 8, 6900 Heidelberg Tel Heidelberg 46289

Language courses for all levels in the historical town of Heidelberg. Ages 17+, individuals only. Intensive courses, 8 weeks, all year, 24 hours per week. Maximum 14 per class. Cost from DM2100. Summer courses, 4 weeks, July-August, 25 hours per week. Maximum 20 per class. Cost DM1300. Also 1:1 lessons throughout the year and tailor-made courses for groups, ages 14+. Audio-visual facilities. Textbooks and materials from DM40 per 8 week course. Social programme of parties, excursions and films. Accommodation can be arranged in student residences, private rooms, hotels or in families, from DM450, 4 weeks or DM730, 8 weeks. Also summer junior programme for ages 12-16. 3 weeks, July. 15 hours language tuition, optional tennis coaching, table-tennis, volleyball, swimming and gymnastics, and excursions and trips around Heidelberg. Cost from DM2100 includes full board college accommodation. Books DM30 and optional tennis coaching DM200.

Applications in the UK can be made to Cultural and Educational Services Abroad, 44 Sydney Street, Brighton, Sussex BN1 4EP Tel Brighton 683304.

DEUTSCH IN DEUTSCHLAND GMBH Hauptstrasse 26, 8751 Stockstadt/Main Tel Stockstadt 20090
Language courses for all levels in 27 language schools throughout the Federal Republic.

Standard summer courses in Aschaffenburg, Bad Kreuznach, Bamberg, Hammersbach, Hanau, Fulda, Ingoldstadt, Obernburg, Oldenburg, Schwabach, and Siegen for all levels. Ages 10-20, individuals and groups. 2-9 weeks, generally 3, June-August. 16 x 45 minute lessons per week, maximum 15 per class. Cost from DM955, 2 weeks, includes course, teaching materials, one full day excursion per week, full board family accommodation, insurance and supervised sports activities.

Language courses for all levels in Augsburg, home to Mozart and Brecht, in Cologne, ancient city famous for its carnival and Gothic cathedral, in Mainz, a 2,000 year-old city on the banks of the Rhine, and in Wiesbaden, seat of the Hessian State Parliament. Ages 16-25, individuals and groups. 2-8 weeks, July-August. 20 x 45 minute lessons per week, maximum 15 per class. Excursions and evening social programme arranged, plus 2 afternoons per week supervised activities, including swimming, riding, tennis, bowling, mini golf, table tennis and rowing. Cost from DM1035, 2 weeks, includes course, enrolment fee, teaching materials, excursions, supervised activities, full board family accommodation and insurance.

Long-term courses in Wiesbaden for all levels; beginners on request. Ages 18 + , individuals and groups. 2-6 months, all year. 20 x 45 minute lessons per week, maximum 15 per class. Cost DM320 per month includes course and liability insurance. Textbooks approx DM25; enrolment fee DM75. Accommodation arranged with families, cost DM210 half board, DM260 full board, per week. Also long-term courses for all levels ig Mainz; beginners on request. Ages 17-25, individuals and groups. 1-6 months, all year. 25 x 45 minute lessons per week, maximum 15 per class. Teaching involves the use of language laboratory. Cost

DM420 per month includes course and liability insurance. Textbooks approx DM25; enrolment fee DM75. Accommodation arranged with families; cost DM210 per week, half board, DM260 per week, full board.

Courses for all levels in Hamburg, the largest city in the Federal Republic. Ages 18 +, individuals and groups. 1-6 months, all year. 15 or 30 x 45 minute lessons per week, maximum 15 per class. Teaching involves use of language laboratory. Cost per month DM300, 15 lessons per week, or DM600, 30 lessons per week, includes tuition and liability insurance. Textbooks approx DM25; enrolment fee DM75. Accommodation arranged with families; cost DM220 bed and breakfast, DM270 half board, per week.

Language courses in Hanover, the trade fair city, and in Würzburg, centre of the wine-growing industry, for all levels. Ages 17 +, individuals and groups. 2-8 weeks, July and August. 25 x 45 minute lessons per week, maximum 15 per class. 1 excursion and 2 afternoon programmes arranged per week. Sports available include swimming, tennis, sailing, surfing, rowing, bowling, mini golf, table tennis, badminton and squash. Cost from DM1035 for 2 weeks includes course, enrolment fee, teaching materials, excursions, spare-time programme, half board family accommodation, full board at weekends, and insurance. Also long-term courses for all levels; beginners on request. Ages 17 +, individuals and groups. 2-6 months. 25 x 45 minute lessons per week, maximum 15 per class. Cultural programme arranged each week. Cost DM850 per month includes course and liability insurance. Textbooks approx DM25, enrolment fee DM75. Accommodation arranged with families, half board Monday-Friday, full board at weekends; cost DM920 per month.

Language courses for all levels in Mannheim, on the Rhine. Ages 16-18, individuals and groups. 3 weeks, July. 16 x 45 minute lessons per week, maximum 15 per class. 1 excursion and 3-4 afternoon programmes arranged per week. Cost DM1375 includes course, teaching materials, excursions, activities, full board family accommodation and insurance.

Language courses in Munich for all levels. Ages 18 +, individuals and groups. 2-8 weeks, July and August. 30 lessons per week, maximum 12 per class. Cost from DM1035, 2 weeks, includes course, teaching materials, bed and breakfast family accommodation, half board at weekends, and insurance. Excursions can be booked. Sports available include swimming, tennis, bowling, minigolf, table-tennis, skating and squash. Also courses for students and young business people. All levels; beginners on request. Ages 18 +, individuals and groups. 2 + weeks, all year. 30 lessons per week, maximum 8 per class. Language laboratory and video system. Cost DM380 per week includes course and teaching materials. Enrolment fee DM75. Family bed and breakfast accommodation from DM190 per week; other accommodation available.

Language courses for all levels in Nuremburg, birthplace of Albrecht Dürer. Ages 16-20, individuals and groups. 2-8 weeks, June-August. 20 lessons per week, maximum 15 per class. Excursions and evening social programme arranged, plus 2 afternoons per week supervised activities, including swimming, bowling, mini golf and skating. Cost from DM1035, 2 weeks, includes course, enrolment fee, teaching materials, excursions, supervised activities, full board family accommodation and insurance.

Also combined language/sports courses in Aschaffenburg, Bamberg, Fulda, Oldenburg and Siegen for all levels. 15 x 45 minute lessons of language tuition plus 6 hours per week sports tuition. Cost from DM955, 2 weeks, plus sports tuition fees, per week: tennis DM80, riding DM110, sailing and windsurfing DM130. Those playing tennis or riding should have their own kit. Sports insurance not included.

Language courses for executives in Frankfurt, birthplace of Goethe. All levels. Ages 25 +, individuals and groups. 2 weeks, all year. 30 x 45 minute lessons per week, maximum 10 per class. German for business, German for conferences and negotiations, banking German and German language and culture courses. Teaching involves the use of language laboratory and audio-visual equipment, with strong emphasis on oral practice. Cost from DM888 per week includes course, teaching materials, enrolment fee and insurance. Family bed and breakfast accommodation from DM290 per week; half board and hotel accommodation also available.

Also individual tuition for all levels, in Cologne, Frankfurt, Hamburg, Hanover, Munich and Wiesbaden. Ages 18 +. 1 + weeks, all year. 4-12 x 45 minute lessons per day. Cost from DM1020 plus DM75 enrolment fee. Bed and breakfast family accommodation from DM190.

Insurance can be arranged. Approved by the Ministry of Education. **PH**
1:1 tuition can be arranged with families.

Applications in the UK can be made through Euro-Academy, 77A George Street, Croydon, Surrey Tel 01-681 2905. Cost from £290 per week; individual tuition from £365 per week. Enrolment fee £28. Bed and breakfast family accommodation from £115 per week.

DEUTSCHKURS FÜR AUSLÄNDER BEI DER UNIVERSITÄT MÜNCHEN Adelheidstrasse 13, 8000 Munich Tel Munich 271 26 42

Language course for beginners and advanced levels in Munich. Applicants should have qualification equivalent to Abitur. 7 weeks, July-August and August-October. 20/25 hours per week. Average 20 per class. Cost DM670, 20 hours, DM850, 25 hours, plus DM40 registration fee. Also evening courses for beginners and advanced levels. 10 weeks, August-October. 4, 6, 10 or 13 hours per week. Average 17 per class. Cost DM205-DM670 depending on hours. No accommodation provided; average cost DM950 per month.

EF EUROPÄISCHE FERIENSCHULE GMBH Annagasse 3, 1010 Vienna, Austria Tel Vienna 512 14 69

Language courses for all levels in Munich. Ages 16 +, individuals and groups. Main courses 2-50 weeks, all year. 24 lessons per week. Average 13 per class. Cost AS9900, 2 weeks. Also intensive courses 2-50 weeks, all year. 30 lessons per week. Average 12 per class. Cost AS11900, 2 weeks. Summer courses 2-12 weeks, May-August. 20 lessons per week. Average 14 per class. Cost AS8900, 2 weeks. Courses also available for students wishing to take the EF examinations, the Kleines Deutsches Sprachdiplom for university entrance, or the Grosses Deutsches Sprachdiplom. 8-12 weeks; examinations take place in April, May and November. 30 lessons per week. Cost from AS47600, 8 weeks. Teaching involves the use of language laboratory and audio-visual materials. Also opportunity to learn business German. Costs include course, teaching materials, map and guided tour, membership and discount cards, preparatory language practice cassette, personal care throughout the course and full board family accommodation. Extra-curricular activities also arranged.

EUROCENTRES Sedanstrasse 31-33, 5000 Cologne 1 Tel Cologne 720831

Language courses for all levels in Cologne. Ages 16 +, individuals and groups. Intensive courses, 2, 3, 4, or 10-12 weeks, all year. 25 hours per week. Maximum 12 per class. Holiday courses, 4 weeks, July-August. 20-25 hours per week. Also refresher course for teachers, 3 weeks, July. 25 hours per week. Examinations of the Goethe-Institut and the Cologne Chamber of Commerce may be taken during certain courses. Language laboratory, video facilities and computer-assisted learning available; also multi-media self-study centre. 5 hours per week of special options include the land, people, museums and churches of Cologne, conversational exchange with local people, German cinema, and creative computing; and translation practice for the Chamber of Commerce examination on long courses. Extra-curricular events include excursions, film shows, parties and discos. Tandem system, whereby students are linked with local people during their stay. Costs from £363, 2 weeks intensive course, and £705, 4 weeks holiday course, include course, 1 textbook, teaching materials and half board family accommodation. Students receive an information pack to help them during stay. *Some scholarships available.* **PH** accommodation available for wheelchair students

Applications in the UK can be made to Eurocentres, 21 Meadowcourt Road, London SE3 Tel 01-318 5633, or Cultural and Educational Services Abroad, 44 Sydney Street, Brighton, Sussex, BN1 4EP Tel Brighton 683304. Cost from £491 includes 2 week course, half board family accommodation, insurance and return flight from London.

EUROPA COLLEG KASSEL EV Wilhelmshöher Allee 19, 3500 Kassel Tel Kassel 77 6788
Language courses for all levels in Kassel, famous for its art gallery. Ages 16+, individuals and groups. 2 weeks, all year, or 3 weeks, June-September. Also 11 week courses, starting January, April and September. 25 hours per week. Average 13 per class. Teaching includes the use of language laboratory and audio-visual facilities. Extra-curricular activities include excursions to Marburg, Göttingen, Fulda and Hanover, sightseeing tour of Kassel, visits to theatre, art galleries and local places of interest, plus sports, filmshows and folk singing. Cost DM500 per week includes course, teaching materials, excursions, activities and full board family accommodation. Hotel accommodation also available. Cost DM250 per week, course only. Also 4 week summer seminars on German literature, 2 week advanced courses for teachers and university students of German and 2 week courses in German for business and academic purposes.

EUROPA-SPRACHCLUB GMBH Stuttgarter Strasse 161, 7014 Kornwestheim Tel Kornwestheim 6028
Language courses for all levels in 10 main centres and many other small towns in the centre and south.

Language courses for all levels in Augsburg. Ages 14+, individuals and groups. 2, 3, 4, 8 and 12 weeks, all year. 20-25 x 45 minute lessons per week. Maximum 16 per class. Introduction to modern literature for advanced classes. Weekly excursions to local places of interest. Extra-curricular activities include soccer, swimming, bowling, table tennis and mini golf. Riding and tennis also available at extra cost. Cost from DM1010, 2 weeks, includes course, excursions, activities, full board family accommodation and insurance. Also 1:1 and small group tuition for adults. Cost from DM15 per lesson.

Language courses for all levels in Cologne. Ages 16 +, individuals and groups. 2, 3, 4, 11 and 12 weeks, all year. 20-30 lessons per week. Maximum 16 per class, or 10 per classs during 2 week courses. Cost from DM1095. Optional excursions arranged to Amsterdam, the German Democratic Republic and Cologne countryside. Students on longer courses can take the Goethe-Institut and Cologne Chamber of Commerce and Industry examinations. Also refresher course for teachers of German. 3 weeks, July. 30 lessons per week. Maximum 16 per class. Cost DM1640. All costs include course, teaching materials, insurance and half board family accommodation.

Language courses in Düsseldorf, capital of North-Rhine-Westphalia, for advanced beginners to upper intermediate level. Ages 18 +, individuals and groups. 2, 3, 4, 8 and 12 weeks, all year. 20 lessons per week. Maximum 15 per class. Cost from DM1000, 2 weeks. All costs include course, teaching materials, full board family accommodation and insurance. Holiday courses include excursions such as a tour of Düsseldorf and a trip on the Rhine.

Holiday course in German in everyday life for those with at least 2 years' school German, in Munich. Ages 17 +, individuals and groups. 2 or 4 weeks, July-August. 20 x 40 minute lessons per week. Maximum 12 per class. Emphasis is placed on practical use of the language. Cost DM1530, 2 weeks or DM3050, 4 weeks.
Intensive course in business German for those with some knowledge of the language. Ages 18 +, individuals and groups. 2 weeks, all year. 40 x 40 minute lessons per week. Maximum 6 per class. Tuition includes simulating business situations, making phone calls, sales talks, conferences and negotiations. Cost DM3240. Special course in German for secretaries, for those with some knowledge of the language. Ages 18 +, individuals and groups. 2 weeks, April and July. 30 x 40 minute lessons per week. Maximum 10 per class. Tuition includes essentials for fairs, exhibitions and conferences, business letters and making phone calls. Cost DM1960. All costs include course, teaching materials, tour of Munich, cultural visit, lectures and discussions relating to course, bed and breakfast family accommodation and insurance. Also individual tuition for all levels, ages 18 +. 2-4 weeks, all year. Cost from DM3290, 2 weeks, includes tuition, teaching materials, bed and breakfast family accommodation and insurance.

Language courses for those with at least 2 years' school German, in Stuttgart, capital of Baden-Wurttemburg. Ages 15-19, individuals and groups. 3 weeks, June and JUly. 20 x 45 minute lessons per week. Maximum 15 per class. Introduction to modern literature for advanced students. Extra-curricular activities organised on 7 afternoons include visits and tours to places of interest. Cost DM1520 includes course, teaching materials, supervised activities, full board family accommodation, transfers and insurance. Optional tennis course available.

Also course in Tubingen, for those with at least 1 year's school German. Ages 16+ or 14+ during July and August. 2, 3, 4, 8 or 12 weeks, all year. 26 x 45 minute lessons per week. Maximum 16 per class. Language laboratory available. Cost from DM1280, 2 weeks, includes course, teaching materials, full board family accommodation and insurance. Alternative school accommodation available. City tour, excursion, table tennis and film evening also include for July/August courses. Also special 8 day Easter course for A level students, cost DM1250.

Course at Todtmoos for those with minimum 2 years' German. Residential centre specially designed to enable young Europeans to meet and mix. Ages 14-18. 3 weeks, June-August. 15 x 45 minute lessons per week. Maximum 14 per class. Leisure programme includes excursion, discos, barbeques, swimming, table tennis, museum visit, video and workshop evenings. Cost DM1500 includes course, teaching materials, leisure programme, full board school accommodation and insurance. Special interest courses in tennis, photo/video, windsurfing and canoeing also available, DM250, 15 hours.

Also 1:1 German at a teacher's home programme in towns and villages in the Düsseldorf, Karlsruhe, Regensburg and Stuttgart areas. Reasonable knowledge of German required. 15, 20 or 25 x 45 minute lessons per week. Student lives with the teacher and becomes part of the family, with total immersion in the language. Cost per week DM1200, 15 lessons, DM1350, 20 lessons and DM1500, 25 lessons.

EUROPA-SPRACHCLUB GMBH Stuttgarter Strasse 161, 7014 Kornwestheim Tel Kornwestheim 6028

HEIDELBERGER FREMDSPRACHEN-INSTITUT Wilhelm-Blum-Strasse 12/14, 6900 Heidelberg Tel Heidelberg 43629

Apply to either of the above for language courses for all levels in Heidelberg; beginners on request. Ages 16+, or 15+ during July/August; individuals and groups. 3/4 weeks, all year, 2 weeks, December. 20 hours per week. Maximum 18 per class. Advanced level courses include introduction to modern literature. Courses in July/August also include 2 day and 5 afternoon excursions to local places of interest. Cost from DM990 includes half board family accommodation, or from DM305, course only. Textbooks included.

EUROPA-SPRACHCLUB GMBH Stuttgarter Strasse 161, 7014 Kornwestheim Tel Kornwestheim 6028

INTERNATIONAL HOUSE Lehrgemeinschaft für Sprachen, Bismarckallee 4, 7800 Freiburg/Breisgau Tel Freiburg 34751

Apply to either of the above for language courses for all levels in Freiburg, near the Black Forest. Ages 18+, individuals and groups. 2, 3, 4, 8 and 12 weeks, all year. 25 lessons per week. Maximum 7 per class. Introduction to modern literature for advanced classes. Cost from DM1700, 2 weeks, includes course, teaching materials, half board family accommodation, transfer from station and insurance. Holiday language courses for ages 10-13 and 14-21. 2-4 weeks, starting March, June and July. 15 lessons per week. Maximum 15 per class. Extra-curricular activities include tours of the city, excursions, sports and cultural programmes. Cost from DM1160, 2 weeks, includes course, teaching materials, activities, full board family or guest house accommodation, transfer from station and insurance. Supervision around the clock for lower age group. Also individual courses for all levels. 2-3 weeks, all year. Ages 18+. 25 or 30 lessons per week, plus 5 hours per week guided self-access to language laboratory and video sessions. Cost from DM4700, 2 weeks, includes course, teaching materials, half board family accommodation, transfer from station and insurance.

Applications in the UK can be made to Kate Naameh, Marketing Director, International House, 106 Piccadilly, London W1V 9FL Tel 01-491 2598, or through any International House school.

FERIENKURSE FÜR AUSLÄNDER FRANK KARS Postfach 1311, 7770 Überlingen-Bodensee Tel Überlingen 61960

Summer language and literature courses for all levels at Überlingen on Lake Constance. Ages 16+, individuals and groups. 1 month, July and August or 3 weeks, September. 18 hours per week. Cost DM450, July and August, DM400, September, plus DM100 registration fee. Textbooks DM30. Language classes include folk singing. Excursions arranged around Überlingen, to the city of Konstanz, Reichenau Island, Bernau monastery and other local sights; transport costs only. Accommodation can be arranged with local families for DM20 per day bed and breakfast or DM40 per day full board, or in hotels and guesthouses.

FREMDSPRACHEN-INSTITUT COLON Colonnaden 47, 2000 Hamburg 36, Tel Hamburg 345850
Language courses for all levels at private language school in Hamburg. Ages 16+, individuals and groups. Courses can be of any length, starting throughout the year. 10 or 25 hours per week, maximum 12 per class. 1:1 courses, plus combined group and 1:1 courses also available. Specialised language needs catered for. Excursions to Lübeck, Bremen, Berlin and the Baltic and North Sea coasts can be arranged. Cost from DM1600, 10 hours tuition, and DM1900, 25 hours tuition, per month includes course and half board family accommodation. Hotel/apartment accommodation also available. Textbooks not included. Approved by the Hamburg School Board.

GOETHE-INSTITUT Zentralverwaltung, Postfach 2010 09, Lenbachplatz 3, 8000 Munich 2 Tel Munich 59990
German courses offered at 16 branches throughout the Federal Republic, and at 7 summer centres. These include compact courses, refresher courses, language, games and sport courses for young people, and language, culture and leisure courses for adults. Also special courses in German for business, technology and medicine, seminars for teachers of German abroad, and 1:1 courses. Courses for school or other special interest groups arranged on request.

Compact courses for all levels in Berlin, Bonn, Boppard, Bremen, Düsseldorf, Frankfurt, Freiburg, Göttingen, Iserlohn, Mannheim, Munich, Murnau, Prien, Rothenburg, Schwäbisch Hall and Staufen. Ages 18+, individuals and groups. 8 weeks, January, February, March, April, May, June, July, August, October and November, depending on centre. 24 x 45 minute lessons per week. Average 15-22 per class. Cost DM2060, January-June or DM2160, July-December, includes course, textbooks and materials. Goethe-Institut examinations may be taken. Also at Freiburg, Göttingen and Mannheim, Mittelstufenprüfung, approved by the universities.

Refresher courses for all levels except complete beginners in Boppard, Ludwigsburg, Prien and Rothenburg. 4 weeks, all year, depending on centre. Cost DM1150, January-June or DM1210, July-December, including textbooks.

Centres are equipped with language laboratories, audio-visual facilities and other modern aids. Courses include study visits to urban and rural areas prepared and evaluated during class time, lectures about Germany, cultural activities, films, parties and one full day excursion per course. Sports facilities also available. In addition students are expected to spend at least 12 hours per week in private study.

Family/student hostel accommodation from DM300, 4 weeks. Meals available from DM500, 4 weeks, for breakfast, lunch and dinner. Can also arrange cheap health insurance and advise students on all aspects of their stay.

Language, games and sport courses for all levels at Marienau in North Germany and Mossingen near Stuttgart; for all levels except beginners at Altensteig in the Black Forest, Oberurff near Kassel, and Marquartstein and Neubeuern in Bavaria. Ages 14-18, individuals and groups. 3 weeks, June-August. 24 x 45 minute lessons per week. Average 15-22 per class. Extensive supervised leisure programme includes excursions, barbecues, plays, films, discos, opportunities to meet German families, artistic and sporting activities. Cost DM2095 includes course, leisure programme, textbooks and teaching materials, full board school accommodation and health and accident insurance.

Language, culture and leisure courses for all levels except complete beginners in Staufen. 4 weeks, all year. 90 x 45 minutes lessons. Maximum 12 per class. Programme of excursions, sightseeing, theatre visits, wine tasting and other cultural events. Cost DM3350 includes course, programme, textbooks and teaching materials, and bed and breakfast accommodation in the Institut's guest house.

Also arrange various courses for teachers and lecturers of German. Limited number of scholarships available from Goethe-Instituts in the UK and other countries. **PH** Mannheim

Applications in the UK can be made through Goethe-Instituts in London, Glasgow, Manchester and York, see below.

HOME LANGUAGE LESSONS LTD 12-18 Royal Crescent, Ramsgate, Kent CT11 9PE Tel Thanet 590300
1:1 German lessons for all levels in the Stuttgart, Frankfurt and Black Forest regions. No age limits. Lessons take place in the home of the teacher, where the student also stays, with total immersion in German and no contact with other students. Choice of 15, 20 or 25 hours of classes per week; cost DM1350, DM1500 or DM1650 respectively. Also weekend crash courses, 5 hours per day, cost DM440. Courses may be taken together by 2 people; 25% reduction if from the same family. Five star immersion course for business and professional people. 25 hours per week language tuition and superior accommodation. Cost DM2250 per week. Given notice, it is possible to place students with teachers who share their interests, and on 5 star immersion courses to arrange suitable contacts in the local community. Full board accommodation included in all costs. **PH**

HOURMONT LTD Brunel House, Newfoundland Road, Bristol BS2 9LU Tel Bristol 426961

Young Reporter language courses in Andernach and Kamp Bornhofen, on the banks of the Rhine near Koblenz. All levels except beginners. School groups only. 6+ days, all year. Hours vary depending on requirements. Pupils work in teams of 5 to research a chosen theme. Time is spent interviewing, conducting surveys, observing, recording information, sketching and taking photographs. Material is then reviewed and condensed into a report which reflects aims and linguistic ability of the team. Completed reports can be presented to the rest of the group or back at school. Cost from £149. Also Hi-Fi German course for all levels in Kamp Bornhofen and nearby Bad Salzig. School groups only; 5+ days. Pupils are provided with personal hi-fi systems, pre-recorded cassettes and booklets on a selection of topics at varying levels. Cost from £120. Costs are based on 35 pupils and include return coach travel, collective passport, travel insurance, necessary recording/ photographic equipment, service of resident courier, teachers' notes and full board guesthouse accommodation.

HUMBOLDT-INSTITUT Schloss Ratzenried, 7989 Argenbühl 3 Tel 07522-3041

Language courses in Hohenfels, Meersburg, Ratzenried and Spetzgart, all in the vicinity of Lake Constance, in Cappel, and on Spiekeroog, one of the East Frisian islands.

Junior courses for levels up to intermediate in Hohenfels Castle, part of Salem, Germany's famous boarding school. Ages 10-14. 2/4 weeks, July-August. 20 hours per week. Average 10 per class. 24 hour supervision. Extra-curricular activities include basketball, volleyball, football, gymnastics, jogging, swimming, pottery, painting, music, dance and theatre. Excursions include visit to a nearby holiday park. Cost DM1380, 2 weeks or DM2760, 4 weeks includes course, teaching materials, excursions, activities and full board school accommodation.

Main courses for levels up to intermediate held in the Baroque castle in Meersburg. Ages 15+. 3, 4, 7, 8 and 11 weeks, June-August. 25 hours per week. Average 10 per class. Lessons are usually in the morning, with time available for leisure activities, including films, hiking, sailing, windsurfing, swimming, waterskiing, jogging, tennis and mini golf. Excursions arranged to places of interest, and to exhibitions and concerts. Cost from DM2010, 3 weeks, includes course, teaching materials, activities, excursions and full board family accommodation. Half board accommodation also available; inclusive cost from DM1740, 3 weeks.

Intensive course for levels up to intermediate in Spetzgart. Ages 15+. 3 weeks, July-August. 30 hours per week. Average 10 per class. Facilities for tennis, squash and other sports; excursions arranged to local places of interest, plus visits to the theatre, cinema, exhibitions and concerts. Cost DM2070 includes course, teaching materials, excursions, activities and full board school accommodation.

Intensive courses for all levels in Ratzenried Castle. Ages 16+, or 18+, June-August. 3+ weeks, all year. 30 hours per week. Average 10 per class. Sports facilities available locally include sailing, hiking, cycling, volleyball, basketball, badminton, tennis, table-tennis, squash and swimming. Excursions include visits to the castles of Neuschwanstein and Linderhof, and trips to the mountains for skiing, November-April. Cost DM640 per week includes course, teaching materials, excursions, some activities and full board school or family accommodation. Surcharge of DM50, June-August. Also 1:1 and 1:2 tuition.

Language courses for levels up to intermediate in Cappel, a part of the old university city of Marburg. Ages 15+. 3 weeks, July-August. 25 hours per week. Average 10 per class. Lessons are usually in the morning, with time available for leisure activities, including swimming, rowing, tennis, use of the school's gym, plus visits to exhibitions, theatre and concerts. Excursions include trips to Frankfurt and Koblenz. Cost DM2040 includes course, teaching materials, excursions and full board school accommodation. Students can continue studies here after course in Spiekeroog. Accompanied transfer fee DM80.

Language course on Spiekeroog, in the North Sea near Bremen, for levels up to intermediate. Ages 15+. 4 weeks, July. 25 hours per week. Average 10 per class. Lessons are usually in the morning, with time available for leisure activities, including swimming, surfing or sailing in the North Sea, tennis, riding, hiking, ball games and crafts. Excursions include trips to neighbouring islands and to Emden on the mainland. Cost DM2760 includes course, teaching materials, excursions and full board school accommodation. Students can continue studies at Cappel, see above. Accompanied transfer fee DM80.

INLINGUA SPRACHSCHULE Spitaler Strasse 1, 2 Hamburg 1 Tel Hamburg 33 08 34
Language courses in Hamburg for all levels. Ages 16+, individuals and groups. 2+ weeks, all year, starting monthly for beginners and weekly for other levels. 15 x 45 minute lessons per week. Maximum 9 per class. Cost DM125 per week, course only. 1:1 tuition also available. Accommodation can be arranged in families, pensions or hotels.

INLINGUA SPRACHSCHULE Tal 73, 8000 Munich 2 Tel Munich 220354

Language courses for all levels in the heart of Munich. Ages 16+, individuals and groups. 2+ weeks, all year. 20 or 34 x 45 minute lessons per week. Maximum 15 per class. Also courses in business, technical German, and 1:1 tuition. Teaching involves the use of audio-visual facilities and interactive computer-video programme. Cost DM990, 20 lessons per week, DM1150, 34 lessons per week, 2 weeks, includes course, teaching materials, textbooks and bed and breakfast family accommodation. Half board on request. Course only DM470, 20 lessons per week, and DM645, 34 lessons per week, 2 weeks. Approved by the Government of Bavaria.

INLINGUA SPRACHSCHULE Rosgartenstrasse 29-31, 775 Konstanz Tel Konstanz 2 73 52

Language courses for all levels in Konstanz. Ages 16+, individuals and groups. 4+ weeks, January, April, June, September-October and by request. 25 x 45 minute lessons per week. Maximum 10 per class. Cost from DM135 per week. Half board family accommodation available at extra cost. Also holiday courses for all levels. Ages 14+, individuals and groups. 2+ weeks, April-August. 20 x 45 minute lessons per week. Maximum 10 per class. Cost DM220 per week. Half board student hostel accommodation available at extra cost. 1:1 tuition also available.

INLINGUA SPRACHSCHULE Poststrasse 42-44, 6900 Heidelberg Tel Heidelberg 29076

Language courses for all levels in Heidelberg. Ages 16+, individuals and groups. 4+ weeks, all year. 20 x 45 minute lessons per week, maximum 10 per class. Cost DM387 per week includes course, textbook, and bed and breakfast family accommodation; DM218, course only. Also holiday courses for all levels except beginners. Ages 16+, individuals and groups. 4+ weeks, June-August. 20 x 45 minute lessons per week, average 8 per class. Cost DM538 per week includes course, textbook, various excursions and activities, and bed and breakfast family accommodation. 1:1 tuition also available.

INSTITUT FÜR LERNFÖRDERUNG, Schumannstrasse 32, 6000 Frankfurt am Main Tel Frankfurt 749795

Summer course for all levels at a private house in Frankfurt. Ages 15-17. 3 weeks, August. 20 hours per week, maximum 10 per class. Computer-assisted learning. Some textbooks and materials provided. Cost DM1600 includes course, full board family accommodation, a tour of Frankfurt, a day river trip, sports and other activities and insurance. Course tutor specialised in dealing with dyslexic students. Also arrange 1:1 courses for business executives in association with the University of Frankfurt.

Applications can also be made through Anne Von Gleichen, Von Gleichen Travel, Goethestrasse 23, 6 Stock, 6000 Frankfurt am Main 1 Tel Frankfurt 293733/284253.

INTERNATIONAL HOUSE MUNICH Weissenburger Platz 8, 8000 Munich 80 Tel Munich 488446

Language courses for all levels in Munich. Ages 17+, individuals and groups. 2, 4, 6, 8 or 10 weeks, April-August. 20 hours per week, maximum 12 per class. Courses arranged for groups with specialised needs. Extra-curricular activities include invited speakers, seminars, exhibitions at the school, theatre trips and tours of Munich and the surrounding area guided by teachers. Students may also take part in events at Munich University and the Goethe Institut. Cost DM550 per week includes course, bed and breakfast family accommodation, lunch at the school, excursion and theatre trip per week, social/cultural events and travel pass for Munich area. Also courses leading to Goethe Institut examinations, for executives, au pairs, and in teaching German as a foreign language. Accommodation can also be arranged in shared flats, hostels, pensions or hotels. **PH**

Applications in the UK can be made through Kate Naameh, Marketing Director, International House, 106 Piccadilly, London W1V 9FL Tel 01-489 2598 or through Casale & Casale Ltd, 17 Lingfield Road, London SW19 4QD.

INTERNATIONAL STUDY PROGRAMMES The Manor, Hazleton, Cheltenham, Gloucester GL54 4EB Tel Cheltenham 60379

Language courses for A level students of German in Wolfhagen, near Kassel, 3 weeks, Easter, and in Cuxhaven and Wolfsburg in Lower Saxony, and in Osnabrück, 3 weeks, August. 15 hours per week, average 20 per class. Course consists of 10 hours of classes per week with a German teacher, and 5 hours per week with a British teacher of German, and includes study of literature, culture, history and current affairs. Also opportunity to attend school classes together with German pupils. Excursions, local visits and social activities arranged. Cost from £233 includes course, return travel from London, full board family accommodation, textbooks and insurance. Organised in conjunction with the government of the Federal Republic. *Apply by mid-January.* **PH**

INTERNATIONALE SOMMERKURSE DER UNIVERSITÄT FREIBURG Akademisches Auslandsamt, Werthmannplatz, 7800 Freiburg im Breisgau Tel Freiburg im Breisgau 203-4243

Language courses for intermediate and advanced level students in Freiburg. Ages 18+, individuals only. 3.5 weeks, July/August.

Maximum 15 per class. Teaching involves the use of language laboratory. Intermediate course, 5 hours per day of language study plus 2 hours of lectures on the culture, history and society of the Federal Republic. Advanced course, 3 hours per day of language study, plus 6 hours of seminars covering German language and literature, state and society, and economics and politics. Excursions, cultural visits and social events organised. Cost DM450 covers course and some extra-curricular activities, but not teaching materials or insurance. Accommodation arranged locally or in student hall of residence; cost from DM250. *Early application advised.*

INTER-SPRACHSCHULE INTERNATIONAL LANGUAGE SCHOOLS, PO Box 1168, 6800 Mannheim 1 Tel Mannheim 28786
Language courses for all levels in Mannheim, Neustadt, Weinheim and Heidelberg. Ages 15+, individuals and groups. 4 weeks, all year. 20 hours per week. Maximum 10 per class. Cost DM550 per course, plus DM30 registration fee and DM45 textbooks and materials. Special language courses available for engineering, import-export, public relations, sales, banking, finance, tourism and leisure. 1:1 tuition also available, DM35 per hour. Chamber of Commerce examinations may be taken, and students can prepare for entrance examinations for German universities. Extra-curricular seminars on culture and other topics. Excursions organised to local places of interest. Bed and breakfast family accommodation arranged, cost DM300 per month. Hotel accommodation, travel and insurance can also be arranged. Approved by the Ministry of Education and the Chamber of Commerce.

KASSELER SPRACHENSCHULE Obere Königsstrasse 47A, 3500 Kassel Tel Kassel 15715
Summer language courses for all levels at converted farmhouse in Gottsburen, a village in a forestry region near Kassel. Ages 16+, individuals and groups. 1-6 weeks, June-July. 30 lessons per week. Average 8 per class. Advanced students may take an examination leading to the Deutsch als Fremdsprache certificate of the German Association for Extra-Mural Studies. Also special courses for family groups, and 1:1 tuition. Advice given on excursions and other extra-curricular activities. Opportunities for swimming, riding, walking and boating. Cost DM495 per week includes half board accommodation.

KATHOLISCHE UNIVERSITÄT EICHSTÄTT Akademisches Auslandsamt, Ostenstrasse 26, 8078 Eichstätt Tel Eichstätt 20-1
Language and cultural course in Eichstätt near Augsburg for intermediate and advanced level students and teachers of German. 3

weeks, July-August. 25 hours per week. Average 15 per class. Teaching methods involve use of language laboratory. Lectures on various aspects of literature and society in the Federal Republic, including modern religious literature. As the beginning of the course overlaps with the end of the academic year, participants may attend university lectures and activities. Excursions are arranged to local places of interest. Extra-curricular events include music and theatre evening courses, slide show and literary evening. Cost DM620 includes course, teaching materials, activities, excursions and half board student residence accommodation.

KLARTEXT Zentrum für Sprache und Kultur eV, Schmied-Kochel-Strasse 8, 8000 Munich 70 Tel Munich 773401
Language courses in Munich for all levels combined with seminars on contemporary German society and culture. Ages 16+, individuals and groups. 2, 3, or 4 weeks, July-October. 20 hours per week. Maximum 10 per class. Cost from DM320, 2 weeks. Teaching materials DM20. Registration fee DM30. Also business courses, 1:1 tuition and courses for groups of 8+ students, all year. Seminars and meetings in afternoons on German film, literature, songwriters, women's liberation, the peace movement, ecology and other alternative movements, history and social studies and the media. Social programme includes a first week party, excursion, and opportunities for contact with Germans. Accommodation arranged in communal flats, sharing with German students; cost approx DM380, 4 weeks. Pension or hotel accommodation also available from DM60 per day.

NOVALIS – SCHULE FÜR SPRACHEN Aachener Strasse 24, 5000 Cologne 1 Tel Cologne 5740323
Language courses at private language school in Cologne. Ages 16+, individuals and groups. 3-4 weeks, all year. 20-30 hours per week. Maximum 10 per class. Cost DM620, 3 weeks or DM790, 4 weeks, for 20 hours, and DM1260, 3 weeks and DM1680, 4 weeks, for 30 hours. 1:1 lessons also available, DM34 per lesson. Specialised courses can also be organised, including preparation for examinations. Textbooks and materials included. Extra-curricular activities include lectures, guided tours of the city, trips to the countryside, boat trips on the Rhine, picnics, theatre and films, and meetings with people involved in fields such as ecology, women's liberation and the peace movement. Accommodation with breakfast arranged by the school for DM100 per week.

REKTORAT DER CHRISTIAN-ALBRECHTS-UNIVERSITÄT, Akademische Auslandsamt, Olshausenstrasse 40, 2300 Kiel 1 Tel Kiel 880-3715
German language in Germany course for intermediate and advanced levels in the Baltic coastal town of Kiel. Ages 20-50. 4 weeks,

July/August. 16 hours per week language tuition plus 4 afternoons per week of lectures. Maximum 20 per class. Afternoon lectures cover historical development, politics, economics and culture of today's Federal Republic. Extra-curricular events include excursions to local places of interest, sailing and bathing in the Baltic. Cost DM1000 includes course, teaching materials, excursions, activities and full board student residence accommodation. Also opportunity to study Middle High and Low German, at extra cost. *Apply by 1 April.*

RUHR-UNIVERSITÄT BOCHUM Internationaler Ferienkurs, Akademisches Auslandsamt, Universitätsstrasse 150, 4630 Bochum Tel Bochum 700 63 97
Course in contemporary German language and culture for advanced level students in the Ruhr town of Bochum. Ages 18 + . 3 weeks, August. 36 hours per week. Teaching involves the use of language laboratories. Lectures are held on themes of contemporary German language, literature and society. Excursions arranged to local places of interest, and social events organised. Sports facilities available. Cost DM780 includes course, teaching materials, excursions, activities and full board student residence accommodation. *Apply by 15 June.*

SCHOOL JOURNEY ASSOCIATION 48 Cavendish Road, London SW12 0DG Tel 01-673 4849
Language study visit to Pinneberg near Hamburg specifically aimed at British GCSE and A level students. Ages 15-20, individuals and groups. 10 days, Easter. 20 hours language classes. Average 10 per class. As well as translation and comprehension exercises, the course includes games, puzzles, and for A level students, discussion of set texts. Excursions organised to Hamburg, Lübeck and the border. Cost £260 includes course, full board family accommodation, flight, insurance, excursions, textbooks and materials. **PH**

SPRACHEN- UND DOLMETSCHER-INSTITUT MÜNCHEN Amalienstrasse 73, 8000 Munich 40 Tel Munich 288397
Holiday language course for all levels in Munich. 4 weeks, July/August. 20 hours per week. Class sizes from 15 to lecture groups of 40. Cost DM400. Textbooks from DM30. Excursions/social activities often arranged. Students arrange their own accommodation. The Institut also arranges courses in German as a foreign language, suitable for those who may wish to enter higher education in the Federal Republic. Applicants should be educated to at least O level/GCSE standard. Courses last up to 5 terms, beginning September, January or April. 20-23 hours tuition per week. Class sizes from 15 to lecture groups of 40. Cost DM900 per term. Textbooks from DM30. As well as language

tuition, course includes geography, politics, history, literature, and business/technical German. Examinations are taken at end of terms 3 and 5; final examination equivalent to Goethe-Institut's *kleiner Sprachdiplom.* Accommodation office, canteen and library, and advice can be given on courses and insurance. **PH**

SPRACHZENTRUM EINE WELT EV Barfusserstrasse 5, Postfach 3309, 3400 Göttingen Tel Göttingen 485055
Language courses for all levels in Göttingen, in a nearby village, or at a conference centre in the forest. Courses are designed to give an insight into the political, economic and cultural realities of Germany from an alternative/Green point of view. Ages 16 + , individuals and groups. 2-3 weeks, March-September. 30 hours per week. Average 5-10 per class. Also arrange special courses for teachers of German, and for school and special interest groups. Lectures by guest speakers and discussions organised on themes including ecology, peace movement, media, political parties and women's rights. Social programme consists of theatre and cinema trips, concerts, walks and opportunities to meet local people. For courses taking place in the village or forest centres, there is an additional emphasis on communal living, giving constant practice in German. Cost for Göttingen course DM430, 2 weeks and DM645, 3 weeks, includes course, teaching materials and social programme. Self-catering accommodation available in local families or shared flats, cost DM170, 2 weeks and DM220, 3 weeks. Cost for village and forest courses DM600, 2 weeks and DM900, 3 weeks includes course, books and project materials, social programme and self-catering residential accommodation. **PH** First course of the year takes place in a centre with facilities for disabled students.

Applications in the UK can be made to Martin Farrel, 48 Hydethorpe Road, London SW12 0MZ Tel 01-673 1882.

STUDENTENHEIM SCHWEIDT Weinsbergstrasse 74, 5000 Cologne 30 Tel Cologne 525061
Summer language course in Cologne under the auspices of the non-profitmaking Catholic organisation Opus Dei. All levels, false beginners to advanced preferred. Ages 15-23, individuals and small groups. 3 weeks, July/August. 25 hours per week. Maximum 8 per class. Extra-curricular activities include excursions, Rhine cruises, cultural and company visits, film shows and parties with students from other countries. Sports include football, badminton, swimming, basketball, tennis and walks. Cost from DM1380, 3 weeks and DM2600, 6 weeks, includes full board student residence accommodation, laundry, social events, excursions, learning materials and meeting younger participants at airport or station.

STUDIES MUNICH EV Amalienstrasse 67, 8000 Munich 40 Tel Munich 284022/23
Language courses for all levels at non-profitmaking school in Munich. Specialises in courses for executives with language needs, but also offers general courses. Specialised course for ages 18 + available 1:1 or in small groups of maximum 5 or in a combination of both. 9 days-3 weeks, all year. 20-35 hours per week. Cost from DM2570, 2 weeks. General courses for ages 16 + include intensive courses of 4 + weeks, all year, 20 hours per week. Cost from DM1030, 4 weeks. Also summer vacation courses of 3 + weeks, June-August, 15 hours per week. Cost from DM680, 3 weeks. All textbooks and materials included. Visits to cultural and business organisations according to interests of students, plus excursions. Accommodation arranged in private homes from DM190 with breakfast and DM250 half board per week plus insurance at DM55 for 4 weeks. The school is approved by the government and works in close cooperation with the University of Munich.

Applications in the UK may be made to Mrs Viviane Steiner, Language Studies London (LSL), 10-12 James Street, London W1M 5HN.

UNIVERSITÄT BONN FERIENSPRACHKURS Akademisches Auslandsamt, Nassestrasse 15, 5300 Bonn 1
Language and literature summer course for all levels in Bonn. 3 weeks, August. 15 hours language tuition per week. Also lectures and seminars on linguistics, literature, German culture, history, politics, art, history of the German language, and singing and playing old and modern German folksongs. Excursions arranged to places of historic interest; concerts and international meetings also organised. Cost DM500 includes course and registration fees. Accommodation in student residence by prior arrangement. *Apply by 15 June; early application advised.*

UNIVERSITÄT BREMEN Akademisches Auslandsamt, Bibliothekstrasse, 2800 Bremen 33 Tel Bremen 21 82 7 32
Course in contemporary German language, literature and society for intermediate levels upwards in Bremen. Ages 18+. 3 weeks, July-August. 20 hours language tuition per week. Teaching methods involve the use of language laboratory. 4 hours lectures per week for advanced students covering themes of German culture and society. Excursions arranged to local places of interest. Extra-curricular activities include visits to the theatre, cinema and concerts, theatre workshop and sports. Cost DM650 includes course, registration fee, excursions and activities. Accommodation in student residence cost DM200, or with local families, DM450 bed and breakfast, DM650 half board. *Apply by 30 April.*

UNIVERSITÄT HAMBURG Sommerkurs Deutsch als Fremdsprache, Zentrales Fremdspracheninstitut (ZFI), Von-Melle-Park 5, 2000 Hamburg 13 Tel Hamburg 4123-5388

Summer course in Hamburg for teachers, lecturers and advanced students of German. Ages 18+, individuals only. 2 weeks, August/September. 25 hours per week. Conversation class maximum 8-10, lecture groups around 40. Laboratories used in conversation classes. Lectures and seminars cover themes from literature, linguistics, didactics and innovations in language-teaching; also possibility of observing morning lessons in Hamburg schools. Extra-curricular activities include sightseeing tour of Hamburg, full-day excursion, visit to museum, theatre and exhibition, and farewell dinner. Cost DM150 includes course, teaching materials, lectures and extra-curricular activities. Accommodation arranged on half board basis with families, or in a pension/hostel; cost from DM10 per night. *Apply by 16 July. Early application advised.* **PH**

UNIVERSITÄT OSNABRÜCK Internationaler Sommersprachkurs, Akademisches Auslandsamt, Postfach 4469, 4500 Osnabrück Tel Osnabrück 608-4106

Language course for intermediate and advanced levels in Osnabrück. Ages 20+, individuals only. 4 weeks, August. 25 hours per week. Maximum 15 per class. Language laboratory and audio-visual facilities. As well as language and conversation, themes covered at advanced level include history, politics, literature, education, environment, economics, media and art. Cost DM600 includes course, text books and materials, excursions to local places of interest and a 5-day study tour of Northern Germany. Extra-curricular events include concerts, film shows, walks, sporting activities, discos, barbecues and a farewell party. Accommodation arranged in self-catering university halls or with families; cost from DM180. Students arrange own insurance. *Apply by 30 April: early application advised.*

UNIVERSITÄT DES SAARLANDES Internationaler Feriensprachkurs, Akademisches Auslandsamt, Gebäude 28, 6600 Saarbrücken 11 Tel Saarbrücken 302-2569

Course in German language and culture for advanced levels in Saarbrücken, on the French border. Ages 18+, individuals and groups. 3 weeks, September. 20-25 hours per week. Average class size 30. Language laboratory facilities available. Course covers 20th century history, economic development, social structure and politics of the Federal Republic. Three excursions arranged to local places of interest. Social programme includes barbecues, film shows and opportunities to meet other students. Cost DM710 includes course, student hostel accommodation, excursions, social programme, text books and teaching materials. *Apply by 15 June.*

UNIVERSITÄT STUTTGART Internationaler Sommersprachkurs, Keplerstrasse 7, 7000 Stuttgart 1
Language course for intermediate and advanced levels in Stuttgart. Ages 18-35. 4 weeks, June-July. 25 hours per week. Conversation class size 4, course total of 60. Language laboratory and audio-visual facilities. Classes on literature and society, and lectures on contemporary problems of politics, economics and culture. Extra-curricular activities include excursions, concerts, theatre visits and social events; and as the course takes place during termtime there are opportunities to meet German students. Cost DM760 includes course, bed and breakfast family/student residence accommodation, excursions and extra-curricular activities. *Apply by 15 May.*

UNIVERSITÄT TRIER Akademisches Auslandsamt, Postfach 38 25, 5500 Trier Tel Trier 201 28 06
Course in language, culture and society in the Federal Republic, held in the ancient Roman town of Trier for students and teachers with good knowledge of German. Ages 18 + . 3 weeks, August-September. 20 hours language tuition per week. Maximum 15 per class. Teaching involves use of language laboratory. Seminars and lectures on current German linguistics, culture and society. Also special course for teachers and students of German on teaching German as a foreign language. Extra-curricular activities include tours and excursions, films, concerts and wine-tasting. Cost DM450 includes course, teaching materials and activities. Accommodation arranged in student residence or private rooms; cost from DM290. Optional trip to Berlin available at end of course; cost DM300 includes travel, guided tours, entrance fees and half board guest house accommodation. *Apply by 1 June; early application advised.*

UNIVERSITY OF HEIDELBERG INTERNATIONAL VACATION COURSE Seminarstrasse 2, 6900 Heidelberg Tel 542338
Summer language and culture courses at the ancient University of Heidelberg. Ages 18 + . 4 weeks, mid July-August. 16-22 hours per week depending on level. Average 15-20 per class. Special course for teachers of German and advanced students also organised, 16 hours per week. Audio-visual facilities and language laboratory used. Cultural courses consist of lectures, seminars and study groups on themes such as modern German culture and literature. Also chamber music and theatre workshops. Extra-curricular activities include excursions, dances

evenings, folk singing, meeting local people and films. Cost DM450 includes language and culture courses, plus extra-curricular activities. Textbooks cost approx DM35. Accommodation available in student halls of residence, cost from DM150. *Apply by 1 June.*

INFORMATION

Austrian Embassy
18 Belgrave Mews West, London SW1X 8HU Tel 01-235 3731

Embassy of the German Democratic Republic
34 Belgrave Square, London SW1X 8QD Tel 01-235 9941

Embassy of the Federal Republic of Germany
23 Belgrave Square, London SW1X 8PZ Tel 01-235 5033

British Embassy
Reisnerstrasse 40, 1030 Vienna Tel Vienna 731575

108 East Berlin, Unter den Linden 32/24

Friedrich-Ebert Allee 77, 5300 Bonn Tel Bonn 234061

Tourist office
Austrian National Tourist Office, 30 St George Street, London W1R 9FA Tel 01-629 0461

Berolina Travel Ltd, 20 Conduit Street, London W1 Tel 01-629 1664

German National Tourist Office, 61 Conduit Street, London W1R 0EN Tel 01-734 2600

Youth hostels
Österreichischer Jugendherbergsverband, Gonzagagasse 22, 1010 Vienna

Deutsches Jugendherbergswerk, Bulowstrasse 26, PO Box 220, 4930 Detmold

Youth and student information
Austrian Foreign Students' Service, Universitat, Dr Karl Lueger-Ring 1, 1010 Vienna

Buro für Studentenreisen, Schreyvogelgasse 3, 1010 Vienna

Jugendtourist, Jugendreisebüro der DDR, 1020 East Berlin, Alexanderplatz 5, PSF 57

Artu Berliner Gesellschaft fur Studenten und Jugendaustausch GmbH, Hardenbergstrasse 9, 1 Berlin 12

Jugendinformationszentrum, Paul-Heyse-Strasse 22, 8000 Munich 2

Resources

Austrian Institute, 28 Rutland Gate, London SW7 1PQ Tel 01-584 8653 can provide information on grants for study in Austria.

Anglo-Austrian Society, 46 Queen Anne's Gate, London SW1H 9AU Tel 01-222 0366 is a charity whose aims are the promotion of Anglo-Austrian relations. It acts as an agent for language courses in Graz, Kitzbuhel, Salzburg and the University of Vienna, offering inclusive packages including travel. Also arranges exchange visits for individuals and groups, offers cheap travel to Austria, and can book accommodation. In London it runs intensive German courses at Christmas and Easter.

Deutscher Akademischer Austauschdienst, Kennedyallee 50, 5300 Donn 2 Tel Bonn 88 21/German Academic Exchange Service, 17 Bloomsbury Square, London WC1A 2LP Tel 01-404 4065 is an organisation of higher education institutions in the Federal Republic. It awards scholarships to foreign and German students, student trainees, junior academic staff and professors, and promotes the exchange of information between the Federal Republic and other countries.

Pädagogischer Austauschdients, Sekretariat der KMK, Nassestrasse 8, 5300 Bonn 1 aims to foster international understanding through exchange and visitors' programmes for teachers, pupils, language assistants and educationalists. Also organises group tours, language courses and links for schools, and acts as an information bureau for school exchanges.

Goethe-Institut, Zentralverwaltung, Postfach 201009, Lenbachplatz 3, 8000 Munich 2 Tel Munich 59990
Goethe-Institut, 50 Princes Gate, Exhibition Road, London SW7 2PH Tel 01-581 3344/7
Goethe-Institut, Ridgefield House, 14 John Dalton Square, Manchester M2 6JR Tel 061-834 4635

Goethe-Institut, The King's Manor, Exhibition Square, York YO1 2EP Tel York 55222

Scottish-German Centre, Lower Medway Building, 74 Victoria Crescent Road, Glasgow G12 9SC Tel 01-334 6116

A non-profitmaking organisation aimed at promoting German language and culture, with branches throughout the Federal Republic and representation in 67 other countries. It runs German courses, issues diplomas, develops teaching materials, advises teachers of German, and grants scholarships for the study of German, as well as being involved in cultural exchanges.

Publications

Internationale Hochschulferienkurse für Germanistik in der Deutschen Demokratischen Republik is an annual booklet giving information on summer courses in the GDR for teachers, lecturers, translators and students of German. Also *Intensive Courses – German as a Foreign Language in the German Democratic Republic,*
an annual leaflet on courses for academics, research workers, specialists with academic qualifications, and students. Both available from the Embassy of the German Democratic Republic, see above.

Welcome to Germany, is a general folder with information on entry and visa regulations, advice on travel, accommodation, customs and other useful information for visitors. *Rendezvous in Germany: Germany Live* is a booklet containing useful information for young travellers, including accommodation, leisure and place and events. Both available from the German National Tourist Office, see above.

Young People's Guide to Munich, DM50 is an indispensable guide containing notes on where to stay, eating and drinking, walks in the Old City, public transport, maps, entertainment, places of interest, where to meet young people, special events and other useful information. Published by the Tourist Office of the City of Munich, Sendlinger Strasse 1, 8000 Munich 2.

International Youth Meetings in Germany lists services offered by German organisations to young visitors, and includes details of language courses, international workcamps, environmental protectior programmes and social services. Available from Studienkreis für Tourismus eV, Dampfschiffstrasse 2, PO Box 1629, 8130 Starnberg.

Travel

The Austria Ticket allows unlimited travel for 9/16 days on railway and postal bus networks, and a reduction on certain steamship services, and is available from YHA Travel, 14 Southampton Street, London WC2E 7HY Tel 01 836 8541.

DB Tourist Card offers unlimited travel for 4/9/16 days on the Federal Railways network, and on certain coach services. Cost £55/£82/£113. Also available to those under 26; cost £51/£68 (9/16 days). Tramper ticket offers unlimited rail travel for 1 month in the Federal Republic with free use of Intercity trains; for ages under 23, or students under 27. Cost £87.50. Details from DER Travel Service, 18 Conduit Street, London W1R 9TD Tel 01-408 0111.

STA Travel, 74 Old Brompton Road, London SW7 3LQ Tel 01-581 8233 operate flexible, low-cost flights between London and destinations throughout the Federal Republic.

Transalpino Ltd, 117 Euston Road, London NW1 2SX Tel 01-388 2267 offer up to 50% off full rail fares to destinations in Austria and the Democratic and Federal Republics for those under 26.

Accommodation

Youth hostel accommodation in Vienna and hotel accommodation in Vienna, Innsbruck, Graz and Salzburg is available through the Anglo-Austrian Society, see above. For accommodation in student residences in Vienna, Salzburg, Innsbruck, Graz and Linz contact Buro für Studentenreisen or ÖKISTA, see above.

Camping in Germany lists over 400 campsites with a map indicating the locations. Available from the German National Tourist Office, see above.

Christlicher Verein Jünger Menschen, Jugend-Gästehaus, Landwehrstrasse 13, 8000 Munich 2 offers YMCA accommodation in 1-3 bedded rooms for both sexes at Christian centre situated close to the station. Cost from DM27 per night includes breakfast and shower.

Haus International/Youth Hotel, Elisabethstrasse 87, 8000 Munich 40 offers cheap accommodation in 1-5 bedded rooms. Facilities include swimming pool, games room, bar and restaurant. Cost from DM28 includes breakfast. Reservations should be made in advance. **PH**

Large sleeping tent with space for 350, cooking area, canteen, showers, information bureau and recreation tent. Ages up to 23. Cost DM5 per night includes bedding and morning tea. Maximum stay 3 nights, 26 June-7 September. Details from Jugendlager am Kapuzinerhozl, Kreisjugendring München, Franz-Schrank-Strasse, In den Kirschen, 8000 Munich 19.

GREEK

Modern Greek, one of the Indo-European group of languages, is the official language of Greece and one of the official languages of Cyprus, and is the mother tongue of approx 12-13 million people worldwide. It is also one of the official languages of the European Community. Greek-speaking people moved from the Balkan peninsula into the areas of the Greek Peninsula in the 2nd millenium BC. Four distinct dialects developed, the Aeolic, Arcado-Cyprian, the Doric and Ionic. Homer's epic poems of the 9th century BC were written in Ionic. With the rise of Athens the Attic dialect of Ionic became dominant in literature, and formed the basis of the common language. After the conquests of Alexander the Great, Greek was spoken far and wide. It became the second language of the Roman Empire, and was the language in which the New Testament was written. From the 4th-15th centuries Greek was the official language of the Byzantine Empire. This early common language or Koine, *and modern Greek are related to each other much in the same way as Latin and Italian, though linguistically they are separate languages. Modern Greek began to develop in the 9th century and became the official language of Greece in the 19th century.*

COURSES IN GREECE

THE ATHENS CENTRE 48 Archimidous Street, 116 36 Athens Tel Athens 701 5242

Language courses for all levels in Athens. Ages 16+, individuals and groups. 4. 8 or 10 weeks, all year. 6-20 hours per week depending on course. Average 8-14 per class. Cultural events, including lectures, seminars and film evenings. Extra-curricular activities include excursions to places of interest, film, theatre and exhibition visits. Cost Drc30000. Textbooks Drc1500. Information provided on accommodation.

HELLENIC AMERICAN UNION 22 Massalias Street, 106 80 Athens Tel Athens 360 7305
Language courses for all levels in Athens. Ages 18 +, individuals and groups. 60 hour classes all year. 6 hours per week, 10 weeks or 4 hours per week, 15 weeks. Average 12 per class. Also special courses in Greek for executives, Greek literature, Minoan and classical Greece, Greek translation, preparatory course for the Greek Universities Proficiency Examination and conversational course. Audio-visual facilities. Extra-curricular activities include field trips, museum visits and excursions to places of interest. Social events organised to encourage contact with Greek students. Cost Drc14800. Textbooks extra. Hotel accommodation available.

HELLENIC LANGUAGE SCHOOL ALEXANDER THE GREAT Delta Educational Organisation, 4 Zalogou Street, 106 78 Athens Tel Athens 364 0514
Language courses for all levels in Athens. 2-15 weeks, all year. Approx 30 hours per week. Average 5-12 per class. Audio-lingual approach. Also courses in teacher training, business Greek, ancient Greek, Latin, seminars on special historical and archaeological topics and 1:1 tuition. Cost Drc19900, 60 hours, 2 weeks, to Drc116900, 360 hours, 12 weeks. Accommodation can be arranged. Also 2 week summer courses for beginners on the islands of Crete and Rhodes. 30 hours per week, 1 day excursion per week. Information provided on accommodation. Also language course in youth camps for 7-16 year olds in picturesque, coastal region north of Athens. 3 weeks, 4 hours per day. Group living, sports, organised entertainment, cultural activities and sightseeing excursions. Cost Drc138000.

INFORMATION

Greek Embassy
1a Holland Park, London W11 3TP Tel 01-727 8040

British Embassy
1 Ploutarchou Street, Athens

Tourist office

National Tourist Organisation of Greece, 195-197 Regent Street, London W1R 8DL Tel 01-734 5997

Youth hostels

Greek YHA, 4 Dragatsaniou Street, Athens

Youth & student information

British Travel and Student Service, 10 Stadiou Street, Athens

International Student and Youth Travel, 11 Nikis Street, Syntagma Square, Athens

STS, 1 Felellinin Street, Syntagma Square, Athens

Resources

Centre for Information on Language Teaching and Research (CILT), Regent's College, Inner Circle, Regent's Park, London NW1 4NS Tel 01-486 8221 publish *Modern Greek Language & Culture Guide* £4.25 including postage, with details on the provision and use of language teaching and learning resources, covering an introduction to the language, useful addresses, libraries and special collections to consult, opportunities for learning, and examinations which can be taken.

Information centres

International Student & Youth Travel Service, 11 Nikis Street, 2nd Floor, Syntagma Square, 105 57 Athens is the official student and youth travel service specialising in tickets for domestic and international air, sea and land travel, plus information on cheap hotel accommodation, excursions, tours, cruises and festivals. Also issues student cards and provides free welcome and poste restante service.

Travel

STA Travel, 74 Old Brompton Road, London SW7 3LQ Tel 01-581 8233 operate flexible low cost flights between London and destinations throughout Greece.

Transalpino Ltd, 117 Euston Road, London NW1 2SX Tel 01-388 2267 offer up to 50% off full rail fares to destinations in Greece for those under 26.

The Greek Tourist Card allows unlimited travel on rail and bus services of the Greek State Railways. Reduced rates available where 2-5 travel together. Cost from £23.70 (10 days). Available from YHA Travel, 14 Southampton Street, London WC2E 7HY Tel 01-240 5236.

The Rough Guide to Greece £3.95 is a practical, unpretentious handbook with full details on historic sites, including some of the less well-known ones, plus a wealth of practical information on how to get around the country and on cheap places to stay. Published by Routledge & Kegan Paul Ltd, 11 New Fetter Lane, London EC4P 4EE.

Accommodation

National Tourist Organisation of Greece, 195-197 Regent Street, London W1R 8DL Tel 01-734 5997 issues *Camping*, a booklet listing sites run by them, situated by the sea and equipped with modern facilities.

Young Women's Christian Association of Greece, 11 Amerikis Street, 106 72 Athens offers accommodation at Heliopolis YWCA centre near Athens for all young people. Can also provide bed and breakfast hostel accommodation in 1-3 bedded rooms for females only travelling through Athens or Salonika.

HUNGARIAN

Hungarian, or Magyar, is the national language of Hungary, but there are large numbers of Hungarian speakers in the neighbouring regions of Transylvania (Romania), the Banat (Yugoslavia), Burgenland (Austria) and Slovakia. It is one of the Finno-Ugric languages, which includes Finnish, Estonian and a number of languages spoken in the USSR. However Hungarian belongs to the Ugric branch, and the only other languages to which it is closely related are the Ostyak and Vogul languages of Siberia. The original Hungarians came from Asia, migrating between the 5th and 9th centuries, and settling in the Danube area in 896. Since that time they have become Europeanised, only their language revealing eastern roots. A substantial literature has evolved, reflecting cultural developments seen throughout western Europe, the vocabulary being enriched at various times by Slavonic, Turkic and Latin elements. The Magyar vocabulary being largely Asian, the grammar contains a number of complex features not found in Western languages. Hungarian displaced Latin as the official language only as late as 1844.

COURSES IN HUNGARY

THE BRITISH COUNCIL Specialist Tours Department, 65 Davies Street, London W1Y 2AA Tel 01-499 8011
Offer places at summer schools under Cultural Exchange Programmes. Ages 18-35. Course in Hungarian language, literature and culture at Kossuth Lajos University, Debrecen. 2-3 weeks, July/August. Lectures

on achievements of contemporary Hungary, scientific and artistic life, plus seminar groups, round table discussions and excursions. Board and lodging provided, but travel paid by applicant. Bursaries available. Applications should be submitted through an academic or professional referee; candidates applying from a university, college or school must submit their application through a supervisor of studies or head of department. *Closing date mid February.*

INTERNATIONAL HOUSE LANGUAGE SCHOOL CHC, PO BOX 95, Budapest 1364 Tel 361 111 306
Group courses in Hungarian language for all levels in the heart of the Buda side of Budapest. 3 or 6 weeks, July and August. Half board accommodation arranged at the school in rooms shared with Hungarians learning a foreign language. Flat, hotel and family accommodation also available. Campus facilities include a gymnasium, table tennis, jogging track, hard tennis courts, swimming pool and thermal baths. Excursions include sightseeing tours of Budapest, tours to the Danube Bend and Lake Balaton, plus riding and weekend trips to the countryside. Cost, on request, includes course, accommodation, concert or theatre ticket, some excursions and use of library. *UK applications can be made to Kate Neemah, Marketing Director, International House, 106 Piccadilly, London W1V 9FL Tel 01-491 2598.*

COURSES IN AUSTRIA

GESELLSCHAFT FÜR OST UND SÜDOSTKUNDE Bismarkstrasse 5, 4020 Linz Tel 27 33 80
Courses in Hungarian for all levels at Unterweissenbach. Ages 14 + . 2 weeks, August. Maximum 15 per class. Classes and lectures on geography and history delivered in Hungarian by university lecturers, with explanations given in German, English or French if necessary. Opportunities to learn Hungarian folk songs, talks, discussions and concerns, plus sports including tennis, riding, swimming, walking and saunas. Cost AS5000 includes tuition and learning materials. Accommodation arranged at guesthouse; cost from AS210 half board, AS260 full board.

OSTAKADEMIE Ost-und Sudost Europa-Institut, Josefsplatz, 1010 Vienna Tel 512 18 95
International seminar in East European languages at Eisenstadt in the Burgenland, for university students with a prior knowledge of Hungarian. 3 weeks, July-August. Intensive language courses in small

groups. 6 hours tuition per day, plus 2 hours individual study. Specially developed teaching materials. Cost AS8800 includes course, teaching materials and full board accommodation.

INFORMATION

Hungarian Embassy
35 Eaton Place, London SW1 Tel 01-235 4048 Visa section: Tel 01-235 2664/4462

Austrian Embassy
18 Belgrave Mews West, London SW1X 8HU Tel 01-235 3731

British Embassy
1051 Budapest, Harmincad Utca 6

Reisnerstrasse 40, 1030 Vienna

Tourist office
Danube Travel, 6 Conduit Street, London W1R 9TG Tel 01-493 0263

Austrian National Tourist Office, 30 St George Street, London W1R 9FA Tel 01-629 0461

Youth hostels
Hungarian YHA, Semmelweis utca 4, 1395 Budapest V

Österreichischer Jugenherbergsverband, Gonzagagasse 22, 1010 Vienna

Youth & student information
International Bureau for Youth Tourism & Exchange (BITEJ), PO Box 147, Budapest 62

Express Youth & Student Travel Bureau, Semmelweis utca 4, 1395 Budapest V

Austrian Foreign Students' Service, Universitat, Dr Karl Lueger-Ring 1, 1010 Vienna

Resources
Centre for Information on Language Teaching and Research (CILT), Regent's College, Inner Circle, Regent's Park, London NW1 4NS Tel 01-486 8221 publish *Hungarian Language and Culture Guide* £4.25

including postage, which provides full details on the provision and use of language teaching and learning resources, covering an introduction to the language, useful addresses, libraries and special collections to consult, opportunities for learning, and examinations which can be taken.

The Great Britain/East Europe Centre, 31 Knightsbridge, London SW1X 7NH Tel 01-245 9771 aims to promote closer understanding between the British and the peoples of Bulgaria, Czechoslovakia, Hungary, Romania, Poland and the German Democratic Republic. Organises colloquia, symposia and seminars to permit informal exchanges of views between people who have the same professional interest. Also arranges individual visits for academic and professional people.

Travel

Transalpino Ltd, 117 Euston Road, London NW1 2SX Tel 01-388 2267 offer up to 50% off full rail fares to destinations in Hungary for those under 26.

Hungary Tourist Information is a free annual booklet giving information on Hungary including travel, entry formalities, customs, insurance, transport, accommodation, historic monuments, entertainment, sports and other useful information and addresses. Available from Danube Travel, see above.

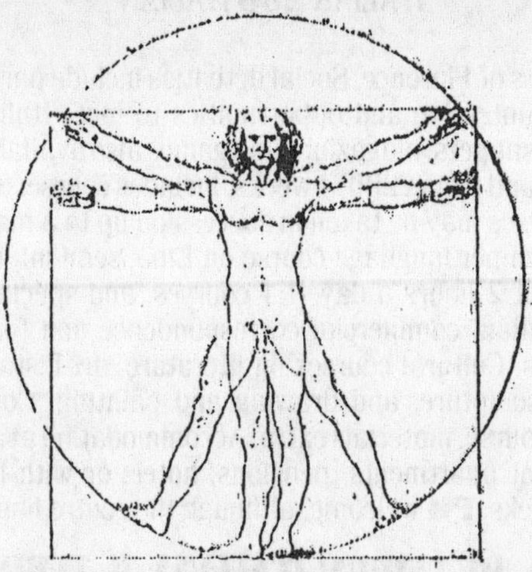

ITALIAN

Of all the Romance languages, Italian is regarded as the closest to Latin, the original language of the Romans. As the language of the Renaissance the influence of Italian on the other western European languages was major. Today it is spoken by approximately 90 million people, mainly in Italy and southern Switzerland, where it is one of the four official languages. It gained recognition as a literary language when Dante used it instead of Latin for his Divine Comedy, *and through him, Petrarch and Boccaccio, it became instrumental in giving Italians a sense of national identity. As they used the dialect of Tuscany, particularly Florentine, modern Italian is essentially Tuscan. The highest concentration of schools of Italian is still in Florence, even though since the late 19th century the Rome dialect has gained prestige. Although the wide-ranging regional dialects are less widely spoken nowadays, their extremes often make cross-communication difficult.*

COURSES IN ITALY

ABC CENTRO DI LINGUA E CULTURA ITALIANA Borgo Pinti 38, 50122 Florence Tel Florence 2479220
Language and culture courses for elementary to advanced levels in Florence. Ages 14 +, individuals and groups. 2 or 4 weeks, all year. 20 or 30 hours per week. Maximum 8 per class. Seminars on Italian culture, plus 20 hours per month of extra-curricular activities including films

and guided tours of Florence. Social activities include parties, cookery, trips to the countryside and opportunities to meet Italians. Library, television, newspapers, magazines and games also available. Cost from £130, 2 weeks and from £200, 4 weeks, includes course, textbooks and activities. Courses may be taken in succession up to a maximum of 24 weeks. Also summer language course on Elba, semi-intensive 2 and 4 week courses of 2 hours a day, 1:1 courses, and special courses for teachers of Italian, commercial correspondence and for business or technical needs. Cultural courses on literature, art history, ceramics, earthenware, sculpture, and drawing and painting. Cost £45-£165, depending on course, materials extra. Accommodation available in self-catering student apartments, pensions, hotels or with families from L270000, 4 weeks. **PH** welcome, although the centre has no lift.

ACCADEMIA DI LINGUA ITALIANA E TURISMO LUIGI PIRANDELLO Via Colombo 30, 90100 Palermo Tel Palermo 361290
Language and culture courses for all levels in Palermo/Cefalù, on the Sicilian coast. 2-4 weeks, March-October. Also lessons on various aspects of Italian and Sicilian society, including politics, art, literature, history, geography and customs. Social programme includes excursions and visits to concerts, the cinema and the theatre. Cost from L700000 includes course and half board accommodation.

THE BRITISH INSTITUTE OF FLORENCE Palazzo Lanfredini, Lungarno Guicciardini 9, Florence Tel Florence 284031
Language and culture courses for all levels in two ancient palazzos on either side of the Arno in Florence. General courses, 4 weeks, all year. 10 hours per week. Cost £190. Also intensive courses, 4 weeks, all year, beginners only or 2 weeks, April, August and November, all levels. 20 hours per week. Cost £320, 4 weeks and £190, 2 weeks. 1:1 courses and year-long A level courses in Italian and history of art available. Cultural courses of 2 or 4 weeks can be taken in the Florentine Renaissance, January-October, Etrusco-Roman civilisation in Tuscany, April and September, High Renaissance, Mannerism and Baroque, February, May and November, and drawing and watercolour painting, March-June and September-October. Costs £55-£105. For language course students there may be reduced fees for culture courses. All students may attend the cultural events organised by the Institute and use its library. The Institute also teaches English to Italians, and regular receptions and class exchanges are organised to enable students to meet. Accommodation in families, hotels or pensions from £8 per day.
UK applicants can apply to Cultural and Educational Services Abroad, 44 Sydney Street, Brighton, Sussex BN1 4EP Tel Brighton 683304. Cost

for 4 weeks, July, £993 including course, half board family accommodation and flight.

CENTRO DI CULTURA PER STRANIERI University of Florence, Via Vittorio Emanuele 64, 50134 Florence Tel 472139
Language and culture courses for all levels run by the University of Florence. Ages 18+, university entrance standard, individuals only. 10 weeks, starting January, June and October, 12 hours language tuition per week. Cost L350000. Also 6 weeks, starting end June, 14 hours language tuition per week. Cost L300000. Average 25 per class. Textbooks approx L20000. Courses include conversation classes at the lowest level, language laboratory practice at intermediate level, and the history of the Italian language at advanced level. Cultural lectures conducted in Italian on Italian literature and history, history of art and Etruscan civilisation, illustrated by visits to museums in Florence and to nearby places of interest, Dante and his times, Renaissance art and culture, the history of music, Italian film, and modern Italy. Accommodation addresses provided, but arrangements made by students. Cost from L40000 per day. *Scholarships may be available from the Ministerio degli Affari Esteri, DGRC Ufficio IX, 00100 Rome.*

CENTRO DI CULTURA ITALIANA BOLOGNA Via Pier de Crescenzi 12 40131 Bologna Tel Bologna 523486
Language and culture courses for all levels in Bologna. Ages 16+, individuals and groups. 2, 3, 5 or 6 weeks, May-January. 20 hours language and 13 hours cultural programme per week. Average 6 per class. Audio-visual facilities. Seminars cover various aspects of Italian life and culture, visits to artists studios, radio stations and publishing houses, walks and social activities. Lectures on Italian literature for more advanced levels. Cost from L200000, 2 weeks. Also 4 week intensive courses, February-May and October-December. 80 hours language and 20 hours cultural programme per week. Maximum 10 per class. Cost from L288000. Also individual courses all year, and 4-10 week preparatory courses for entrance to Italian universities, July-October. All costs include teaching materials. Registration fee L190500 includes insurance. Accommodation available in families, student residences, hotels, flats and villas from L7000 per day. Childcare service. Approved by Bologna Bureau for Culture. *Scholarships available.*

CENTRO CULTURALE GIACOMO PUCCINI Via Ugo Foscolo 36, 55049 Viareggio Tel Viareggio 44238
Summer language course for all levels in Viareggio, a coastal resort near Pisa. Ages 16+. 2-4 weeks, June-September. 15 hours per week.

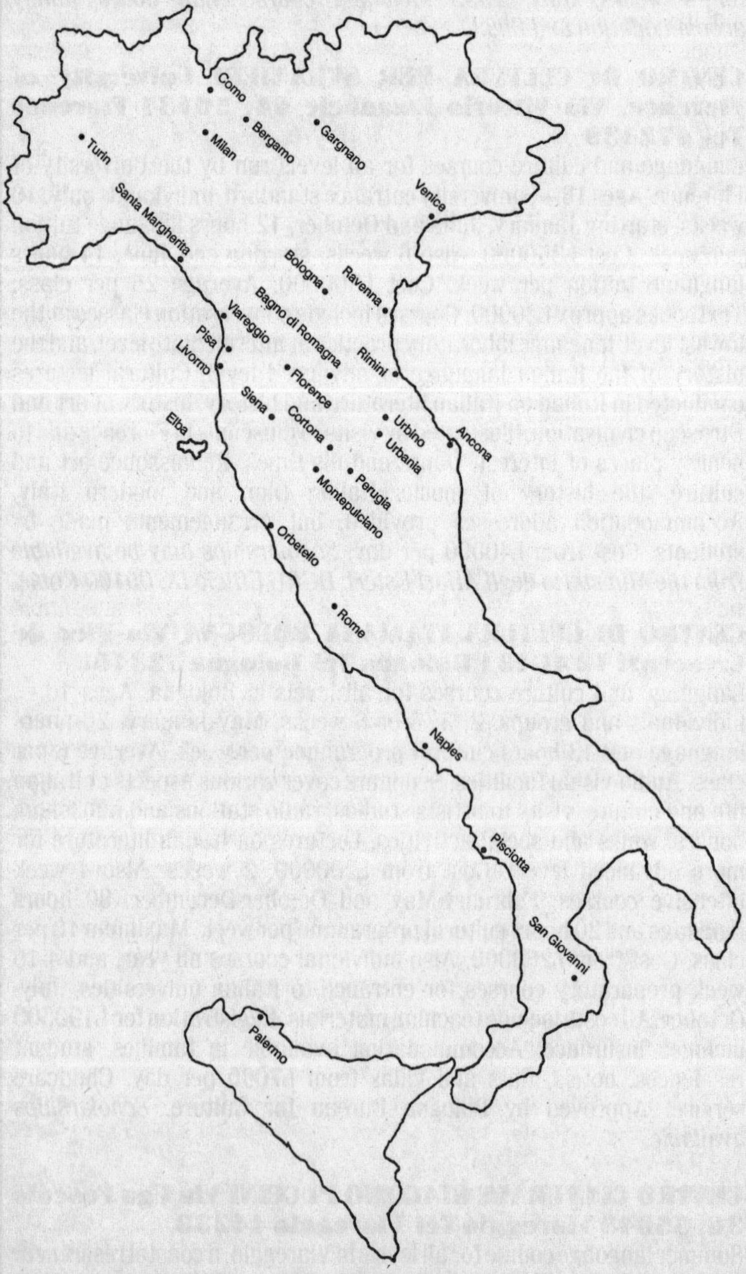
Como
Bergamo
Gargnano
Milan
Turin
Venice
Santa Margherita
Bologna
Ravenna
Viareggio
Bagno di Romagna
Pisa
Livorno
Rimini
Florence
Siena
Cortona
Elba
Urbino
Urbania
Ancona
Perugia
Montepulciano
Orbetello
Rome
Naples
Pisciotta
San Giovanni
Palermo

I T A L Y

Maximum 12 per class. Audiovisual facilities. Extra-curricular activities include excursions, visits to theatres and discos, parties at the school and opportunities to learn windsurfing and sailing. Accommodation in hotels with full board, or in apartments. Cost L865000, 2 weeks, includes course, teaching materials and full board hotel accommodation; L540000 with apartment accommodation.

CENTRO IL DAVID Borgo Pinti 20, 50121 Florence Tel Florence 243793/480154
Language and culture courses for all levels in Florence. Ages 16+, individuals and groups. 4 weeks, all year. 20 hours per week. Maximum 8 per class. 2 hours each grammar and conversation, per day; either section may be taken separately as a 4 week, 10 hour week course. Cost L390000, 20 hour week, L250000, 10 hour week. Audio-visual facilities, textbooks and materials included. Also 1:1 courses, preparatory courses for students wishing to study medicine at Italian universities, commercial Italian and courses for teachers of Italian. Cultural courses, which may be combined with language courses, include literature, art history, cinema, cooking and wines, pottery, drawing, painting. 15-24 hours, cost L90000-L260000. Social programme includes films, parties with Italian students of foreign languages, visits to museums, dinners at the school or in restaurants and trips to the seaside. Accommodation available in self-catering apartments, with families or in pensions, from L260000 per month. Advice for students on all aspects of their stay.

CENTRO INTERNAZIONALE DI STUDI ITALIANI, Universita degli Studi di Genova, Via Balbi 5, 16126 Genoa Tel Genoa 299330
Summer language and culture course for elementary to advanced levels in Santa Margherita Ligure, an small town on the Italian Riviera, east of Genoa. 1 month, August-September. 28 hours per week including seminars on conversation and art history at elementary level, and literature and art history at intermediate and advanced levels. Conferences and meetings also organised. Social programme includes cultural activities, excursions, films, sports and walks in the mountains. Help given in finding accommodation. *Scholarships offered by the University of Genoa.*

CENTRO KOINÈ Centro di Formazione Linguistica e di Incontri Culturali, Via Pandolfini 27, 50122 Florence Tel Florence 213881
Course for all levels in language plus Italian culture and society, in Florence. Ages 15-80, individuals and groups. 4 weeks, all year. 20 hours of language plus 2 hours cultural and social course, and 1 hour art history, per week. Maximum 12 per class. Cost L450000 includes course

and teaching materials. Social programme includes guided tours of artistic places of interest, visits to factories and a newspaper office, plus film shows. Accommodation available in apartments, families, pensions, hostels and hotels from L250000. Medical insurance and travel can be arranged. Also courses for small groups with special needs including business, technical Italian, 1:1 courses and courses for teachers of Italian. Recognised by the Region of Tuscany. *Some scholarships available through Italian Cultural Institutes.*

Language and culture courses for all levels in Orbetello, an ancient Etruscan centre situated in the middle of a freshwater lagoon on the Tuscany coast. Ages 15-80, individuals and groups. 2 weeks, June-September. 40 hours language tuition, plus afternoon lessons in the history of art. Excursions include trips to nearby island of Giglio and to the hot springs of Saturnia. Cost L350000 includes course, teaching materials and excursions. Bed and breakfast pension/hotel accommodation from L220000, 2 weeks. Also campsite nearby, from L130000, 2 weeks.

Summer language courses for all levels in Cortona. Ages 15-80, individuals and groups. 3 weeks, June-September. 20 hours per week language tuition. Maximum 12 per class. Also afternoon lessons on Tuscan cooking and the Etruscans, plus a programme of debates and visits to local places of interest. Cost L450000 includes course, teaching materials and activities. Half board hostel or bed and breakfast pension accommodation available, from L280000, 3 weeks.

CENTRO DI LINGUA E CULTURA ITALIANA Vico S Maria dell'Aiuto 17, 80134 Naples Tel 5524331

Language and culture courses for all levels in Naples. Ages 7-14, 14+, individuals and groups. 4 weeks, all year, or 2-4 weeks, July-September. 20 hours per week. Maximum 12 per class. 2 cultural seminars included. Cost L280000, 2 weeks, L450000, 4 weeks. Also quarterly courses, 12 weeks, February and November. 6 hours per week. Maximum 12 per class. Cost L450000. 1:1 courses, special courses in commercial Italian or technical Italian for Italian university entrance and courses in translation. Audio-visual facilities. Social programme includes guided tours, excursions, films and parties. Costs include course, teaching materials and social programme. Optional cultural courses include history of art and archaeology, handicrafts, history and traditions of Naples, Neapolitan music, cookery, literature, cinema and Italian history. Accommodation can be arranged.

CENTRO DI LINGUA E CULTURA ITALIANA PER STRANIERI FIORENZA Via S Spirito 14, 50125 Florence Tel 298274

Language and culture courses for all levels at a palazzo overlooking the Arno in Florence. Age 18+, individuals and small groups. Intensive courses, 4 weeks, all year. 20 hours per week. Maximum 12 per class. Cost £220. Also courses in language, art, culture and Italian cuisine, 2 weeks, all year. 18 hours language classes, 4 hours art/history tours, 1 hour cultural/practical information and 4 hours cooking lessons per week. Maximum 8 per class. Cost £180. Also 1:1 courses for 10, 20, 30 or 40 hours weekly for professionals, businessmen, students, scholars or anyone wishing to learn Italian quickly. Courses in medical terminology for advanced students wishing to study at Italian medical schools. Audio-visual facilities. Cultural courses available on cooking and kitchen theory, Italy of today and yesterday, literature, art history, antique furniture, the theory of painting restoration, business correspondence, weaving, ceramics and terracotta, and enamel techniques. 4-20 hours. Costs £13-£95, including course and teaching materials. Social events include excursions, theatre, films, concerts and guided tours in Florence. Bicycles for rent at low cost. Self-catering apartment, bed and breakfast, half board family, pension or hotel accommodation available from L10500 per day. *Some scholarships available through Italian Cultural Institutes.*

Language courses for all levels on the island of Elba. Ages 18+, individuals and groups. 2 weeks, May-July and September-October. 33 hours language tuition. Maximum 8 per class. Cost £305-£610. Also 1:1 courses of 22, 33 or 60 hours. Cost £420-£1220. Costs include course, teaching materials, use of swimming pool and tennis courts, and self-catering apartment/half board hotel accommodation. Optional excursions include trips to vineyards, country villages or mountains. Other facilities include tennis courts, swimming pools, private beach and fitness centre. **PH**

CENTRO LINGUISTICO DANTE ALIGHIERI Via Marliano 4, 00162 Rome Tel Rome 8320184
Language classes for all levels in Rome. Ages 15-75, individuals and mini groups. 4 weeks, all year. General courses of 20, 40, 60, 80 and 120 hours per month. Cost £44-£290 per month. Also special courses for groups of 3 in business, technical or other special language needs, plus intensive and semi-intensive 1:1 courses. Audio-visual facilities. Textbooks approx L18000. Afternoon cultural courses available include literature, art, cinema/theatre, socio-politics and cooking. 18 or 24 hours per week. Cost £44-£100 per month. In Siena, courses in drawing, painting, Etruscan studies and Tuscan art also available in the nearby 13th century cloister cultural centre. Social programme includes excursions at extra cost, guided tours, aerobics classes and tennis courts. Accommodation available in families, apartments and pensions/hotels, from L600000 per month. Insurance for emergency medical treatment can be arranged, approx L20000 per month.

Scholarships available through Italian Consulates and Dante Alighieri Societies abroad.

UK applicants can apply to Cultural and Educational Services Abroad, 44 Sydney Street, Brighton, Sussex BN1 4EP Tel Brighton 683304. Cost from approx £125 per week includes 15-30 hours per week tuition and family accommodation.

US applicants can apply to US Student Programs, Institute of International Education, 809 United Nations Plaza, New York, NY100017.

CENTRO LINGUISTICO DANTE ALIGHIERI Piazza La Lizza 10, 53100 Siena Tel Siena 49533

Language classes for all levels in a 17th century palazzo in Siena. Ages 15-75, individuals and mini groups. 4 weeks, all year. General courses of 20, 40, 60, 80 and 120 hours per month. Cost £44-£290 per month. Also special courses for groups of 3 in business, technical or other special language needs, plus intensive and semi-intensive 1:1 courses. Audio-visual facilities. Textbooks approx L18000. Afternoon cultural courses available include literature, art, cinema/theatre, socio-politics and cooking. 18 or 24 hours per week. Cost £44-£100 per month. Courses in drawing, painting, Etruscan studies and Tuscan art also available in the nearby 13th century cloister cultural centre. 1 month May-September, from £95. Social programme includes optional excursions, guided tours, aerobics classes and tennis courts. Accommodation available in families, apartments and pensions/hotels, from L600000 per month. Insurance for emergency medical treatment can be arranged, approx L20000 per month.

UK applicants can apply to Cultural and Educational Services Abroad, 44 Sydney Street, Brighton, Sussex BN1 4EP Tel Brighton 683304. Costs for August: 2 weeks £607, 4 weeks £953 includes course, half board family accommodation and group flight.

US applicants can apply to US Student Programs, Institute of International Education, 809 United Nations Plaza, New York, NY100017.

CENTRO LINGUISTICO ITALIANO DANTE ALIGHIERI Via dei Bardi 12, PO Box 194, 50100 Florence Tel Florence 284955

Language classes for all levels in Florence, near the Ponte Vecchio. Ages 15-75, individuals and mini groups. 4 weeks, all year. General courses of 20, 40, 60, 80 and 120 hours per month. Cost £44-£290 per month. Also special courses for groups of 3 in business, technical or other special language needs, plus intensive and semi-intensive 1:1 courses. Audio-visual facilities. Textbooks approx L18000. Afternoon cultural courses available include literature, art, cinema/theatre, socio-politics and cooking. 18 or 24 hours per week. Cost £44-100 per month. Social programme includes excursions at extra cost, guided tours, aerobics classes and tennis courts. Accommodation available in families, apartments and pensions/hotels from L600000 per month. Insurance for emergency medical treatment can be arranged for approx L20000 per month. *Scholarships available through Italian Consulates and Dante Alighieri Societies abroad.*

UK applicants can apply to Cultural and Educational Services Abroad, 44 Sydney Street, Brighton, Sussex BN1 4EP Tel Brighton 683304. Cost, 2 weeks, August £607; 4 weeks, August £953, includes course, half board family accommodation and group flight.

US applicants can apply to US Student Programs, Institute of International Education, 809 United Nations Plaza, New York, NY100017.

CENTRO LINGUISTICO SPERIMENTALE Via del Corso 1, 50122 Florence Tel Florence 210592/263817
Language and culture courses at all levels in a historic palazzo in the heart of Florence. No age limits, individuals and groups. 4 weeks, all year. 20 hours per week. Maximum 10 per class. Cost L490000 includes course and teaching materials. Also 1:1 courses, 20 hours per week. Courses include afternoon and evening classes on aspects of Italian life and the media. Special 4 week cultural courses also available in art history, Italian history, literature and cooking. Cost L115000 per course. Also course for preparation for admission to Italian medical school, for which good knowledge of Italian required. Social programme includes excursions to Tuscan cities, eating out, a weekly guided museum visits, and information on cultural events and festivals. Bed and breakfast or half board family accommodation, self-catering student apartments or bed and breakfast pensions from L300000 per week. *Scholarships available through Italian Institutes.*

CENTRO LORENZO DE'MEDICI Piazza delle Pallottole 1, 50121 Florence Tel Florence 283142
Language and art courses for all levels at school near the cathedral in Florence. Ages 16+, individuals and groups. 4 weeks, all year. 10 or 20 hours per week. Maximum 10 per class. Cost L250000, 10 hours and L480000, 20 hours. Also 2 week courses, 30 hours per week. Cost L370000. 1:1 courses of 6 or 8 hours a day also available, the latter

specially designed for businessmen, including lunch with a teacher. Costs include course and teaching materials. Also, through the Lorenzo de'Medici Art Institute, 1 or 6 month courses in history of art, painting, drawing, sculpture, modern jewellery-making, tapestry, photography, batik, serigraphy, restoration and ceramics. Social programme, some of which is included in the cost, includes seminars on literature, history of art, cinema, Italian popular music, socio-politics of Italy, and current affairs. Also excursions to Rome, Venice, Assisi and the Chianti Hills, guided tours of museums, restaurant meals, cooking evenings and discos. Accommodation available in families, apartments or pensions from L252000 per month. Non-specialised medical treatment included. Member of the Federation Europeene des Ecoles. Approved by the College Consortium for International Studies.
UK applicants may apply to Euro-Academy, 77A George Street, Croydon CR0 1LD Tel 01-686 2363. Cost from £132 for 4 week course, 2 hours per day. Bed and breakfast family accommodation from £136 per week.

CENTRO PONTEVECCHIO SRL Piazza del Mercato Nuovo 1, 50123 Florence Tel Florence 294511
Courses for all levels at language school near the Ponte Vecchio in Florence. No age limit, individuals and groups. 2-4 weeks, all year. 20 hours per week. Maximum 10 per class. Cost from L230000, 2 weeks, L380000, 4 weeks. Also courses for 1 month, 6 hours per week, special courses for small groups in business, technical, medical and commercial Italian, 1:1 courses and courses for teachers of Italian. Examinations for entrance to Italian universities can be taken. Subsidiary courses in cooking, wine, fashion, cinema, politics, music and song, art history, literature and conversation, 4 hours per week. Cost L80000, 4 weeks. Social programme includes films, excursions, visits to tourist sights, and opportunities to meet Italians. Tape and video used. Costs include course, teaching materials and some social activities. Accommodation available in apartments, families, pensions and hotels from L250000 per month. *Scholarships available through the Italian Institute.* **PH**
Also language courses for all levels in the Chianti countryside. No age limits. 1 + week, January-November. Social programme includes films, excursions, visits to tourist sights, and opportunities to meet Italians. Tape and video used. Cost L260000 per week includes course, teaching materials and some social activities. Accommodation L90000-200000 per week. **PH**

CENTRO STUDI ITALIANI Via Ugolini 15/17, 61049 Urbania (PS) Tel Urbania 57169
Language and culture courses for all levels in Urbania, a small town near Urbino in the Marche area. Ages 16 +, individuals and groups. 3 or 4-24

weeks, all year. Maximum 12 per class. 17 hours language tuition per week plus 4 hours conversation for beginners, 14 hours intermediate or 9 hours, advanced. Also 11 and 16 hours per week culture courses for intermediate and advanced levels. Individual tutorials on Saturday mornings deal with any language problems. Social programme includes weekly afternoon excursions, plus guided tours and twice weekly cultural evenings. Cost L550000, 4 weeks, includes course, teaching materials and social programme. Optional extra culture and art/handicraft courses cover local and national history, literature, philosophy, politics, specific art history topics, philology, music, history of the Italian language, drawing and painting, pottery, xylography, engraving and embossing, weaving, restoration of antique books and prints, wrought iron work, embroidery, cookery and sculpture. Cost L100000 per month, 6 hours per week, plus L10000-L30000 for arts materials and textbooks. Also special courses for teachers of Italian and opera singers. Accommodation in families, in self-catering apartments or in pensions, hotels or on campsite, from L250000, 4 weeks. Approved by the Ministry of Foreign Affairs. *Scholarships available through the Dante Alighieri Society in Rome.* **PH**

COOPERATIVA DI SERVIZI CULTURALI IL SASSO Via di Voltaia nel Corso 74, 53045 Montepulciano Tel Montepulciano 758311

Language courses for all levels in Montepulciano, a fortified hill town to the south east of Siena. Ages 16 +, individuals and groups. 2 or 4 weeks, March-October. 20 hours per week. Maximum 10 per class. Cost £120, 2 weeks, £220, 4 weeks. Also at Christmas, 10 days with 36 hours language classes. Different dates and prices for group applications. 1:1 courses all year. Students get to meet representatives of local organisations and to practice Italian on local people. Textbooks loaned free to students, but may also be purchased. Extra-curricular excursions to places of interest, and visits to farms or other local organisations arranged, from L5000, plus weekly cookery evenings, cost L18000. Also swimming in local pools, sailing or windsurfing on Lake Trasimeno, walks in the Tuscan countryside, local summer festivals and tennis. Accommodation available in self-catering flats, with families, or in pensions/hotels from L10000 per day.

UK applicants can apply to Mr Norman Jopson, 1 Chichester Drive, Purley, Surrey CR2 4LR Tel 01-668 3429.

CORSI CAZZULANI DI LINGUA ITALIANA PER STRANIERI Via Rovelli 41, 22100 Como Tel Como 270068

Language courses for all levels in Como, near the Swiss border. Ages 12-40, individuals and groups. 4 weeks, October-May and August. 15

hours a week. Maximum 10 per class. Cost L430000 per month includes course and teaching materials. Excursions and study tours organised, and opportunities for sports. Full board family accommodation can be arranged. Approved by the Ministry of Foreign Affairs. Diploma Firenze may be taken. Also summer courses up to intermediate levels in Loano, on the Italian Riviera, 80 km from Genoa. Ages 12-40, individuals and groups. 4 weeks, July. 15 hours a week. Maximum 10 per class. Cost L430000 includes course and teaching materials. Excursions and study tours organised, and opportunities for sports. Full board family accommodation can be arranged. Approved by the Ministry of Foreign Affairs. **AI** Diploma Firenze may be taken.

DILIT (INTERNATIONAL HOUSE) Via Marghera 22, 00185 Rome Tel Rome 492602/492592

Language courses and cultural seminars in Rome for all levels. Ages 16+, individuals and groups. 4 weeks, all year. 15 or 20 hours per week. Maximum 15 per class. Cost from L490000. Also 1:1 courses, 4 weeks, 7 hours per day, or on an hourly basis. Also training courses for teachers of Italian. Teaching facilities include video, computers and language laboratory. Course textbooks cost L16000, but all other materials included. Cultural seminars on history of art, literature, history, pronunciation, cooking and wine. Social programme includes excursions, guided tours, parties, films, social get-togethers and bilingual workshops with Italian students learning English. Access to language laboratory and self-study centre during leisure time. Accommodation available in self-catering apartments, families, or bed and breakfast in pensions/hotels from L330000, 4 weeks. Approved by the Ministry of Education. *Scholarships available through Italian Cultural Institutes.* **PH** welcome.

UK applicants can apply through Kate Naameh, Marketing Director, International House, 106 Piccadilly, London W1V 9FL.

EUROCENTRO Palazzo Guadagni, Piazza S Spirito 9, 50125 Florence Tel Florence 213030/294605

Language and culture courses for all levels at a palazzo in the heart of Florence. Ages 16+, individuals and groups. Intensive courses, 3-12 weeks, all year. 30 hours per week includes cultural seminars. Maximum 15 per class. Also holiday courses 4 or 12 weeks, July-September. 20-25 hours per week. Maximum 15 per class. Also refresher courses for teachers and special courses for small groups. Facilities include audio-visual, language laboratory computers, and a multi-media self-study centre open to students during leisure hours. All textbooks and materials included. Cultural seminars include literature, archaeology, history of art, Italian history and everyday life in Italy. Social programme of films and guided tours of museums in Florence. Cost £527, 3 weeks, £2352, 12 weeks for intensive courses, and £708, 4 weeks, £2292, 12 weeks, for holiday courses. Costs include course, teaching materials, social programme and half board family accommodation. Costs excluding accommodation from £293, 3 weeks, intensive, and £400, 4 weeks, holiday courses. Approved by the Ministry of Education. *Scholarships available from Eurocentres Scholarship Department, Seestrasse 247, 8038 Zurich, Switzerland.*

UK applicants can also apply through Cultural and Educational Services Abroad, 44 Sydney Street, Brighton, Sussex BN1 4EP Tel Brighton 683304. Cost approx £150-£200 per week includes 25-30 hours per week tuition and family accommodation.

HOME LANGUAGE LESSONS LTD 12-18 Royal Crescent, Ramsgate, Kent CT11 9PE Tel Thanet 590300
1:1 Italian lessons for all levels in the Turin area. No age limits. The lessons take place in the teacher's home, where the student also stays, giving total immersion in the language, with no contact with other students. 15, 20 or 25 hours of lessons per week. Cost L800000, L900000 or L1000000 per week respectively. Also weekend crash courses of 5 hours per day, cost L260000. The course may also be taken together by two people; if both are of the same family a 25% reduction applies. Five star immersion course for business and professional people, with 25 hours per week language tuition and superior accommodation in fashionable residential areas, cost L500000 per week. Given notice it is possible to place students with teachers who share their interests, and on immersion courses to arrange suitable contacts in the local community. Full board accommodation included in all costs. **PH**

INLINGUA SCHOOL OF LANGUAGES Via Menicucci 1, 60121 Ancona Tel Ancona 53625/204020
Language courses for all levels in Ancona, on the Adriatic coast. Ages 7 +, individuals and groups. General courses, 4 weeks, February, May, September and October. 30 x 45 minute lessons per week, maximum 8 per class. Cost L270000 per week. Holiday courses, 2 weeks, June-July. 15 x 45 minute lessons per week, average 3 per class. Cost L220000 per week. Also 1:1 courses. Video and computer facilities. Textbooks and materials included. Accommodation arranged with families, or in pensions/hotels. Cost from L200000 per week. Recognised by the Ministry of Public Instruction.

Applications in the UK can be made to Inlingua School of Languages, 8-10 Rotton Park Road, Edgbaston, Birmingham B16 9JJ Tel 021-454

0204 or Inlingua School of Languages, 55-61 Portland Road, Brighton, Sussex BN3 5DQ Tel Brighton 721612.

ISTITUTO DELLA LINGUA ITALIANA GALILEO GALILEI Via Guelfa 84, CP 1811, 50129 Florence Tel Florence 294680
1:1 courses at a school in central Florence, at a teacher's home in the Chianti countryside, and on Elba, for all levels. Specialises in courses for managers, executives, businessmen, secretaries, stewardesses, lawyers, doctors and other professionals, and also for interpreters, translators, opera singers and those wanting to learn Italian quickly. No age restriction. 1 + weeks, all year. 20, 30 or 40 hours per week, with a variety of morning or afternoon timetables. Barbecues twice a month to enable students to meet local people. Cost L670000-L2000000 per week includes course, textbooks, teaching materials, activities and tours. Bed and breakfast accommodation from L18000 per day. **PH** wheelchair students accepted.

ISTITUTO DI LINGUA ITALIANA VITTORIO ALFIERI Via dell'Oriuolo 20, 50122 Florence Tel Florence 2340669
Language and culture courses for all levels at school close to the cathedral in Florence. Ages 16+, individuals and groups. Standard courses, 4-16 weeks, all year. 20 hours per week. Cost from £210, 4 weeks. Also compact morning or afternoon courses, 4 weeks, January-June and October-December. 10 or 15 hours per week. Cost from £90, 10 hours or £155, 15 hours, 4 weeks. Also summer courses, 2 or 4 weeks, July-September. 25 hours per week. Cost £150, 2 weeks or £265, 4 weeks. Average 12 per class. Textbooks approx L18000. Also 1:1 courses 4, 6, or 8 hours per day, special courses for small groups and special business and technical courses. Cultural courses include history of art, literature, history, cooking, and Italian wines. Cost £65 per course. Wide variety of art courses also available through the International School of Art and Humanities, same location. Social programme includes guided tours of museums and galleries, excursions, meals in local trattorias and spaghetti parties in the school where students can meet invited Italian guests. Accommodation available in apartments, with families and in pensions, from £195 with breakfast, 4 weeks.

ISTITUTO LINGUISTICO MEDITERRANEO Via Marradi 30, 57126 Livorno Tel Livorno 804326
Language courses for all levels in Livorno on the Tuscany coast, historically famous as Europe's first seaside resort. No age limits. 2 + weeks, April-September. 20 hours per week. Maximum 12 per class. Cost L250000, 2 weeks, L450000, 4 weeks. L130000 each additional

week. 4 week grammar course, 40 hours total, cost L250000. Also 1:1 tuition, 20-40 hours per week, L700000, 20 hours, L1500000, 40 hours. Pre-university language courses in medicine and surgery, veterinary medicine, biology and engineering. Optional excursions to various towns in Tuscany, sailing trips along the coast and a course in sailing and windsurfing. Bed and breakfast/half board accommodation available in families, pensions or hotels, or self-catering student apartments from L70000 per week.

ISTITUTO LINGUISTICO MEDITERRANEO Via C Battisti 3, 56100 Pisa Tel Pisa 598066
Language courses for all levels in Pisa. No age limits. 2+ weeks, February-December. 20 hours per week. Maximum 12 per class. Cost L250000, 2 weeks, L450000, 4 weeks. L130000 each additional week. Also 2 week intensive courses of 30 hours per week, cost L390000. 4 week grammar course, 40 hours in total, cost L250,000. Also 1:1 tuition, 20-40 hours per week, cost per week L700000, 20 hours, L1500000, 40 hours. Also pre-university language courses in medicine and surgery, veterinary medicine, biology and engineering. Optional excursions to various towns in Tuscany, and sailing trips along the coast. Bed and breakfast/half board accommodation available in families, pensions, hotels or self-catering student apartments, from L70000 per week.

ISTITUTO A MARVELLI GIOVENTÙ STUDIOSA Via Cairoli 69, 47037 Rimini Tel Rimini 24704
Language and culture courses for elementary to advanced levels in Rimini, on the Adriatic coast. 3 weeks, July or 4 weeks, August. 4 hours per day, includes language tuition and lessons on Italian literature, cinema, theatre, history of art and institutions. Cultural activities and excursions organised, and students have use of the beach. Cost L180000, July or L230000, August. Bed and breakfast, half board and full board accommodation available from L320000. Organised under the auspices of the School of Tourist Studies and the University of Bologna.

ISTITUTO MONDO ITALIANO Via delle Quattro Fontane 33, 00184 Rome Tel Rome 4746916/4741357
Language courses with cultural seminars for all levels in Rome. Ages 16+, individuals and groups. 3 or 4 weeks, January-November. 15 or 20 hours per week. Maximum 12 per class. Cost L300000, 3 x 15 hours per week, L550000, 4 x 20 hours per week. Textbooks and materials included. Also semi-intensive courses, 4 or 6 hours per week, courses for teachers of Italian, 2 x 20 hours per week, August. Specialised courses for groups of 3, 1:1 courses, and preparatory courses for Italian university entrance. Audio-visual facilities and language laboratory.

Cultural seminars include cinema, theatre, mask and gesture, mask making, music, design, and fashion. 2 weeks, 6 or 9 hours per week. Cost from L200000. Social activities run by student club include evenings out in Rome, trips to museums, films, and social gatherings. Accommodation available with families self-catering, half board, or in apartments shared with other students, from L250000 per month. Travel can be arranged. *Scholarships available through the Italian Cultural Institute in London.*

Also organises special combined language courses/holidays in Rome, Ventetone, an island off Naples, or Lake Trasimeno near Perugia. 2 weeks in Rome, or 1 week in Rome plus 1 week in Ventotene/Lake Trasimeno. 15 hours per week language classes. Maximum 20 per class. Cost for Rome, L480000, includes self-catering accommodation; for Rome/Ventotene, L1200000, includes self-catering accommodation, brunch and dinner, boat trips, scuba diving, use of sail boards, catamarans, sail boats, canoes and sea buggies; for Rome/Lake Trasimeno, L1450000, includes full board accommodation, visits to Etruscan sites, excursions, trekking, cooking lessons and a trip on the lake. Insurance and transfers included in all costs. Courses also organised combining a week in Rome followed by the Venice Carnival or Venice Film Festival.

UK applicants can apply to Centro Turistico Studentesco, 33 Windmill Street, London W1P 1HH Tel 01-580 4554.

ISTITUTO UNIVERSITARIO DI BERGAMO Curso Estivo di Italiano, Via Salvecchio 19, 24100 Bergamo Tel Bergamo 217195
University summer language and culture course for all levels in the Lombardy town of Bergamo. Ages 18+. 3-4 weeks, June-July. 25 hours per week. Maximum 12 per class. Audio-visual facilities and language laboratory. Cultural lectures for intermediate and advanced levels on art, literature, cinema, socio-economic aspects of Italy, and cultural aspects of Bergamo and Lombardy. Also seminar on socio-linguistics for teachers of Italian. Excursions to places of interest organised at weekends, plus trips to industrial establishments in the area. Cost L480000, 3 weeks or L580000, 4 weeks, includes course, teaching materials and excursions. Full board student residence accommodation available for the first 40 applicants. Inclusive cost L950000, 3 weeks or L1150000, 4 weeks. *Apply by mid May.*

ITALIAIDEA CULTURAL ASSOCIATION Piazza della Cancelleria 85, 00186 Rome Tel Rome 6547620
Language and culture courses for all levels at school in a quiet piazza in the centre of Rome. Ages 17-80, individuals and groups. 2 or 4 weeks,

January-November. 15 hours per week. Maximum 15 per class. Cost L230000, 2 weeks, L370000, 4 weeks. Also holiday courses for all levels except beginners, 4 weeks, January-November. 80 hours, including 15 hours of cultural visits and excursions designed to practice Italian in a fun way. Cost L450000. Non-intensive courses of 4 weeks, 6 hours per week, and 1:1 courses of 25 or 40 hours per week including lunch with a teacher. Teaching aids include slides and video. Textbooks and materials included. Cultural courses for intermediate and advanced levels in literature, history of art, cinema or commercial Italian. 20 hours total. Cost L250000, 4 weeks. Social programme includes guided visits, excursions, dinner parties, films and lectures. Accommodation available in apartments from L350000, 4 weeks. *Scholarships offered for 60 hour courses through Italian Cultural Institutes and Italian Departments of various universities, as well as through the Italian Ministry for Foreign Affairs.*

ITALIAN LANGUAGE HOLIDAY (TRENTO) Mr O D'Alberta, Tours Manager, Citalia, Marco Polo House, 3-5 Landsdowne Road, Croydon, Surrey CR9 1LL Tel 01-686 0677

Language courses in Civezzano, a mountain village near Trento. Ages 14 + . 2 weeks, July-August. 15 hours per week. Audio-visual facilities available, plus language laboratory for spare-time practice. Lectures on Venice, Verona and Trento, plus lectures by a local journalist, librarian, parish priest and craftsman. Excursions to Venice and the Dolomites, and half day tour of Trento. Leisure facilities include swimming in nearby lakes, tennis, mountain walking, table tennis and gymnasium. Open-air opera performances in the Roman arena at Verona can also be booked. Cost £686 includes course, teaching materials, extra lectures, excursions, full board school accommodation, return flight and transfers. Insurance can be arranged. Approved by the Ministry of Education.

JACQUELINE FAGET Vicolo Casilino 3, 00039 Zagorolo (Roma) Tel Rome 9525382

Language classes for all levels in Rome. Ages 15-21, individuals and groups. 3 weeks, July/August. 12 hours per week. Average 10 per class. Cultural activities, sports and excursions organised in the afternoons and every Wednesday, including debates, poetry/drama readings, swimming, jogging, cycling, judo, and visits to places of interest in and around Rome. Cost L850000 includes course, teaching materials, excursions and full board family accommodation. Extra excursions/cultural activities also available, including course in Italian cooking, L25000 per lesson; tennis lessons, L25000 per hour; and riding lessons, L15000 per hour.

LA BOTTEGA DELL'ITALIANO Corso Vittorio Emanuele 39, 00186 Rome Tel Rome 6798896/6795185
Language and culture courses for all levels in Rome. Ages 16+, individuals and groups. 2+ weeks, all year. 15-40 hours per week. Average class size 10. Cost from L450000, 2 x 20 hour weeks. Textbooks and materials included. Also conversation courses, 2 weeks, 15 hours per week, plus evening language courses, 1:1 courses, courses in business Italian or to prepare for Italian university or medical school entrance. Audio-visual and video facilities. Cultural courses include cooking, wine, history of art, and politics and economics. Cost from L120000, 2 weeks. Also Italian cinema course for advanced levels, 4 weeks, 50 hours, including a visit to the Cinecitta film studios. Cost L450000. Social programme includes guided tours, visits to parliament and other public buildings and to TV stations, plus films, parties and meals at the school. Accommodation available in self-catering apartments, or on bed and breakfast or half board terms with local families, or in pensions, from L13000 per day. Approved by the Italian Government. **AI** Diplomas may be taken. *Scholarships available through Italian Cultural Institutes.*

UK applicants can apply to Professor Eric Brentini, 201 Willesden Lane, London NW6 7YR.

MACHIAVELLI SCUOLA Piazza S Spirito 4, 50125 Florence Tel Florence 296966
Language and cultural courses for all levels at school run by a teachers cooperative in central Florence. Language courses include optional seminars on Italian life and culture designed to put language lessons in context. Ages 16+, individuals and groups. 1-6 months, all year. 10-20 hours language classes plus 5 hours optional seminars per week. Maximum 12 per class. Cost L440000 per month. Also super intensive courses, 2-4 weeks, including 4 hours per day normal classes and 2 hours per day in small groups reviewing lessons and practicing language in real-life situations out of school. Cost L380000, 2 weeks, L760000, 4 weeks. Also 1:1 courses of up to 8 hours per day. Audio-visual facilities. Textbooks from L14000, but other materials included. Extra cultural courses available for those with basic knowledge of Italian on Italian culture in the 80s, history of art and Italian literature, plus photography, graphic arts, and film production. Can also enrol students on art and craft courses at various centres in the city. Social programme includes bicycle tours of Florence to visit hidden works of art, cycling round the Chianti countryside, trips to restaurants and walks in the mountains near Florence. Accommodation available in families, apartments, pensions or hotels from L340000 per month. Also 2-4 week summer and Easter courses at Jesi, near Ancona and Volterra, near Pisa, in

cooperation with local authorities, plus a summer language and yoga course at Radicondoli, near Siena.

ST CLARE'S 139 Banbury Road, Oxford, England OX2 7AL Tel Oxford 52031
Summer language and culture course for all levels in Venice. Ages 15 +, individuals and groups. 2 or 4 weeks, August. 15 hours per week. Maximum 12 per class. Audio-visual facilities. Opportunities to study history, art restoration, jewellery making, mask and lace making, modern/Renaissance/studio art. Tennis coaching also available. Lectures on the medieval world, Machiavelli, the European rediscovery of Italy, and aspects of modern Italy. Excursions organised to Vincenzo, Verona, Ravenna, Mantua, Florence, Bologna, Padua, and Yugoslavia. There are also guided tours of Venice, barbecues, receptions and parties, and video showings. Cost £660, 2 weeks or £1300, 4 weeks, includes course, teaching materials, basic art materials, half board student hostel accommodation, excursions and return flight from London. Approx £15 needed for art materials in Venice. Course only £510, 2 weeks or £1150, 4 weeks. **PH**

US applicants may apply through Academic Study Abroad, 400 Main Street, Armonk, New York 10504

SCHOOL JOURNEY ASSOCIATION 48 Cavendish Road, London SW12 0DG Tel 01-675 6636
Language study visit to Rome specifically aimed at GCSE or A level UK students of Italian. Ages 15-20, individuals and groups. 2 weeks, all year. 15 hours per week language classes. Average 12 per class. Daily educational visits organised to places of interest in Rome. Cost £334 includes course, educational visits, bed and breakfast family accommodation, textbooks and teaching materials, escorted flight, airport charges, transfers and insurance. **PH**

SCUOLA BOTTICELLI Via Aretina 120, 50126 Florence Tel Florence 665544
Language courses for all levels in a teacher's home in the centre of Florence. Ages 14 +, individuals and groups. 1 + months, all year. 20 hours per week. Maximum 5 per class. Cost L450000, 1 month or L1250000, 3 months, includes course and teaching materials. Family, apartment or pension accommodation available from L280000, bed and breakfast, per month. Also 1:1 courses. 1 + weeks, all year. 30 hours per week. Cost L790000 per week includes course, teaching materials, lunch with teacher and bed and breakfast family accommodation. Hotel accommodation available. Courses in literature, 16 hours, history of art, 20 hours and cookery, 4 hours. Cost L90000 per course. Free monthly

guided tour of museums and art galleries in Florence; other excursions also arranged. Also language courses in the south of Elba for all levels. Ages 14 + , individuals and groups. 4 weeks, July and August. 15 hours per week. Maximum 5 per class. Cost L920000 includes course, teaching materials and self-catering apartment accommodation.

SCUOLA DI LINGUA E CULTURA ITALIANA PER STRANIERI DI SIENA, Piazzetta Grassi 2, 53100 Siena Tel Siena 49260
Language and culture courses for elementary to advanced levels at an old palace in Siena. Open to those at university entrance level, individuals and groups. 3 months, January, April, July and October. 15-20 hours per week. Maximum 25 per class. Cost L300000, plus L3000 for diploma and L6000 examination fee. Cultural courses for advanced levels include language and literature, the language of architecture, medieval/contemporary history, economic history, Italian political system, institutions and economy, history of art, medieval/modern art, ethnic traditions, teaching Italian, linguistics, the history of the Italian language, Italian dialects, Roman history, Italian law, archeology, history of the theatre, history of music, history of the cinema and Etruscology. Summer course for all levels, ages 14 + . 4 weeks, July-August, cost L200000. Also courses for teachers of Italian, and special courses in commercial Italian on request. Audio-visual facilities, language laboratory and computer assisted learning used. Free entrance to university library. Textbooks and materials not included. Social programme includes excursions and films. Accommodation available in student halls of residence in summer, and in private houses, from L250000 per month. Health insurance available from L20000. Approved by the Ministry of Education. *Scholarships available from Italian Cultural Institutes, the Italian Ministry of Foreign Affairs through Italian Embassies and Consulates and from Dante Alighieri Societies.* **PH**

SCUOLA LEONARDO DA VINCI Via Brunelleschi 4, 50123 Florence Tel Florence 294247
Language, culture and craft courses for all levels at a school near the cathedral in central Florence. Ages 16 + , individuals and groups. 2-24 weeks, February-November. 20 or 30 hours per week. Maximum 12 per class. Cost L400000-L670000, up to 4 weeks. Extra weeks from L100000 per week. Also 4 week semi-intensive courses, 10 hours per week, cost L250000. 2 week small group intensive courses, 30 hours per week, cost L700000. 1:1 courses from L525000, 15 lessons. Also special courses in Italian for business and trade, for medical students and for teachers of Italian. The Certificato de Italiano of the International Certificate Conference may also be taken. Audio-visual facilities. All

materials included. Cultural and craft courses offered include history of art, general culture in Italy, drawing, painting, pottery, weaving, Italian cooking/wine, and current affairs. Cost L135000-L300000, 20-30 lessons. Social programme comprises daily excursions, visits to potteries and wine cellars, guided tours of Florence, eating out and parties. Accommodation available in self-catering apartments or bed and breafast/half board in families, pensions and hotels from L70000 per week. *Scholarships available through Italian Cultural Institutes, the Italian Foreign Affairs Ministry, and the Association of Teachers of Italian, London.* **AI** Diploma Firenze may be taken.

UK applicants can apply to Cultural and Educational Services Abroad, 44 Sydney Street, Brighton, Sussex BN1 4EP Tel Brighton 683304. Cost approx £150-£200 per week includes 20-30 hours per week tuition and family accommodation.

US applicants can apply through US Student Programs, Institute of International Education, 809 United Nations Plaza, New York, NY 10017.

SCUOLA PALAZZO MALVISI Via Florentina 36, 47021 Bagno di Romagna (Forli) Tel Bagno di Romagna 911170/917140

Language courses for all levels in spa village in the Apennines. Ages 17-80, individuals and groups. 3-12 weeks, March-October. 32 hours per week. Maximum 10 per class. School is equipped with video and computerised teaching aids. Lectures on cookery, wine, geography and history of the region. Also 1:1 courses, and special courses for small groups on Italian for tourism, banking and commerce, and for teachers of Italian. Social programme includes excursions, parties, visits to local firms and wine shops and activities designed to offer students the chance to meet local people. Also opportunities for walking, fishing, swimming and tennis. Cost from L1390000 (3 weeks) includes course, teaching materials, social programme and accommodation. Scholarships are offered by the school and by the Communita Montane dell'Appennino Cesenate, 47026 S Piero in Bagno, (Forlì). Recognised by the local Chamber of Commerce. **AI** Diploma Firenze may be taken.

SCUOLA PALAZZO MALVISI Via Ponte Marino 10, 48100 Ravenna Tel Ravenna 36261

Language courses for all levels, at a palazzo in Ravenna. Ages 17-80, individuals and groups. Courses 2-12 weeks, March-October. 20 or 25 hours per week. Maximum 10 per class. Cost L350000, 2 weeks, 20 hours per week, L2150000, 12 weeks, 25 hours per week, includes course and teaching materials. Also 1:1 courses, 2-3 weeks, 20 hours per week, and special courses on request for small groups of Italian for tourism, commerce, banking and for teachers of Italian. Teaching aids include video and computers. Lectures on cultural subjects include cookery, wine, and the geography and history of the region. Social programme includes excursions, visits to local firms, parties, and activities to help students meet local people. Wide range of sporting facilities includes tennis, windsurfing, riding and swimming. Accommodation available in self-catering apartments, families or bed and breakfast in hotels, from L13000 per day. Recognised by the Chamber of Commerce. **AI** Diploma Firenze may be taken. *Scholarships offered by the school.*

SOCIETÀ DANTE ALIGHIERI Via Gino Capponi 4, 50121 Florence Tel Florence 2478981

Language and culture courses for all levels in Florence. Ages 15+, individuals and groups. 2-8 weeks, all year. 40, 60, 80 or 120 hours total. Maximum 10 per class. Cost from L295000, 2 weeks, 40 hours, L650,000, 8 weeks, 120 hours. Materials, cassette tape and books included. Also 1:1 courses and courses for teachers of Italian. Special courses for groups on request. Registration fee L50000. Audio-visual facilities. Also 4 week cultural courses in archaeology, literature, and history and socio-economics of Tuscany. May, June, July and September. Cost L1000000, 3 hours per week. Social programme includes concerts, conferences and art exhibitions. Accommodation available in families, pensions or hotels. Approved by the Ministry of Education and the Ministry of Foreign Affairs. *Some scholarships offered through the national committee of the Dante Alighieri Society in Rome.*

SOCIETÀ DANTE ALIGHIERI Via Torriani 10, 20124 Milan Tel Milan 669216

Language and culture courses in Milan for three levels. Normal courses, 7 months, October-May. 4 hours per week. Intensive courses, 3 months, January-May and October-January. 9 hours per week. Also lessons in Italian literature, culture, contemporary writers. Cultural activities, guided visits and theatre/music evenings also arranged. Cost L403000 each course, plus L100000 enrolment fee. Help given in finding accommodation. Courses can lead to the Diploma of the Dante Alighieri Society.

SOCIETÀ DANTE ALIGHIERI Piazza Firenze 27, 00186 Rome Tel Rome 6873722

Language and cultural courses for all levels in Rome. 2 months, February-March, April-May, October-November and December-January. Hours per week: language 4, literature 2, history of music 2, history of art 3, history of theatre 4, and Italian history 4. Cost per 2 month session L80000, language courses and from L50000, cultural courses. Registration fee L20000. Extra fees for attendance certificates and examinations. Extra courses on various subjects also organised, free of charge. Two 3 week summer courses in June/July. 10 hours per week language classes plus history of art. Students arrange their own accommodation. Approved by the Ministry of Education and the Ministry of Foreign Affairs. *Some scholarships offered through the national committee of the Dante Alighieri Society.*

SOCIETÀ DANTE ALIGHIERI Fondamenta Arsenale, Ponte de Purgatorio, 30122 Venice Tel Venice 5289127
Language courses in Venice for all levels. Ages 17 +, individuals and groups. 4 weeks, January-June and October-December. 10 hours per week. Maximum 15 per class. Cost L250000. Intensive summer courses, 3 weeks, July-September. 20 hours per week. Cost L400000. Other courses can be organised for groups of 5 minimum. Teaching facilities include audio-visual and educational games. Advanced level courses include an introduction to Italian culture and literature. Social programme includes visits to local tourist sights, exhibitions, films and opportunities to meet local people. Accommodation available in pensions, hotels or families. Approved by the Ministry of Foreign Affairs. *Scholarships available through the Italian Foreign Affairs Ministry or Società Dante Alighieri, Rome, see above.*

TORRE DI BABELE CENTRO DI LINGUA E CULTURA ITALIANA Via Bixio 74, 00185 Rome Tel Rome 7008434
Language courses for all levels in Rome near the Colosseum and the Basilica of San Giovanni. Ages 18 +, individuals and small groups. 2-5, 8 or 12 weeks, February-December. 20 hours per week. Maximum 10 per class. Cost L280000, 2 weeks, L1400000, 12 weeks, includes course and teaching materials. Special courses at Christmas and Easter. Also 1:1 intensive courses for 10 or 20 hours per week. Facilities include slides and video. Optional cultural seminars include Italian literature, art history, architecture, music from the 60s to the 80s, plus theatre workshop. Social programme includes guided tours, excursions, cinema, theatre and meals in restaurants. Accommodation arranged in private homes and self-catering student flats or bed and breakfast in pensions/hotels from L12000 per day. *Some scholarships offered through Italian Cultural Institutes and also through LEAs in the UK.*

Summer language and culture course for all levels in Pisciotta, a small coastal town south of Salerno. Ages 18 +, individuals and small groups. 2 or 4 weeks, July-September. 20 hours per week. Maximum 10 per class. Extra-curricular activities include boat trips, tours of archaeological sites and meetings with local political representatives. Excursions arranged at extra cost. Cost L280,000, 2 weeks or L500,000, 4 weeks includes course, teaching materials and extra-curricular activities. Sports facilities available. Accommodation in self-catering apartments from L100000 per week.

UNIVERSITA DEGLI STUDI DI MILANO Segretaria dei Corsi Internazionali di Cultura, Via Festa del Perdono 7, 20122 Milan Tel Milan 8846226
Summer courses run by the University of Milan at Gargnano on Lake Garda. Aimed at those with a good level of Italian who can demonstrate a special interest in deepening their knowledge of Italian language and culture. Ages 21 + . 3 weeks, July and August. 3 hours each of language classes and cultural lectures, per day. The course is free subject to attendance at all classes, and includes meals, Monday-Friday. Accommodation arranged in private rooms, cost approx L10000 per night. Social/cultural activities organised during the course. *Applications, supported by relevant institutions and giving reasons why the candidate would benefit from the course should be submitted by 15 April.*

UNIVERSITA DEGLI STUDI DI URBINO Corso Estivo per Stranieri, via Saffi 2, 61029 Urbino Tel Urbino 45250/2289
Language and culture course for all levels at the University of Urbino. Ages 18 + , individuals only. 1 month, August. 15-20 hours per week language tuition. Maximum 20 per class. Also includes 10 hours per week cultural courses covering linguistics and socio-linguistics, contemporary music, philosophy, Italian cinema, history and the Renaissance in Urbino. Cost L300000 includes course, teaching materials and social programme of films and local guided tours. Audio-visual facilities and language laboratory. University library available. Accommodation available in student halls of residence, private houses, pensions and hotels, and there is a student restaurant. *Some scholarships are available through Italian Cultural Institutes.*

UNIVERSITA ITALIANA PER STRANIERI Palazzo Gallenga, Piazza Fortebraccio 4, 06100 Perugia Tel Perugia 64344
Language and culture courses for all levels at university for foreigners in a palazzo in Perugia. 1, 2 or 3 months, January-November. 20 hours per week. Maximum 20 per class. Cost from L180000 per month. Also intensive courses, 1 month July-September. 27 hours per week. Maximum 20 per class. Cost L350000. Also linguistic-cultural and

technical-commercial courses for those with a reasonable level of Italian. 3 months, January, April, July and September. 28/29 hours per week language classes, plus lectures on literature, history, art history, cinema, phonetics and phonology (linguistic-cultural course) or economic history, commercial institutions, commercial correspondence and economics (technical-commercial course). Also intensive 1 month intermediate language course, July-September. 27 hours per week. Cost L350000. Also 9 month courses in language or culture for advanced students, 3 month courses for teachers of Italian, 1 month refresher course in August for teachers of Italian, courses for admission to Italian universities, 1 month courses on 15th century Italy, Nova Lectura Dantis, Italy today, contemporary Italian language, history of art and etruscology. Language laboratory facilities. The university runs a social programme, shows free films, and offers free sporting facilities including gymnasiums, tennis courts and and indoor swimming pools. Excursions and guided tours also arranged. Accommodation available in private homes, religious colleges, hotels and pensions, and in halls of residence during August. *Scholarships are awarded by the unversity, the Italian Ministry for Foreign Affairs, and the Dante Alighieri Society. Details from Italian Cultural Institutes.*

COURSES IN SWITZERLAND

THE AMERICAN SCHOOL IN SWITZERLAND Admissions Office, 6926 Montagnola-Lugano Tel Lugano 546471
Organise summer language programme for all levels on campus in a village near Lugano. Ages 12-18, individuals only. 4 weeks, June-August. 3 hours language tuition per day, supplemented by computer assisted language learning programmes, plus 2 hours per day of activity periods including language laboratory work, drama classes video film making, art and singing. Maximum 12 per class. Excursions and activities include mountain hikes, visits to open air markets and trips to Milan and Locarno. Campus social activities include weekly videos and firework displays. Optional weekend trips to main cities. Daily sports programme. Facilities include library, theatre, arts centre and photographic studio. Cost SF3600 includes full board campus accommodation, excursions. books, accident insurance and laundry.

ISTITUTO SANTO CATERINA Via Santa Caterina 4, 6600 Locarno Tel Locarno 311784
Language courses for all levels in Locarno. Ages 14+, individuals and groups. 3 weeks, July. 19 hours per week. Maximum 12 per class. Cost SF600 includes course, teaching materials and enrolment fee. Audio visual facilities. Excursions arranged to places of interest. Facilities for swimming, tennis and golf. Accommodation available includes full board at school for female students or in small hotels with meals at school, from SF1000. Advice and help given on problems and free time activities. Also year-long course starting January, April or September. 16 hours Italian, 8 hours French, English or German, 2 hours computing, per week. Cost SF600 per month plus SF100 enrolment fee. Accommodation arranged.

INFORMATION

Italian Consulate General
38, Eaton Place, London SW1X 8AN Tel 01-235 9371

Swiss Embassy
16-18 Montagu Place, London W1H 2BQ Tel 01-723 0701

British Embassy
Via XX Settembre 80A, 00187 Rome Tel Rome 4755441

Thunstrasse 50, 3005 Bern

Tourist office
Italian State Tourist Office (ENIT), 1 Princes Street, London W1R 8AY Tel 01-408 1254

Swiss National Tourist Office, Swiss Centre, 1 New Coventry Street, London W1V 8EE Tel 01-734 1921

Youth hostels
Associazione Italiana Alberghi per la Gioventu, Palazzo della Civilta del Lavoro, Quadrato della Concordia, 00144 Rome

Schweizerischer Bund fur Jugendherbergen (SJH), Postfach 2232, Wildhainweg 19, 3001 Bern

Youth & student information

Centro Turistico Studentesco e Giovanile (CTS), Via Nazionale 66, 00184 Rome

ESTC, Largo Brancaccio 55, 00184 Rome.

Swiss Student Travel Office, SSR-Reisen, Backerstrasse 40, PO Box, 8026 Zurich

Resources

Accademia Italiana di Lingua, Via Pellicceria 6, Casella Postale 815, 50123 Florence Tel Florence 294820/263382 is a professional organisation of language schools teaching Italian, which binds its members by a code of conduct and researches new methods and materials for the teaching of the language. The Accademia has also introduced the Diploma Firenze to provide a standardised certificate of competence in Italian. Member schools are indicated above by **AI**

Dante Alighieri Society, St Patrick's International Centre, 24 Great Chapel Street, London W1V 3AF Tel 01-385 2800 is the London branch of a non-profitmaking society founded in Rome in 1889 to promote Italian language and culture all over the world and to act as a point of contact for Italian expatriates. Offers evening courses in Italian for all levels; cost £75 for 30 lessons.

The Italian Institute, 39 Belgrave Square, London, SW1X 8NX Tel 01-235 1461 acts as the cultural section of the Italian embassy in that it promotes Italian language and culture in Britain, organises cultural events and language classes, and handles scholarship applications for schools in Italy. Scholarships are granted by the Italian government, usually to university students of Italian, and by individual schools themselves who offer a limited number of free courses to those with a special reason for learning Italian. The Institute publish a leaflet *Italian Government Scholarships and Grants,* which gives details on how to apply for summer bursaries, short-term research grants and long-term scholarships and research grants. Also publish an annual booklet *Cultural and Language Courses in Italy,* and can provide current brochures on most of the listed courses.

Servizio Turistico Sociale (STS), Via Zanetti 18R, 50123 Florence Tel Florence 292067/268396 provides a reception and information service for visitors to Florence. It can book language, culture and craft courses in the city, find accommodation, arrange study tours and holidays in Tuscany, and offer discount travel.

Information on courses in the Italian-speaking cantons of Switzerland can be found in *Holidays and Language Courses* a free leaflet produced by the Swiss National Tourist Office, see above.

Publications
Italy, Travellers Handbook is a free booklet containing useful information for visitors with notes on accommodation, culture and leisure, sports and travel. Also includes general information and addresses of provincial and local tourist boards. Available from the Italian State Tourist Office, see above.

Young Rome is a source of information containing advice on where to sleep and eat, health and public services, details on museums, galleries and monuments, universities and cultural institutions, transport, excursions, maps and a host of other useful information and addresses. Available free from the Regional Tourist Organisation, Region of Latium, Tourist Assessor's Office, Via Rosa Raimondi Garibaldi 7, Rome.

Travel
Centro Turistico Studentesco UK Ltd, 33 Windmill Street, London W1P 1HH Tel 01-580 4554 offers low cost rail and air travel to Italy, and reductions on Mediterranean shipping lines, for students and young people. Can also book accommodation in major Italian cities.

CIT (England) Ltd, 50-51 Conduit Street, London, W1R 9FB Tel 01-434 3844 issues a kilometric ticket valid for 3000 km (maximum 20 journeys) which can be used by up to 5 people at the same time. Valid 2 months. A Travel at Will ticket is also available for unlimited travel on the Italian rail network for various periods.

STA Travel, 74 Old Brompton Road, London SW7 3LQ Tel 01-581 8233 operates flexible, low cost flights from London to Italy and Switzerland.

Transalpino Ltd, 117 Euston Road, London NW1 2SX Tel 01-388 2267 offers up to 50% off rail fares to 55 destinations in Italy and Switzerland for those under 26.

Swiss National Tourist Office, see above, issues the Swiss Holiday Card which gives unlimited travel on rail, lake boat and postal coach networks, plus reductions on mountain railways and cable cars. Cost SF145-SF285, 4-31 days. Also issue *Travel Tips for Switzerland*, a booklet containing information on travel formalities and facilities including accommodation, sports, culture and general information and advice.

Accommodation

Federazione Italiana per Campeggio e del Caravanning, Via V Emanuele 11, PO Box 23, 50041 Calenzano, Florence operates an international campsite booking centre and publishes a list of member campsites which can accept bookings, with details of costs, opening dates and facilities. *Apply by 15 May.*

Student Lodgings at University Cities in Switzerland is a booklet giving the addresses of student accommodation in Basle, Bern, Fribourg, Geneva, Lausanne, Neuchatel, St Gall and Zurich. Available from the Swiss National Tourist Office, see above.

The Swiss Student Travel Office, see above, offers cheap but comfortable accommodation in international student hostels at Klosters, St Moritz, Scuol, Lucerne, Wengen and Davos. Cost approx SF36 per day, half board.

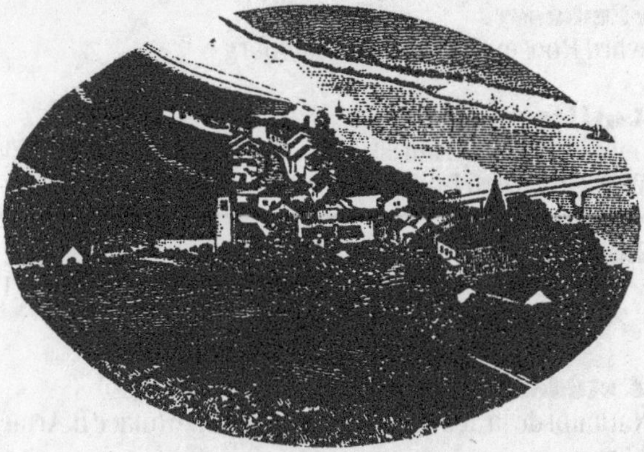

LUXEMBOURGIAN

Luxembourgian, or Letzeburgesh is one of the minor languages of the western branch of the Germanic Indo-European language family. It is basically a dialect of German, but as Luxembourg is an independent country, is generally considered as a separate language.

COURSES IN BELGIUM

INSTITUT PRO LINGUIS Place de l'Eglise 19, 6719 Thiaumont, Belgium Tel Arlon 22 04 62
Courses in Letzeburgesh for all levels in country house at Thiaumont, near Arlon in Belgium, close to the Luxembourg border. Ages 10+, individuals and groups. 1+ weeks, all year. 8 hours per day includes 4 hours in language laboratory and 4 hours in conversation groups. Maximum 7 per class. Cost from BF8650, 1 week, includes course, textbooks, transfer from station and full board accommodation at school or in village. Also weekend courses, Easter and summer holiday language/sports courses and intensive courses including private tuition for conversation practice. Business and science language programmes available on request.

INFORMATION

Luxembourg Embassy
27 Wilton Crescent, London SW1X 8SD Tel 01-235 6961

British Embassy
14 boulevard Roosevelt, 2450 Luxembourg

Tourist office
Luxembourg National Tourist and Trade Office, 36/37 Piccadilly, London W1V 9PA Tel 01-434 2800

Youth hostels
Centrale des Auberges de Jeunesse Luxembourgeoises, 18 place d'Armes, 2013 Luxembourg

Youth & student information]
Service National de la Jeunesse, 1 rue de la Poste (place d'Armes), 2346 Luxembourg

Union Nationale des Etudiants Luxembourgeois, 20 avenue Marie-Therese, 2132 Luxembourg

Travel
The Benelux Tourrail Card is available for 5 days within a period of 17, allowing unlimited travel on the national railway networks of Luxembourg, Belgium and the Netherlands and on the Luxembourg bus services of CFL and CRL. Valid mid March- mid September and Christmas; cost from £90. Details from YHA Travel, 14 Southampton Street, London WC2E 7HY Tel 01-836 8542.

Transalpino Ltd, 117 Euston Road, London NW1 2SX Tel 01-388 2267 offer up to 50% off full rail fares to destinations in Luxembourg for those under 26.

Grand Duchy of Luxembourg contains practical information for visitors covering entry requirements, climate, transport, accommodation, outdoor activities, museums, special events and places of interest. Available from the Luxembourg National Tourist and Trade Office, see above.

Accommodation
Gites d'Etape Luxembourgeois, Caritas, 23 boulevard Prince Henri, 1724 Luxembourg have rest houses and vacation homes available throughout Luxembourg. All year; cost approx FB120-FB180 per night, self- catering.

The Luxembourg National Tourist & Trade Office, see above, can provide a booklet listing accommodation in Luxembourg City. Also a leaflet *Camping* which lists all the authorised camping sites in the Grand Duchy, together with facilities available.

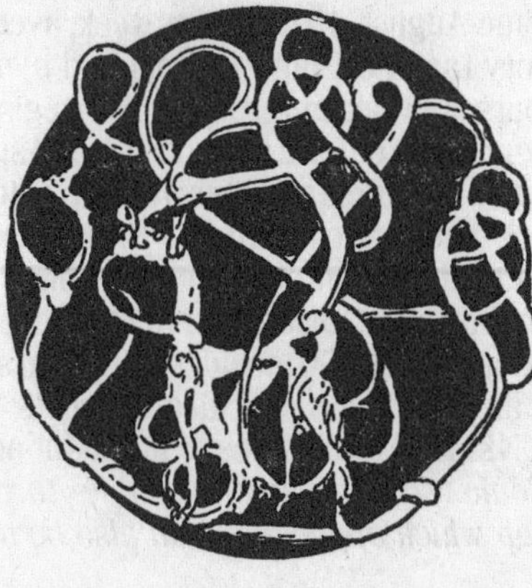

NORWEGIAN

Norwegian is a member of the Scandinavian group of languages, which share a common root in the Old Norse language spoken throughout Scandinavia from 6th-11th centuries. As Germanic languages they are members of the Indo-European group. From the late 14th century until 1814 Norway was under Danish rule, with Danish as the official court language and Norwegian spoken in rural areas. After 1814 the desire for recognition of Norwegian as the national language led to the gradual transformation of Danish vocabulary and spelling into riksmal *or state language. At the same time there was a more radical attempt to develop Norwegian as a language distinct from Danish, which led to* landsmal *or country language, based on the rural dialects. At present these two languages, now known as* bokmal *or book language and* nynorsk *or New Norwegian, have equal status. Both are learned in schools and have a strong literary tradition. Attempts to combine them into* samnorsk, *a united Norwegian have so far been unsuccessful. However the languages are gradually becoming closer, and it may be a matter of time before they merge.*

COURSES IN NORWAY

INTERNATIONAL SUMMER SCHOOL University of Oslo, PO Box 3, Blindern, 0313 Oslo 3 Tel Oslo 45 63 85
Language and culture courses for all levels at Oslo University. Good academic or professional record required. Ages 19 +, individuals and

groups. 6 weeks, June-August. 15 hours per week, average 12 per class. Language laboratory facilities. Both *bokmal* and *nynorsk* are taught. Also additional courses in peace research, Norwegian literature, art, folklore, history, education, culture and society, and special courses for teachers of Norwegian language and literature. Evening lectures on life in Norway, politics and current affairs. Extra-curricular activities include excursions to the mountains, to museums and optional long weekend in Bergen, barbecue, disco, and folklore evening. There is no actual tuition fee. Cost NKr10200 includes full board student residence accommodation, an excursion, incidental costs and insurance. Textbooks approx NKr120. Excursions required for additional courses from NKr200. *Some scholarships available through Norwegian Embassies, through which application can also be made. Apply by 1 March.*

INFORMATION

Royal Norwegian Embassy
25 Belgrave Square, London SW1X 8QD Tel 01-235 7151

British Embassy
Thomas Heftyesgate 8, 0264 Oslo 2

Tourist office
Norwegian National Tourist Office, 20 Pall Mall, London SW1Y 5NE Tel 01-839 6255

Youth hostels
Landslaget for Norske Ungdoms-herberger, Dronningensgate 26, Oslo 1

Youth & student information
Universitetenes Reisebyra (Norwegian Student Travel Office), Universitets-sentret, Blindern, Boks 55, Oslo 3

Norwegian Youth Council (LNU), Osterdalsgata 17, Oslo 6

Resources
Anglo-Norse Society, 25 Belgrave Square, London SW1 Tel 01-235 7151 aims to promote contact, friendship and understanding between Britain and Norway. Holds meetings, lectures and slideshows on aspects of Norwegian life, culture and society. Publishes quarterly newsletter and twice yearly *Anglo-Norse Review.*

Centre for Information on Language Teaching and Research (CILT), Regent's College, Inner Circle, Regent's Park, London NW1 4NS Tel 01-486 8221 publish *Norwegian Language & Culture Guide* £4.25 including postage, with details on the provision and use of language teaching and learning resources, covering an introduction to the language, useful addresses, libraries and special collections to consult, opportunities for learning, and examinations which can be taken.

Travel

The Nordic Tourist Ticket entitles the holder to unlimited travel on trains in Norway, Denmark, Finland and Sweden, and is also valid on some inter-Scandinavian ferries. Valid for 21 days; cost £128. Details from Norwegian State Railways, 21-24 Cockspur Street, London SW1Y 5DA Tel 01-930 6666.

Transalpino Ltd, 117 Euston Road, London NW1 2SX Tel 01-388 2267 offers up to 50% off full rail fares to destinations in Norway for those under 26.

POLISH

Polish is spoken by almost all of the 35 million people in Poland, by over 2 million citizens of the United States, and by smaller groups in the USSR, the UK, Canada and South America. It is a member of the western group of the Slavic languages which forms part of the Indo-European family, and structurally is related to Czech and Slovak. No early texts have survived to provide linguistic evidence on the evolution of the Polish language, but by around 1550 a literary language of sorts had emerged on the basis of converging influences emanating from the dialect areas and from Czech. Principal dialects are Little-Polish, Silesian, Great-Polish/Pomoranian, Mazovian and Kashubian. The vocabulary resembles that of the other Slavic languages, and many words in Polish, Bulgarian, Czech, Russian and Serbo-Croatian are identical.

COURSES IN POLAND

Applications from the UK for any of the courses below may be made to the the Consulate General in London, see under information heading.

ADAM MICKIEWICZ UNIVERSITY ul H Wieniawskiego 1, 61-712 Poznan Tel 699 251

Course in Polish culture and language for people of Polish origin, in Poznan. 4 weeks, July/August. 36 hours language classes and 20 hours lectures on Polish culture and language and contemporary social issues.

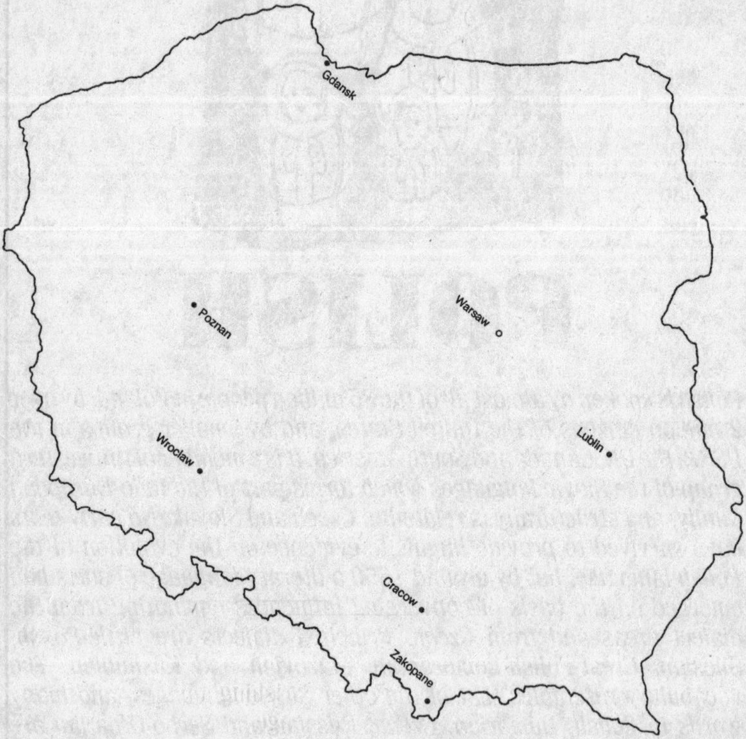

P O L A N D

Classes are held in French by staff members of the University. Cultural and tourist programme arranged. Also organise course in Polish economy and trade for lecturers and students of economics. Cost $480 includes full board student accommodation, didactic, cultural and tourist programme, books and other teaching aids.

BOLESLAW BIERUT UNIVERSITY Pl Nankiera 15, 50-140 Wroclaw Tel 40 25 59
Course in Polish culture and literature at Wroclaw, one of Poland's youngest universities, for people of Polish origin. 4 weeks, July/August. Curriculum includes 45 hours language classes and 31 hours lectures given in German on Polish films, theatre, music, literature, history of Silesia over the past centuries, Silesian architecture and art, folklore and material culture. Theatre performances and concerts, plus sightseeing tours of the city and vicinities. During last week there is a tour of Poland visiting Cracow, Zakopane and Warsaw. Cost $480 includes full board student accommodation, didactic, cultural and tourist programme, books and other teaching aids.

JAGIELLONIAN UNIVERSITY Institute for Polonian Studies, Rynek Glowny 34, 31-010 Cracow Tel 22 77 01
Course in Polish language and culture for people of Polish origin, at summer schools at university in Cracow. 6 weeks, July-August. 60 hours language classes and 36 hours lectures on Polish history, literature, music, economics, sociology, contemporary social problems and state-church relations, plus 6 hours seminars devoted to selected problems of Polish history and culture. Cost $550. Also 4 week course including 36 hours language classes and 20 hours lectures on Polish history and language, the economic and political system and contemporary social problems. Cost $480. Also 6 week intensive course in Polish language for graduates of these courses or those wishing to improve their command of Polish, with 120 hours language classes and lectures delivered in Polish and English. Cost $590. All programmes include an extensive presentation of Poland, its past and contemporary culture. Costs include full board student accommodation, didactic, cultural and tourist programme, books and other teaching aids.

Also course in Polish culture for teachers of the UNESCO Associated Schools. 3 weeks, August. 36 hours lectures on Polish history, art, literature, modern music, contemporary theatre, film, geography, economy, international relations, structure and education system. Also afternoon excursions and cultural events. Optional 1 week trip round Poland at end of course. Participants pay for trips and excursions only; university defrays costs of full board student dormitory accommodation, didactic, cultural and tourist programmes, books and other teaching aids. *Apply by end May to the National Commission for UNESCO who will forward applications.*

LUBLIN CATHOLIC UNIVERSITY Aleje Raclawickie 14, 20-950 Lublin Tel 302 26

Summer school of Polish culture and language for all levels in Lublin, a town dating back to the 10th century. Although intended primarily for students of Polish origin, those seriously interested in the Polish language and culture are welcome. Ages 18-45, individuals and groups. Maximum 12 per class. 6 weeks, July and August. 66 hours Polish language classes, 2 hours daily individual consultations with tutors, and 52 hours lectures on social problems, history, literature, theatre, music, films, history of art and folklore. Seminars on the history of Polish culture and meetings with artists, intellectuals, prominent humanists also scheduled. Audio-visual facilities and language laboratory. Lectures are delivered in English and later repeated in Polish. Cultural programme includes film shows, museum visits, meetings with artists, trips to Cracow, Warsaw, Gdansk and around Lublin. Cost $550 includes full board student dormitory accommodation, didactic, cultural and touristic programme, books and other teaching aids. Free health service provided during course.

MARIA CURIE-SKLODOWSKA UNIVERSITY The Polonian Centre of Culture and Education, Ul Weteranow 18, 20-038 Lublin Tel 32 786

Summer course of Polish culture and language for elementary to advanced levels, in Lublin. Ages 16-17. 4 weeks, July/August. Aims to help young people of Polish origin learn the language and become acquainted with Polish history and culture. Maximum 10 per class. 4 hours per day language classes with lectures conducted in English, French and German. Afternoon activities include sports, games, competitions, trips, learning Polish songs and folk dances, and excursions. Cost $150. Also arrange study course for Polish language teachers, focusing on the theoretical and practical aspects of teaching Polish, plus meetings with representatives of various areas of Polish social and cultural life, sightseeing tours, film shows, theatre performances and teaching practice.

INFORMATION

Polish Embassy

47 Portland Place, London W1N 3AG Tel 01-580 4324 Visa section: Consulate General, 73 New Cavendish Street, London W1N 7RB Tel 01-636 4533

British Embassy
Aleja Roz 1, 00-556 Warsaw

Tourist office
Polorbis Travel Ltd, 82 Mortimer Street, London W1N 7DE Tel 01-637 4971

Youth hostels
Polskie Towarzystwo Schronisk Mlodziezowych, Chocimska 28, 00-791 Warsaw

Youth & student information
Almatur, Travel and Tourism Office of the Polish Student's Association, 9 Ordynacka Street, 00-364 Warsaw

Juventur Youth Travel Bureau, Union of Socialist Polish Youth,Malczewsksiego 54, 02-622 Warsaw

Polish National Committee for the Cooperation of Youth Organisations, Smolna 40, Warsaw

Resources
The Society for Relations with Poles Abroad (POLONIA) Ul Krakowskie Przedmiescie 64, 00-322 Warsaw Tel 26-20-41 is a society established in 1955 with the aim of maintaining mutual and extensive ties between Poland and people of Polish origin. This includes promoting Polish language and culture, encouraging educational, scientific and economic cooperation and disseminating knowledge about Poland and Polish communities. Publish an annual information booklet on meetings, summer schools and courses organised in Poland for people of Polish origin, available free from the Consulate General of the Polish Embassy in London, see above.

Centre for Information on Language Teaching and Research (CILT), Regent's College, Inner Circle, Regent's Park, London NW1 4NS Tel 01-486 8221 publish *Polish Language and Culture Guide,* £4.25 including postage, which provides details on the provision and use of language teaching and learning resources, covering an introduction to the language, useful addresses, libraries and special collections to consult, opportunities for learning, and examinations which can be taken.

The Great Britain/East Europe Centre, 31 Knightsbridge, London SW1X 7NH Tel 01-245 9771 aims to promote closer understanding between the British and the peoples of Bulgaria, Czechoslovakia, Hungary, Romania, Poland and the German Democratic Republic. Organises colloquia, symposia and seminars to permit informal exchanges of views between people who have the same professional interest. Also arranges individual visits for academic and professional people.

Travel

Fregata Travel Ltd, 100 Dean Street, London W1V 6AG Tel 01-734 5101 offer express rail travel London-Poznan/Warsaw from £151 return, including couchettes and luggage service, and a coach service Manchester/Nottingham/Birmingham-Poznan/Warsaw, from £129 return.

The Polrailpass entitles the holder to unlimited travel on local and express trains. Valid for 8/15/21/30 days, cost £29-£72. Available from Polorbis Travel Ltd, 82 Mortimer Street, London W1N 7DE Tel 01-636 2217.

Transalpino Ltd, 117 Euston Road, London NW1 2SX Tel 01-388 2267 offer up to 50% off full rail fares to destinations in Poland for those under 26.

Accommodation

Polorbis Travel, see above, can provide student and youth tourist vouchers which guarantee bed and breakfast in 2-4 bedded rooms in international student hotels in 20 major university cities. Vouchers can be used without advance reservation, provided check is in before 16.00. July-August. Cost approx £7-£10 per night. Vouchers can also be used in payment for Almatur services, equipment hire and tickets for cultural events.

PORTUGUESE

Portuguese is the national language of Portugal and Brazil, and is the third most widely spoken of European languages after English and Spanish. It is closely related to, but distinct from Spanish, and belongs to the Romance group of languages that evolved from Latin, implanted in a large part of Europe as a result of military victories of the Romans and their subsequent political and cultural domination. The Roman occupation of the Iberian peninsula was total, and Latin gradually became established there, replacing all the native languages with the exception of Basque. A large number of Arabic words were incorporated into both the Portuguese and Spanish vocabularies when the Moors invaded in the 8th century. The Porto region was the first linguistic centre of Portugal, and its own language gradually became the national language. The Portuguese began the expansion of European influence around the world, setting up numerous trading posts and settlements, and acquiring a colonial empire. As a consequence, Portuguese is still spoken in the islands of the Azores and Madeira in the Atlantic, some parts of India and Sri Lanka, Africa and Asia. Galician, a dialect of Portuguese is also spoken in northwest Spain.

COURSES IN PORTUGAL

CENTRO AUDIO-VISUAL DE IDIOMAS Praca Luis de Camoes 36-3 esq, 1200 Lisbon Tel Lisbon 364988
Language courses for all levels in Lisbon. No age limits, individuals and groups. 5-8 weeks, all year. 10 hours per week. Maximum 6 per class.

Cost from Esc21620, 5 weeks. Also 1:1 tuition and language laboratory lessons by the hour. Excursions and family, pension or hotel accommodation can be arranged. Project materials provided, textbooks extra. Recognised by the Ministry of Education. **PH**

CENTRO DE INICIACAO E APERFEICOAMENTO DE LINGUAS Avenida da República 41-8o, 1000 Lisbon Tel Lisbon 730231
Language courses for all levels in Faro, capital of the Algarve, and in Lisbon and Porto. No age limits, individuals and groups. 1, 2 and 4 weeks, April-November. 10 or 15 hours per week, Faro and Porto, 15 or 30 hours per week, Lisbon. Maximum 6 per class. Extra-curricular activities include lectures and discussions on Portuguese life and culture, videos and afternoon visits to place of interest. Audio-visual facilities and language laboratory. Cost from Esc13350, 1 week (10 hours) and Esc20000, 1 week (15 hours) includes course and teaching materials. Also offer 1:1 tuition, courses in Portuguese art, history, literature and culture. Bed and breakfast family accommodation available from Esc20000, 2 weeks, to Esc35000, 4 weeks. Hotel accommodation available on request. Recognised by the Ministry of Education.
UK applicants for the Lisbon courses can apply to Cultural and Educational Services Abroad, 44 Sidney Street, Brighton, Sussex BN1 4EP Tel Brighton 683304, cost approx £125 includes tuition and family accommodation, or to Euro-Academy, 77A George Street, Croydon, Surrey CR0 1LD Tel 01-686 2363.

INLINGUA ESCOLA DE LINGUAS Rua Goncalo Cristovao 217, 4000 Porto Tel Porto 319313
Language courses for all levels in Porto. 2 weeks, summer. 15 hours per week. Average 3-5 per class. Language laboratory. Costs on request. Also 1:1 tuition throughout the year in general or business Portuguese, and tailor-made courses for groups. Sightseeing tours to Port cellars and local industry. Advice given on sport and leisure activities. Family, pension or hotel accommodation available. Recognised by the Ministry of Education.
UK applicants can apply to Inlingua School of Languages, 8-10 Rotton Park Road, Edgbaston, Birmingham B16 9JJ Tel 021-454 0204 or 55-61 Portland Road, Brighton, Sussex BN3 5DQ Tel Brighton 721612.

INTERNATIONAL HOUSE Rua Marques de Sa da Bandeira 16, 1000 Lisbon Tel Lisbon 571496
Language courses for all levels in Lisbon for executives, diplomats, businessmen, doctors, technicians, teachers and students. Ages 18+, individuals and groups. 3-4 weeks, all year. 20 hours per week.

Maximum 10 per class. Also 1:1 tuition and courses for special groups. Video and computer facilities, courses for special groups. Video and computer facilities. Lectures on Portuguese history, legal system, literature and politics. Extra-curricular activities include excursions to Coimbra, Oporto and Viseu, visits in Lisbon, parties and film shows. Cost Esc75000, 4 weeks, includes course and teaching materials. Apartment, pension or hotel accommodation available.
UK applicants can apply to Kate Naameh, Marketing Director, International House, 106 Piccadilly, London W1V 9FL Tel 01-491 2598.

UNIVERSIDADE DE COIMBRA Secretariado do Curso do Ferias, Gabinete de Relacoes Internacionais, Facultade de Letras, 3049 Coimbra Codex Tel Coimbra 34613
Summer language courses for all levels at the ancient university of the picturesque city of Coimbra. Ages 16+. 5 weeks, June-August. 20-23 hours per week. Intermediate and advanced level courses include study of Portuguese literature, history and society. Additional optional courses in Portuguese art, art, music, geography and cinema, and the literature of Brazil and Portuguese-speaking African countries. Extra-curricular activities include excursions, cultural activities and sports. Also academic year course in Portuguese language and culture. Cost from Esc25000. Accommodation list provided. *Subsidised by the Institute of Portuguese Language and Culture (ICALP), Praca do Principe Real 14-1, 1200 Lisbon, who offer some grants, and the State Secretariat for the Portuguese Communities (SECP).*

INFORMATION

Portuguese Embassy
11 Belgrave Square, London SW1X 8PP Tel 01-235 5331

British Embassy
35/39 Rua S Domingos a Lapa, Lisbon 3

Tourist office
Portuguese National Tourist Office, New Bond House, New Bond Street, London W1Y 0NP Tel 01-493 3873

Youth hostels
Associacao das Pousadas de Juventude, Avenida Duque de Avila 137-7, Lisbon 1

Youth & student information
Associacao de Turismo Estudantil e Juvenil, PO Box 586, 4009 Porto Cedex

Centro de Documentacao e Informacao Juvenil-FAOJ, Avenida Duque d'Avila 137, 1097 Lisbon

Turicoop, Turismo Social e Juvenil, Rua Pascoal de Melo, 15-1, Dto, Lisbon 1

Resources

Calouste Gulbenkian Foundation, 98 Portland Place, London W1N 4ET Tel 01-636 5313 was founded in 1956 in Lisbon, and is concerned with grant-giving throughout the world. Maintains cultural and educational centres in Portugal. The London branch offers grants for projects in the fields of arts, education, social welfare and Anglo-Portuguese cultural relations.

Hispanic & Luso Brazilian Council, Canning House, 2 Belgrave Square, London SW1X 8PJ Tel 01-235 2303 was founded in 1943 to advance the knowledge of the culture, languages, history and economics of Latin America, Spain and Portugal, in Britain. Organises lectures, offers information on courses, runs cultural events and can advise on grants. Also the base of the Anglo-Portuguese Society, which gives advice on all aspects of travel and study in Portugal and Brazil.

Centre for Information on Language Teaching and Research (CILT), Regent's College, Inner Circle, Regent's Park, London NW1 4NS Tel 01-486 8221 publish *Portuguese Language & Culture Guide* £4.25 including postage, with details on the provision and use of language teaching and learning resources, covering an introduction to the language, useful addresses, libraries and special collections to consult, opportunities for learning and examinations which can be taken.

Travel

STA Travel, 74 Old Brompton Road, London SW7 3LQ Tel 01-581 8233 operate flexible low-cost flights between London and destinations throughout Portugal.

Transalpino Ltd, 117 Euston Road, London NW1 2SX Tel 01-388 267 offer up to 50% off full rail fares to destinations in Portugal for those under 26.

Accommodation

The Portuguese National Tourist Office, see above, can provide a brochure listing *pousadas* (state tourist inns) in historic houses, castles, palaces, convents and monasteries, and situated in areas of natural beauty. Also publish a leaflet with map showing the location of campsites with information on dates and facilities. Information sheet on accommodation for the disabled available. **PH**

ROMANIAN

One of the Romance languages descended from Latin, which include French, Italian, Portuguese, Spanish, Catalan and Sardinian, Romanian is the official language of the Socialist Republic of Romania, and spoken by about 19 million people. A variety of the language is also spoken in the Moldavian republic of the USSR, but written in the Cyrillic alphabet. Romanian derives from the Latin introduced by the emperor Trajan when he conquered the region in the 2nd century, and although much influenced by Hungarian, Albanian, Turkish and Greek, it is more archaic than the other Romance languages. From the 16th century when the first written and literary texts emerge, borrowings from Latin and later from Italian and French re-Romanised the vocabulary. Romanian was generally written in the Cyrillic alphabet until 1860, when the use of the Roman script became universal.

COURSES IN ROMANIA

THE BRITISH COUNCIL Specialist Tours Department, 65 Davies Street, London W1Y 2AA Tel 01-499 8011
Offers places at summer schools under Cultural Exchange Programmes. Ages 18-35. All levels. 3-4 weeks, July/August. Course in Bucharest includes language tuition and lectures on language, literature, history,

art and folklore of the Romanian people. Also language tuition in Cluj, with lectures on historical, cultural and literary aspects of Romania provided in Romanian, with translated summaries. Excursions arranged. Knowledge of French/Romanian required. Board and lodging provided, but travel paid by applicant. Cost of course covered for Bucharest, but not Cluj. Bursaries available. Applications should be submitted through an academic or professional referee; university, college or school students must submit their application through a supervisor of studies or head of department. *Apply by mid February.*

INFORMATION

Embassy of the Socialist Republic of Romania
4 Palace Green, London W8 4QD Tel 01-937 9666

British Embassy
24 Strada Jules Michelet, Bucharest

Tourist office
National Tourist Office of Romania, 98/99 Jermyn Street, London SW1Y 6EF Tel 01-930 8812

Youth and student information
Youth Tourist Bureau, Onesti Street 4-6, Bucharest 1

Resources
Centre for Information on Language Teaching and Research (CILT), Regent's College, Inner Circle, Regent's Park, London NW1 4NS Tel 01-486 8221 publish *Romanian Language and Culture Guide,* £4.25 including postage, which provides details on the provision and use of language teaching and learning resources, covering an introduction to the language, useful addresses, libraries and special collections to consult, opportunities for learning, and examinations which can be taken.

The Great Britain/East Europe Centre, 31 Knightsbridge, London SW1X 7NH Tel 01-245 9771 aims to promote closer understanding between the British and the peoples of Bulgaria, Czechoslovakia, Hungary, Romania, Poland and the German Democratic Republic. Organises colloquia, symposia and seminars to permit informal exchanges of views between people who have the same professional interest. Also arranges individual visits for academic and professional people.

RUSSIAN

Throughout the USSR over 140 million people have Russian as their mother tongue and another 42 million have it as a fluent second language. Together with Arabic, Chinese, English, French and Spanish it is one of the six official languages of the United Nations. Russian is the most important of the Slavic languages, and its library of literature places it amongst the world's great. It is written in the Cyrillic script which was created in the 9th century by two Greek missionary brothers, Cyril and Methodius, and as such is based largely on the Greek alphabet. Russian is a member of the eastern Slavic language family, together with Ukrainian and Belorussian, and is known for its unusual consonant groupings, lengthy words, and long personal and place names.

COURSES IN THE USSR

THE BRITISH COUNCIL Specialist Tours Department, 65 Davies Street, London W1Y 2AA Tel 01-499 8011
Offer places on summer course at the Herzen Institute, Leningrad. 5 weeks, July/August. Course concentrates on improving language abilities and teaching skills, with visits to places of interest. Cost approx £220 for travel and visa arrangements. Hotel accommodation, tuition

and subsistence provided by the USSR. Applicants should normally be British citizens with established careers in the UK who have taught, or who are intending to teach, Russian at any level. *Apply by 4 March.*

INTERCHANGE Interchange House, 27 Stafford Road, Croydon, Surrey CRO 4NG Tel 01-681 3612
Study visits to the Soviet Union organised under the terms of the Cultural Agreement and subsidised by the British Council. 30 days, March/April. Groups are attached to the Herzen Institute in Leningrad. Language tuition seminars, cultural activities and meetings with students and teachers at various educational institutions, plus local visits of historical interest. Cost £549 includes flight, briefing information and visa. The cost of accommodation, food, travel and visits on the programme are met by the USSR. Participants are required to write a report/essay on some aspect of their visit on their return. Applications only from British students with a good knowledge of Russian, at colleges of education, departments of education, or at departments of Russian or Slavonic Studies at universities or polytechnics, and must be submitted through colleges or departments.

REGENT HOLIDAYS (UK) LTD 13 Small Street, Bristol BS1 1DE Tel Bristol 211711
Arrange courses in the Russian language in conjunction with university departments, in Oryol and Novo Sibirsk, for intermediate levels and above. All ages, individuals and groups. Maximum 10 per class. 4 weeks, July. 24 hours tuition per week. Full tourist/social programme arranged. Cost from £800 includes full board hotel accommodation, textbooks and project materials, flight and excursions.

SOCIETY FOR CULTURAL RELATIONS WITH THE USSR 320 Brixton Road, London SW9 6AB Tel 01-274 2282
Annual intensive Russian course for all levels, from near beginners to postgraduates, at the Moscow Motor Road Institute. All ages. 3 weeks, July. 3 hours per day language classes, with singing or dancing lessons plus art lectures given by leading specialists and performers, with slides, music of the balalaika, domra and guitar with demonstrations, Soviet literature, home and foreign policy. Optional afternoon programme includes excursions to places of interest, visits to concerts, theatre, circus, cinemas, exhibitions and museums. Informal discussions with students, meetings with writers, poets and translators. Hotel accommodation and meals provided in cooperation with Intourist. Cost £750. Organised in conjunction with Progressive Tours Ltd, 12 Porchester Place, London W2 2BS Tel 01-262 1676. *Apply by May. Scholarships available through the British-Soviet Educational Trust.*

COURSES IN AUSTRIA

GESELLSCHAFT FÜR OST- UND SÜDOSTKUNDE Bismarkstrasse 5, 4020 Linz, Austria Tel Linz 27 33 80
International Russian language seminars for all levels at Unterweissenbach, in Upper Austria, north of Linz. 2 or 3 weeks, July-September. 7 hours per day. Maximum 15 per class. Also lessons in Russian literature and commercial correspondence. Extra-curricular activities include excursions, walking, swimming, tennis, table tennis, riding, mini golf, evening lectures, concerts and discussions. Cost AS5000, 2 weeks or AS6500, 3 weeks, includes course, teaching materials and extra-curricular activities. Accommodation available in hotels or families, from AS195 half board, AS245 full board, per day. Also Russian winter seminar for all levels. Location varies each year, but always in an Upper Austrian ski resort. 2 weeks, February-March. Approx 5 hours per day, small groups. Classes in Russian literature for intermediate and advanced levels. Social programme arranged in evenings. Opportunities for downhill and cross country skiing, tobogganing, skating, swimming and bowling. Accommodation available in hotels, from AS310 half board, AS390 full board, per day; also bed and breakfast in private rooms, cost AS170 per day.

ÖSTERREICHISCHES OST- UND SÜDOSTEUROPA-INSTITUT Ostakademie, Josefsplatz 6, 1010 Vienna, Austria Tel Vienna 512 1895
International seminar in East-European languages in Eisenstadt, a village near the Hungarian border, south east of Vienna. Aimed at university level students with some knowledge of Russian. 3 weeks, July-August. 6 hours language tuition and 2 hours private study per day, small groups. Also special lessons in phonetics, lexis, syntax, translation and literature, and special courses for translators and more advanced students. Social activities arranged. Cost AS8800 includes course, teaching materials and full board school accommodation. Also international seminar in Russian language in Dienten, an alpine village south of Salzburg. Aimed at university level students with some knowledge of Russian. 2 weeks, February. 5 hours language tuition, 2 hours private study and 2 hours skiing, per day. Maximum 10 per class. Special classes in Russian for economics. Extra-curricular activities include films and singing/dancing evenings. Cost AS7700 includes course, teaching materials, ski instruction in Russian and full board school accommodation.

SALZBURG INTERNATIONAL LANGUAGE CENTRE Moosstrasse 106, 5020 Salzburg Tel 84 44 85
Intensive introductory courses arranged at language school in Salzburg, aimed at students who have no background in Russian. Ages 15+, individuals and groups. Maximum 15 per class. 3 week compact courses, July-September. 25 x 45 minute lessons per week. Course includes basic structures of the spoken and written language, enhanced by audio-visual aids, language laboratory, computer groups and conversation groups with native speakers. Library available. Lectures in Russian culture and life. Daily excursions and afternoon hikes to places of interest including ice caves, boat trips, salt mines, and castles, sports activities such as windsurfing and skiing, social events on campus, plus folklore and theatre evenings. Cost AS14000 includes full board campus accommodation, social events plus all textbooks and instructional material. Family accommodation also available. Medical insurance available at AS80 per week. Participants can be met at airport/station. Advisory office can assist students plan enrolment at Salzburg University, travel, theatre and concert visits and provide extensive visitors guide. Approved by the Department of Education.

INFORMATION

Embassy of the USSR
13 Kensington Palace Gardens, London W8 4QX Tel 01-299 3628
Consular section: 5 Kensington Palace Gardens, London W8 4QS
Tel 01-229 3215

Austrian Embassy
18 Belgrave Mews West, London SW1X 8HU Tel 01-235 3731

British Embassy
Naberezhnaya Morisa Toreza 14, Moscow 109072

Reisnerstrasse 40, 1030 Vienna

Tourist office
Intourist Moscow Ltd, 292 Regent Street, London W1 Tel 01-631 1252

Austrian National Tourist Office, 30 St George Street, London W1R 9FA
Tel 01-629 0461

Youth & student information

Sputnik, Youth & Student Tourist Bureau of the USSR, 15 Kosygin Street, Moscow 117946

Society for Cultural Relations with the USSR, 320 Brixton Road, London SW9 6AB Tel 01-274 2282

Austrian Foreign Students' Service, Universitat, Dr Karl Lueger-Ring 1, 1010 Vienna

Resources

Great Britain-USSR Association, 14 Grosvenor Place, London SW1X 7HW Tel 01-235 2116, founded in 1959 with the aim of fostering on a politically impartial basis professional, cultural and human contacts of all kinds between the UK and Soviet Union. Offers members introductions to opposite numbers in the Soviet Union, receptions to meet Russian visitors, an extensive library, lectures and film shows, the provision of information and advice to researchers and to those visiting the USSR.

Society for Cultural Relations with the USSR, 320 Brixton Road, London SW9 6AB Tel 01-274 2282, a charity founded in 1924 to further Anglo-Soviet cultural exchanges, with offices in Cambridge, Devon, Kent and Wiltshire. Plays an active part in the promotion and extension of cultural relations and exchanges with the USSR. Services include providing contacts with cultural organisations and institutions and with Soviet teachers, scientists, artists and writers; film shows, visual aids and display material for teachers, students and lecturers, reading lists, reference and music library. Can answer enquiries for information about the USSR, has extensive holdings of Russian reference books for consultation, can provide advice on study tours in education, science and medicine, theatre, cinema, architecture, law, history, archaeology and the social sciences. Also sponsors lectures by experts in the field and arranges for speakers to address meetings at educational institutions in a wide variety of subjects. Can provide advice to school groups together with pre-trip preparation material and variety of competitions on themes of Soviet culture, plus assistance in arranging study courses, contacts and youth meetings. Also organises evening classes in Russian, plus an intensive Easter course in London with Soviet teachers. Publishes *SCR Guide to Russian Classes in the UK* £1.75, a guide for part-time or adult students, which includes details on evening classes, short courses in the UK and USSR, cultural activities, private study facilities and useful addresses.

SERBO-CROATIAN

Serbian and Croatian are generally considered one language. Serbo-Croatian is the common language of modern Yugoslavs and the Serbs, Croats, Montenegrins, Dalmatians and the peoples of Bosnia and Herzegovina, despite differences of dialect and varying historical development. Croatian is the majority language in Yugoslavia, spoken by about 15 million people, and is known to most Slovenes and Macedonians, though Slovenian and Macedonian are also officially recognised Yugoslav languages. These, together with Bulgarian belong linguistically to the southern branch of the Slavic group of languages. The Cyrillic alphabet, based on Greek, was adopted by the Eastern Orthodox religious Serbs. The Croats, Roman Catholics influenced by the West, have used a modified form of the Roman alphabet since the 14th century. The Croatian and Serbian alphabets have precise equivalents so that one can be exactly transliterated into the other.

COURSES IN YUGOSLAVIA

THE BRITISH COUNCIL Specialist Tours Department, 65 Davies Street, London W1Y 2AA Tel 01-499 8011
Offer places at summer schools under Cultural Exchange Programmes. Ages 18-35. Courses in language, combined with choice of classes on

literature, art, history and culture. Courses include seminar for Slovenian language, literature and culture organised by the Faculty of Philosophy at the University of Ljubljana. 2 weeks, July. Also Yugoslav seminar for foreign Slavists in Zadar and Sarajevo organised by the Faculty of Philosophy, Sarajevo. 3 weeks, August. Seminar for Macedonian language, literature and culture in Skopje and Ohrid organised by the University Kiril I Metodij, Skopje. 3 weeks, August. Seminar at the Zagreb Slavistic School in Dubrovnik and Zagreb organised by the Faculty of Philosophy at Zagreb University. 3 weeks, July/August. Visits and excursions arranged. Board and lodging provided, but travel paid by applicant. Bursaries available. Applications be submitted through an academic or professional referee; candidates applying from a university, college or school must submit their application through a supervisor of studies or head of department. *Closing date mid February.*

MEDUNARODNI SLAVISTICKI CENTAR Filoloski fakultet, Studenteski trg 3, 11000 Belgrade Tel 011/187-662
Annual seminar in the Serbo-Croat language, literature and culture for foreign slavists, organised by the International Centre for Slavistic Studies. 3 weeks, September. Seminars and meetings take place in Belgrade, Novi Sad, Pristina and Trsic and provide an opportunity to improve language skills.

MEDUNARODNI SLAVISTICKI CENTAR SR HRVATSKE Filoloski fakultet, Dure Salaja 3, 41000 Zagreb Tel 041/513-155]
Annual seminar of the Zagreb School of Slavistics for foreign Slavists, including students, professors and assistants, in Dubrovnik and Zagreb. 3 weeks, July/August. Course in Croatian language, literature and culture of Yugoslav people, with lectures in the Croatian language, seminars and exercises. Opportunities to meet local writers, translators and cultural and public workers. Also courses on Old Church Slavonics, Macedonian and Slovenian. Excursions arranged. Hotel accommodation provided. *Scholarships available.*

SEMINAR SLOVENSKEGA JEZIKA, LITERATURE IN CULTURE Filolofski fakultet, Askerceva 12, 61000 Ljubljana Tel 061/332-611
Annual seminar of Slovenian language, literature and culture for foreign Slavists in Ljubljana, including students, professors, scientists and translators. 2 weeks, July. Lectures of language, literature and culture, plus visits to cultural events and institutions.

UNIVERZITET KIRIL I METODJ VO SKOPJE Krste Misirkov bb, 91001 Skopje
Annual seminar on Macedonian language, literature and culture for students, cultural workers and foreign slavists in Skopje and Ohrid. 3 weeks, August. Lectures on the development and present situation of the Macedonian language.

COURSES IN AUSTRIA

OSTAKADEMIE Ost-und Sudost Europa-Institut, Josefsplatz, 1010 Vienna Tel 512 18 95
International seminar in East European languages at Eisenstadt in the Burgenland of Austria. 3 weeks, July-August. For university students with a prior knowledge of Serbo-Croat. Intensive language courses in small groups. 6 hours tuition per day, plus 2 hours individual study. Specially developed teaching materials. Cost AS8800 includes course, teaching materials and full board accommodation.

INFORMATION

Yugoslav Embassy
5-7 Lexham Gardens, London W8 5JU Tel 01-370 6105

British Embassy
46 Ulice General Zdanova, Belgrade

Tourist office
Yugoslav National Tourist Office, 143-147 Regent Street, London W1R 8AE Tel 01-734 5243

Youth hostels
Ferijalni Savez Jugoslavije, Mose Pijade 12/1, 11000 Belgrade

Youth & student information
Karavan-Naromtravel, Organisation for International and Domestic Youth Travel, Knez-Mihailova 50, 11000 Belgrade

Resources
Centre for Information on Language Teaching and Research (CILT), Regent's College, Inner Circle, Regent's Park, London NW1 4NS Tel 01-486 8221 publish *Serbo-Croat Language and Culture Guide* £4.25 including postage, which provides details on the provision and use of language teaching and learning resources, covering an introduction to the language, useful addresses, libraries and special collections to consult, opportunities for learning, and examinations which can be taken.

Travel
STA Travel, 74 Old Brompton Road, London SW7 3LQ Tel 01-581 8233 operate flexible low cost flights between London and destinations throughout Yugoslavia.

Transalpino Ltd, 117 Euston Road, London NW1 2SX Tel 01-388 2267 offer up to 50% off full rail fares to destinations in Yugoslavia for those under 26.

Accommodation *Private Accommodation Rates* gives details of accommodation available throughout the year in private homes, including rented apartments, family houses and bungalows. *Camping Yugoslavia* provides a list of all official campsites with details of facilities and a map. Both available from the Yugoslav National Tourist Office, see above.

SPANISH

Spanish is one of the Romance languages, and one of the most widely spoken languages in the world, spoken today by between 250 and 300 million people in Spain, Central and South America, and southern areas of the United States. It is also one of the six official languages of the United Nations. Ladino, a variation of Spanish, is also spoken in Turkey and Israel by descendants of Jews expelled from Spain in the late 15th century. The pronunciation and method of the language vary between countries, but not so greatly as to make cross-communication impossible. The purest form of Spanish, Castilian, was originally one of the dialects developed from Latin after the Roman occupation of the 3rd century. The Moors conquered most of Spain in the 8th century, adding Arabic as a language influence, but by the 15th century the Christian reconquest had established Castilian as the major dialect.

COURSES IN SPAIN

Members of the Federacion Espanola de Centros de Ensenanza de Idiomas – Spanish Federation of Language Schools – are denoted by **FECEI**, *and members of the Asociacion de Centros de Ensenanza de Idiomas de Madrid – Association of Language Schools in Madrid – by* **ACEDIM**.

AC IDIOMAS Plaza Frances Macia 2 entlo 3, 08021 Barcelona Tel Barcelona 2000263
Language courses for all levels in Barcelona. No age limits, individuals and groups. 1 month, all year. 20 hours per week. Maximum 8 per class. Cost Pts43000. Also courses in business and technical Spanish. Audio-visual facilities. Textbooks Pts2000 per course. Debates and seminars with guest speakers, and study of cultural topics, including the architecture of Gaudi. Courses in riding, tennis, gymnastics and other sports, and Spanish dancing available through affiliated organisation. Extra-curricular activities include guided tours of Barcelona and visits to radio and TV stations, theatres and museums. Accommodation with families Pts97000 per month. Also superintensive course for executives, 10 days, 8 hours per day, staying in a 3 star hotel, cost Pts179150. **PH**

AL-ANDALUZ, Herrera 12, 29017 Malaga Tel Malaga 291741
Language courses in a typical Andalusian house near the beach in Malaga. Ages 16 + , individuals only. Multiples of 2 weeks, all year, or 3 weeks, November-March. 20 hours per week. Maximum 7 per class. Cost Pts20000, 2 weeks, Pts31000, 3 weeks, Pts35000, 4 weeks. Intensive courses, 25 hours per week, cost Pts2500 extra per week. For advanced students the course has a strong cultural element covering Spanish culture, history, art, geography, literature and folklore. Extra lessons using audio-visual methods, and remedial classes for students needing help to keep up. Also business correspondence courses and 1:1 tuition. All textbooks included. Social activities include 2 excursions per month to local villages and towns, 1 guided tour of Malaga, parties with opportunities to meet local people, visits to museums 2 or 3 times a month, films followed by discussions and free flamenco dance lessons. Opportunities for sports. Family, apartment or pension accommodation available, from Pts20000. Can offer advice on all aspects of student's stay. **PH**

ALBA CENTRO INTERNACIONAL DE INTERCAMBIOS, Triana 4 – 1 dcha, 28016 Madrid Tel Madrid 4586016
Language courses for all levels in Madrid. Ages 15 + , individuals and groups. 1 + weeks, all year. 10, 15 or 20 hours per week. Maximum 10 per class. Also 2 weeks, Easter, 10 hours per week, and 3 weeks, July and August, 10 hours per week. 1:1 courses of 20, 30, 40 or 50 hours per week also available, plus 1:1 courses of 10 or 20 hours per week in teacher's home. Special courses can also be organised for groups of 45 + . Students may study for the examinations of the Escuela Oficial de Idiomas. Audio-visual and language laboratory facilities. Group courses include programmes on modern Spanish culture and civilisation,

including geography, history, politics, discussion groups, visits to museums and excursions. Optional classes in flamenco dancing and guitar, and cooking. Facilities for tennis and swimming available, and opportunities to meet Spanish people. Cost from Pts54000, 2 weeks, Pts66000, Easter course or Pts96000, summer course includes course, teaching materials, full board family accommodation plus some extra-curricular activities and excursions. 1:1 courses Pts 2500 per hour. Approved by the University of Madrid. **PH**

THE AVILA CENTRE OF ENGLISH Bajada de Don Alonso 1, 05003 Avila Tel Avila 213719

Language and culture courses for all levels in the small ancient city of Avila. No age limits, individuals and groups. 1-3 weeks, Easter and July-August. 15 hours per week. Classes in colloquial Spanish, literature, and contemporary issues and customs of Spain. Audio-visual, video and computer aids. Extra-curricular activities include film, drama, music and games evenings where participants can mix with Spanish students of English. Also talks on local crafts and industry, excursions to Madrid, Salamanca and Segovia, and free use of sports facilities. Cost £120, 1 week, £220, 2 weeks and £320, 3 weeks, includes course, teaching materials, excursions, sports facilities, and full board family accommodation. **PH**

CASA INTERNACIONAL Rodriguez Sanchez 15-17, 14003 Córdoba Tel Córdoba 470350

Language courses for all levels in Córdoba. Ages 16+; younger students by arrangement. Individuals and groups. 1+ weeks, all year. 1:1 tuition also available, 15 hours per week. Cost Pts43000 includes full board family accommodation. Also courses for school/college groups. 1+ weeks, February-April and September-October. 15 hours per week. Maximum 12 per class. Lectures on Spanish art and architecture, history and civilisation. Audio-visual and language laboratory facilities. Social activities include excursions to local places of interest, guided tours of Córdoba, opportunities to meet Spanish students at the school and films. Cost Pts700000, group of 24 students, or Pts900000, group of 36 students, includes course, teaching materials, social activities and full board family accommodation. Recognised by the city council of Córdoba.

Applications in the UK can be made to Kate Neemah, Marketing Director, International House, 106 Piccadilly, London W1V 9FL Tel 01-491 2598.

Santiago de Compostela
Oviedo
Llanes
Santander
Laredo
Leon
Pamplona
Jaca
Barcelona
Valladolid
Zaragoza
Salamanca
Avila
Madrid
Navalcarnero
Toledo
Valencia
Picassent
Alicante
Murcia
Cartagena
Cordoba
Seville
Almunecar
Granada
Malaga
Marbella
Cadiz

S P A I N

CENTRO DE CULTURA Y ESTUDIOS CARMEN DE LAS CUEVAS Cuesta de los Chinos 15, Albayzin, 18010 Granada Tel Granada 221062
Courses for all levels in the heart of the famous old quarter of Granada, overlooked by the Alhambra and on the slopes of the Sierra Nevada. Ages 18+, individuals and groups. 2, 3 or 4 weeks, March-September. 15 hours per week. Maximum 8 per class. Audio-visual and video facilities. Talks given on subjects such as the Civil War, modern Spain, art in Granada, Garcia Lorca, Latin-America, and the world of flamenco. Also extra 3 hour per week courses on literature and flamenco dancing, cost Pts2000 per course. Extra-curricular activities include 1 or 2 day trips on foot, accompanied by an expert mountain guide, or by Land Rover to places off the beaten track, plus visits to local cultural sights, parties and video films. Facilities include self-service bar, library, terraces for relaxing, and a television. Cost Pts36300, 2 weeks, Pts52800, 3 weeks, and Pts60500, 4 weeks, includes course, teaching materials and self-catering apartment accommodation. Cost excluding accommodation from Pts22000, 2 weeks.
UK applicants can apply to Rachel Thalman, 11 Kennington Park Place, London SE11.

CENTRO DE ESTUDIOS DE CASTELLANO Avenida Juan Sebastian Elcano 110, 29017 Malaga Tel Malaga 290551
Language courses for all levels at school in residential district of Malaga near the sea. Ages 16+, individuals only. 1 month, all year. 20 hours per week. Maximum 8 per class. Cost Pts34000. Special courses for businessmen, secretaries and interpreters. Textbooks from Pts3000, depending on course. Lectures on Spain and Latin America. Social activities include barbecues, paellas and excursions to places near Malaga. Accommodation in families or self-catering apartments available, from Pts25000 per month.
UK applicants can apply to Gabbitas, Truman & Thring, 6-8 Sackville Street, Piccadilly, London, W1X 2BR Tel 01-734 0161, or to Cultural and Educational Services Abroad, 44 Sydney Street, Brighton, Sussex BN1 4EP Tel Brighton 683304.

CENTRO DE ESTUDIOS Y VACACIONES ALMUNECAR La Victoria 28, Almunecar (Granada) Tel Granada 633380/229181
Language, commercial and cultural courses for all levels in the typically Andalusian town of Almunecar, on the Costa del Sol. No age limits, individuals and groups. Intensive courses, 2-8 weeks, March-October. 20 lessons per week. Maximum 9 per class. Cost from Pts45000, 2 weeks, Pts62000, 3 weeks and Pts77000, 4 weeks. Also 4 week summer

courses of 20 lessons per week. Commercial Spanish course, July, covers business in Spain, commercial correspondence, business administration, and banking and finance. Hispanic history and art course, August, covers the history of Spain, the history of Latin-America, the history of art in Spain, and modern Latin America. Hispanic literature and civilisation course, September, covers classical and modern Spanish literature, civilisation and culture in Spain, modern Latin American literature, and civilisation and culture in Latin America. Cost Pts77000. May be taken simultaneously with intensive language course. Programme of complementary activities organised, including discussions, visits to banks, commercial enterprises, Granada and other places of interest, slide shows, films and poetry recitals. Extra-curricular activities for all courses include lectures, films, music recitals, parties, visits to places of interest, beach paella parties, and excursions to Granada, the Sierra Nevada and other localities. Sports can be practised using school equipment, and the school also has bicycles and mopeds to rent. Free lessons on flamenco and passadoble dancing. Also optional short courses in pottery, painting, dancing, flamenco or classical guitar, gastronomy and other crafts, cost from Pts2500. Library, collection of Spanish and Latin American recorded music and newspapers, magazines and videos also available. All costs include most of the above activities and self-catering apartment accommodation. *10 half scholarships a year are granted to school or university students. Applications should be made by the Spanish teacher of the student concerned.* **PH** but no special facilities.

CENTRO DE IDIOMAS SAGASTA Sagasta 27, 28004 Madrid Tel Madrid 4466979

Language courses for all levels at school in an old area near the centre of Madrid. Ages 17 + , individuals and groups. 4 weeks, all year. 20 or 30 hours per week language tuition. Maximum 8 per class. Cost from Pts56000, 20 hours per week, and Pts84000, 30 hours per week. 10 hours per week afternoon classes on culture, institutions and history of Spain. Also 2-3 week summer courses, June-August. Cost from Pts36000, 2 weeks, 20 hours per week, or Pts76000, 3 weeks, 30 hours per week. Special courses in commercial Spanish for intermediate levels and above. 6 weeks, 20 hours per week, leading to Madrid Chamber of Commerce examinations. Specialised courses can also be arranged for executive, financial, medical or school groups, and on a 1:1 basis. Audio-visual facilities. Textbooks cost average Pts1000 per course. Extra-curricular activities include sightseeing tours, meals out, films and parties, all accompanied by a teacher and designed to encourage the use of Spanish in natural surroundings. Family accommodation available from Pts8500 per week, bed and breakfast. Can also recommend hotel and apartment accommodation. **ACEDIM FECEI**

UK applicants can apply to Ms Psyche Kennett, 99 Milton Road, Cambridge.

CENTRO DE LA LENGUA ESPANOLA FEDERICO GARCIA LORCA, Alonso Carillo de Albornoz 14–1C, 29017 Malaga Tel Malaga 298046
Language courses for all levels in school in old part of Malaga. Ages 16+, individuals and groups. 3-4 weeks, February-November. 20 hours per week. Maximum 8 per class. Classes consist of 2 hours per day study based on textbook, followed by 2 hours chosen from Spanish and Latin-American music and cooking, acting plays by Garcia Lorca, discussions, conducting opinion polls in the street, editing a school newspaper, word games, or studying aspects of life and culture in Malaga and Andalusia, all with the aim of learning through creating. Cost Pts26000, 3 weeks and Pts32000, 4 weeks, includes course and teaching materials. Extra-curricular activities include parties and weekend expeditions to remote places. Sports club near the school. Accommodation available families or in self-catering apartments from Pts17000, 3 weeks. Approved by the Ministry of Education and Science.

CENTROS EUROPEOS GALVE Principe 12-6 A, 28012 Madrid Tel Madrid 2327230/5216076
Language courses for all levels in Alicante, Madrid and Valencia. Ages 12+, individuals and groups. 4+ weeks, October-June. 20 hours per week. Also 2-12 weeks, July-September. 15 hours per week. Maximum 12 per class. Study of literature and civilisation included at advanced levels. Summer courses at universities, ages 17+, 4 weeks, July. 20 hours per week includes language and culture. Also 1:1 tuition, business language courses and tailor-made courses for groups. Video facilities. Extra-curricular activities include excursions, museum visits, visits to newspapers, companies and other organisations, cinema and theatre trips, and in summer a range of sports. Cost Pts44000, 2 weeks and Pts89000, 4 weeks, includes course, teaching materials, weekly excursions in the summer, and half board family/student residence accommodation. Full board Pts2000 per week extra. Approved by the Spanish government. **PH**

CILCE – CENTRO INTERNACIONAL DE LENGUA Y CULTURA ESPANOLAS Bordadores 10, 46001 Valencia Tel Valencia 3310463/3321678
Language courses for all levels in Valencia. Ages 16+, individuals and groups. 2, 3, 4 or 11 weeks, January-November. 20 hours per week. Maximum 14 per class. Special courses for groups of 15-17 year olds, university or polytechnic groups, and in business and commercial Spanish. Also 1:1 courses and 2 week Easter course. Video and audio-

visual facilities. Study of Spanish literature and culture included in each course. Extra-curricular activities include guided tours, excursions, films, parties and meetings with local people. Also information on sports facilities and classes in Spanish dancing and crafts. Major fiestas in the city in March and July. Study room equipped with magazines, books and games for self-study. Cost from Pts46645, 2 weeks, includes course, teaching materials, extra-curricular activities and half board family accommodation. Cost excluding accommodation Pts24396, 2 weeks. Approved by the University of Valencia.

Applications in the UK can be made to Cultural and Educational Services Abroad, 44 Sydney Street, Brighton, Sussex BN1 4EP Tel Brighton 683304. Cost from £125 per week includes tuition and family accommodation.

CLUB DE RELACIONES CULTURALES INTERNACIONALES Calle de Ferraz 82, 28008 Madrid Tel Madrid 4796303
Language courses for all levels in Madrid, Salamanca and Toledo. Ages 18+, individuals and groups. 4, 8 or 12 weeks, all year. 20 or 30 hours per week. Average 8 per class. Also courses for teachers of Spanish, businessmen and diplomats, and non-intensive courses for au pairs resident in Madrid. Examinations of the Polytechnical University of Madrid may be taken. Extra-curricular activities include study of literature, visits to the Prado museum to study art, theatre visits, excursions and opportunities to meet young Spaniards. Cost Pts48000, 2 weeks and Pts82000, 4 weeks, includes course, teaching materials, and full board family, pension or student residence accommodation. Reduced price air or rail travel and insurance arranged on request. Approved by the Ministry of Interior Affairs, the Ministry of Culture and the Ministry of Education. *Some scholarships available.* The school has an affiliated organisation which assists disabled students during their stay **PH**

COLEGIO DE ESPANA San Juan Bosco 7-2, 03005 Alicante Tel Alicante 214406
Language and culture courses for all levels in Alicante. Ages 14+, individuals only. Intensive courses, 1+ months, all year. 20 hours per week. Maximum 15 per class. Cost Pts22500 per month. Special intensive courses, 2 or 4 weeks, all year. 25 hours per week. Maximum 7 per class. At intermediate level and above, course includes 5 hours per week cultural courses on the language and customs of Latin America, geography, history, literature, and politics. Cost Pts16500-Pts30500, 2-4 weeks. Also 1 and 2 month courses in commercial Spanish, and 1:1 tuition. Audio-visual facilities. Intermediate and advanced students may enrol on optional extra courses on contemporary Spain,

conversation, commercial Spanish, written Spanish, and general culture. 1 hour per day. Cost from Pts5000. Also 4 week summer courses in Spanish language and civilisation, 15 hours per week, and Hispanic studies for teachers of Spanish. All costs include textbooks and teaching materials. Extra-curricular activities include guided tours, excursions, meetings with Spanish students, and film shows. Accommodation available in families, student residences, and in self-catering apartments and pensions from Pts1250 per month. Insurance can be arranged.

COLEGIO DE ESPANA Compania 65, 37008 Salamanca Tel Salamanca 214788
Language and culture courses for all levels in Salamanca. Ages 14+, individuals only. Intensive courses, 1+ months, all year. 20 hours per week. Maximum 15 per class. Cost Pts22500 per month. Special intensive courses, 2 or 4 weeks, all year. 25 hours per week. Maximum 7 per class. At intermediate level and above, course includes 5 hours per week cultural courses on the language and customs of Latin America, geography, history, literature, and politics. Cost Pts16500, 2 weeks to Pts30500, 4 weeks. Also 1 and 2 month courses in commercial Spanish, and 1:1 tuition. Audio-visual facilities. Intermediate and advanced students may enrol on optional extra courses on contemporary Spain, conversation, commercial Spanish, written Spanish, and general culture. 1 hour per day. Cost from Pts5000. Also special 4 week summer courses in Spanish language and civilisation, 15 hours per week, and Hispanic studies for teachers of Spanish. All costs include textbooks and teaching materials. Extra-curricular activities include guided tours, excursions, meetings with Spanish students, and film shows. Accommodation available in families, student residences (summer only) and apartments. Can arrange insurance.

COLEGIO DE ESTUDIOS HISPANICOS Bordadores 1, 37002 Salamanca Tel Salamanca 214837
Language and culture courses for all levels in the ancient centre of Salamanca. Ages 16+, individuals and groups. 2 weeks-9 months, all year. 15-30 hours per week. Maximum 5-16 per class, depending on course chosen. Courses include intensive language, language and culture, courses in small groups, summer, Christmas and Easter courses, Hispanic studies, commercial Spanish and special courses for students and EC officials. Also academic year courses. Varying degrees of study of literature, history, art and modern Spain. Cost from Pts14500, 2 weeks to Pts120000, 9 months. Audio-visual and video facilities. Textbooks and materials approx Pts4500 per course. Extra 1 hour per day courses in grammar, art and history also available, cost Pts7000 per month. Also in Spanish songs, guitar and folklore, cost from

Pts4500 per week. Extra-curricular activities include visits to Salamanca, sports, films, music and poetry recitals and parties. Accommodation available in families, self-catering residences, flats, pensions or hotels, from Pts9000, 2 weeks. *Scholarships available through the Ministry of Foreign Affairs or occasionally from the school itself.* **FECEI PH**

COLEGIO INTERNACIONAL GEORGE WASHINGTON Cervantes 15, 33004 Oviedo, Principado de Asturias Tel Oviedo 257491
Language and culture courses for all levels in an ancient palace set in 260 acres of woodland in Oviedo. Ages 12 +, individuals and groups. 1 week-9 months, January-October. 10-25 hours per week. Maximum 10 per class. Special courses for teenagers, teachers, and in the language of business, commerce or technical subjects. Language laboratory, video, audio-visual facilities, computer-assisted learning and television recording studio. Courses include study of Spanish history, art, music, literature and geography. Regular programme of cultural activities includes exhibitions, talks, lectures, colloquia and concerts. Also craft classes, cinema and television, dancing, meetings with local people and excursions. Facilities for sports, plus sauna. Cost from Pts15000, 1 week, Pts60000, 4 weeks, includes course, teaching materials, and full board family accommodation. Produces an information booklet with practical information for students.

COLEGIO MARAVILLAS Avenida La Paloma 1, Arroyo, Benalmadena, Malaga Tel Malaga 445829/443326
Language courses for all levels in Benalmadena, a village on the Costa del Sol near Malaga. Ages 14-60, individuals and groups. 2 + weeks, all year. 10, 20 or 30 hours per week. Maximum 11 per class. Cost from Pts18000, 2 weeks, 20 hours per week. Also courses in business Spanish, 1:1 courses, and tailor-made courses for specialised groups. Audio-visual and video facilities. Textbooks from Pts1000. At higher levels cultural subjects include art, literature, customs, history, geography, theatre and politics of Spain. Social programme includes meals, beach parties, slide and film shows, guided tours of local sights, and excursions to Andalusian cities. Sporting facilities available. Family, apartment or hotel accommodation available from Pts42000, 2 weeks half board with family.

UK applicants can apply to Euro-Academy, 77A George Street, Croydon, Surrey CR0 1LD Tel 01-686 2363. Cost £378, 2 weeks, 20 hours per week, includes tuition and full board family accommodation.

COLEGIO MIGUEL DE CERVANTES Rua Mayor Principal 46, 37001 Salamanca Tel Salamanca 248582
Language and culture courses for all levels in Salamanca. Ages 16+, individuals and groups. General and intensive courses, 2, 4, 8 or 12 weeks, all year. 15, 20 or 25 hours per week. Maximum 7 or 20 per class, depending on course chosen. Cost for a 4 week, 20 hour per week course Pts35000, small class and Pts20500, large class. Cultural element to the courses. Commercial Spanish, 4 or 8 weeks, 25 hours per week. Maximum 7 per class. Cost Pts30000, 4 weeks. Also specialised courses for public employees and students of the EC, intensive courses in Spanish philology, courses for teachers, courses in Spanish history and literature, and 1:1 tuition. Audio-visual aids. Textbooks approx Pts1200 per course. Complementary courses include folklore and traditions (8 hours total, Pts5800), and lessons in Spanish dance (12-20 hours total, from Pts5800). Art and craft lessons also available. Extra-curricular activities include meals, parties, guided tours of Salamanca and video showings, plus excursions and free tickets for swimming pools, concerts and theatre during the summer. Accommodation available in families, apartments, residential centres, pensions or hotels, cost from Pts18700, 4 weeks, bed and breakfast. Recognised by the Spanish Government.

COLEGIO NUEVA UNIVERSIDAD DE GRANADA Cuesta del Aljibetrill 4, 18010 Granada Tel Granada 229181/633380
Language, commercial and cultural courses for all levels at private school situated in the famous old quarter of Granada, beneath the Alhambra. No age limits, individuals and groups. 1, 2 or 3 months, March-December. 20 hours per week. Maximum 12 per class. Cost Pts40000, 1 month, Pts75000, 2 months and Pts110000, 3 months. Special 4 month course also available for those with good knowledge of Spanish, October and March, cost from Pts110000. Christmas/New Year and Easter courses also run. Social activities include seminars, discussions, slide shows, parties and visits to places of interest in Granada and its surroundings. Courses in flamenco dance and various crafts organised in conjunction with local community centres. Opportunities for walking in the Sierra Nevada, riding, sailing and many other sports. Accommodation available in families, student residences or self-catering apartments from Pts16000 per month. *Offers 50 full and 100 75% scholarships a year through schools and universities or through the Spanish Foreign Ministry.* **PH** but no special facilities.

CURSOS INTERNACIONALES DE LA UNIVERSIDAD DE SALAMANCA Patio de Escuelas 2, 37008 Salamanca Tel Salamanca 216689/213506
Language courses for all levels at the University of Salamanca, the oldest university in Spain. Ages 16 + , individuals and groups. 4 weeks, January-June and October-November. 15 hours language classes plus 5 hours literary, linguistic or composition classes, per week. Cost Pts33000. Also 10 weeks, January, April and October. 10 hours language classes plus 5 hours conversation classes (beginners) or study of modern Spanish culture (other levels), per week. Cost Pts54000. Maximum 25 per class (advanced level) or 20 (others), both courses. 1:1 tuition also available. Language and culture course, 4 weeks, July-August. 10 hours language classes plus 5 hours language laboratory (beginners) or cultural classes (other levels) per week. Cost Pts29000. Language course, 4 weeks, July-September. 15 hours language classes, plus 5 hours language laboratory (beginners) or options (other levels), per week. Options from literary Spanish, business Spanish, writing or translation workshop. Cost Pts33000. Maximum 25 per class (advanced level) or 20 (other levels), both courses. Intensive language course, 4 weeks, July-September. 22.5 hours per week language classes, including language laboratory practice for beginners or options for other levels, plus 1 hour each afternoon real life language practice in a cafe, accompanied by a tutor. Maximum 8 per class. Cost Pts96000. Philology course for advanced students, 4 weeks, July-August. 15 hours seminars per week, dealing with different topic each week on literary themes. May be taken on a weekly basis. Cost Pts39000 per month, Pts13000 per week. Also courses for teachers of Spanish, 4 weeks, July-August. 20 hours per week, covering language problems and teaching methods. Cost Pts50000. Examination for Diploma de Espanol de la Universidad de Salamanca may be taken. Participants in summer courses may also enrol in 3 hours per week supplementary courses in guitar, Pts4500 per month, Spanish dance, Pts3500 per month, or Spanish songs, free. Audio-visual facilities. Textbooks and materials included in all costs. Extra-curricular activities include excursions, guided tours, parties, dances, sports, photography competitions, and preparing a summer school newsletter. Programme of cultural activities organised in the city, particularly in the summer, including theatre, music, film, ballet and other performances. Accommodation available in families or student residences from Pts1425 per day. Medical insurance available, Pts1800 per month. *Scholarships available via Spanish Embassies abroad.*
The Faculty of Philology also offers courses in the language, literature and history of Spain for advanced levels only. 2 months, March-May or October-December, cost Pts50000, or 9 months, October-June, cost

Pts105000. 15 hours per week. At the end of 9 month course, a diploma in Spanish studies may be obtained. Applications for these courses only should be made to Secretaria de la Facultad de Filologia, Palacio de Anaya, 37008 Salamanca, Spain Tel Salamanca 216534. *Some scholarships available for teachers of Spanish.* **PH**

DINAMICA ACADEMIA DE IDIOMAS Francisco Silvela 21-3, 28028 Madrid Tel 4017522
Language courses for all levels at private language school in a modern part of Madrid. Ages 16 + , individuals and small groups. 1 month, all year. 20 hours language classes per week. Maximum 5 per class. Audio-visual facilities. 10 hours per week complementary programme includes visits in Madrid, a guided tour of the Prado museum, discussions on Spanish life and customs, slide shows, recitals of folk music, a concert or play in Madrid, and trips to *tascas* and *mesones*. Excursions include visits to famous cities and towns near Madrid, and to the Sierra de Guadarrama. Cost Pts19500 per month includes course, complementary programme, 2 excursions per month, family accommodation, and breakfast and lunch at school. Textbooks Pts1500-Pts2000 extra. Approved by the Ministry of Education.
Applications in the UK can be made to Cultural and Educational Services Abroad, 44 Sydney Street, Brighton, Sussex BN1 4EP Tel Brighton 683304. Cost approx £150-£200 per week includes tuition and family accommodation.

EF EUROPÄISCHES FERIENSCHULE GMBH Annagasse 3, 1010 Vienna, Austria Tel Vienna 512 14 69
Courses for all levels in Barcelona and Madrid. Main courses, 2-50 weeks, all year. 24 lessons per week. Average 13 per class. Cost AS7500, 2 weeks. Also intensive courses, 2-50 weeks, all year. 30 lessons per week. Average 12 per class. Cost AS8600, 2 weeks. Summer courses, 2-12 weeks, May-August, 20 lessons per week. Average 14 per class. Cost AS6800, 2 weeks. Courses also available for students wishing to take the EF examinations or the Cerfificado Europeo de Espanol: 8 weeks, with examinations taking place in Barcelona in April. Cost AS34400. Language laboratory and audio-visual facilities. Costs include courses, teaching materials, preparatory language cassette, personal care throughout the course and full board family or student residence accommodation. Extra-curricular activities also arranged.

ESCUELA COOPERATIVA DE IDIOMAS MONTALBAN Montalban 13-3E, 18002 Granada Tel Granada 276874
Language courses for all levels at a cooperative language school in Granada. No age limits, individuals and groups. 3 weeks, all year. 15 or 25 hours per week. Maximum 6 per class. Audio-visual facilities. Aims to offer an alternative to traditional language schools, and to relate the

teaching of the language to the realities of everyday life in Spain. Courses include discussions on political and social aspects of modern Spain, and students can choose from special options such as Andalusian culture, literature, theatre, history and Francoism. Cost Pts20000, 15 hours per week, or Pts35000, 25 hours per week, plus Pts5000 registration fee. All textbooks and materials included. Extra-curricular activities include twice weekly excursions or guided tours and visits to films and art exhibitions, prepared beforehand in class. Can put students interested in special themes in touch with like-minded people in Granada. Bed and breakfast accommodation arranged sharing with Spanish students, cost Pts18000. Cheap hotel accommodation also available. Approved by the University of Granada. **PH**

ESCUELA MUNICIPAL DE IDIOMAS Carretera de Ojen s/n, 29600 Marbella (Malaga) Tel Malaga 778295
Summer language courses for all levels at the municipal language school of Marbella. Ages 14 +, individuals only. 4 weeks, July. 15 hours per week. Average 15 per class. Cost Pts25000. Audio-visual facilities. Textbooks Pts2000 per course. Extra-curricular activities include lectures on Spanish and Andalusian art, history and politics, and trips to the theatre, cinema and concerts. Also 4 month, 5 hour per week courses, starting October and February. Advice given on accommodation.

ESITI – ESCUELA DE TRADUCTORES E INTERPRETES, Calle de la Paz 23-4, 46003 Valencia Tel Valencia 3310454/3310455
Language and culture courses for all levels in Valencia. Ages 16 +, individuals and groups. 2, 3 or 4 weeks, July-August. 15 hours per week. Maximum 15 per class. Audio-visual facilities. Classes in colloquial Spanish, literature, and translation into Spanish. Also academic year course leading to diploma in translation approved by the Universidad Complutense de Madrid. Extra lectures on Valencia and its gastronomy and modern Spanish politics. Extra-curricular activities include museum visits, guided tours, excursions, films, opportunities to meet local people, and sports. Cost Pts108075, 4 weeks, includes course, teaching materials and full board family accommodation. Cost Pts94035 including half board family accommodation, Pts38450 excluding accommodation. Registration fee Pts4000. **FECEI**

ESTUDIO GENERAL LULIANO DE MALLORCA Instituto de Lenguas Modernas, Estudio General y San Roque 4, 07001 Palma de Mallorca, Balearic Islands Tel Palma 711988
Language courses for all levels on Majorca. Ages 18 +, individuals and groups. 3 weeks, July. 20 hours per week. Lectures on the history, art and

literature of Spain, and excursions to places of interest. Cost from Pts54000 includes course and full board hotel accommodation; half board or bed and breakfast also available. Cost Pts20000 excluding accommodation. Textbooks Pts1500 extra. Approved by the Universities of Barcelona and the Balearic Islands.

ESTUDIO INTERNACIONAL SAMPERE Castello 50 bajo derecha, 28001 Madrid Tel Madrid 2754025/ 2768264/2759790
Language courses for all levels in modern area of central Madrid. 2-32 weeks, all year. 20-22 hours per week. Maximum 9 per class. Also courses of 30 hours per week. Maximum 5 per class. Video facilities, plus tape recorders for self-study. Special courses in commercial Spanish, translation, for secretaries and 1:1 tuition for specialised needs. Preparation for Chamber of Commerce and university examinations. Extra-curricular activities include seminars on Spanish society and civilisation, visits to sights in Madrid, excursions and cookery classes. Cost from Pts63000, 2 weeks, includes course, teaching materials, extra-curricular activities and half board family accommodation. Full board available. Cost excluding accommodation Pts32000, 2 weeks.
FECEI

EURO-ACADEMY 77A George Street, Croydon, Surrey CRO 1LD Tel 01-686 2363
Courses for all levels in school close to the sea in Alhambra. Ages 18+, individuals and groups. Aimed at adults, executives and undergraduates. 3 weeks, all year. 5 lessons per day. Maximum 9 per class. Cost £245. Bed and breakfast pension accommodation available from £160, 3 weeks.

EUROCENTRO – INSTITUTOS MANGOLD Rambla de Catalunya 16, 08007 Barcelona Tel Barcelona 3012539
Language courses for all levels in the heart of Barcelona. Ages 16+, individuals and groups. Intensive courses, 2-12 weeks, January-May and September-December. 20 hours per week. Summer courses, 3 weeks, July-September. 20 hours per week. Maximum 16 per class. Both courses also have 5 hours per week of special options, including Spanish for business, commercial correspondence, Spanish and Latin American art and literature, and Spain in the EC. A further 5-10 hours a week can be spent in self-study in the multi-media centre, with video, audio and computer assisted learning facilities. Also refresher courses for teachers of Spanish. Language laboratory. Textbooks and materials included. Social activities include lectures, excursions, film shows and

parties. Cost £287-£1722, intensive courses and £415, summer courses, includes half board family accommodation. Cost excluding accommodation £162-£945 intensive, and £228 summer. *Some scholarships available; details from Eurocentre, Seestrasse 247, 8038 Zurich, Switzerland.*

Applications in the UK can be made to Eurocentre London, see below, or to Cultural and Educational Services Abroad, 44 Sydney Street, Brighton, Sussex, BN1 4EP Tel Brighton 683304.

EUROCENTRO – INSTITUTOS MANGOLD Gran Via 32-2, 28013 Madrid Tel Madrid 5228300

Language courses for all levels in the heart of Madrid. Ages 16+, individuals and groups. 4-13 weeks, all year. 20 hours per week, plus 5 hours special business, technical and cultural options, including study of Latin American culture. Refresher courses for teachers and study leading to examinations of the Sociedad Cervantina also available. Language laboratory. Extra-curricular activities include excursions, sightseeing in Madrid, sports, lectures, song recitals and social activities. Cost from £593, 4 weeks, includes course, teaching materials and half board accommodation.

UK applicants for the Eurocentro courses in Barcelona and Madrid, see above, can apply to Eurocentre, 21 Meadowcourt Road, Lee Green, London SE3 9EU Tel 01-318 5633, or through any Eurocentre school.

EUROLINGUA Prats de Mollo 6 (junto Plaza Adriano), 08021 Barcelona Tel Barcelona 2013307

Language courses for all levels in Barcelona. Ages 15+. 4, 8 or 12 weeks, all year. 20 hours per week. Also summer courses, 4 weeks, July/August. 16 hours per week. Audio-visual facilities. The courses include some study of literature and the arts. Summer courses include free excursions. Also 1:1 courses for executives. Opportunities to practise sports including tennis, sailing, riding and cycling. Half or full board accommodation in families or student residences. Cost including course, teaching materials and accommodation from Pts77874, half board or Pts86937, full board. Courses may also be booked by the week.

FICDE – FEDERACION INTERNACIONAL DE CENTROS PARA LA DISFUSION DEL ESPANOL Colegio Ausias March, Tancat de l'Alter s/n, Picassent, Valencia Tel Valencia 1230566

Language and culture courses for all levels at school at Picassent, near the coast south of Valencia. Ages 14+, individuals and groups. 2+ weeks, all year. 15-20 hours per week. Maximum 13 per class. Audio-visual and computer facilities. Programme of afternoon sports activities, plus seminars on gastronomy, Spanish customs, colloquial Spanish and other themes. Also folk music recitals, films, excursions to beaches and local sights, boat trips and meetings with local young people. Cost Pts23700 per week, summer and Pts17950, rest of the year, includes course, textbooks, extra-curricular activities, full board family, student residence or apartment accommodation and accident insurance. Approved by the Ministry of Education and Science. *Scholarships may be available via Spanish Embassies.* **PH**

GRAN CANARIA SCHOOL OF LANGUAGES Tomas Morales 54, 35003 Las Palmas, Canary Islands Tel Las Palmas 371957
Language courses for all levels in Las Palmas and Playa del Ingles on the island of Gran Canaria. Ages 16+, individuals and groups. 1-16 weeks, all year. 20 hours per week. Group 10 courses, cost SF100 per week, 12 students maximum; Group 5 courses, SF 160 per week, 6 students maximum. 1:1 and 1:2 tuition also available. Textbooks approx Pts1400 per 4 week course. Weekly excursion plus monthly visit to theatre, restaurant or nightclub. Can also help book cultural courses such as guitar, ballet, yoga or ceramics, and all types of watersport courses and boat excursions. Accommodation available in families, beach studios or apartments from SF125 per week.

Applications in the UK can be made to Cultural and Educational Services Abroad, 44 Sydney Street, Brighton, Sussex, BN1 4EP Tel Brighton 683304. Cost from £125 per week includes tuition and half board family accommodation.

HARVEN SCHOOL (LANZAROTE) c/o The Mascot, Coley Avenue, Woking, Surrey, GU22 7BT Tel Woking 70969
Language courses at school near seafront on the island of Lanzarote. Ages 18+, younger with parent's consent. 1-2+ weeks, all year. 15 hours per week. Video facilities. Leisure programme includes barbecues, discos, jeep excursions, beach activities and sports. Cost from £195 per week includes course, teaching materials, sports and activities, transfers, full time services of leisure leader and accommodation in self-catering hotels with swimming pool.

HISPALENGUA San Miguel 16, 50001 Zaragoza Tel Zaragoza 221810
Language courses for all levels in Pamplona and Zaragoza. Ages 16+, individuals and groups. 2+ weeks, all year. 10-35 hours per week. Maximum 12 per class. Study of literature and history of Spain. Language laboratory and video facilities. Excursions and opportunities

to meet local people. Cost Pts116000, 4 weeks, includes course and full board family accommodation. Textbooks Pts1200. Approved by Ministry of Culture.

HISPANICA Colegio Internacional de Estudios Practicos de Lengua y Cultura Espanolas, Hernando de Carabeo 89, Apartado de correos 19, Nerja (Malaga) Tel 522096
Language courses for all levels at a language school in Nerja, a small town on the Costa del Sol near Malaga which has preserved its traditional Andalusian character. School specialises in teaching Spanish to foreigners. Ages 16+, individuals and groups. Intensive courses, 4 or 8 weeks, all year. 20 hours per week. Maximum 10 per class. Cost Pts39300, 4 weeks, Pts76200, 8 weeks. Super-intensive courses, multiples of 2 weeks, all year. 30 hours per week. Maximum 6 per class. Cost Pts35600, 2 weeks, Pts66800, 4 weeks. Both courses include performing real life tasks in the town in order to practise Spanish by talking to local inhabitants, plus a strong cultural component. 1:1 courses, and courses for two students together or for small groups with business or other special interests also available. Video facilities and textbooks included. Also courses in flamenco dancing and Spanish cooking. Extra-curricular activities include parties, meals and excursions to Andalusian cities, small villages and places such as the Alpujarras and the famous caves of Nerja. Accommodation available in families or apartments, from Pts5300 per week.

UK applicants can apply to Cultural and Educational Services Abroad, 44 Sydney Street, Brighton, Sussex BN1 4EP Tel Brighton 683304. Cost from £125-£150 per week includes tuition and family accommodation.

HOME LANGUAGE LESSONS LTD 12-18 Royal Crescent, Ramsgate, Kent CT11 9PE Tel Thanet 590300
1:1 Spanish lessons at all levels in the Canary Islands, Madrid, Granada, Valencia and throughout southern Spain. No age limits. Lessons take place in the teacher's home, where student stays, giving total immersion in the language, and no contact with other students. 15, 20 or 25 hours of lessons per week. Cost from Pts70000 per week. Also weekend crash courses of 5 hours per day, cost Pts24000. The course may also be taken together by two people; 25% reduction if both are of the same family. For business and professional people there is a 5 star immersion course, with 25 hours per week language tuition and superior accommodation, cost Pts150000 per week. Given notice it is possible to place students with teachers who share their interests, and on immersion courses suitable contacts in the local community can be arranged. All costs include full board accommodation. **PH**

IBERLENGUA SA Torpedero Tucuman 26, 28016 Madrid Tel Madrid 4588257
Language courses for all levels at small language school in residential area of Madrid. Ages 16 +, individuals and groups. 4, 6, 8, or 12 weeks, all year. 15, 20 or 25 hours language classes per week. Maximum 8 per class. 1:1 tuition also available. Special course on Spanish life and culture for CNAA students January-June, 9 hours per week, and part time courses in Spanish for long term residents. Video facilities. Extra-curricular activities organised on request. Cost Pts120760, 15 hours per week, Pts137260, 20 hours per week or Pts153760, 25 hours per week, 4 weeks, includes course, teaching materials and full board family or hotel accommodation. **ACEDIM FECEI**

IDIOMAS CASTILLA Sol 9-2, 37002 Salamanca Tel Salamanca 217435
Language courses for all levels in Salamanca. Ages 14 +, individuals and groups. 4 weeks, all year. 10 or 20 hours per week. Maximum 10 per class. 20 hours per week courses include 5 hours per week culture classes. Cost from Pts17000 includes course and teaching materials. Special courses include Spanish for diplomats, commercial Spanish for secretaries and businessmen, 1:1 tuition, and tailor-made courses for specialised groups. Video facilities. Full board family accommodation available from Pts1700 per day. Summer language and civilisation courses, 3 or 4 weeks, July-August. 20 hours per week. Maximum 15 per class. 5-10 hours per week on Spanish literature and culture, depending on level. Extra-curricular activities include 3 day excursions, guided tours of Salamanca, video shows, trips to swimming pool, bowling alley and discotheques. Cost Pts76000, 3 weeks and Pts97000, 4 weeks, includes course, activities and full board family accommodation. Cost excluding accommodation Pts42000, 3 weeks and Pts53000, 4 weeks. Also 10, 12 or 15 days, Easter. Cost Pts37000, 10 days, Pts43000, 12 days and Pts48000, 15 days, includes course, programme of activities and full board family accommodation.

INLINGUA IDIOMAS C/31 de Diciembre 7, 07003 Palma de Mallorca, Balearic Islands
Language courses for all levels on Majorca. Ages 18 +, individuals and groups. 2 + weeks, all year. 20 or 30 hours per week. Average 5-6 per class. Extra-curricular activities include visits to places of interest, concerts, festivals and theatre. Cost per week Pts18645, 20 hours and Pts22625, 30 hours, includes course and bed and breakfast pension accommodation. Cost per week excluding accommodation Pts8845, 20 hours and Pts12825, 30 hours. 1:1 tuition also available.

INLINGUA IDIOMAS Rambla de Cataluna 33, 08007 Barcelona
Language courses for all levels in Barcelona. Ages 16+, individuals and groups. 4+ weeks, January-November. 24 hours per week. Average 7 per class. Lectures on Spanish art, cinema and politics, and on regional music. Cost Pts17475 per week including course and bed and breakfast family accommodation, Pts10600 excluding accommodation. 1:1 tuition also available.

INLINGUA IDIOMAS Paseo de Tomás Morales 28, 35003 Las Palmas, Canary Islands Tel Las Palmas 360671
Language courses for all levels in Las Palmas and Playa del Inglès on the island of Gran Canaria. No age limits, individuals and groups. 2 weeks-3 months, all year. 15 lessons per week. Maximum 10 per class. Audio-visual facilities. Specialised courses and 1:1 tuition also available. Cost Pts12000 per week includes course and teaching materials; discounts for groups of 6+. Accommodation available with local families, Pts10000, bed and breakfast, or Pts24000, half board, per week.

INLINGUA IDIOMAS Avenida de los Castros 36-1, 39005 Santander Tel Santander 277295
Courses for all levels at school in Santander, near the beach. Ages 16+, individuals and groups. 2, 3 or 4 weeks, all year. 15-20 hours per week. Average 5-6 per class. Also summer courses, June-September, 15 hours per week. 1:1 courses of 20, 25 and 30 hours per week and tailor-made courses for specialised groups also available. Guided tours and excursions organised, plus film shows on video. Cost Pts32100 per week, includes course, teaching materials and half board family accommodation.

INLINGUA IDIOMAS Arenal 24, 28013 Madrid Tel Madrid 2413246
Language courses for all levels in the heart of Madrid. Ages 17+, individuals and groups. 2-12 weeks, all year. 25 hours per week. Maximum 5 per class. Lectures on current themes, art and music; discussions on Spanish film and theatre. Cost Pts16500 per week. Also 1:1 tuition. Bed and breakfast family accommodation Pts7500 per week.

INLINGUA IDIOMAS C/Ribera 13, 46002 Valencia Tel Valencia 352 97 73
Language courses for all levels in Valencia. Ages 16+, individuals and groups. 2+ weeks, all year. 20 hours per week. Average 6 per class. Afternoon study of Spanish cinema, literature, music, art, and programme of cultural visits. Cost Pts37000, 2 weeks, includes course,

teaching materials and half board family accommodation. Cost Pts11500 per week excluding accommodation. 1:1 tuition also available.

Applications in the UK for any of the Inlingua Idiomas courses above can be made to Inlingua School of Languages, 8-10 Rotton Park Road, Edgbaston, Birmingham B16 9JJ Tel 021-454 0204 or 55-61 Portland Road, Brighton, Sussex BN3 5DQ Tel Brighton 721612

INSTITUTE OF SPANISH STUDIES El Bachiller 13, 46010 Valencia Tel Valencia 3696168
Summer courses for all levels in Valencia. Ages 17+, individuals and groups. 3 weeks, June and 4 weeks, July. Maximum 15 per class. Textbooks approx Pts4000 per course. American college credit system, with students choosing up to 3 courses, each taught daily, from a range including language classes, phonetics, literature, civilisation, history of Spanish, Latin-American culture, modern Spain, art, commercial Spanish and translation. Most courses are taught in Spanish. Also year-long course primarily for American college students. Programme of excursions organised to Sagunto, Gandia and other local places of interest. Optional post-course tour of Spain. Cost Pts107600 – Pts125200 includes course, excursions and full board family or student residence accommodation. Cost Pts57000 – Pts66400 excluding accommodation.
US applicants can apply to the Institute's office at 1315 Monterey Boulevard, San Francisco, CA 94127.

INSTITUTO CASTELLANO LEONES DE LINGUISTICA APPLICADA PO Box 12, Soria Tel Soria 227323
Language courses at historic monastery in Avila run by the regional government of Castille and Leon. Ages 11-17, individuals and groups. 2 weeks, July-August. 15 hours per week. Maximum 12 per class. Courses are attended by both Spanish and British students, who participate jointly in afternoon sports, team games, competitions, arts and crafts, lectures on local customs and excursions. Cost Pts58000 includes full board residential accommodation. Also courses for advanced students in Aranda del Duero and Soria, towns in the heart of old Castille. 3 weeks, July-August. 15 hours per week. Maximum 12 per class. Extra-curricular activities include excursions, lectures on local customs and sports. Opportunities to meet local people and integrate into the life of the town. Cost Pts66000 includes full board family accommodation.

INSTITUTO CERVANTES Avenida Juan Sebastian Elcano 69, 29017 Malaga Tel Malaga 299047
Language courses for all levels near the beach and town centre in Malaga. Ages 16+. 2, 3, 4, 8 or 12 weeks, all year. 20-30 hours per week.

Maximum 8 per class. Cost from Pts33000, 4 weeks. Also commercial Spanish, 4 weeks, 20 hours per week. Cost Pts45000. 1:1 tuition also available. There is a cultural element to the more advanced courses. Audio-visual facilities. Extra-curricular activities include parties, cooking classes, guided tours of Malaga, 2 excursions per month, local fiestas, flamenco dancing lessons, trips to flamenco shows and acting plays. Accommodation available in families or apartments from Pts32000, 4 weeks.

INSTITUTO DE ESPANOL PABLO PICASSO Plaza de la Merced 10 – 1, Apartado de Correos 552, 29080 Malaga Tel Malaga 213932
Courses for all levels at a school in Malaga, near the old quarter and castle. Ages 16+, individuals and groups. 4 weeks, all year (December course, 3 weeks). 20 hours per week. Maximum 8 per class. Video facilities. Introduction to Spanish life and culture, including Spanish and Latin-American songs, literature, films, radio and television programmes, depending on level. Visits to places of cultural interest included at advanced level. Cost Pts32000 (December Pts25000) includes course and teaching materials. Extra course of 10 hours per week with options including economics, commercial Spanish, remedial studies on grammar, Spanish culture, films, theatre, debates, cooking, special visits, songs and flamenco dancing. Cost Pts15000. Social activities include parties, beach barbecues in summer, guided tours and excursions, films and a weekly class in Flamenco dancing. Accommodation available in families, shared apartments or studios, from Pts15000 per course. **PH** but no lift or special facilities.

INTERNATIONAL HOUSE Trafalgar 14 entlo, 08010 Barcelona Tel Barcelona 3188429
Language courses for all levels at school in the centre of Barcelona. Ages 15+, except in special groups. Individuals and groups. 2 or 4 weeks, February-November. 15 hours per week Maximum 8 per class. Cost Pts19000, 2 weeks or Pts36000, 4 weeks. An extra 5 hours per week of special skills classes may also be taken, cost Pts6000, 2 weeks. 1:1 classes also available. Training courses for teachers of Spanish and tailor-made courses for specialised groups. Lectures on regions of Spain, South America through its music, the history of the Spanish language, difficult aspects of Spanish, and the Civil War. Social programme includes parties, video films and opportunities to meet Spanish students studying English at the school. Also excursions, Easter-September. Cost from Pts22000, 2 weeks and Pts45000, 4 weeks includes course, teaching materials and bed and breakfast family accommodation. Half board also available.

INTERNATIONAL HOUSE Jesus y Maria 9, 38004 Santa Cruz de Tenerife, Canary Islands Tel Tenerife 287009
Language course for all levels on the island of Tenerife. Ages 18+, individuals and groups. 2, 3, 4 and 6 weeks, July-August. 20 hours per week. Maximum 12 per class. Cost Pts18850 per week, plus Pts2500 enrolment fee, includes course and teaching materials. Also organises O/GCSE and A level courses for schools, tailor-made courses for companies and other special groups, and 1:1 tuition at any time of year. Social activities include barbecues, excursions, opportunities to meet local people, films and sports. Half board family accommodation Pts12000 per week, or in hotels from Pts1800 per night.

INTERNATIONAL HOUSE Zurbano 8, 28010 Madrid Tel Madrid 4101314
Language courses for all levels in Madrid. Ages 16+, individuals and groups. 2 weeks, all year. 15 hours per week. Maximum 10 per class. Cost Pts19000. Special courses in commercial Spanish. Audio-visual facilities. Opportunities to study culture, literature, history and art of Spain. Social programme includes films, parties, and sightseeing trips. Family and university residence accommodation available, from Pts1600 per day, bed and breakfast.

Applications in the UK for any of the International House courses above can be made to Kate Neemah, Marketing Director, International House, 106 Piccadilly, London W1V 9FL Tel 01-491 2598.

LANGUAGE STUDIES SA Luchana 31, 28010 Madrid Tel Madrid 4460999
Language courses for all levels in Madrid. Ages 16+, individuals and groups. 2, 3, 4 or 5 weeks, all year. 20 or 30 hours per week. Maximum 12 per class. Cost from Pts30000, 20 hours per week, and Pts40000, 30 hours per week, 2 weeks. Also courses for businessmen. 35 hours per week. Maximum 6 per class. Cost Pts85000, 2 weeks. 1:1 tuition also available. Examinations of the Spanish Chamber of Commerce and the Escuela Oficial de Idiomas may be taken. Audio-visual facilities. Textbooks and teaching materials included. Extra-curricular activities include 2 excursions per week with teachers involving sightseeing, meals, fiestas and shows. Optional weekend excursions also organised to places such as El Escorial, Toledo and other famous cities of Castille. Family or hotel accommodation available. Travel arrangements on request. **ACEDIM FECEI PH**

UK applicants can apply to Language Studies Ltd, Woodstock House, 10-12 James Street, London, W1M 5HN.

LISTEN AND LEARN Narvaez 15, 28009 Madrid Tel Madrid 2762528
Language courses for all levels in Madrid. Ages 14+, intensive courses, 6-11 or 12+, semi-intensive. Individuals and groups. Intensive courses, 2 or 4 weeks, all year. 15 or 20 hours per week. Maximum 6 per class. Cost from Pts 11100, 2 weeks, 15 hours per week. Semi-intensive courses, 4+ weeks, all year. 4, 5, 6 or 10 hours per week. Maximum 6 per class. Cost from Pts7400, 4 hours per week, per month. Also 1:1 tuition and specialised courses including Spanish for commerce, business correspondence and the tourist trade. In May and December the examinations of the Madrid Chamber of Commerce may be taken. Audio-visual and language laboratory facilities. Textbooks and materials Pts700-Pts1500 per course. Intensive and 1:1 courses include additional seminars on various aspects of present day and historical Spain, including literature, politics, art and history, as well as sightseeing trips to the Prado, National Institute of Industry, the Royal Palace and other places of interest in Madrid. Dinners, social events in cafes, and accompanied trips to theatres, cinemas and concerts also organised, plus weekend excursions to places of interest outside Madrid. Family or pension accommodation available. **PH**

MAYFLOWER ACADEMY Juan Martinez Ruiperez, Reina Victoria 34, 30204 Cartagena Tel Murcia 507322
Summer language courses for all levels in Cartagena in the south east of Spain. Ages 18+, or 10-18 if in organised groups. Individuals or groups. 1 month, July-August. 15 hours per week. Average 25 per class. The course combines language lessons with a seaside holiday. Extra-curricular activities include excursions, boat trips, sports and trips to beaches. Cost Pts75000 includes course, teaching materials, excursions and full board family/residential centre accommodation. Licensed by the Ministry of Culture and approved by the Cartagena Chamber of Commerce.

UK applicants can apply to Mrs M Carmichael, 83 Milehouse Road, Stoke, Plymouth Tel Plymouth 560816.

RAPIDIDIOM Castillo 15, Santa Cruz de Tenerife, Canary Islands Tel Tenerife 242101
Language courses for all levels on the island of Tenerife. Ages 12+, individuals only. 2 or 4 weeks, July-September. 10 or 15 hours per week. Cost Pts9100, 10 hours per week, to Pts15000, 15 hours per week, per 4 week course. Also runs year courses of 5 hours per week. Audio-visual and video facilities. Textbooks approx Pts2000 per course. Hotel/apartment accommodation available from Pts2270 per night.

SALMINTER – ESCUELA SALMANTINA DE ESTUDIOS INTERNACIONALES Toro 34/36 – 2, 37002 Salamanca Tel Salamanca 211808
Language and culture courses for all levels in Salamanca at cooperative school specialised in the teaching of Spanish. Ages 13 +, individuals and groups. 1 month, all year. 10 or 20 hours per week. Maximum 10 per class. Cost Pts14000, 10 hours per week to Pts26000, 20 hours per week, per month. Also 3 month courses, starting January, April and October. Total of 100 hours language and 48 hours civilisation classes, including art, history, theatre, literature and modern Spain. Cost Pts59000. Also special courses in business and administrative Spanish, and in translating from English or German into Spanish. Audio-visual and video facilities. Textbook Pts1200 per course. Extra cultural courses offered on literature, history, art, geography, and modern Spain. Cost from Pts4500 depending on course length. Extra-curricular activities include excursions, guided tours of Salamanca, language exchanges with Spanish students, discussions on Spanish society, weekly films, concerts and opportunities to practise sports. Many of the activities are specifically designed to improve language skills. Information provided on local dance and craft classes. Accommodation available in families or shared apartments from Pts1450 per day. **PH**

SCHOOL JOURNEY ASSOCIATION 48 Cavendish Road, London SW12 0DG Tel 01-675 6636
Inclusive language study visit to Córdoba for GCSE and A level students of Spanish. Ages 15-20, individuals and groups. 15 days, Easter. 17 hours per week. Average 12 per class. Course includes literature classes for A level students, and lectures in the evenings by local officials and academics on background topics. Guided tours of the Mezquita and other sights of Córdoba included, as well as excursions to Seville, Medina Azahara, and Castillo de Almodovar, plus opportunities to see the Holy Week processions. The courses take place at Casa Internacional in the centre of the old city, and students will be introduced to Spanish students studying English at the school. Cost £385 includes course, lectures, teaching materials, tours, full board family accommodation, return flight, transfers, insurance and escort throughout the journey and stay by British teachers. *Apply by December/January.* **PH**

THE SPANISH COUNCIL Department of Castilian Studies, Apartado 2372, 46080 Valencia Tel 3514011/3514015
Language, culture and special interest courses for all levels in the centre of the old part of Valencia. Ages 4 +, childrens' courses and 16 +, adults. Individuals and groups. Basic language courses 1 week-1 year,

starting any time. 10, 20, 30 or 40 hours per week. Video and audio-visual aids. Specialised options include business, commerce and banking, a bilingual secretarial workshop, Spanish for tourism, history of Spanish language and culture, South and Central America history and culture, Spanish for the medical profession, Catalan in Valencia, workshop for literary creation, and courses for teachers of Spanish. A wide range of supplementary courses also available on historical, political, artistic, cultural and scientific subjects. Extra-curricular activities include cultural visits, excursions, fiestas, cinema, theatre, parties, plus opportunities for sports. Participants have free membership of the Valencian Society of Fine Arts, with use of its social facilities. Classes in ceramics, pottery, other handicrafts, classical and flamenco guitar, other musical instruments, yoga, dance and photography available at extra charge. Cost Pts80000, basic 1 month course, includes course and half board family accommodation; Pts40000 excluding accommodation. Registration fee Pts8500. Students are met at station or airport on arrival. Teaching staff from the University of Valencia Philology Department. Recognised by the Ministry of the Interior and the Ministry of Education and Sciences. *Scholarships available from The Spanish Council, Programa de Becas, at the address above.* **PH**

THE TRINITY CENTRE LANGUAGE CONSULTANTS, Avenida de la Constitucion 10, Navalcarnero, Madrid Tel Madrid 8110091

Language classes for all levels in a typical Castilian market town near Madrid. Ages 18+, individuals and groups. 2 weeks, all year. 15 hours per week. Average 10 per class. Cost Pts21000. Special business and teachers courses and 1:1 tuition also available. The school prepares students for the examinations of the Universidad Complutense de Madrid and the Madrid Chamber of Commerce. Audio-visual facilities. All textbooks included. Classes in Spanish culture, literature and history. Social programme includes excursions and trips to bodegas and restaurants. Sports facilities for gymnastics, jogging and judo also available. The small town atmosphere gives plenty of opportunity to speak with local people. Accommodation available in small hotel with swimming pool, cost from Pts1500 per day.

UK applicants can apply to Mr Joseph Speight, 19 Clifton Drive, Cliftonville Road, Belfast BT14 Tel Belfast 746991.

UNIVERSIDAD DE ALICANTE Catedra Rafael Altamira Cursos Internacionales, 03690 San Vicente del Raspeig, Alicante Tel Alicante 661150

Language course for all levels at the University of Alicante. 3-6 weeks, July-August. 17.5 hours per week. Additional seminars held on art, geography, literature, history and anthropology. Extra-curricular activities include video showings, visits to museums and other places of interest, archaeological excursions, and a nightly programme of cultural events including discussions, film shows, theatre performances and concerts. Cost Pts15000-Pts30000, 3-6 weeks. Campus has swimming pool and sports facilities. Accommodation available in university residences or families from Pts1650 per day, full board.

UNIVERSIDAD DE BARCELONA CURSOS DE VERANO Plaza de la Universidad, 08071 Barcelona Tel 3184266
Summer language and culture course at the University of Barcelona. Ages 16+, individuals only. 3 weeks, August. 15 hours per week. Maximum 20 per class. 2 hours language plus 1 hour Spanish culture, per day. 24 hours per week afternoon seminars and lectures on various Hispanic themes. Visits to museums and places of interest, theatre and music performances, and excursions organised, and access to university library and sporting facilities. Cost from Pts60000 includes course, social programme and bed and breakfast student residence accommodation; from Pts36000 excluding accommodation.

UNIVERSIDAD DE CADIZ Secretaria de los Cursos de Verano, Calle Ancha número 16, 11001, Cadiz Tel Cadiz 223808
Summer language and culture course for all levels at the University of Cadiz. 4 weeks, July-August. 10 hours language tuition per week. Maximum 20 per class. Also lessons on Spanish linguistics, literature, geography, history and Andalucian folksongs. Weekend excursions arranged to places of interest, and various cultural activities organised during the course. Cost Pts35000 includes course, teaching materials and extra-curricular activities. Full board accommodation available in student residences, cost Pts47600.

UNIVERSIDAD DE CANTABRIA Secretaria de Cursos de Verano, Pabellon de Gobierno, Avenida de Los Castros s/n, 39005 Santander
Summer language and culture course for beginner and intermediate levels at Laredo, near Santander on the northern coast of Spain. 4 weeks, July-August. 22.5 hours per week. Cost from Pts35000. Evening cultural activities include seminars, concerts and videos. Excursions are made to Burgos, Santanilla del Mar and Santo Domingo de Silos. Students may use the university sports facilities. Full board accommodation available in student residence, cost from Pts90000. Organised by the University of Cantabria and the Fundacion Ponce de Leon, in conjunction with the local council of Laredo.

UNIVERSIDAD COMPLUTENSE Secretaría de los Cursos para Extranjeros, Facultad de Filosofía y Letras (Edificio A), Cuidad Universitaria, 28040 Madrid Tel 2433448
Language and culture courses for all levels at the Universidad Complutense de Madrid. Ages 16-60. 10 weeks, October, January and April. 20 hours per week. 1 hour per day each of language practice, grammar, textual commentary, and cultural seminars on literature, philosophy, history, modern Spain, Latin-American literature, music and folklore, art, and modern Spanish thought. Examinations may be taken leading to university diplomas in Spanish culture and language. Cost Pts45000. Also summer courses in July. Intensive courses, 2-3 weeks, 25 hours per week, covering grammar, conversation, textual commentary, and seminars on aspects of modern Spain. Cost Pts22000-Pts30000. General language and culture courses, 4 weeks, 20 hours per week, covering grammar, conversation, textual commentary, and seminars on the literature, art, and history of Spain. Students may also attend the cultural seminars on the intensive course for 1 hour each day. Cost Pts40000. Language and literature course, advanced levels only, 4 weeks, 15 hours per week, covering a range of literary and linguistic subjects, with opportunity to attend cultural seminars on other summer courses for 2 hours each day. Cost Pts42000. Examinations leading to official university diplomas may be taken at the end of summer courses. Also Spanish studies course, October-June, covering language, literature, history, geography and philosophy of Spain. Extra-curricular activities include guided visits in Madrid, films and excursions to various cities in Castille. Free use of university library and sporting facilities. The University produces a special guide book for course participants. Accommodation available in university residences on summer courses. Medical insurance can be arranged.

UNIVERSIDAD DE GRANADA Cursos para Extranjeros, Palacio de las Columnas, Puentezuelas 55, 18002 Granada Tel Granada 262584
Language courses for all levels, and language and culture courses for those with a good knowledge of Spanish at the University of Granada. Ages 16+, individuals and groups. Intensive courses, 1 month, July-September and 2 months, October, January and March. 15 hours per week. Average 15 students per class. Cost Pts30000-Pts42000. Also language and culture course for those with a good level of Spanish, 1 month, September. 20 hours per week. Includes the study of the history, art, geography and literature of Spain, plus business, colloquial and scientific Spanish. Cost Pts36000. Also 8 month course in Hispanic Studies for advanced students, starting October. 1 or 2 terms. 18 hours per week. Average 25 per class. Cost Pts60000, 1 term or Pts110000, 2 terms. Special courses for groups organised on request. Audio-visual

facilities. Textbooks approx Pts1200 per month. Students may attend all lectures, talks and seminars organised by the University, and to use all its sports and other facilities. Accompanied excursions organised to places of interest. Student accommodation service available. *Scholarships available through the Ministry of Foreign Affairs, via Spanish Embassies.*

UNIVERSIDAD INTERNACIONAL MENENDEZ PELAYO Isaac Peral s/n, Antiguo Edificio del Instituto Psicotecnico, 28040 Madrid Tel Madrid 4495000
Summer language and culture courses for all levels in Santander. Ages 17+, individuals and groups. 4 weeks, July and August, or 3 weeks, September. 25 hours per week. Cost Pts30000, 3 weeks or Pts35000, 4 weeks, includes course and teaching materials. Study of Spanish and Latin-American literature and culture, history of art, geography of Spain, and commercial Spanish, for those with a good knowledge of the language, and language laboratory sessions at elementary levels. Also special course in Latin American philology for teachers of Spanish and post-graduate students, consisting of conferences and seminars. Students may also take part in other summer courses run by university if places available. Extra-curricular activities include excursions to local towns and to the mountains of the Picos de Europa, cultural activities including concerts, theatre and cinema, gatherings and meetings, singing and sports competitions. Facilities for football, basketball and tennis. Limited amount of full board student residence accommodation available, cost from Pts50000. Families and hotel accommodation also available. Practical information booklet for all participants. Insurance available. *Approx 10 scholarships awarded annually; apply by 1 April.*

After 26 June apply to Residencia de Las Llamas, Avda de los Castros, s/n 39005 Santander

UNIVERSIDAD DE LEON Cursos de Verano para Extranjeros, Vicerrectorado de Extension Universitaria, Apartado de Correos 1258, 24080 Leon
Summer language and culture course for intermediate and advanced levels at the University of Leon. 4 weeks, July-August. 18 hours per week. Maximum 15 per class. Afternoon seminars on Spanish culture, also attended by Spanish students. Extra-curricular activities include social events, guided tours and excursions accompanied by course teachers, theatre, cinema and music recitals organised by the city of Leon, and free access to municipal sporting facilities. Cost Pts81000 includes course, teaching materials, excursions, full board family or student residence accommodation and medical insurance.

UNIVERSIDAD DE MALAGA Cursos para Extranjeros, Apartado 310, 29080 Malaga Tel Malaga 214007
Language and culture courses for all levels at the University of Malaga. Intensive courses, 2, 3 or 4 weeks, all year. 25 hours per week. Average 5 per class. Cost Pts30000 – Pts50000. Also courses in commercial Spanish. Summer courses, 1, 2 or 3 months, July-September. 20 hours per week. Average 18 per class. Courses include study of the art, literature, geography, history and folk dances of Spain, and additional lectures on Spanish cinema, society, politics and folklore. Cost Pts27000 – Pts75000. Also 8 month Spanish studies course, October-May. 15 hours per week. Language classes and cultural subjects. Cost Pts111500, 8 months, Pts65700, 1 term and Pts26700, 1 month. On all courses an examination leading to an official university certificate of competence in Spanish may be taken, after minimum 2 months study. Audio-visual and language laboratory facilities. Textbooks approx Pts2000 per course. Extra-curricular activities include guided tours of the city, excursions to Andalusian cities and to Morocco, concerts, films and beach parties. Can provide addresses of accommodation in families or apartments, but students must make arrangements. Cost from Pts550 per day, room only. *Scholarships available for summer courses from the Ministry of Foreign Affairs.*

UNIVERSIDAD DE MURCIA Cursos para Extranjeros, Granero 4, 37001 Murcia Tel Murcia 210566
Language courses for elementary-advanced levels at the University of Murcia in south-east Spain. Ages 16 +, individuals and groups. 3 weeks, July. 20 hours per week. Extra-curricular activities include seminars and visits. Beaches nearby. Can also arrange courses for special groups. Cost Pts55000 includes course, teaching materials and full board university residence accommodation. *Limited number of scholarships available from the University or from the Spanish Government. Information from Spanish Embassies.*

UNIVERSIDAD DE NAVARRA Secretaria del Instituto de Lengua y Cultura Espanola, Campus Universitario, 31080 Pamplona Tel Pamplona 252700
Summer language and culture courses for intermediate levels and above at the Catholic University of Navarra in Pamplona. Ages 19-40, individuals and groups. General course, 2 or 4 weeks, July. 25 hours per week. Cost Pts22500 or Pts32500. Intensive course, 4 weeks, September. 30 hours per week. Cost Pts37500. Average 30 per class. Both courses include study of culture, literature and modern Spain. Intensive course includes classes on colloquial Spanish. Audio-visual facilities. Textbooks from Pts2000 per course, but may be borrowed from university library. Also 2 week course for teachers of Spanish in

July, cost Pts25000, 4 month language and culture course October-February, and specialist courses February-May, cost Pts62500. Accommodation available from Pts1200 per day. Students may use university canteen. There is a system of advisors and tutors offering personal advice and assessment. Approved by the Ministry of Education and Science. *Grants available from the Ministry of Foreign Affairs.* **PH**

UNIVERSIDAD DE OVIEDO Secretaria de los Cursos de Verano, Negociado de Extension Universitaria, Edificio Palacio de Quiros 2 planta, Plaza de Riego, 33003 Oviedo
Summer language course for all levels at Llanes on the northern coast of Spain, organised by the University of Oviedo. 4 weeks, July. 20 hours per week. Classes include 5 hours per week of conversation on cultural themes. Extra-curricular activities include seminars, guided tours, excursions, and local fiestas. Cost Pts23000 includes course, teaching materials and activities. Accommodation can be arranged in pensions, campsites, hostels and hotels.

UNIVERSIDAD PONTIFICIA DE SALAMANCA Cursos Intensivos de Lengua y Cultura Espanolas, Apartado 541, 37080 Salamanca Compania 5, 37008 Salamanca Tel Salamanca 218316
Language and culture courses for all levels at the Catholic university of Salamanca. No age limits, individuals only. 4 weeks, January-December. 20 hours per week. Maximum 20 per class. Includes 5 hours per week commentaries on texts, commercial Spanish, and translations. Specialised courses for students, translators, interpreters, teachers of Spanish, doctors, businessmen, banking and technology. Audio-visual facilities. Extra lectures on Spanish and Latin American culture, film shows, music recitals, meetings with Spanish students, excursions, guided tours and opportunities for sports. Students may also attend university classes for Spanish students. Cost from Pts65000 includes course, extra-curricular activities and full board family accommodation. Textbooks Pts1000 per level. Medical insurance available at Pts2000 per month. *Some scholarships available through the Ministry of Foreign Affairs: information from Spanish Embassies.* **PH**

UNIVERSIDAD DE SANTIAGO DE COMPOSTELA Secretaría de los Cursos para Extranjeros, Facultad de Filología, Plaza de Mazarelos, 15703 Santiago de Compostela
Summer language courses for elementary levels and above in Galicia. 4 weeks, July-August or 3 weeks, September. 20 hours per week. Maximum 15 per class. Lectures and seminars on art, geography,

history and literature. Also excursions, video films and sports facilities. Cost Pts20000, 3 weeks or Pts26000, 4 weeks, includes course, teaching materials and excursions. Help given in finding accommodation; student residence accommodation available in July and August, females only.

UNIVERSIDAD DE SEVILLA Secretaría de las Facultades de Filologia y Geografia e Hitoria, Cursos de Extranjeros, Dona Maria de Padilla s/n, 41004 Seville
Language and culture courses for elementary levels and above at the University of Seville. Ages 17 + . 4 weeks, September. 20 hours per week. Maximum 20 per class. Lectures on literature, history, geography, anthropology, music and art of Spain, with special emphasis on themes relating to Andalusia. Extra-curricular activities include discussions, visits to museums, monuments and art centres in Seville. Cost approx Pts20000. Excursions arranged at extra cost, approx Pts5000, to Cordoba, Arcos and La Rábida. Accommodation available in pensions, hotels or private homes.

UNIVERSIDAD DE VALLADOLID Secretario de Estudios para Extranjeros, Facultad de Filosofía y Letras, 47002 Valladolid Tel Valladolid 250458 extension 11
Summer language and civilisation course at the University of Valladolid in central Spain for those with some knowledge of Spanish. Ages 17 + , individuals and groups. 1 month, August. 20 hours per week. Maximum 20 per class. 10 hours language classes, 2 hours conversation, 3 hours literature and 5 hours lectures per week. Lecture subjects include cinema, philosophy, geography and cultural subjects. Also study of art, history and civilisation in the form of guided excursions to Salamanca, Burgos, Segovia, La Granja and local castles. Cost Pts39000, includes course, lectures and excursions. Textbooks Pts2000. Full board student residence accommodation available, cost Pts45000. Also 5 month Spanish Studies course, January-May. 15 hours per week. Includes study of language and culture. Cost Pts80000 for course, Pts198000 for full board accommodation.

UNIVERSIDAD DE ZARAGOZA Secretaría de los Cursos de Verano, Ciudad Universitaria, Zaragoza Tel Zaragoza 45 46 48
Language and culture courses for all levels in the Pyrenean summer resort of Jaca, organised by Zaragoza University. Ages 18 + . 4 weeks, July and August. 20 hours per week. Maximum 25 per class, 15 for beginners classes. Lectures on Spanish culture, civilisation, literature, history, geography, art and traditions. Extra-curricular activities include special courses in Spanish singing and dancing, concerts and

discussions, and excursions in the Pyrenees and to places of artistic and cultural interest. Sports facilities available. Cost approx Pts65000 includes course, teaching materials and full board student residence accommodation, approx Pts30200 excluding accommodation.

After 25 June apply to Cursos de Verano para Extranjeros de la Universidad de Zaragoza, Residencia Universitaria, Jaca (Huesca) Tel Jaca 36 01 96.

INFORMATION

Spanish Embassy
24 Belgrave Square, London SW1X 8OA Tel 01-235 1484

British Embassy
Fernando el Santo 16, 28010 Madrid Tel Madrid 4190200

Tourist office
Spanish National Tourist Office, 57/58 St James's Street, London SW1 Tel 01-499 0901

Youth hostels
Red Espanola de Albergues Juveniles, Jose Ortega y Gasset 71, 28006 Madrid

Youth & student information
TIVE, Oficina Nacional de Intercambio y Turismo de Jovenes y Estudiantes, Jose Ortega y Gasset, 28006 Madrid

Resources
The Spanish Institute, 102 Eaton Square, London, SW1 Tel 01-235 1484/5 was established in 1947 with the aim of spreading Spanish language and culture within the UK. Arranges Spanish language courses and cultural activities, and provides and information service and a library. Holds consultation copies of *Cursos de Lengua y Cultura para Extranjeros en Espana,* see below, an annual publication giving details of Spanish language courses in Spain arranged by both public and private colleges.

The Hispanic and Luso Brazilian Council, Canning House, 2 Belgrave Square, London SW1X 8PJ Tel 01-235 2303 gives information and advice on all matters relating to Spain and Latin America, including language courses and travel. Produces leaflets with practical information for visitors to Spain and Latin America, including *Courses in Spain.* Also runs a programme of events throughout the year for its members, organises courses in the UK for teachers of Spanish and for GCSE and A level students, and can advise on sources of grants.

Publications

Cursos de Lengua y Cultura para Extranjeros en Espana, is an annual guide to Spanish courses, published by Servizio de Publicaciones, Ministerio de Educacion y Ciencia, Ciudad Universitaria, 28040 Madrid, Spain Tel Madrid 4497700.

Travel

STA Travel, 74 Old Brompton Road, London, SW7 3LQ Tel 01-581 8233 operate flexible, low cost flights between London and destinations throughout Spain.

Transalpino Ltd, 117 Euston Road, London NW1 2SX Tel 01-388 2267 offer up to 50% off full rail fares to over 50 destinations in Spain for those under 26.

SWEDISH

Swedish is the official language of Sweden and one of the official languages of Finland, and there are over 9 million speakers worldwide. It is closely related to both Danish and Norwegian, with its beginnings in the Viking Age when the national states came into being and the Scandinavian languages first became distinct from one another. The oldest forms of Swedish writing are runic inscriptions of the 11th and 12th centuries, following which Latin remained the only written language in use in Sweden. Modern Swedish dates from the early 16th century. During the Middle Ages the trade links and immigration resulting from the formation of the Hanseatic League led to an important German influence, which continued with the introduction of Lutheran doctrines. There are also a number of French borrowings dating from the 17th century, with roots in the court of Louis XIV and Huguenot migrants to Sweden.

COURSES IN SWEDEN

INTERNATIONAL SWEDISH UNIVERSITY PROGRAMS (ISUP), Kursverksamheten, Skomakaregatan 8, 223 50 Lund Tel Lund 151784

Summer language course for all levels in Lund. Ages 18+, individuals and groups. 3 weeks July-August. 25 hours per week. Maximum 25 per class. Lectures on Swedish culture and society. Extra-curricular activities include study visits and excursions to places of interest. Cost SKr3800 includes course, teaching materials and excursions. Student residence accommodation available, cost SKr1500.

INTERNATIONAL SWEDISH UNIVERSITY PROGRAMS (ISUP) Kursverksamheten, Skomakaregatan 8, 223 50 Lund Tel Lund 151784

SWEDISH INSTITUTE Section for Swedish Language Instruction Abroad, Box 7434, 103 91 Stockholm Tel Stockholm 789 20 00

Apply to either of the above for beginners courses in language and culture at the Folk High Schools of Södra Vätterbygden in Jönköping, and at Skinnskatteberg, northwest of Västeras in central Sweden. Aimed at English-speaking students. Ages 18+, individuals and groups. 3 weeks, June-July. 16/25 hours per week. Maximum 25 per class. Lectures in English on Swedish culture, history and society. Extra-curricular activities include participation in midsummer festivals, folk music and dancing, and excursions to places of interest. Cost SKr4500 includes course, teaching materials, excursions and full board school accommodation. *Apply by end March/April.*

INTERNATIONELLA SOMMARKURSER Kursverksamheten vid Stockholms Universitet, Box 7845, 10398 Stockholm Tel Stockholm 789 4100
Summer language course for all levels in Stockholm. Ages 16+, individuals and groups. 4 weeks, June-September. 15 x 45 minute lessons per week. Average 16 per class. Cost SKr2250. Textbooks approx SKr250 per course. Students arrange own accommodation. University affiliated.

UPPSALA UNIVERSITY INTERNATIONAL SUMMER SESSION Box 513, 751 20 Uppsala Tel Uppsala 15 54 00
Summer language courses for all levels at Uppsala. Applicants should be eligible for university entrance or requiring Swedish for their career. Ages 18+, individuals and groups. 4, 6, 8 and 10 weeks, June-August. First 2 weeks in June session held at Folk High School in Vardinge, 60 km southwest of Stockholm. 28-32 x 45 minute lessons per week. Maximum 15 per class. Optional seminars on Swedish art, history, films and Scandinavian literature, and evenings lectures with writers, politicians and experts on economics and film. Extra-curricular activities include folk dancing and singing, weekly sports activities, films, excursions and study trips, and opportunities to meet local people. Cost from SKr6900,

4 weeks, to SKr14600, 10 weeks, includes course, excursions, study trips, entrance fees, social events and student residence or apartment accommodation with 1 meal per day except weekends. Cost at Vardinge includes course, some course material, study trips and school accommodation, half board except weekends. *Some scholarships available. Apply by mid March.*

INFORMATION

Swedish Embassy
11 Montagu Place, London W1H 2AL Tel 01-724 2101

British Embassy
Skarpogatan 6, 115 27 Stockholm

Tourist office
Swedish National Tourist Office, 3 Cork Street, London W1X 1HA Tel 01-437 5816

Youth hostels
STS, Vasagatan 48, 101 20 Stockholm

Youth & student information
SFS Resor, Kungsgatan 4, 103 87 Stockholm

International Youth Centre, Valhallavagen 142, 115 24 Stockholm

Resources
Svenska Institutet (Swedish Institute), PO Box 7434, 103 91 Stockholm Tel Stockholm 789 20 00 is a government financed foundation responsible for providing general information on Sweden to other countries. Its tasks consist of supplying materials and services in order to build knowledge abroad about Swedish society and culture, and encouraging the exchange of ideas and experiences across national boundaries. Organises summer courses in association with various Folk High Schools in Sweden, information on which is published in the annual guide *Svenska Institutets Internationella Sommarkurser,* available from the Institute or from Swedish Embassies.

Centre for Information on Language Teaching and Research (CILT), Regent's College, Inner Circle, Regent's Park, London NW1 4NS Tel 01-486 8221 publish *Swedish Language & Culture Guide* £4.25 including postage, with details on the provision and use of language teaching and learning resources, covering an introduction to the language, useful addresses, libraries and special collections to consult, opportunities for learning, and examinations which can be taken.

Travel
Norwegian State Railways, 21/24 Cockspur Street, London SW1Y 5DA Tel 01-930 6666 issue the Nordic Tourist Ticket which entitles the holder to unlimited travel on trains in Sweden, Norway, Denmark and Finland, and is also valid on some inter-Scandinavian ferry services. Valid 21 days; cost £128.

Transalpino Ltd, 117 Euston Road, London NW1 2SX Tel 01-388 2267 offer up to 50% off full rail fares to 28 destinations in Sweden for those under 26.

Sweden is a free magazine providing general information on travel to and around the country, public services, medical treatment, eating, accommodation, outdoor activities, useful words and phrases, plus maps and colour photographs. Also *Holiday Guide for the Disabled.* Both available from the Swedish National Tourist Office, see above. **PH**

Accommodation
International Youth Centre Hostel, Valhallavagen 142, 115 24 Stockholm has accommodation available for young people. Facilities include information centre, washing machines, lockers, bike hire, kitchen and coffee shop. 5 consecutive nights only, June-August. Cost Skr35 per night, bed and shower; membership Skr10.

TURKISH

Turkish is the official language of Turkey, which has a population of approx 50 million, and is also the mother tongue of minority groups in Bulgaria, Cyprus, Greece and Yugoslavia, and of Turkish/Cypriot immigrants and their descendants in Britain and the Federal Republic of Germany. It is a member of the Turkic group of languages, a branch of the Altaic family. Turkey's location partly in Asia and partly in Europe means that it has been a melting pot of different cultures and races since prehistoric times. It is thought that the Turks, originally woodland hunters in the Altay Mountains, arrived in Anatolia in eastern Turkey during the 11th century. Since the Islamic conversion Turkish was written in Arabic script; however since 1928 a modified version of the Roman alphabet has been used.

COURSES IN TURKEY

ANKARA UNIVERSITY, TOMER (Turkish Language Centre), Dil ve Tarih-Cografya Fakultesi, Sihhiye, Ankara Tel 10 32 80/384

Language courses for all levels in Turkey's modern capital, Ankara. 4 weeks, July-September or 8 weeks, October-June. 8-20 lessons per week. Language laboratories and audio-visual facilities. Extra-curricular activities include sightseeing tours, tea parties, Turkish folk dancing and music. Contact with Turkish students encouraged. Use of University's sports facilities. Cost US$190, summer, includes bed and breakfast hotel accommodation; or from US$64, winter, course only. Information provided on accommodation.

GENCTUR TURIZM VE SEYAHAT ACENTASI LTD Sirketi, Yerebatan Cad 15/3, 34410 Sultanahmet, Istanbul Tel 526 54 09/512 04 57
Language courses for beginners and intermediate levels in the cultural and historic city of Istanbul. Ages 18+, individuals and groups. 2 weeks, March-April, 55 hours total. Average 3-8 per class. Cost DM693 includes half board family accommodation and museum entrance. Also 3 weeks, July-September, 60 hours total. Cost DM805 includes 5 days half board family accommodation in Istanbul and 13 days full board hotel accommodation in Ackay, on the Aegean coast. Sightseeing tours and visits to places of interest offered in the afternoons. Also language course for beginners and intermediate levels in the tourist resort of Kas. 2 weeks, Easter, 20 hours per week. Cost approx DM600 includes course, travel from Istanbul and bed and breakfast accommodation.

ISTANBUL UNIVERSITY (Turk Dili ve Kulturu yaz Kurlari Burosu), Istanbul Tel Istanbul 520 13 65/528 69 04
Language courses for beginners and intermediate levels in Istanbul. 2 months, July and August. 16 hours per week plus 1 day of films and lectures. Language laboratory facilities. Cost DM700. Hostel accommodation available.

INFORMATION

Turkish Consulate General
Rutland Lodge, Rutland Gardens, London SW7 1BW Tel 01-589 0360

British Embassy
Sehit Ersan Caddesi 46/A Cankaya, Ankara

Tourist office
Turkish Tourist Office, 1st Floor, 170-173 Piccadilly, London W1V 9DD Tel 01-734 8681

Youth hostels/youth & student information

Genctur, Tourism and Travel Agency, Yerebatan Caddesi 15/3, Sultanahmet, Istanbul Postal address: PO Box 1263, Sirkeci-Istanbul

Resources

Centre for Information on Language Teaching and Research (CILT), Regent's College, Inner Circle, Regent's Park, London NW1 4NS Tel 01-486 8221 publish *Turkish Language & Culture Guide* £4.25 including postage, with details on the provision and use of language teaching and learning resources, covering an introduction to the language, useful addresses, libraries and special collections to consult, opportunities for learning, and examinations which can be taken.

Travel

North-South Travel Ltd, Room 1A, 6 Brondesbury Road, London NW6 6AS Tel 01-624 4416 arrange competitively priced, reliable planned flights to all parts of Turkey. Profits are paid into a trust fund for the assignment of aid to projects in the poorest parts of the South.

STA Travel, 74 Old Brompton Road, London NW1 2SX Tel 01-388 2267 offer up to 50% off full rail fares to destinations in Turkey for those under 26.

Turkey Travel Guide is a booklet containing information on frontier formalities, youth and student travel and accommodation, recreation, traditions plus a plus a detailed list of useful addresses and practical information. Also *Youth & Student Tourism in Turkey* providing information on student residences in main towns and travel reductions. Both available from the Turkish Tourist Office, see above.

Turkey – A Travel Survival Kit £5.95, is a handbook for travellers, with comprehensive information on where to stay, what to eat, the best places to visit and how to travel around. Available from Trailfinders Travel Centre, 42-48 Earls Court Road, London W8 6EJ Tel 01-937 9631.

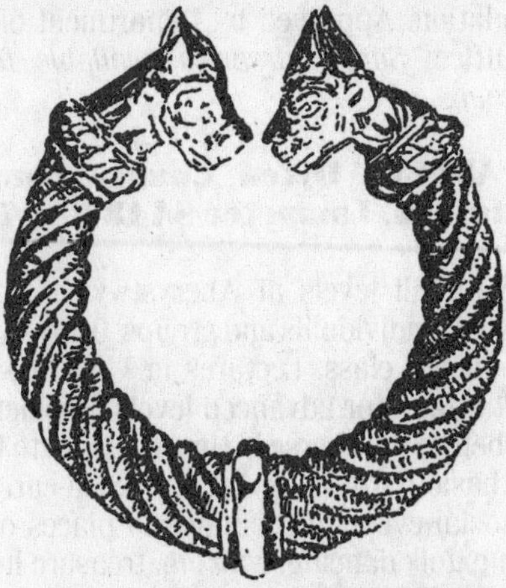

WELSH

Welsh, like Gaelic is a Celtic language, and a member of the Indo-European group. Celtic tribes came to Britain sometime after the 5th century BC, and Welsh began to emerge after the Romans had left. For a while it was spoken in parts of England and Scotland until Anglo-Saxon invasions drove the Welsh into the west. Today, apart from individual speakers worldwide and a small Welsh-speaking community in Patagonia, Welsh is confined to Wales, where it is spoken by about 20% of the population. The earliest Welsh literature dates from the 6th century, and a standard literary form was in use from the Middle Ages. This was used in translating the Bible in 1588, which had an important effect on the status of the language and Welsh consciousness. Currently there is a strong growth of interest in Welsh and it is now used extensively in Welsh schools and broadcasting services.

COURSES IN WALES

COLEG HARLECH Harlech, Gwynedd LL46 2PU Tel Harlech 780363

Summer course in Harlech for those with some knowledge of Welsh. No age limits, individuals only. 1 week, July. Approx 25 hours per week. Average 10 per class. Audio-visual facilities. At advanced levels, works of contemporary Welsh writers are studied and discussed. Social events arranged. Cost £130 includes course, teaching materials and full board college accommodation. Approved by Department of Education and Science Welsh Office. *Some bursaries available for members of disadvantaged groups.*

WELSH FOR ADULTS Dyfed County Council, Theatr Felinfach, Felinfach, Lampeter SA48 8AF Tel Lampeter 470 005
Language course for all levels at Aberystwyth College of Further Education. Ages 16 + , individuals and groups. 9 days, July. 7 hours per day. Average 12-15 per class. Lectures in Welsh history, literature, music and current affairs for advanced levels. Booklets and cassettes sent to beginners before the course in time for them to become familiar with sounds and basic patterns of Welsh. Extra-curricular activities include evening social events, excursions to places of interest, pony trekking, swimming, folk dancing, walking, treasure hunt and visits to private homes. Cost £35, £20 for unemployed, includes course and teaching materials. Bed and breakfast college accommodation available, cost £10.40 per day. Sponsored by Dyfed local education authority with the support of University College of Wales. **PH**

INFORMATION

Tourist office
Wales Tourist Board, Brunel House, 2 Fitzalan Road, Cardiff CF2 1UY Tel 0222 499909

Youth hostels
YHA, Trevelyan House, 8 St Stephen's Hill, St Albans, Hertfordshire Al1 2DY Tel St Albans 55215

Youth & student information
National Union of Students, 461 Holloway Road, London N7 6LJ Tel 01-272 8900

Resources
Centre for Information on Language Teaching and Research (CILT), Regent's College, Inner Circle, Regent's Park, London NW1 4NS Tel 01-486 8221 publish *Welsh Language & Culture Guide* £4.75 including postage, with details on the provision and use of language teaching and learning resources, covering an introduction to the language, useful addresses, libraries and special collections to consult, opportunities for learning, and examinations which can be taken.

STUDY HOLIDAYS REPORT FORM

Up-to-date reports of study courses enable us to improve the accuracy and standard of information in this guide. Your replies to the questions below would therefore be very much appreciated. Please send the completed form to: Information Services Department, Central Bureau, Seymour Mews House, Seymour Mews, London W1H 9PE. **All reports will be treated in strict confidence.**

Name and address of organisation(s)

Country and course attended, and dates

Was correspondence prompt? Yes ☐ No ☐
Comments:

Were you sent enough accurate information about what to expect? Yes ☐ No ☐
Comments:

If travel was arranged by you, were you able to find a cheap and efficient way of arriving at your destination?
Yes ☐ No ☐
Comments:

If travel was arranged by the organisation, was it efficient? Yes ☐ No ☐
Comments:

What type of accommodation was provided?

Was it satisfactory? Yes ☐ No ☐
Comments:

Were meals satisfactory? Yes ☐ No ☐
Comments:

Was the standard of teaching satisfactory? Yes ☐ No ☐
Comments:

Were you satisfied with the content and planning of the programme? Yes ☐ No ☐
Comments:

What was the age range of participants?

Were you able to meet local people? Yes ☐ No ☐
Comments:

Were you able to meet people from other countries?
Yes ☐ No ☐
Comments:

Do you think that you got value for money? Yes ☐ No ☐
Comments:

Would you recommend this course/organisation to other people? Yes ☐ No ☐
Comments:

Did your language skills benefit? Yes ☐ No ☐
Comments:

Any other comments:

Signed Date

Name

Age

Home address

Telephone